Garden of the World

Garden of the World

*Asian Immigrants and the Making of Agriculture
in California's Santa Clara Valley*

CECILIA M. TSU

OXFORD
UNIVERSITY PRESS

OXFORD
UNIVERSITY PRESS

Oxford University Press is a department of the University of
Oxford. It furthers the University's objective of excellence in
research, scholarship, and education by publishing worldwide.

Oxford   New York

Auckland   Cape Town   Dar es Salaam   Hong Kong   Karachi
Kuala Lumpur   Madrid   Melbourne   Mexico City   Nairobi
New Delhi   Shanghai   Taipei   Toronto

With offices in

Argentina   Austria   Brazil   Chile   Czech Republic   France   Greece
Guatemala   Hungary   Italy   Japan   Poland   Portugal   Singapore
South Korea   Switzerland   Thailand   Turkey   Ukraine   Vietnam

Oxford is a registered trade mark of Oxford University Press
in the UK and certain other countries.

Published in the United States of America by
Oxford University Press
198 Madison Avenue, New York, NY 10016

Library of Congress Cataloging-in-Publication Data
Tsu, Cecilia M.
Garden of the world : Asian immigrants and the making of agriculture in California's Santa
Clara Valley / Cecilia M. Tsu.
pages cm.
Includes bibliographical references and index.
ISBN 978-0-19-973477-1 (alk. paper)—ISBN 978-0-19-973478-8 (pbk. : alk. paper)   1. Asian
Americans—California—Santa Clara Valley (Santa Clara County, Calif.)—History.   2. Santa Clara Valley
(Santa Clara County, Calif.)—Ethnic relations.   3. Agriculture—California—Santa Clara Valley (Santa
Clara County, Calif.)—History.   4. Fruit trade—California—Santa Clara Valley (Santa Clara County,
Calif.)—History. 5. Fruit growers—California—Santa Clara Valley (Santa Clara
County, Calif.)—History.   I. Title.
F868.S25T78 2013
338.1089'95079473—dc23
2012048607
Portions of this book were published in earlier forms as the following articles:
"'Independent of the Unskilled Chinaman': Race, Labor, and Family Farming in California's Santa Clara Valley,"
Western Historical Quarterly 37 (Winter 2006): 474–495. Copyright by the Western History Association.
Reprinted by permission.
"Sex, Lies, and Agriculture: Reconstructing Japanese Immigrant Gender Relations in Rural California,
1900–1913," *Pacific Historical Review* 78 (May 2009): 171–209. Copyright by the Pacific Coast Branch,
American Historical Association. Reprinted by permission of the University of California Press.

1 3 5 7 9 8 6 4 2

Printed in the United States of America
on acid-free paper

To my parents, Rex and Teresa Tsu

CONTENTS

ACKNOWLEDGMENTS

The journey to the publication of this book has taught me the true meaning of collaboration and community. First and foremost, my graduate advisors Gordon Chang and Estelle Freedman at Stanford University were exceptional mentors who guided and challenged me with penetrating insight at each stage of this project's development. I am also grateful to other faculty members at Stanford who helped shape this project with their expertise, especially Richard White, Al Camarillo, and Kären Wigen. I extend deep thanks to my graduate school friends who read multiple chapter drafts of the dissertation and book, Andrea Davies, Malgorzata Fidelis, Kim Warren, and Jared Farmer, and to Shana Bernstein, Gabriela González, Benjamin Greene, Rachel Jean-Baptiste, Benjamin Lawrance, Hyung-Suk Lee, Shelley Lee, Beth Lew-Williams, Dawn Mabalon, Rachel St. John, and Tamara Venit-Shelton for their support and friendship at Stanford and beyond. In all honesty, I would not have become a historian in the first place if not for the inspired teaching and mentorship of Bruce Dorsey at Swarthmore College. In addition, I am indebted to Lillian Li for encouraging me to pursue my interests in Asian American history as an undergraduate. For the past six years, my colleagues in the Department of History at the University of California, Davis, have graciously given me valuable feedback on this project, especially Ari Kelman, Kathy Olmsted, and Louis Warren; I also thank Tori Langland, Lisa Materson, Lorena Oropeza, and Clarence Walker for their sharp advice on many matters. A number of scholars have offered comments and multiple forms of assistance with the book, including Eiichiro Azuma, Mark Brilliant, Tom Guglielmo, Richard Kim, Valerie Matsumoto, Glenna Matthews, Michael Meloy, Gary Okihiro, Nayan Shah, Julie Sze, David Vaught, and Grace Wang.

Generous funding in the form of fellowships and research grants contributed to the completion of this project. At Stanford, the Department of History, the Research Institute of Comparative Studies in Race and Ethnicity, and the Institute for Research on Women and Gender all provided fellowships. I also received awards from the Whiting Foundation and the Andrew W. Mellon Foundation. A University of California President's Research Fellowship in the Humanities allowed me to make substantial progress during a sabbatical year, while grants from the Hellman Family Foundation, the Academic Senate Committee on Research, the Davis Humanities Institute, the Office of Research, and the Office of the Dean of Social Sciences at UC Davis helped greatly with research and publication costs.

Many archivists and librarians provided research assistance and helped uncover essential sources. I extend my sincere thanks to Jim Reed at History San José, Stephen Fugita and Jimi Yamaichi at the Japanese American Museum of San Jose, Lisa Christiansen at the California History Center, Michael Griffith and Trista Raezer, formerly of the Santa Clara County Archives, Ralph Pearce at the California Room of the San Jose Public Library, Margaret Kimball in the Department of Special Collections and University Archives at Stanford, David Piff at the National Archives and Records Administration in San Bruno, and the staff at the Santa Clara County Recorder's Office and Santa Clara County Superior Court. I thank Paula Jabloner for showing me the county coroner's inquest files for the first time when I was a graduate student. Special thanks to those who shared their family stories and photographs with me, especially Patricia Catolico, Curt Fukuda, Will Kaku, and Connie Young Yu. A team of enthusiastic and talented research assistants helped me mine a huge body of sources: Bonnie Montgomery has been the most superb, perceptive, and knowledgeable assistant I could have ever asked for. Justin Baker, Kevin Dobiles, Stephanie Ellingson, Yu Hirayama, Jennifer LaFleur, Erin McNichol, Jean-Franco Romualdez, Tracey Ross, and Wing-Yan So, all bright, energetic former UC Davis students and a joy to work with, combed through newspapers and trade journals, entered census data, and provided a variety of research help. Thanks to John Daniels at the UC Davis Social Science Data Center for his help with the quantitative analysis of my sources, and to Maki Yama for her indispensable translation work.

In terms of transforming this longstanding research interest into a book, I am very grateful for the expert guidance of Susan Ferber, my editor at Oxford, and all of the astute editing, thoughtful comments, and all-around support she has offered from the beginning. My appreciation also goes to Oxford's fine production team, especially Marc Schneider, and to copyeditor Brenda Griffing for her terrific attention to detail, as well as John Grennan and Bonnie Montgomery for their fine work in the late stages of production. Many thanks to the reviewers of this manuscript, who imparted wide-ranging, perceptive, and thorough suggestions that helped me significantly improve the final product.

Portions of this book are drawn from my previously published articles in the *Western Historical Quarterly* and the *Pacific Historical Review*. I thank the editors and staff of these journals, especially David Rich Lewis, Colleen O'Neill, David

A. Johnson, Carl Abbott, and Susan Wladaver-Morgan, for their editorial advice and support, and for permission to reprint the work in revised form.

My family and friends outside academia have given incredible encouragement throughout this long process, and above all, have kept me grounded and attuned to what is truly important. For their kindness, patience, and willingness to listen over the span of many years, I thank Kyung Ahn, Thanh Barretto, Sonali Chakravarti, Angela Chang, Jacqueline Gu, Roger Mar-Tang, and my brother, Vincent Tsu. My in-laws from the Lee and Villamil families, plus sister-in-law Cindy Lee, have contributed much tangible and intangible help to facilitate the publication of this book. My uncle Glen Tsu, along with my aunt and uncle Jeanine and Kai Liang, have been lifelong pillars of support in my life. My grandparents, Wai-Ying and Tin-Pa Tsu, did not live to see this project come to fruition, but they inspired me in countless ways. It is only in recent years since I have become a parent that I can begin to understand the depths of my parents' love and sacrifice. I dedicate this book to them and am thankful beyond measure for everything they have taught and given me. I met my husband, Jackson Lee, in the early stages of this project, and since then, have relied continuously on his unwavering confidence in me, along with his steadfast care and comic relief. The arrival of our daughter, Carissa, has been an extraordinary gift, an infinitely rich source of new inspiration.

Garden of the World

Introduction

Nestled between two branches of the Coast Range mountains, the Santa Clara Valley lies at the southern edge of the San Francisco Bay, in the center of California. To the west, the Santa Cruz mountains, dense with coastal redwoods, Douglas fir, madrone, laurel, and varieties of oaks, separate the Valley from the Pacific Ocean, visible from the crest of the range, which extends to nearly four thousand feet above sea level. The Diablo range lies to the east of the Valley, dry and barren in appearance for most of the year save for scattered oak trees that dot its lower altitudes. Winter rains fill the mountain streams and creeks that wind through the Valley floor, enriching the topsoil and turning the hillsides to a bright velvet green each spring. The protective arms of these mountain ranges shield the Valley from severe frosts and storms, and the Mediterranean climate remains mild year-round, temperatures rarely below freezing in the winter or excessively warm during the clear, rainless summers. Passing through the Santa Clara Valley in 1872, naturalist John Muir remarked the weather was "the best we ever enjoyed. Larks and streams sang everywhere; the sky was cloudless, and the whole valley was a lake of light."[1]

When Muir visited the Valley, it was just beginning to shift from wheat growing to intensive orchard fruit production. Capitalizing on an ideal growing climate, fertile soil, and plentiful water supply from artesian wells, agricultural entrepreneurs transformed the area into the lush agrarian landscape of manicured fields and flowering trees that would make it an international fruit capital, called the Valley of Heart's Delight and the Garden of the World. Specializing in the cultivation and processing of apricots, prunes, pears, and cherries, the Santa Clara Valley in its horticultural heyday was undeniably beautiful, covered with row upon row of fruit trees that created a canopy of delicate, sweetly perfumed pink and white blossoms, flanked by hillsides awash in orange California poppies and other native wildflowers. At the turn of the twentieth century, visitors flocked to behold this annual spring display, the profusion of orchards in full bloom interspersed with neat farmhouses, berry patches and vegetable gardens, pastures of hay and alfalfa. Each year the orchard blossoms gave way to a no less spectacular sensory experience, leafy treetops laden with sweet, luscious fruit ripening in the warm summer sun. It was no wonder that Santa Clara Valley boosters scarcely hesitated to use superlatives to describe their region, calling it "the most pleasant land in the world in which to live…the garden of the continent," "an embarrassment of beauty," "nearest Paradise," and "the best spot in the whole world." To promoters and visitors, the Santa Clara Valley was "the Eden of vine and tree," a "God-favored spot," and "God's favorite valley," fertile, lush, and prosperous.[2]

The bucolic fruited Valley appeared to embody par excellence the American agrarian ideal, Thomas Jefferson's vision of white citizens tilling the soil and con-tributing to the stability and virtue of the new nation.[3] John P. Nilson, a Swedish immigrant who arrived in San Jose in 1870, owned one of these lauded Santa Clara Valley orchards, a 50-acre ranch between First Street and the Guadalupe River, and seemed to exemplify this highly touted vision of American agrari-anism. Before he purchased his own farm, Nilson spent several years as a nursery foreman in the Orchard District of San Jose. By 1900, he and his wife, Maria, had seven children, including two young adult sons who worked with their father on the ranch, which was planted mostly in pears and apples. The orchard was by all accounts a thriving family enterprise, to the point that John Nilson was able to purchase an additional 43 adjacent acres in 1911, nearly doubling his property.

Yet the Nilson farm did not quite conform to Jefferson's ideal in one key respect: for more than several decades, the people who operated it were not whites of Swedish extraction, but Asian immigrants who arrived in California from China, Japan, and the Philippines during the nineteenth and twentieth centuries. In 1910, a Japanese farmer named Tsunejiro Iwasaki signed a lease to farm all of the Nilsons' property except the family homestead. Two years later, Iwasaki and John Nilson renewed their lease for six more years, Nilson placing Iwasaki in charge of the newly purchased tract as well. In 1921, Chinese cannery owner Thomas Foon Chew, to whom Iwasaki regularly mortgaged his crops for loans, took over the lease on the Nilson ranch and employed Iwasaki as ranch foreman.[4] After John and Maria Nilson died in 1926, their children left the prop-erty under Chew's management. When Iwasaki died of a stroke in 1927, Chew appointed another Japanese farmer, Heikichi Ezaki, as foreman. Until Ezaki, his wife, Yukino, and their children were interned during World War II, the family hired over a dozen Filipino laborers during harvest season, boarding them in bunkhouses on the ranch. In 1936 and 1942, two of the Nilson brothers (who used the spelling Nelson for their surname) sold their shares of the farm to the American-born sons of Heikichi and Yukino Ezaki.[5]

Even though many white farm owners throughout California and the American West like the Nilsons relied on Asian immigrant farmers, the cultural lore that celebrated farming as a native-born white American pursuit erased Asians altogether from the narrative of success associated with the region's orchard fruit economy. Indeed, the Jeffersonian agrarian ideal central in the American cultural imagination left out many Americans who spent their lives farming: slaves on Southern plantations, Native American cultivators, European immigrant farmers initially considered to be of inferior races and not quite "white," black sharecroppers, Mexican agricultural laborers, and farmers and farm workers of various Asian ethnicities. The deep-rooted conception of the American family farm, according to which white European-American, male-headed households operated farms requiring only the labor of family members to maintain, was at odds with rural realities.

This book tells that national story in a regional setting by examining how overlapping waves of Chinese, Japanese, and Filipino immigrants fundamentally altered the agricultural economy and landscape of the Santa Clara Valley as well as white residents' ideas about race, gender, and what it meant to be an American family farmer. From 1880 to 1940, the region's peak decades of horticultural production, the participation of Asian immigrants in agriculture challenged, modified, and consolidated the white family farm ideal. Asians who labored in agriculture also redefined this ideal for their respective communities, eschewing the exclusive white American version. For Chinese immigrant men, who espoused a trans-Pacific view of family farming, their labor on California farms became a means to support immediate and extended families in rural villages in southern China. Japanese immigrants, increasingly intent on settling permanently in California as family units, came to see farming as the basis of a secure, thriving immigrant society. In the Japanese incarnation of the American dream, the ability of an immigrant man to succeed as a farmer and thereby support a wife and children in California signified his status among his countrymen and became a means of bolstering his community standing. For Filipino migrants, the majority of whom struggled as poorly paid seasonal agricultural laborers during the Great Depression, the search for work on dignified terms led them to form multiracial coalitions in the farm labor movement.

In California by the 1880s, boosters promoted orchard fruit growing as one of the most idyllic incarnations of the family farm ideal, and the Santa Clara Valley as the finest location to live out this agrarian dream. As the advent of industrialized agriculture threatened the American dream of independent family farming, white residents of regions still amenable to small farms became more adamant in proclaiming their agricultural self-sufficiency in racialized and gendered terms. While whites persisted in their reliance on Asian farm labor, they attempted to reify what historian Neil Foley has called "agrarian whiteness" and strove to hold onto fruit growing as the last bastion of the American agrarian ideal.[6] Within California agriculture alone, the exigencies of diverse forms of land tenure and crop specialization produced region-specific patterns of racial formation and class stratification. The prevalence of small family farms in the

Figure I.1 Santa Clara Valley in spring, c. 1900.
Alice Iola Hare Photograph Collection, The Bancroft Library, University of California, Berkeley.

Santa Clara Valley contrasted with, for example, the large-scale industrial farming that characterized the Sacramento–San Joaquin Delta region, where the extensive construction of levees to handle frequent flooding made land prices prohibitive for farmers of middling means. In this context, the Delta became conducive to Chinese and Japanese tenancy, viewed by white agribusiness in the early twentieth century as indispensable rather than a threat to the independence and livelihoods of white rural families.[7] Well into the twentieth century, however, white farmers in the Santa Clara Valley maintained relatively small farms (in 1900, the typical unit was under 50 acres; in 1920, the average farm size was 40 acres), owing to the profitability of deciduous fruits like prunes and apricots, which yielded a high crop value per acre.[8] Thus white growers in the Valley could pride themselves on being proprietors of family farms, decidedly not the maligned "factories in the field" journalist Carey McWilliams later described, and ideas about mobility through the farm ladder and the intrinsic value of independent family farming dominated the culture there.[9]

But the rhetoric of family farming contradicted the stark reality that family labor was insufficient for white growers. From the start, white families relied on hired help, which in the late nineteenth and early twentieth centuries was largely provided by Asian laborers. The area consistently ranked among the top five California counties with the highest percentages of Asian residents before World War II. From 1880 to 1940, though Asians made up between 2 percent and 7 percent of the total population of Santa Clara County, the overwhelming majority engaged in agricultural work. Moreover, Asian immigrants in the Santa Clara Valley, Chinese and Japanese in particular, made contributions not only as agricultural laborers—hired to harvest, plant, irrigate, spray, and pack crops as the seasons dictated—but also as tenant farmers and sharecroppers.[10] The variety of horticultural production that characterized the Santa Clara Valley included its acclaimed orchard fruits, as well as less profitable, more labor-intensive berries, numerous vegetable crops, and garden seed, all of which Asians cultivated.

As Asian immigrants staked their livelihoods in agriculture, they posed a major challenge to the white family farm ideal. In response, white residents developed new ways of defining themselves vis-à-vis Asians, employing crops and family structure to mark racial difference between whites and "Orientals" in agriculture. The family farm itself became a malleable site of racialization for Asians in the United States. For example, whereas in the late nineteenth century, white residents considered the labor of all family members, including women and children, critical to the success of the family farm enterprise, by 1920, they accused Japanese farm families of denigrating Japanese women and exploiting their children by employing them in the fields, castigating such practices as decidedly "Asiatic" and aberrant. Thus popular perceptions of Asian immigrants incorporated a belief in their inability to adhere to notions of proper American family ideology and their association with more marginal agricultural products, crops other than the region's renowned deciduous fruits.

The inclusion of Asians as menial itinerant agricultural workers in "inferior" crops and their exclusion as aliens unfit not only for U.S. citizenship but also American family life ultimately preserved and reproduced white supremacy and American national identity.[11] With each successive influx of Asian immigrant farm labor, the white family farm ideal was deployed to inscribe racial difference and perpetuate the belief that only white families rightfully belonged in the sanctified realm of American agriculture. Building on works that investigate agriculture in America as an arena of contested racial interactions and bringing the study of rural Asian Americans in dialogue with whiteness studies and gender history, this book demonstrates how white growers made both racial and gendered claims to justify their dependence on nonwhites as "independent" family farmers, and how those claims expanded and changed over time, forcing a transformation of the family farm ideal itself.[12]

Far from indicating that the arrival of Asian immigrants in the United States heralded a direct march to the path of alien land laws and exclusion, however, the experiences of Chinese, Japanese, and Filipino immigrants who formed close working relationships with white growers in intensive agricultural regions like the Santa Clara Valley show a remarkable tolerance and unspoken understanding of mutual dependence. As this history reveals, racial constructions and race relations are dependent on local context. What happened in the Santa Clara Valley

Table I.1 Asian Population of Santa Clara County (SCC), 1870–1940

Year	Number of Chinese	Percentage of SCC population	Number of Japanese	Percentage of SCC population	Number of Filipinos	Percentage of SCC population
1870	1,525	5.8	—	—	—	—
1880	2,695	7.7	—	—	—	—
1890	2,723	5.7	27	0.06	—	—
1900	1,738	2.9	284	0.5	—	—
1910	1,064	1.3	2,299	2.8	—	—
1920	839	0.8	2,981	3.0	45[a]	0.04
1930	761	0.5	4,320	3.0	857[a]	0.6
1940	555	0.3	4,049	2.3	600[a]	0.3

[a] Exact totals not available. Based on estimates from census and other quantitative data.

Source: U.S. Census.

had national and global implications as the everyday interplay of events and individuals' experiences in their immediate surroundings contributed to an evolving racial ideology. That is, local negotiations mattered. Exposing these negotiations illustrates the limits of broader national frameworks for understanding racism and racial formation. As much as state and federal laws, immigration policy, and episodes of racial conflict and violence throughout the American West seem to suggest monolithic, sweeping anti-Asian sentiment overwhelmingly sanctioned by state and society, the complexities of agitation against Asian immigrants in the Santa Clara Valley also reveal that it was not simply a product of economic competition or "yellow peril" fears.[13] Anti-Asian activity existed there, but it tended to lag behind more intense conflicts that erupted elsewhere and usually originated not from white farmers but from politicians, the press, and working-class whites. In fact, white growers frequently found themselves adopting precarious, contradictory stances on the issue of Asian immigration, their positions reflecting their adherence to prevailing views of white superiority as well as their conflicted feelings about Asian agricultural labor. Viewed on the ground in a localized community context, individuals' motives and behaviors were far more nuanced than macro-level policy suggests.

But this is not just a story of how whites marginalized Asian immigrants in California agriculture and constructed new ideologies to uphold white racial hegemony. Although most Asian immigrants and their children lived outside urban areas before World War II, the rural Asian American experience remains, as historian Gary Okihiro noted in 1989, an area "uncultivated yet rich with possibilities," overshadowed by other developments in the field, the "transnational turn," a sustained focus on the urban dimension of Asian American history, and theoretical interventions.[14]

This book explores how Chinese, Japanese, and Filipino agriculturalists in the Santa Clara Valley constantly sought out and negotiated opportunities for themselves within the rural economy and society, forced white growers to acknowledge their dependence on Asian labor, and maintained their right to earn a living in agriculture even as oppressive laws and occasional mobs threatened to drive them out of the industry. As historian Chris Friday notes, while Asian laborers in the American West "tacitly accepted the boundaries set by economic, political, and social forces beyond their control," they also participated in the creation of distinctive work cultures and within those boundaries refused to be treated as a docile, subservient labor force.[15] For example, as the image of Asians as diligent farmers with uncanny talents for reaping abundant crops from the soil solidified by the 1920s, Chinese and Japanese immigrants in the Santa Clara Valley co-opted such notions for their own benefit to secure favorable terms of labor and cultivation from white growers. Well aware of the niche they occupied and the reality of the Valley's agricultural needs, Asian agriculturalists also understood dominant racial stereotypes that depicted them as exacting, precise, and industrious farmers (white perceptions that ultimately formed the basis of a broader model minority stereotype) could work to their advantage and contribute to their economic survival.

Moreover, departing from scholarship on rural Asian Americans, which has heretofore been limited to ethnic-specific studies, *Garden of the World* uncovers an intricate world of rural intra-Asian relations characterized by interethnic cooperation and conflict against the omnipresence of white racism.[16] In the Santa Clara Valley, three Asian immigrant groups succeeded each other in terms of comprising the majority of farm laborers in the county in a given decade, but the lives of Chinese, Japanese, and Filipino residents also constantly overlapped (these three groups represented the only significant Asian populations in the Santa Clara Valley at that time; South Asians, Koreans, and other Asian immigrants in the state for the most part tended to reside in the Central Valley and other regions of California). Japanese and Filipino residents patronized Chinese-owned businesses and boarded in San Jose Chinatown; Chinese and Japanese day laborers and tenant farmers worked for the same white landowners; Japanese growers often employed Filipino laborers, as on the Nilson ranch; and the American-born children of Asian immigrants attended the same rural schools and encountered the same racial stereotypes. This book joins the disparate experiences of several Asian ethnic groups through a comparative perspective, bringing these multiethnic interactions to light while also illuminating how each group developed distinct yet interlinked and mutually informed patterns of migration, community formation, and race relations. Each of these groups, this work demonstrates, also deployed unique strategies to survive and retain livelihoods in California agriculture under the ascendancy of the white family farm ideal.

The story of race, gender, and agriculture in the Santa Clara Valley, as Chapter One describes, begins with the articulation of the white family farm ideal, which called for a labor system that relied exclusively on the toil of white men, women, and children within the family unit in the late nineteenth century. White growers needed Asian labor but felt compelled to maintain the family farm ideal and to defend themselves against accusations of supporting Asian immigration. The Valley's white residents resolved this dilemma in part by asserting that Chinese immigrants, as sojourning bachelors, were suited only for the tedious, labor-intensive cultivation of berries, truck crops, and garden seed, not fit for the more prestigious task of growing orchard fruit. Japanese immigrants, as detailed in Chapter Two, initially fit into this framework as well, appearing to be another community of single Asian men. As white promoters and settlers placed a higher cultural premium on orchard fruit growing, setting it apart from the variety of horticultural production in the region, they envisioned a labor system divided along the lines of race, gender, and crop. In reality, the Japanese, like their Chinese counterparts, engaged in all types of horticulture and were essential to the Valley's agricultural landscape. In contrast to the Chinese, however, the early Japanese immigrant community found itself mired in intra-ethnic conflict and occasionally violent episodes stemming from gender imbalance and the exceptional conditions of rural immigrant life in California, as Chapter Three discusses.

By the late 1910s, the settlement of Japanese farm families, some of which came to operate their own orchards, disrupted the entrenched framework of racialized crops and family structure, setting off a prolonged anti-Japanese movement centered on allegations of deviant Japanese family labor practices. While the preponderance of men and the scarcity of families in the earlier world of Japanese immigrants conformed to Valley residents' understanding of racial hierarchy, Chapter Four contends that the formation of Japanese families by 1920 became a flashpoint of conflict, forcing new definitions of the white family farm ideal. Family structure could remain a clear-cut marker of race only with modifications: gendered labor and the exclusion of women from field work came to define the new family farm ideal, which by the 1920s no longer sanctioned using the labor of all family members.

Race relations and cultural constructions of Asians in agriculture took another direction during the 1920s and 1930s. Chapter Five explores how in the aftermath of institutionalized legislative discrimination, whites began to adopt positive views of the Asians in their midst, particularly second-generation, American-born children of Chinese and Japanese immigrants, considered high-achieving and rapidly assimilating. Social scientists studying the "Oriental Problem" in the Santa Clara Valley during the mid-1920s discovered that residents' racial attitudes, largely formed through interactions in the agricultural industry, were characterized by class distinctions and comparisons of Asian ethnic groups, as well as comparisons among Asians and Europeans, Mexicans, and blacks.

Chapter Six shifts the focus to the 1930s and Filipino migrant farm laborers, who initially had been welcomed as another bachelor population capable of serving white growers' labor needs. Filipino men soon came under fire for their association with white women, but their participation in farm labor unions and strikes during the 1930s was even more problematic for white residents, since labor organization pitted Filipinos squarely against growers desperate to preserve some semblance of horticultural prosperity in the "Garden of the World." Filipino laborers' affiliation with the farm labor movement led to their racialization as disruptive "radicals" threatening the livelihoods of struggling farmowners, already hit hard by the Depression. In this context, Japanese farm families, some of whom also employed Filipino workers, evaporated from public view, overshadowed by the popular discourse on the farm labor problem.

Today the Santa Clara Valley is better known as Silicon Valley, and its current residents would hardly associate the region with fruit, though they might call to mind a company named Apple, headquartered in Cupertino. From Palo Alto in the Valley's northwest corner to the sprawling metropolis of San Jose, and stretching to Gilroy in the south, urbanization, enormous population growth, and the entrenchment of an economy rooted in high technology have obliterated nearly all signs that the area was once one of the nation's premier producers of deciduous fruits.[17] In many ways, the rise of Silicon Valley in recent decades has obscured two important, intersecting histories: the Santa Clara Valley's rich agricultural past and the history of the Asian farmers and laborers who cultivated the land.

Growing up in the suburbs of Sunnyvale and Cupertino when there were just a few orchards left and Silicon Valley was developing in full force, I caught glimpses of the receding glory days of agriculture, listened with puzzled amusement to stories from grade-school teachers who recalled what the area had looked like in the springtime when it was blanketed in pastel blooms. I savored the juicy cherries my family bought from Olson's Sunnyvale fruit stand in the summer and looked forward to our favorite holiday treats: chocolate-covered prunes from a local confectioner that has since closed. But by the time my family and I moved to the Valley in the 1980s, agriculture had ceased to be its most important industry or characterize the majority of its residents' way of life.

Nor was the history of rural Asian Americans apparent to many people who lived there, as the emergence of Silicon Valley produced the popular impression

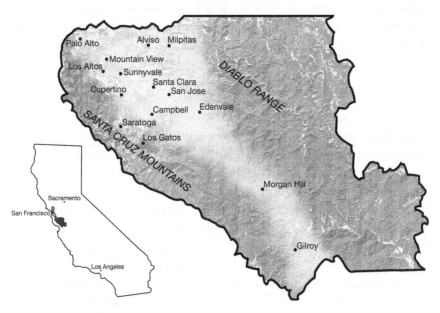

Figure I.2 Santa Clara County map.

that Asians were relative newcomers to Santa Clara County and arrived primarily as employees in the high-tech industry during the late twentieth century. As a child reared in the Valley, I assumed the same, seeing that the Asians I knew worked for firms like Hewlett-Packard, Sun Microsystems, IBM, and Intel, or in other middle-class professions. Like my own family, most of these individuals had arrived in the United States during the 1970s and 1980s with no former ties to the area, much less to its agricultural roots. I was surprised to discover that while the demand for high-tech workers in Silicon Valley had indeed brought a new wave of Asian immigrants to the area, another group of Asian Americans had laid claim to the region as farmers and farm laborers long before the arrival of Asian computer engineers and dot-com entrepreneurs. Just as intensive agriculture and the rising demand for farm labor lured Chinese, Japanese, and Filipino immigrants to the Valley in the past, the high-tech sector and the region's reputation as one of the world's top centers of research and development continues to draw immigrants from numerous countries in Asia today.

Recovering the intertwined history of the Santa Clara Valley when it was known as the Garden of the World along with the history of the Asian immigrants who farmed its famed crops, this book illuminates the importance of agriculture in shaping American racial, regional, and national identity. The rural lens brings into view unique patterns of Asian-white relations and suggests the need to examine forms of racialization more subtle than blatant discrimination and organized anti-Asian movements. The white family farm ideal, a fluid construct that never reflected the Santa Clara Valley's agricultural reality, imbued crops, gender roles, and family structures with racial meaning, responding to waves of Chinese, Japanese, and Filipino migration in the nineteenth and twentieth centuries. The farms and orchards that once graced the Valley may have faded away, but the complex legacy of race relations remains rooted in its soil.

"Independent of the Unskilled Chinaman"

Race, Labor, and Family Farming

In a thick, extensively illustrated book that combined promotional writings for Santa Clara County with a history of the region and biographies of its prominent citizens, Horace S. Foote wrote about Andrea Malovos, a prosperous Austrian immigrant who owned the Light-house Farm on Alviso Road north of San Jose, where he lived in "one of the finest residences of the section" with his wife and nine children. In this 1888 account, Foote noted that Malovos grew a variety of orchard fruits, grapes, asparagus, hay, and grain on his 286-acre property with the assistance of "from ten to sixty men, as the exigencies of the season require." Foote claimed that Malovos, "a man of intelligence and enterprise," hired "none but white labor," opposing workers who did not "enrich and build up the country of his adoption."[1]

As Foote may have been dismayed to discover, Malovos was apparently not so strict about his "white labor only" rule. According to the Santa Clara County recorder's office, in January of 1883, Malovos leased two parcels of land, one for 20 acres, the other for 24 acres, to four Chinese growers, Yuk Lun, Peh Yee, Ah Yee, and Ah Jim, to cultivate asparagus and grapes on a sharecropping basis for terms of six and ten years. Malovos agreed to furnish "lessees and employees house and water, transportation to Rail Road Depot on Steamboat landing, boxes for asparagus," along with two horses and multiple farm implements. After Malovos died in 1899, his widow continued to lease land to Chinese immigrants for growing asparagus under a sharecropping arrangement with a farmer named Hi Loy; the net proceeds were to be divided equally between the landowner and lessee, and expenses for canneries and commissions shared. The 1900 census documented six Chinese farmhand employees in residence, who had emigrated between 1877 and 1899, along with a Chinese cook. Years later, memories of "Chinese washing asparagus at the artesian well" in the early twentieth century stood out in the minds of the youngest Malovos children when they recalled their upbringing on Light-house Farm.[2]

Whether Foote suffered from a case of sloppy fact-checking or knowingly included false information to appeal to would-be settlers, central to his portrayal of the Santa Clara Valley as an ideal fruit growing region and place of settlement was an insistence on the whiteness of those who worked and lived there. The disjuncture between Foote's assertion that only whites operated a flourishing Santa Clara Valley farm and the reality of the Malovos family's dependence on Chinese tenant farmers and laborers reveals the contest over constructing and reconstructing racial ideology in California agriculture. Despite vigilante efforts to expel Chinese immigrants from many parts of the West, particularly in cities and mining districts, white growers in agricultural regions like the Santa Clara Valley largely welcomed and needed Chinese labor. In fact, the anti-Chinese movement in the late nineteenth century had the effect of sending more Chinese immigrants into farm labor as they sought refuge in agricultural areas located a safe distance from urban mobs.[3] But at a time when controversy over the "Chinese question" raged and occasionally erupted in violent conflict throughout California and the American West, whites also made every effort to avoid accusations of supporting Chinese "cheap labor" and violating the sanctity of white family farming and white labor.[4]

During the peak decades of orchard fruit production, Santa Clara Valley boosters and growers attempted to reconcile the white family farm ideal with the prevalence of Asian farm labor. To this end, they constructed a racialized and gendered discourse of labor that confined the Chinese to certain types of agricultural work and tried to write them out of orchard fruit growing. Though this discourse hardly bore a resemblance to everyday farm labor relations, the multifaceted nature of horticultural production in the enormously fertile Santa Clara Valley made it possible for whites to imagine a labor system segmented by race and crop. Nevertheless, Chinese immigrant farmers and field hands comprised the vast majority of the approximately 2,700 Chinese residents of Santa Clara County, and despite attempts by white boosters like Foote to erase them from promotional tracts, they made themselves an indispensable part of the agricultural landscape. Far from Foote's insinuation that the Chinese constituted a "labor element" that did not "enrich and build up" the country, the Chinese engaged in all facets of Valley agriculture and found inventive ways to farm and prosper.

"An Ideal Home Place"

One of the original twenty-seven counties of California established in 1850, Santa Clara County contains 832,256 acres (about 1,300 square miles), mostly rolling hills and mountains. Roughly 250,000 acres (390 square miles) comprise the famed Santa Clara Valley. Though cattle ranching, wheat and grain growing, and quicksilver mining all flourished in the Valley during the nineteenth century, by the 1880s, the county had become "one vast orchard" as deciduous fruit cultivation emerged as the dominant industry of the region and its claim to national and international prominence. Fruit growing became so renowned that the California Board of Horticulture in 1892 called Santa Clara County "preeminently the horticultural county of the State," after it produced a record 22 million pounds of prunes in the previous growing season. A booster wrote with pride that it was not merely the quantity of fruit cultivated that made the Valley impressive, but "of greater importance, Santa Clara Valley raises the very best of each of these fruits." Indeed, the "Santa Clara Grade" became synonymous with the highest quality prunes in the world, characterized by an abundant sugar content, "clear amber meat, thin skin and fine color," surpassing its competition from France within a few years of cultivation.[5]

At the turn of the twentieth century, Santa Clara County ranked first in acreage devoted to apricot and prune production among California counties, and second in acreage of pears and cherries. Prunes were by far the dominant crop, with the Santa Clara Valley supplying one-third of prunes in the world by the early twentieth century (California supplied nearly three-quarters of the world's total prune production). In addition to prunes, apricots, pears, and cherries, orchardists cultivated peaches, plums, and apples in smaller quantities. At its horticultural peak in the 1920s, the Santa Clara Valley led the state in fruit production as well as fruit canning and packing, with nearly all of its output canned or dried.[6] The presence of growing urban centers such as San Jose and the Valley's proximity to San Francisco made it a more populated region than other rural areas in the West and provided readily accessible markets for produce. Bolstered by the steady stream of settlers who helped increase the population of Santa Clara County by approximately one-third each decade from 1880 to 1910, promoters firmly held that the Valley was extraordinary in its offerings and attractions, not just another rural community in California.[7]

Who actually lived in the Santa Clara Valley before American boosters and fruit growers? The Ohlone Indians, for one, had inhabited the region for at least 6,000 years prior to the coming of the Spanish and numbered 7,000 to 26,000 before European contact. Part of the Penutian-speaking people, who included the Miwok, Wintun, Maidu, and Yokuts of northern California, the Ohlone subsisted on acorns harvested from local oaks, hunted wild game, fished, and gathered clams from San Francisco Bay.[8] In 1777, the government of Spain sent 66 representatives, most hailing from the Mexican regions of Sonora and Sinaloa, to establish the first *pueblo*, or civilian town, in Alta California to provide food for remote mission outposts and *presidios* (garrisons) in San Francisco and Monterey. José Joaquín Moraga, who led the group, named the new settlement after his patron saint. Hence San José de Guadalupe, California's oldest city, was built on the site of an abandoned Ohlone village. The pueblo and nearby Missions Santa Clara and San José established the Santa Clara Valley as the heart of Spanish colonial society in Alta California. When Mexico threw off Spanish colonial rule in 1821, the mercantilist system ended and foreign trade flourished, with cattle becoming the leading industry. The Mexican inhabitants, called Californios, increased their cattle herds to meet the trade demand, stepping out of the subsistence economy. Since traders sought only hides and tallow, Californios gave up on other manufacturing enterprises to focus on cattle, thereafter buying finished goods at inflated prices.[9]

In the 1840s, American emigrants stripped Valley Californios of their property at a growing rate, squatting on their land, killing cattle, and stealing horses on communal grounds. The initial "gringo" population in the Santa Clara Valley consisted in significant part of successful Irish Catholic immigrants, such as the prominent landowning family of Martin Murphy, and the region never experienced a period of Anglo-Protestant hegemony.[10] After the Treaty of Guadalupe Hidalgo ended the Mexican-American War and officially made the region an American settlement in 1848, white settlers resolved to rid the land of any vestiges of the Californio economy and replace it with one based on family farms producing goods for the market. The new American residents continued with the cattle economy to some extent, but only to produce meat to feed miners who flocked to the area during the gold rush. When the California Land Act of 1851 placed the burden of proof on Californios to establish rights to their land, many found themselves on the losing side of land claims, lacking both extensive knowledge of the American justice system and adequate funds for litigation. The destruction of the Californios' land base facilitated the creation of a new low-wage labor force in the Santa Clara Valley, the beginning of a succession of non-white laborers who would provide seasonal employment in mining and agriculture in the nineteenth and twentieth centuries.[11] In the 1850s and 1860s, many displaced Californios and immigrants from Latin America sought work in the New Almaden mercury mines. Located about fifteen miles south of San Jose, New Almaden became the second largest producer of mercury in the world and was key to the gold rush, increasing the amount of gold extracted from the Sierras and reducing the cost of its recovery.[12]

Key to Santa Clara Valley promoters' understanding of themselves and the role of Anglo-Americans in producing the remarkable changes that had occurred by the turn of the century was their narrative of the Spanish and Mexican landholding period. Presented as a foil to the lush orchards that white settlers planted and the bustling towns they built, the Spanish missions, Mexican cattle ranches, and sparsely settled pueblos were no match for the prosperous American fruit-growing economy in the minds of local promoters. Though the Santa Clara Valley through the nineteenth century had been home to four major populations—the native Ohlone, Spaniards, Mexicans (or Californios), and white Americans—boosters in the late nineteenth and early twentieth centuries tended to conflate Spanish missionaries with Mexican ranchers and Indians, indiscriminately labeling the many decades that preceded Anglo settlement as one long, unproductive "Spanish period" or "mission era." The boosters' narrative failed to take into account historical events like Mexican independence from Spain or the subsequent mandated secularization of missions.

An 1896 promotional publication described "an easy-going life that was led by the few inhabitants of the State during the mission era. Their wants were few, and easily supplied, and they lived contentedly, raising fruits and vegetables for home consumption, and pasturing their cattle on a thousand hills."[13] It did not matter to boosters that early white American emigrants continued to live and work much as the earlier inhabitants of the Valley had done, growing produce for subsistence and raising livestock. Unlike diligent white fruit growers of the late nineteenth and early twentieth centuries, promoters claimed, the Spanish and Californios sought instead an "easy-going life" of stagnation.

Promotional literature writers cast into question the masculinity of the Spanish and Mexican residents of the Valley, calling them idle and unambitious men who "were content to eat, sleep, ride horseback and roll cigarettes" while the land lay fallow and unimproved.[14] A May 1902 *Sunset* magazine article detailing the growth of the Santa Clara Valley featured a photograph of a Mexican man with two dogs walking outside a small, run-down ranch house, evocatively captioned "Before the Gringo Came." According to another writer, a "primitive manner of living" characterized those days, when there was "no sawed lumber, and houses were universally built of sun-dried bricks; there was not a vehicle in the country that had wheels with spokes in them; there were no fire-places, and no stoves until a few were brought by immigrants in 1846." For white boosters, the Valley was a desolate, unrefined place that had produced little of value before the arrival of the enterprising gringo.[15]

According to Valley promoters, something exceptional replaced the adobes and cattle ranches of Spanish and Mexican California. The area's exalted orchards did not simply represent white racial superiority but also a unique vision of agrarian domesticity and homebuilding, in which families on small farms grew a variety of irrigated crops, trees, and native flowers and thus provided the state with a more balanced form of development than the gold, wheat, or cattle ranching economies. Far from the alleged idleness and lack of agricultural productivity that characterized the lives of Spanish and Californio settlers, boosters and residents of the Santa Clara Valley claimed that Anglo-Americans had established a system of family labor in which white men, women, and children all held productive roles in the horticultural economy. Promoters targeted families as the unit of settlement in the Santa Clara Valley during the late nineteenth and early twentieth centuries, not single men or women. Pamphlet authors called the Valley's women and children "her most attractive advertisement," with the climate being "exactly suitable to them," in the vein of ideas popularized beginning in the 1870s by writer and economist Henry George. An advocate of small farms as a counterweight to wheat cultivation, which he blamed for land monopoly, environmental degradation, and racial strife in California, George argued that land barons and their use of Chinese "coolie" labor created vast social and economic inequalities that could be corrected only with the settlement of white farm families.

Striving to promote rural values against the incursion of industrial capitalism and to defend farmers from railroads and other corporate interests, the Grange movement echoed George's views. The Santa Clara Valley's first Grange chapter formed in San Jose in 1873 and soon the Patrons of Husbandry had a branch in nearly every Valley town.[16] The language of agrarian homebuilding in the American West permeated national discourse well into the early twentieth century, epitomized in the figure of the "homebuilder," the man who would settle the West with his family and improve the value of the land through their labor.[17]

Fruit culture meant the end of wheat cultivation in many California counties, long associated with absentee landlords and land exploitation. In the case of Santa Clara County, which ranked fifth in wheat production in 1870 (behind San Joaquin, Yolo, Solano, Stanislaus Counties) and at its peak in 1874 produced 1.7 million bushels, the large-scale planting of orchards in the 1880s displaced wheat growing, and by the early 1890s, the Valley had become the state's leading horticultural region. In these years, boosters christened the Santa Clara Valley the "Garden of the World," and San Jose the "Garden City."[18] With income per acre of orchards far exceeding the yield of grain farms, Santa Clara County growers enthusiastically embraced specialty crops like prunes. Valley boosters cheerfully noted the establishment of "innumerable homesteads surrounded by orchards and in which hundreds of happy families repose, literally under their own vines and fig trees." As San Jose orchardist Simon Leib told an audience of California fruit growers in 1892, the Santa Clara Valley was "one vast grain field" just a quarter-century ago when he arrived to settle, but "Now, behold the change!"[19]

Beginning in 1881, as specialty crop agriculture took root in California, hundreds of fruit growers gathered annually, and sometimes twice a year, to discuss issues ranging from pest control and cultivation techniques to marketing and advertising. At the 1892 convention where Leib spoke, two San Jose men were chosen as vice presidents of the state growers' organization, reflecting the area's prominence in horticultural affairs. Leib claimed that visitors who had not been to the Valley within the past decade would be "astonished" at the number of new orchards and vineyards.[20]

As specialty crop cultivation predominated by the turn of the twentieth century, boosters of the Santa Clara Valley reduced the region's Spanish and Mexican past to quaint relics, "whitewashing" an adobe past in nostalgic narratives and public displays that expunged the violence and injustice of recent decades.[21] Valley settlers replaced the area's adobes with orchards and afterward pointed to those few remaining Mexican structures to underscore how far the Valley had progressed since the arrival of "enterprising Americans." The missions and "here and there an old adobe building and a liberal sprinkling of the descendants of the Spanish and Mexican inhabitants" gave "interesting and pleasant suggestions of former times and conditions," but mission days were decidedly over. "Prosperous Americanism" took their place, heralded as "the results of fertility of soil, perfection of climate and labor intelligently and diligently applied." Promoters described the descendants of the early Californio inhabitants as if the latter were mere remnants, like the old adobe structures that formerly dotted the Valley. Spanish place names like "Santa Clara" and "San Jose" remained, but promoters felt such names sounded so foreign and unfamiliar to Anglo prospective settlers that they had to give pronunciation instructions for "the soft Spanish accent which is distinctive; 'j' has the sound of 'h,' and 'e' the sound of 'a': San-ho-say."[22]

A 1902 poem illustrated with a montage of Santa Clara Valley scenery summed up the view of many native-born white residents on the progress of the region. Beautiful pictures of blooming trees, a cherry orchard on Los Gatos–Campbell Road, pear blossoms near Santa Clara, prune and almond trees flowering in other local spots, flanked Jeanette Campbell's poem, "California Orchard Bloom," which closes with this stanza:

> While over it all is floating,
> Like an Indian summer haze,
> The lost romance and glory
> Of the vanished mission days.[23]

For Campbell and other turn-of-the-century promoters who delighted in the orchard culture and economy of the Valley, "mission days," the period they associated with subsistence farming and cattle ranching were certainly "lost" and "vanished" forever. So few were the remnants of this period since the orchards had taken over that Campbell chose to term those vestiges a nebulous floating "haze," without concrete shape or form. The presence of orchards helped white residents erase the real history of missions and ranchos and replace it with a hazy, romantic myth of Hispanic California, complete with Spanish colonial revival buildings, pageants, and fiestas.[24] In the new founding narrative Valley promoters told about the transformation of the region, white Americans by virtue of their enterprising racial attributes and productive agricultural labor legitimately crowded out the idle nonwhites who had occupied the land previously, and the Santa Clara Valley fulfilled its destiny as a lush paradise for American home seekers and fruit growers.

The "Right Kind" of Men, Women, and Children

At a time when urban wage earners were steadily becoming more numerous than farmers in the United States, fruit growers viewed their occupation with great pride, as a virtuous, honest way to earn a living. Contrary to popular stereotypes of unscrupulous growers bent on cutting costs and maximizing profits, many California horticulturists of the late nineteenth century were informed, public-minded farmers who believed their labors contributed to improving society. They viewed fruit growing as "more than manufacturing" and "a higher order of agriculture," which they enthusiastically promoted in their own writings and convention speeches, complementing booster publications.[25] The marked confidence in their burgeoning identities as orchardists may have also contributed to their lack of interest in the Farmers' Alliance and the Populist Party of the late nineteenth century. While some Farmers' Alliance members in California were fruit growers who participated in various cooperative organizations, most specialty crop farmers paid little attention to the Populist movement, which was short-lived and weak in the state, composed of largely isolated small wheat growers.

Mass protest did not appeal to California fruit growers, who were content with the economic benefit and moral meaning of their occupation.[26] Addressing the 1888 annual meeting of the American Horticultural Society in San Jose, association president Parker Earl called fruit growing "one of the noblest occupations of the world.... The results of our work contribute directly and powerfully to the betterment of mankind." Without hesitation, Earl tied the cultivation of fruits with improving the human race. These ideas resonated with the white boosters and orchardists of the Santa Clara Valley, who resided in one of the preeminent fruit-growing regions in the state and did not require much convincing to believe that horticulture was a noble, edifying way of life.[27]

To sell prospective emigrants on the advantages of settling in the Santa Clara Valley, authors of promotional literature drew on white middle-class American apprehensions about the strength of the family, gender roles, and racial identity at the turn of the twentieth century. As the nation became increasingly industrialized and urbanized, boosters insisted that the revered Jeffersonian vision of family farms, updated and improved for the new century, was still attainable in this California valley. Promotional literature for the Santa

Clara Valley encapsulated the ideology of turn-of-the-century American romantic agrarianism and appealed to the notion that individuals could recapture a lost paradise by escaping to land often described as "unspoiled." For anyone wishing to flee overcrowded cities, strained family life, meaningless occupations, racial conflict, and unclean air, boosters offered the Valley as a viable solution and encouraged the settlement of family farmers to cultivate orchard fruits.[28]

Santa Clara Valley boosters' emphasis on family life and their targeting of male household heads meant that gender ideals surfaced repeatedly in the body of promotional literature they produced at the turn of the twentieth century. Beyond hyperbolic descriptions of the Santa Clara Valley and its attractions for settlers was the gendering of the Valley itself. In his San Jose Chamber of Commerce brochure, pamphleteer and booster Leigh Irvine personified the Santa Clara Valley as a "sleeping maiden, fragrant with perfume and intoxicatingly beautiful, lying in a carven bed formed by the mountains of Santa Cruz, curtained by fleecy clouds; her coverlet of eiderdown, tinted with rose, quilted with green, edged with yellow; her pillow the sun-kissed water of San Francisco Bay."[29] Akin to Puritan settlers in New England who used virgin land metaphors linking the "subjugation of wilderness and the subjection of women," Irvine constructed the Valley to his male readers as an alluring maiden. The suitors who came to woo her were potential fruit growers, presumed to be enterprising, intelligent men hailing from all parts of the nation to settle down with this prized "maiden." Transformed from oak plains to cattle ranches, and from wheat farms to orchards, the Santa Clara Valley by the early twentieth century was not exactly virgin land, as New England had appeared to English settlers in the seventeenth century. Nonetheless, promotional literature inviting fruit growing men to "court" the Valley continued to draw on gendered earth rhetoric and images of male cultivation domesticating the land.[30]

Promoters of the Santa Clara Valley as a place for settlement linked manhood to family farming and associated fruit growing with an elevated type of man. Directing his sales pitch to male household heads, Irvine assured would-be settlers of the self-sufficiency and a comfortable living they would find on a few acres of orchard land, if they were "the right kind of men." Speaking to fellow fruit growers in San Jose in 1892, N. P. Chipman railed against those he admonished "Need Not Apply" to become fruit growers: "A slothful, or lazy, or unambitious man has no business with an orchard." Growers and promoters concurred that fruit growing required certain masculine qualities, and an orchardist must be "observant, industrious, intelligent, a reading man, and he must have to some extent the mercantile faculty." Given these selective requirements, Chipman concluded that fruit growers were indeed "a very superior body of men."[31]

Related to appeals to American masculinity was the repeated assertion in promotional literature that men could fulfill their appointed breadwinning roles by settling in the Valley. Unemployment, economic depression, and the advent of corporate work in the late nineteenth century produced anxiety about manhood and the ability of American men to carry out their responsibility as providers.[32] Making a living from the land, some perceived, was far more autonomous and manly than holding "soft" white-collar jobs or working for large, bureaucratized companies. Self-employed and not reliant on the favors of other men in the corporate world, as one booster pronounced, "he who owns a few acres of good fruit land in this county...is one of the most independent men on God's footstool." Fruit growers were not corporate employees who had lost touch with the product of their work, putting their hands "only on the typewriter, the account books, the documents."[33]

Targeted at anxious heads of household, booster materials brimmed with talk of the wealth to be had by running a small orchard, juxtaposed with mentions of inadequate urban salaries. One promoter chided the man who would live in crowded cities "to make a small salary, confront the vices of congested population, and spend all you earn in doing it" when, as a San Jose Chamber of Commerce pamphleteer put it, "the right investment in Santa Clara County will earn money faster than a man can make it by working."[34] At the 1901 convention of state growers, San Francisco farmer J. W. Nelson declared that the Santa Clara Valley was "The Richest Spot on the Globe," with its orchard districts producing "more money than any other tract of ground of equal area on the face of the globe."[35] While California growers were not fixated solely on material advancement, they nonetheless saw their orchards and farms as profitable investments.

For some commentators, achieving this dream of owning a small, prosperous farm in the Santa Clara Valley denoted true manliness, as exemplified by certain decidedly masculine paragons. An 1899 real estate advertisement cited the late politician, railroad baron, university founder, and Palo Alto gentleman farmer Leland Stanford as proof that living in Santa Clara Valley was the epitome of manliness. After all, the pamphlet's author gushed, "that great and noble specimen of American manhood" Stanford, who advocated small-farm settlement as California's governor and as president of the Central Pacific Railroad, located his home in this county, and "there left his monument—the great Stanford University."[36] This tract did not divulge that the Stanfords, hardly typical Valley settlers, could not have run "The Farm" without the employment of numerous Chinese (and later Japanese) laborers on their large estate.

In another testimony to the manliness of farming in Santa Clara Valley, self-proclaimed "globe-trotting" writer E. Alexander Powell told of his encounter with a philosophical sea captain sailing on the Indian Ocean. The captain had announced, during one conversation over brandy on his steamer, that he was going to quit the sea after a few more voyages: "I'm going to build a house for myself and the missis in a valley that I know; a house painted white with green blinds and with a porch as broad as a ship's deck, and I'm going to have a fruit orchard and a flower garden and raise chickens." This "valley that I know," as it turned out, was the Santa Clara Valley, which the captain called "too beautiful." For this seasoned captain, masculinity was bound up with the fulfillment of a fanciful agrarian daydream. Though he drank brandy, commanded a steamer on the high seas, and was indisputably manly, the captain did not hesitate to share his vision of domestic bliss on a Santa Clara Valley orchard farm. Powell proceeded to detail another chance meeting he had, this time in Algiers with an American from the Valley. As they were drinking and waxing nostalgic, the man made a toast: " 'Friend' he said, and his voice was husky, 'here's to God's favorite valley—here's to the Santa Clara.'"[37] From the famous Leland Stanford to the rough sea captain and a homesick, husky-voiced traveler, shining examples of American manhood found themselves entranced with the Santa Clara Valley and dreams of farming in it.

As reflected in the captain's dream of owning a green-and-white farmhouse flanked by a garden, an orchard, and chickens with his "missis," the brand of masculinity linked with fruit growing in the Santa Clara Valley did not exclude women, whose productive labor was welcome in the family farm enterprise. In fact, according to commentators, because horticulture was "essentially a home-making industry," fruit growing was "peculiarly adapted for women," a "light, healthful, interesting and profitable occupation." Speaking on the subject of "A Woman's Orchard" at the 1892 state growers' convention, Georgia McBride of San Jose claimed that a woman could "engage in this work without loss of delicacy, grace, or refinement."[38] The *California Fruit Grower* observed that female fruit growers were actually fulfilling gender roles delineated since the biblical creation: "Women have a natural aptitude for agriculture in its lighter forms, and since the time of Mother Eve herself, have delighted to delve in the garden and prune the shrubs and plants about the home." But male fruit growers would not go so far as to concede their occupation to women entirely. The article noted there remained "some forms of manual work" requiring strength that women could not perform without male help.[39] Thus writers implied that farming had a place only for women who were part of a family unit, in positions of dependence on male support. Rare indeed were suggestions that female-headed farms were a desirable type of settlement.

Valley promoters made exceptions, however, for the widow nobly trying to provide for her children by managing a fruit orchard. McBride told her audience of a widowed "lady from the East" who arrived in "this beautiful valley" with her four young sons, purchased 15 acres of land in the Willow Glen neighborhood of San Jose, and put in an orchard of prized French prune trees, eventually adding

20 more acres to her holdings. McBride attributed this woman's success as an orchardist not to her ambition and intelligence, characteristics that reportedly allowed male fruit growers to thrive in the same pursuit, but praised her ability to transfer maternal instincts to farming: "[S]he found that young trees, like children, need both watchful care and pruning." Hence, the lady fruit grower nurtured the fruit trees as if they were her children, though as McBride pointed out, only "while her boys were at school," implying that the woman would not let her productive role as a fruit grower overshadow her more vital reproductive role. McBride, who was born and raised in Missouri, the mother of four sons, and owner of a fruit orchard in San Jose, was most likely referring to herself in this sketch.[40] In the Santa Clara Valley and elsewhere in the major agricultural regions of California, the presence of female property owners, whether single, married, or widowed, contradicted the vision of male-headed family farms even as promoters claimed that some were legitimate exceptions to the rule.

Like women, children held a distinct place within the vision of orderly agriculture in the Santa Clara Valley and were noted for their productive potential. Promoters recalled East Coast observers marveling at how "ruddy, stout and robust" the children of the Valley looked, supposedly from the wholesome air and surroundings. Beyond the appearance of health, commentators affirmed that children reaped the benefits of contributing to the family income by doing orchard work, available to "[a]ny one who has strength enough to cut open a peach or an apricot and spread it on a tray." As a result, there was "no need for any industrious boy or girl to be idle in Santa Clara County," a venue that provided plentiful opportunities for character-building labor.[41] Those concerned that vice-filled urban areas bred misbehaving children prescribed prune picking, apricot cutting, and other orchard work as an antidote. In a speech met with "great and prolonged applause" among the state's gathered fruit growers in 1889, Flora Kimball proclaimed: "Give a mischievous city lad a dozen fine fruit trees, all for his very own, his to cultivate, and enjoy the fruit thereof, and his early reformation may be safely predicted." Sarah Cooper, wife of the president of the state board of horticulture, Elwood Cooper, concurred that contact with plants in a pleasant landscape could even serve as "a bar against surrounding evils."[42]

Idyllic images of white families picking orchard fruit in the summertime abounded in literature about the Valley. Cherries and apricots in May and June and prunes in August demanded the greatest number of harvesters in the Valley. Apricot cutting in particular, the 1911 Immigration Commission report noted, involved "a large number of white persons, principally women and children." Fruit dryers in Campbell reported white families arrived "from 50 miles around" to enjoy the novelty of working "in the fruit." Fruit-drying associations in the Santa Clara Valley provided campgrounds for families, who had to furnish their

Figure 1.1. Group photograph taken at the Stelling family orchard, Cupertino, 1895.

own tents and meals. School boards even timed summer vacations to coincide with harvests so local children could participate.[43] As Powell wrote, the seasonal employment available in the Santa Clara Valley attracted "an altogether exceptional class of people, for university and high-school students and the wives and daughters of small ranchmen eagerly avail themselves of this opportunity to add to their incomes." Taking a feminist stance on women's fashions, the *California Fruit Grower* told readers that there should be "nothing reprehensible or shocking" about seeing women and girls "clad in overalls and jumpers" in prune orchards, for California growers needed the "willing and agile female.... ambitious to earn a little extra pin-money" to help harvest "the lighter crops." However the harvesters were dressed, Powell noted that during picking season, the county's fruit orchards looked "not so much like a hive of workers, but rather like a gigantic picnic among the shaded orchard rows, in which the whole countryside is taking part."[44]

  A 1904 *Sunset* article showcased diligent young men and women picking and packing the Valley's fruit crop in the summer. An accompanying photograph featured a ten-year-old boy under a tree, picking up ripe prunes, a bucket and fruit boxes nearby. According to the caption, he was "working his way through school by gathering prunes."[45] Growers and observers of California horticulture hoped that white native-born women and children representing the "more desirable class of efficient American labor" would comprise a workforce sufficiently numerous to permit ranchers to dispense with the employment of Asian immigrants in the harvesting and processing of orchard fruits.[46]

In this idealized version of agrarianism, which incorporated white women and children along with white male landowners, there was no place for nonwhite wage labor. At least theoretically, the strategy of putting a white family's women and children to work in the orchards safeguarded fruit growers from having to employ Asian laborers, thereby tainting the family farm venture. Chipman maintained that "the small orchardists" of the state eschewed "alien labor" in favor of family help. According to the *San Francisco Call*, Georgia McBride "did her own pruning," while Valley booster Horace Foote noted that McBride, "by the aid of her sons" managed her orchard "without assistance," suggesting that she, like Andrea Malovos, did not hire Chinese labor.[47]

Writing about the anonymous thriving female orchardist in San Jose whose circumstances uncannily resembled her own, McBride herself emphasized that she had received "willing assistance from her four boys" when she added 20 acres to her orchard, so that even as a widow with sizable holdings, she could manage without "alien labor": "Having raised her own help, she was independent of the unskilled Chinaman."[48] The labor of her offspring, conveniently four male children, saved the widow fruit grower from the stigma of hiring "Chinaman" help and upheld the integrity of her orchard as a family farm in the absence of a male household head. For white residents who depicted their Valley as a place where only virtuous white families grew the region's celebrated orchard fruits, Chinese immigrant men, who to most white Americans constituted a bachelor population without visible families, provided a convenient foil representing the antithesis of family farming.

"Exacting Work"

In reality, Santa Clara Valley growers were neither very independent of "the unskilled Chinaman," nor was the labor Asian immigrants performed truly "unskilled." Though mentions of Chinese in promotional materials were rare, since local chambers of commerce and boosters believed advertising their presence would repel home-seekers, growers' perceived need to point out strategies for avoiding "alien labor" and "the Chinaman" suggested there were many farmers who did not find family labor sufficient. An exploration of sources revealing the nature of rural life in the Valley beyond promotional literature shows that as much as the Chinese population, predominantly male, with few women or children, did not fit the white family farm ideal, the Chinese remained for decades a ubiquitous and significant part of the region's agricultural economy.

Chinese immigrants first migrated to the United States in significant numbers in the mid-nineteenth century during the California gold rush and remained primarily in the gold fields until profits declined in the mid-1860s. Many subsequently entered railroad construction and played a pivotal role in building the transcontinental Central Pacific line, completed in 1869. Thousands of these former railroad laborers then flocked to San Francisco and found opportunities in the manufacturing economy, while others became farm laborers as California agriculture shifted from wheat to fruit growing, the Santa Clara Valley illustrating this trend precisely. In 1870, the Chinese made up 18 percent of all farm laborers in California and 55 percent in Santa Clara County.[49] In 1886, county officials provided the Bureau of the Census with estimates that of the 2,500 Chinese in Santa Clara County, nearly all of whom were male, 1,600, or 64 percent were involved in some type of "agricultural pursuit," and 600, or 24 percent were reported to be domestics.[50] Of Chinese persons engaged in agriculture, the 1900 census showed that 89 percent were laborers and 10.6 percent were farmers. Chinese men who rented or owned farms had resided in the United States an average of two years longer than their countrymen who were farm laborers.[51]

With further emigration of Chinese laborers prohibited by the 1882 Chinese Exclusion Act, Chinese agriculturists in California at the turn of the twentieth century represented an aging immigrant population. Tabulations from certificates of residence filed by Chinese residents of Santa Clara County in the spring of 1894 show that the average age of the men who listed their occupation as "farmer" or "ranch hand" was nearly forty-three years.[52] In 1900, just 47 percent Chinese of males in the U.S. were thirty-nine years of age and under, compared to 87 percent of white males. Even though the Chinese population in Santa Clara County in 1900 was 98 percent male, over one-third of Chinese men enumerated stated they were married, indicating that their wives had not emigrated with them.[53] Despite the presence of a significant number of married Chinese men, many assumed that the Chinese population in the Valley constituted a "bachelor" community of single men; this error, in turn, formed the basis of the notion that the agricultural work of Chinese farmers was inferior to that performed by white families.

While white growers relied on Asian labor, they also created a racial hierarchy of production, classifying Chinese contributions to agriculture as labor too tedious and menial for whites to perform. Berry and seed cultivation, along with vegetable farming, were often cited. In contrast, agricultural work associated with deciduous fruit orchards denoted whiteness, perpetuating the notion that white European family farmers alone cultivated the Santa Clara Valley and accounted for its acclaimed reputation as the center of orchard fruit production. White commentators and Valley promoters consistently referred to the agricultural work that the Chinese, and later the Japanese, did using terms that delineated racial boundaries necessary to maintain the family farm ideal. Chinese labor was "exacting," "careful," "particular," and "hand work." "Exacting work" usually involved tasks related to strawberry growing and garden seed processing, two prominent industries that flourished in the Santa Clara Valley in the late nineteenth and early twentieth centuries alongside the region's famed prunes, apricots, pears, and cherries. Employing Asian farmers and laborers to do marginalized "exacting work" in berries and seed production made possible white growers' constructed identities as independent family farmers who grew orchard fruit. The embrace of the family farm ideal concurrent with the overrepresentation of Chinese immigrants in crops involving stoop labor paralleled the pattern of white working-class tolerance of Chinese as menial or unskilled laborers who often performed dangerous, undesirable work in the mining and railroad industries. As Chinese workers moved into manufacturing, white trade unionists constructed their class-based white racial identity through their anti-Chinese politics and by ensuring that Chinese were constrained to the lowest rungs of urban industries. In the late nineteenth century, Chinese specialization in "inferior" crops in rural California occurred in tandem with their trade-based containment in the industrial sector.[54]

In the late nineteenth century, the Valley's white growers commonly leased their land to Chinese immigrants to grow strawberries. From 1878 to 1906, one-third of the leases recorded in the county between white landowners and Chinese tenants specified terms relating to berry cultivation, mainly strawberries, with some mentions of raspberries, blackberries, and loganberries.[55] Chinese immigrants had cultivated strawberries in the Santa Clara Valley since the 1860s, first in the stretch of land around the southern end of the San Francisco Bay between Alviso and San Jose. According to census data, 17 percent of the Chinese residents listed by census takers in 1870 in Santa Clara County were strawberry growers, as were 13.4 percent of the Chinese population recorded in 1880. A far greater number of Chinese were involved in berry cultivation than indicated by the census, since six times as many workers were hired during harvest season.[56] An 1896 promotional tract unabashedly acknowledged that growers rented out portions of their farms to "Chinamen," as in the case of Augusta Younger, whose husband, Coleman, died in 1890. As a widow in the 1890s, she charged $20 rent per acre and had her Chinese tenants raise onions between rows of young strawberry plants. Coleman and Augusta Younger had made the overland journey from Missouri to California in 1853 and settled in San Jose, where Coleman Younger became a leading cattle raiser and farmer. Between 1868 and 1898 the Youngers and their four children signed a total of eleven leases with Chinese tenants.[57]

Sharecropping arrangements between white growers and Chinese tenants were common in Santa Clara County, as evidenced by numerous leases signed and filed by each group at the county recorder's office. The recorded agreements represented only a fraction of such arrangements. In a lease not entered in official records, Charles Cropley agreed in November 1887 to lease 20 acres of land in Alviso during a term of ten years to Ah Wah, for the purpose of planting "berries, asparagus or such fruits or vegetables as may be agreed upon by the parties." Booster Horace Foote called Cropley a "prosperous farmer" who cultivated a small orchard on his home ranch in Berryessa and grew berries and vegetables on his Alviso property. Under the agreement with Ah Wah, Cropley was to supply plants for the first year and a house for the tenant, as well as water, tools, and transportation to market of "the productions of said land." In exchange, the tenant was to cultivate the land "assiduously and in a workmanlike manner," providing necessary labor for harvest, and maintaining irrigation ditches. As was typical of most sharecropping leases, profits were to be divided equally between the parties.[58]

Whether they were written or oral contracts, filed with the county or privately maintained, sharecropping arrangements involving white landowners and Chinese farmers were an integral part of agricultural life in the Valley during the late nineteenth century. Indeed, the practice of leasing land to Chinese for berry cultivation was mentioned in leases between whites as well. For example, in 1893, widow Mary Cole leased 65 acres of her property at Coyote Creek south of San Jose to William Farrell with the understanding that the latter was "permitted to contract with Chinese to sublet that portion of the ranch planted in raspberries, strawberries, blackberries and asparagus," assuming that Farrell would be responsible for any damage or loss caused by the Chinese tenants.[59]

Lease and property records in Santa Clara County also show a marked frequency on the part of white women in hiring Asian tenants and sharecroppers. In general, agricultural historians have noted that American women who owned land tended to lease a higher percentage of it than men.[60] From 1885 to 1890, women comprised approximately 6 percent of agricultural landowners in Santa Clara County (the figure was as high as 15 percent in some districts).[61] Since community property law in this period was more progressive in California than in other states, a woman had the right to own property individually as well as jointly with her husband. While a female farm ownership rate of 6 percent was not remarkable (e.g., a survey of four rural townships in New York State in 1911 found that women owned 9 percent of all agricultural acreage), women landowners were disproportionately represented as lessors with Asian tenants, signing nearly 31 percent of all leases between whites and Asian tenants (Chinese and Japanese were the only discernible Asian groups in these records) between 1878 and 1921.

Statistical and anecdotal evidence from the Santa Clara Valley indicates a connection between the absence of a male household head and the decision to lease to Chinese and Japanese tenants, but exact reasons for this trend need to be explored in more depth.[62] For example, immediately after Coleman Younger's death in 1890, the Younger women, Augusta and three adult daughters, recorded numerous leases with Chinese and Japanese tenants on their respective inherited parcels (the only son, Edward Younger, recorded just one lease with Japanese tenants, in 1907). Widow Augusta Younger signed multiple leases with Chinese farmers in the 1890s, mainly for berry and vegetable cultivation.[63] The Younger women and other female landowners in the Valley made business decisions about which crops to plant, negotiated the terms of leases with Chinese and Japanese tenants, drew up official agreements at the county recorder's office, collected rent, ensured that lessees followed through with the outlined terms, and tried to maximize the economic benefit they could derive from their property. These women were not just "helpmeets" of their husbands who occasionally dabbled in the garden as prescribed in promotional literature, but pragmatic, enterprising businesswomen in their own right. Furthermore, managing agricultural land through Asian tenancy became a means for single and widowed white women to sustain an affluent middle-class lifestyle, thereby upholding the social and economic order and de-emphasizing both the women's reliance on nonwhite labor and the authority they exercised in agricultural dealings.

White growers defended their practice of leasing land to Chinese for berry culture as acceptable precisely because the work involved was so tedious and labor intensive. An August 1901 article in the *Palo Alto Times* informed readers that strawberry vines required "constant cultivation, the ground being hoed six or seven times during the year," along with "abundant irrigation" after the grueling planting of runners and 15,000 to 16,000 vines per acre. "The field work here is almost wholly done by Chinese," the article noted, under sharecropping arrangements in which the Chinese received one-half of the profits for their labor.[64] According to one Valley booster, Chinese tenant farmers worked "incessantly, early and late, and make money" on the Younger property by ensuring that the rich soil was "most thoroughly utilized." Another writer emphasized that Chinese tenant farmers were not innately talented at growing berries, but the "exacting" nature of the work made it undesirable for anyone else to take it on: "Of course any white man could take the same land and net nearly as much as the Chinamen do, even hiring white help. Few white men care to do it, however, as the work is very exacting. There is always difficulty in securing white men who will perform the work, and many land owners, therefore, lease their land." When discussing berry cultivation, white residents readily admitted to their employment of Chinese immigrants; they did not consider the arduous labor entailed in raising berries, as distinguished from orchard fruits, to be appropriate for white men, women, and children.[65]

The other prime case of "exacting work" undertaken by Chinese agriculturists in Santa Clara County was garden seed processing, described by one commentator in 1902 as a "careful and particular process." In the 1901 growing season, the Valley's seed farms reportedly harvested a staggering 1,035,000 pounds (250 tons) of seed, of which one-half consisted of onion seed, worth a total of approximately $500,000 (equivalent to around $11 million today).[66] Observers remarked that harvesting seed from onions required meticulous, "experienced labor," since the onion tops had to be cut from the stalks by hand, leaving about one inch of stem. Well-known local author Jessie Juliet Knox painted a romantic image of Chinese taking "large, covered baskets" into "the great fields of snowy bloom" to harvest onion seed. The laborers then spread the harvested onion tops on white canvas to dry thoroughly, frequently turning them with wooden forks before carting them to the threshing machine. Next came the cleansing process, in which seeds were again spread out to dry and then raked up and packaged for the market. Photos in *Sunset* magazine showed Chinese workers engaged in every stage of onion seed production, operating threshers and a seed-raking machine, as well as harvesting onion tops in fields.[67]

Although Knox highlighted one of the Valley's larger seed farm operations, many small farmers were involved in production as well. In 1880, William A. Z. Edwards, a farmer in the Alviso area, began raising onions for seed under an agreement with commercial seed grower James Kimberlin of Santa Clara. Edwards's diaries were full of entries documenting business transactions with Chinese farmers in the vicinity and amounts he paid them for sacks of onions ("I paid Ah Yod for 93 sks onions $17.50"; "Paid Ah Jim for 12 Sks onions $3.00.").[68] Another Chinese farmer, Chin Ah Coon, managed multiple seed farms in Santa Clara and Sunnyvale on the property of white landowners at the turn of the twentieth century, including a ranch that had belonged to Austin Kellogg, partner of renowned seed grower C. C. Morse, who eventually formed the Ferry-Morse Seed Company, still in operation today.[69]

Seed ranch owners in the Valley readily praised the proficient skill of the Chinese workers who had been employed since the earliest years of operation of the Morse seed farm, west of Santa Clara. Reportedly the Chinese understood "every detail of care and culture" and thus were able to "distinguish all the delicate differences of varieties." Specialized knowledge of each seed type was critical: during the 1895 season, the Morse farm grew an enormous array of crops for seed, including lettuce, turnips, cabbage, kohlrabi, onions, celery, parsnips, and sweet pea flowers. Seed growers regarded the Chinese as "the best of all races thus far employed," declaring that Chinese laborers gave "the close attention and care required to obtain the best product."

After the passage of exclusionary immigration legislation in 1882, however, Santa Clara Valley seed ranchers had to seek other laborers and experimented with Italian and Portuguese immigrants. Growers found these Europeans "inconvenient to obtain, not organized into groups" and most importantly "not as skillful" as the Chinese. While ranchers considered Chinese laborers gifted with dex-

Figure 1.2. Chinese laborers washing and preparing onion seed in the Santa Clara Valley, c. 1900.
Courtesy of History San José.

terity for "hand work," they thought the Chinese were "not good with teams" (referring to teams of horses or other draft animals), the other type of work involved in garden seed production. Thus the U.S. Immigration Commission reported that members of the "white races," French, German, Portuguese, Swiss-Italian, Spanish, English, and native-born men were engaged in plowing, cultivating, and hauling, receiving markedly higher wages than Chinese workers. Well into the 1920s, however, Asian labor predominated in the seed growing industry of the Santa Clara Valley.[70]

For a shorter period, Chinese farmers in the Valley also dominated the growing and processing of asparagus. Edwards eventually entrusted his entire asparagus patch to Jim Lee, who he noted "called proposing to take my asparagus & c on shares" in late November 1893, possibly with intentions to sell the harvest to the Bayside Canning Company in Alviso, owned by Chinese canner Thomas Foon Chew. This arrangement continued until early 1902, when Edwards decided to plow out the asparagus patch, which had become infested with morning glory weed. Chew owned extensive property in the Sacramento region and in addition to the Alviso cannery, operated a cannery in Isleton.

By the early twentieth century, Santa Clara Valley asparagus growers faced stiff competition from the Sacramento Delta region, where Chinese farmers had

Figure 1.3. Chinese cabin at Morse seed ranch, Mountain View, c. 1890.
Courtesy of History San José.

harvested the first commercial asparagus crops in the area in 1893 and helped
establish asparagus as a major industry there.[71] As late as 1909, Chinese and
white growers in the Valley continued to make arrangements to raise asparagus,
as on the Bellew ranch near Milpitas, where Lee Gun had partnered with Michael
Bellew for over two years. An Irish immigrant who first began farming in Santa
Clara County in 1861, Bellew owned 93 acres at his farm residence on the south
side of Milpitas-Alviso Road, and another 128 acres on the north side of the
road, lying on the west bank of the Coyote Creek, where Lee Gun farmed approximately 20 acres of asparagus.[72]

As much as some promoters strove to depict orchard work as an all-white
endeavor, growers also hired Chinese immigrants for a variety of jobs associated
with orchard fruit production. Santa Clara County lease records reveal that the
Younger family not only leased land to Chinese farmers for strawberry growing
but also rented a parcel of land on Gish Road in San Jose to four Chinese farmers
to grow pears. Coleman Younger agreed to furnish Ah Sing, Ah Hong, Ah Lee,
and Ah John "sufficient yearling pear trees to plant fifteen acres of orchards."[73]
William A. Z. Edwards, the Alviso farmer, planted his first French prune crop in
1897 and easily incorporated his Chinese hired hands into the harvesting of the
fruit and the pruning of trees. In his memoir of growing up in the Santa Clara
Valley during its orchard heyday, Ralph Rambo noted how his father sought out

Chinese to pick prunes on their West Side ranch, ascribing racial characteristics to the work. Rambo explained, "Picking prunes requires either a kneeling or stooping posture, quite natural for the Celestial and almost unendurable for the American, (including the writer)," though he admitted to spending summers in his childhood prune picking as well: "I wasn't a boy coolie but I rented my muscle for five cents a box of prunes for several years."[74]

In a number of cases, Chinese tenants grew deciduous fruits in addition to strawberries on white landowners' property, contradicting boosters' assertions of strict racial division between orchard fruit and strawberry cultivation. In October 1892, German immigrant Henry Rengstorff of Mountain View, who purchased his first parcel of Valley land in 1857, leased 20 acres for a term of five years to Yuen Lee and Company to plant and maintain fruit trees furnished by Rengstorff. He also permitted the tenants to plant strawberries between the trees, with no remarkable distinction in terms between the growing of berries and orchard fruit in the lease.[75] Likewise, San Jose landowner Alice Cohen signed a lease with Ah Hoo in November of 1895 to cultivate on her property one of the Valley's most profitable commodities: French prunes. Ah Hoo stated he would "care for all the cleared land in a workmanlike manner and do everything needed to keep all fruit trees and vines in a healthy condition." Numerous Santa Clara Valley growers would have concurred with the *California Fruit Grower*'s measured support for landowners' widespread practice of leasing their orchards to "Chinamen" and its declaration that "the fruit grows just the same...provided the cultivation and attention are proper," regardless of the ethnicity of the fruit grower.[76]

In the day-to-day operations of farms, precise racialized and gendered categories of labor were difficult to maintain, and white growers did not always distinguish between "exacting work" that only Chinese did and labor fit for white help. Edwards frequently instructed his white hired men to do the same work as his Chinese laborers, though sometimes in separate teams. For a week in late February and early March of 1889, his diary entries featured the same pattern: "Carl and Bradley pruned pear trees in the south orchard, two Chinese pruned pear trees in the east orchard." In late March of 1895, grower and canner John Francis Pyle of Berryessa noted in his journal: "I and 2 Chinamen sacked and loaded 56 Sks of squash." In May, other male members of the Pyle family worked together with Chinese laborers on the same tasks: "Frank and 5 Chinamen reset rhubarb until about 9 o'clock," and "Harry with the Chinamen planted tomatoes."[77]

Daily journal entries of local white growers like Edwards and Pyle demonstrate constant interactions between whites and Asians in agriculture. Pyle's diary entries from the 1890s show him selling berry chests to "Chinamen" and hiring them to work on the various crops grown on his property. He noted: "Five

Figure 1.4. Chinese and white workers in front of loaded fruit truck, San Jose, c. 1910.
Courtesy of History San José.

Chinamen worked all day with the rhubarb and one hour each packing squash";
"made knives for the Chinamen to thin onions forenoon."[78] From the 1870s until
his death in 1908, Edwards, an English immigrant who mined and worked during
the early 1850s in Tuolumne and Plumas Counties in northern California before
settling on a ranch in San Jose in 1857, hired scores of Chinese. In the span of the
1889 growing season, for example, Edwards reported in his diary the use of
Chinese in pruning fruit trees; cutting weeds; cultivating asparagus, berries, and
grass; cooking hay; irrigating crops; hoeing carrots; picking fruits and vegetables; packing produce; and hauling manure. Many Chinese farmers lived on the
Edwards ranch and were involved in practically every aspect of running it. In the
1890s, at harvest time or whenever he needed extra hands, Edwards employed
additional Chinese immigrants to work for a dollar a day, with small pay
increases.

Elected county supervisor in 1884 and appointed county artesian well
inspector in 1893, Edwards was a respected and well-connected citizen of Santa
Clara Valley. His practice of hiring Chinese immigrants for tenant farming and
agricultural work was widely accepted and did not interfere with his rise to
prominence in the region.[79] Though promotional literature perpetuated the
notion that white family farmers alone cultivated the Santa Clara Valley with the
help of some Chinese in menial capacities, the practices of these Valley farmers
belied the boosters' claim. In fact, there was no agricultural work on the ranch
the white farmers felt to be beyond the competence of Chinese immigrants.

The horticultural expertise of Chinese immigrants in the Santa Clara Valley
was not limited to fruit and vegetable raising but expanded to gardening and

flower growing as well. A number of the Valley's well-to-do landowners hired Chinese gardeners to tend their large properties, an occupation that often enabled Chinese to initiate other agricultural enterprises. For example, when the Edwards family went for a visit to "Palo Alto stock farm" one Saturday in October 1893 and saw the "private residence of Mrs. [Leland] Stanford," William Edwards's diary mentions the flowers, which were "found in profusion planted artistically and kept in neatest order."[80] The Edwards family may not have been aware that the impressive garden was cared for by two Chinese flower growers, Jim Mock and Ah King. Yet in a lengthy lease signed at the county recorder's office a few months prior to the Edwards family's weekend visit, Jane Stanford stipulated that the Chinese lessees were to "water and keep in proper condition all the lawns surrounding the said Private Residence, flower beds, growing plants and trees thereon and to replant beds etc."[81]

Jim Mock and other Chinese gardeners in the Valley often negotiated additional horticultural opportunities on white landowners' property. Mock, who arrived in California before the 1880s from a region of the Pearl River Delta formerly known as Huangliang Du (Wong Leung Do) and had supervised Chinese workers on the Southern Pacific Railroad, became a foreman on the Stanford farm, a position that allowed him to begin a flower-growing business on the side. Emigrants from Huangliang Du were among the earliest Chinese to settle in North America, many becoming flower growers and agricultural specialists in California. Up to the early 1920s, practically all Chinese gardeners and cooks on the Stanford estate were natives of this region.

Jim Mock's lease with Jane Stanford stated he and Ah King were to have "the privilege of propagating and raising in portions of the beds in said hot houses such plants and flowers for their own use and disposition as they may see fit," or to sell the flowers they grew, as long as they gave Mrs. Stanford some of those flowers in the "amount asked for or required by her from time to time." By the early 1900s, Mock had left the employ of Jane Stanford to take on flower growing on a full-time basis, cultivating sweet peas, asters, chrysanthemums, and stock near San Carlos in San Mateo County. Before he departed the Stanford farm, Mock helped others who hailed from his native region find work on the estate and on the university campus, either as gardeners or as cooks in Stanford fraternity and sorority houses.[82]

Like Mock, other Chinese gardeners who worked for prosperous Santa Clara Valley landowners secured a fair amount of autonomy to grow their own crops and establish auxiliary businesses. In 1893, Anna B. Rock of San Francisco, owner of a large parcel of land in San Jose, signed a lease with the Quong Lee Company, composed of Ah Wy and Ah Sing of San Jose. The arrangement essentially allowed the Chinese lessees to use her property for a variety of agricultural purposes as long as they also "kept up and preserved in good condition" the

Figure 1.5. Garden at Stanford residence, c. 1890.
Stanford Historical Photograph Collection (SC 1071), Department of Special Collections and University Archives, Stanford University, Stanford, California.

Figure 1.6. Chinese gardener at Stanford residence, 1888.
Courtesy of Palo Alto Historical Association.

flower garden in front of the Rock residence and "in a proper manner, all necessary work in and to the same for the preserving and cherishing, herbs, shrubs, plants, flowers, and roots now growing." In exchange for rent to be collected during the four-year term of the lease, Rock permitted the lessees to "grow all sorts of small fruits and vegetables" along with "seeds for nursery stock," an indication that the tenants cultivated and marketed an array of produce and garden seed. The property owner also gave her lessees use of the farm tools and implements on the premises and specified the names of several horses they could enlist. Her main precondition was that the tenants' crops be planted at a reasonable distance from her fruit trees and not interfere "with the proper development and growth of said trees." The Quong Lee Company was to maintain all fruit trees growing on the property and to plant a new cherry orchard with trees Rock would furnish herself. Jane Stanford offered a similar arrangement with Jim Mock and Ah King, who rented from her an additional 22 acres of "orchard field" at $15 an acre "for vegetable and fruit cultivation."[83]

The existence of multiple leases filed by the same landowners demonstrates lasting economic relationships between white and Chinese growers. Kate D. McLaughlin, owner of a portion of the Stockton Ranch in San Jose, signed a lease in 1884 with Ah Jim, Ah Ou, Doe Sue, and Ah Goh to "put in and cultivate said land in a good and farmlike manner and to use all diligence and care to insure a crop." The lease noted that the 30-acre field under contract bordered on the northwest "land belonging to McLaughlin now rented to Ah Sing," reflecting McLaughlin's established history of leasing farmland to Chinese tenants. The landowner signed two more leases with a total of nine different Chinese tenant farmers in 1886, renting out an additional 50 acres of her ranch near the Guadalupe River.[84] James Farney, a neighbor of William Edwards in Alviso who was mentioned periodically in the latter's diaries, also had a history of multiple leases with Chinese tenants. In 1892 Farney recorded a lease with Quong Wo Lee and Ah Young for 6 acres that the Chinese tenants had already been farming "for the last seven years, under a former contract or lease," this time for an additional ten years from October 1, 1892. Though the crops grown were not specified in detail, the lease mentioned strawberry chests and asparagus boxes, as well as an arrangement for the lessees to prune trees according to Farney's direction.[85] Interactions with Chinese immigrants occupied a substantial part of the daily lives of white farmers in the Santa Clara Valley, who maintained extensive networks of Chinese employment in agriculture.

Indicative of the familiar relationships between them and their Chinese employees, white growers in the Santa Clara Valley commonly provided housing for the Chinese who farmed on their property. Edwards first built a cabin to house his Chinese tenants and day laborers in 1872; numerous workers inhabited it and other dwellings on his farm for over a quarter-century. In his daily journal, grower John Pyle noted that several men in his family prepared a house for Chinese workers in March 1895: "Frank, Harry, and Charley worked on the China house fore noon and I went to town brought out the Chinamen, blankets, bedding, and grub after noon."[86] Jane Stanford's 1893 lease documented the presence of a "China Boarding House" and "China Lodging Building" on land adjoining her private stables, which housed a number of Chinese employed at the Stanford estate.[87] White growers also permitted seasonal workers to set up makeshift camps on ranches. Fruit drying in particular required a large labor force, and while some growers hired white women and children to harvest, cut, and dry fruit, it was often impossible to induce them to camp out on remote farms.

Chinese laborers, however, were willing to set up camp next to sulfur sheds for the duration of the harvest, as they did at the West Side orchard of the Rambo family. Ralph Rambo recalled the Chinese workers who, in the 1900s, camped there during prune season and prepared meals in "heavy, covered black iron pots hung over an open fire." The "Chinese home cooking" he sampled, Rambo recounted, "had a fine flavor," prompting him to share their hospitality "whenever my wondering mother permitted." Among the staples they used were rice, dried fish, salt pork and locally grown "green, hairy cucumbers about a foot long." Some observers believed fruit growers could induce more white men to work for them if they provided accommodations beyond crude campsites: "Let the Chinamen camp and live as they have a mind to, if you'll but give white farm laborers at least a semblance of home comforts . . . the labor question will be . . . solved for a little while."[88]

Though growers permitted Chinese men to board on their property, they were also concerned with the presence there of large numbers of Chinese, which might indicate to outside observers that the farm was overrun with nonwhites. Augusta Younger wrote into an 1890 lease that her Chinese tenants could not establish "any Chinatown, or congregation of residents more than usual and proper for the cultivation of said premises and care and handling of their crops." Furthermore, lessors were influenced by prevailing stereotypes of Chinese vice, whether gambling, smoking opium, or consorting with prostitutes.[89] In addition to banning gambling, Andrea Malovos of San Jose stated that his four Chinese lessees should not engage in any "riotous or disorderly conduct," and moreover could not employ "any known convicted criminals or persons of bad repute." His wife, Maria, years later had similar apprehensions and specified that her tenant asparagus farmer Hi Loy was to hire "none but good honest men to work upon the said premises."[90] The Youngers and Malovos attempted to dissociate the employment of Chinese labor on their property from negative images of Chinatown, clarifying their relationship with the Chinese was an economic one, considered "usual and proper" for the maintenance of their farms.

Figure 1.7. Chinese camp at Mount Hamilton, in the vicinity of San Jose, c. 1900.
Courtesy of History San José.

When Valley growers needed workers in addition to the Chinese laborers who already lived at their ranches, they usually trekked to San Jose's Chinatown, often providing transportation for Chinese workers who did not board on location. After an arson fire destroyed the original San Jose Chinatown at Market and San Fernando streets in May 1887, farmer-turned-businessman John Heinlen helped Chinese leaders build a new Chinatown at Fifth and Taylor Streets, which became known as "Heinlenville."[91] Other local white leaders used the fire as an opportunity to force Chinese refugees into an area on the edge of town, at Hobson and San Pedro Streets where the San Jose Woolen Mills factory was located. Whereas the Chinese population of Heinlenville tended to include more women and children and the neighborhood had a broader economic base, Woolen Mills Chinatown residents were a relatively homogeneous group of older men employed primarily as farm laborers.[92] Until it burned to the ground in the early fall of 1902, this smaller Chinese settlement, along with Heinlenville, was where local growers like Edwards and Pyle went in search of extra laborers. Pyle considered trips to Chinatown a routine part of his daily errands, writing in one 1902 entry, "I took Gertrude to school halled [*sic*] the cherries from Mag-ine's and the Chinamen home to dinner took them back to work and brought them home."[93] Ralph Rambo remembered his father going to Heinlenville to hire Chinese workers during the prune harvest: "Every prune season we drove our one-horse truck to this Chinatown and loaded in four or five coolies and their rice, tea, matting (no blankets) and other Oriental requisites, unknowingly, hidden opium."[94]

Once in Chinatown, white growers relied heavily on English-speaking Chinese contractors to introduce them to laborers. In the Santa Clara Valley town of Gilroy, located 20 miles southeast of San Jose, James C. Zuck and his son James Ralph Zuck made arrangements through Chinese contractor Jim Furlong. Testi-mony by the younger Zuck at a coroner's inquest in May 1904 reveals the fatal consequences of ducking a personnel issue by using a contractor to communicate a stern message. A problem had developed several weeks before the inquest, said Zuck, not long after Furlong had sent two Chinese workers to hoe beets on the senior Zuck's sprawling 810-acre ranch, praised in promotional literature as "one of the largest and finest properties in Santa Clara County." Though they initially performed the task well, Zuck began to notice "there seemed to be some trouble between [the two Chinese], and they didn't wish to work together … and some-times one would be working and sometimes two, and sometimes they wouldn't work at all." Whenever the two had a chance, Zuck continued, "they would tell me that the other fellow was no good," with the younger man saying the older was "heap lazy, and like to smoke opium all the time."[95]

Frustrated with the lack of productivity stemming from what appeared to be personal grudges between his Chinese employees, Zuck complained to Jim Fur-long and asked for a letter in Chinese to "tell them I wanted them to work or get off the job," a message Zuck was evidently unable to communicate himself. In broken English, Furlong testified that he told Zuck he would help dismiss the men as long as Zuck paid the contractor the previously negotiated wage of $1.50 a day for the time they had worked. That evening, when Zuck went to the Chinese workers' bunkhouse to present the contractor's letter to the feuding employees, he found one of them, Chin Yong, dead, in all probability killed by his rival Ah Fook, who had fled the ranch and was unsuccessfully pursued by sheriff's dep-uties. The San Francisco–based *Chung Sai Yat Po* reported that Chin Yong's head had been struck with an ax; the living quarters where Zuck discovered his body were in disarray, chairs and a table overturned.[96]

Despite being tightly knit, the Chinese immigrant community consisted of individuals who sometimes developed serious personal vendettas. Witnesses at the inquest that followed Chin's death also suggested the involvement of tong rivalries. In any event, testimony recorded in connection with the murder high-lighted the go-between role of labor contractors.

The informal, erratic employment of Chinese immigrants for seasonal farm work meant that Chinese men in the Valley often had to piece together various occupations to earn a living. When not performing farm labor, Chinese residents worked as cooks and handymen; they cut hair, fished, and sold clams. Friends reported that Ung Sing Bang, a forty-five-year-old farmhand who hanged himself with a baling rope in Heinlenville Chinatown in 1893, was "a contractor, and sometimes a fruit dealer" but lately, because of sickness, had only "carried chairs and mended broken ones." In a similar case in 1901, county officials who reported on the death of Li Sack listed his occupation as "orchardist"; Chinese acquaintances, however, verified that Li had started a business selling clams around town several months prior to his death from strychnine poisoning.[97]

Cooking for white farmers and crews of workers was a more common supplemental occupation for numerous Chinese in rural California, one that affirmed many whites' opinion that Chinese men were effeminate, though for the immigrants themselves, cooking represented simply another economic opportunity. According to Gilroy resident Ye Tong Yong, Ohn Yen, a fifty-year-old laborer who accidentally drowned in the Pajaro River near the border between Santa Clara and Santa Cruz Counties, "didn't work regular... sometimes he fruit picker and sometimes he cook." In the off-season when most farmers were not hiring, many Chinese took up residence in San Jose Chinatown to await employment. As Ah Ling reported to county officials, "sometimes I go cook, sometimes I no work and I come live in Chinatown." Though Chinese cooks in this period generally earned higher wages and led a more stable life than field hands, those residing in Santa Clara County found seasonal stints for farm crews during harvest times, irregular work that required supplementation with side jobs. Other Chinese followed crop harvests in distant locales. Before he committed suicide in February 1904, forty-year-old Louie Woon was believed to have gone to pick potatoes in the "Stockton Islands" about 60 miles northeast of San Jose in the San Joaquin Delta.[98] While rural Chinese immigrants usually found abundant employment among the Valley's white farmers, they also marshaled other resources and skills to earn extra income and ensure their ability to support themselves and families overseas.

Valley farmers like Edwards who hired Chinese agricultural laborers on a long-term basis and boarded them on their property contended with occasional management problems. A series of events that occurred on the Edwards ranch in the summer of 1893 illustrates Chinese hired workers actively securing their best interests, without regard for their employers. While several Chinese laborers were gathering Bartlett and Hardy pears on the Edwards farm one morning in August 1893, a thief "broke into the cabin stole 2 sacks rice and clothing," along with, as it turned out, a large sum of cash.[99] Ah Kim, the head Chinese hired man, who had been harvesting blackberries for Edwards that season at wages of a dollar a day, lost his possessions and savings and, in the aftermath of the robbery, left the Edwards ranch. His roommate in the cabin, Ah Loy, initiated a deal with Edwards to acquire the "head" Chinese farmhand position for himself. Edwards recorded in his diary what happened several days following the burglary:

> Chinese watchmaker Charley [Kow Kee] acting as interpreter informed me Ah Kim had abandoned the premises and I may pay Ah Loy balance due for Blackberries. That he would occupy the cabin and work for me when I had work for him at $1.00 per day and seek employment else-where when I had no work for him. That thieves had stolen from the cabin money and clothes amounting to $180, leaving him without a nickel.
>
> I assented to his proposition.

Edwards had been employing Chinese farm laborers for over two decades, but he had little control over his employees' decisions to stay or leave his ranch as they pleased. By "abandoning" the premises without notice, Ah Kim displayed a lack of employer loyalty and determination to move on regardless of any prior agreement he might have made with Edwards. Ah Loy took advantage of Ah Kim's absence to obtain job security for himself, enlisting the interpreting skills of a Chinese go-between to convey his proposal to Edwards.

Despite claims that "family farming" was the norm in Santa Clara Valley agri-culture, whites and Chinese relied on and bargained with each other over the terms of labor. In another twist, just over a week after making the agreement with Ah Loy, Edwards recorded in his diary that the Chinese laborer and his associates had "abandoned the cabin" and "sent me the key by George," a white hired man. Perhaps recognizing the possibility that Ah Loy had been dissatisfied with his dollar-a-day wage, two days later, the seventy-year-old grower decided to increase the pay rate for his subsequent workers in hopes of retaining them. Edwards wrote that he went back to Charley Kow Kee and "engaged 2 Chinese to work at $1.20 per day," the first time he paid more than a dollar for Chinese day labor on his farm.[100]

Edwards's travails with his Chinese employees continued through the end of 1893. On December 5, Edwards recorded in his journal that "Two Chinese called and informed me Ah Toy [Loy] was stirring up a row amongst them because I owed them for 10 chests blackberries for which I told them I would pay Ah Loy as per instructions of Ah Kim. The two went to San Jose to harmo-nize the matter."[101] Edwards may not have intended to shortchange Ah Loy over the blackberries, but the incident demonstrated that Chinese farmers and laborers insisted on fair treatment from their employers and effectively commu-nicated their expectations. Edwards's willingness to acquiesce to the demands of his Chinese hired help for fear of jeopardizing future contracts shows the extent to which Valley growers depended on Chinese labor, as well as how the bargaining skills and resourceful calculations of the Chinese paid off.[102]

Anti-Chinese Sentiment and the "White Labor" Question

In the consistently anti-Chinese climate found in turn-of-the-century California, white growers' need for Chinese labor placed the Asians in a precarious position vis-à-vis the white working class and the general public not engaged in farming. California farmers walked a fine line between conceding their utter dependence on Chinese labor and defending themselves from accusations of betraying white labor by supporting the Chinese. Growers leveled bitingly sarcastic complaints at white workers: "White men who sit around on cracker barrels at the village groceries damning the Chinese while refusing to work at fair wages themselves, are a greater nuisance than the Chinese, grasshoppers and jackrabbits combined." Another writer for the *California Fruit Grower* pointed out that while it was "not especially creditable to the white man" that growers considered him "inferior to the despised Chinaman as a fruit packer," this was the reality. Thus if white men insisted upon "supplanting yellow ones in fruit packing or other industries," the author advised them to show themselves "equal to the Asiatics in point of skill, honesty and faithfulness." Otherwise, the journal warned, labor-dependent fruit growers, while avowedly not "Chinese nor Jap lovers," would be engaging in a "suicidal policy to wholly surrender business management to incompetent persons of any color." Self-interested calls for competence across racial lines aside, white growers nonetheless remained concerned that their need for Chinese labor in agricultural enterprises frequently made them unpopular and targets of criticism.[103]

In response to questions about their racial allegiance, white growers in California asserted their belief, at least in theory, in the inherent integrity and superiority of white labor, especially as related to the support of white families. When asked in 1886 by Commissioner John Enos of the California Bureau of Labor Statistics how Chinese and white labor compared "as to Quality and Quantity," the Santa Clara County clerk and assessor replied unambiguously: "Whites are best." As fruit culture grew rapidly in California from the 1880s on, so did hopes that reliable white help would also migrate to intensively cultivated regions.[104] In response to the economic downturn of 1893, the *California Fruit Grower* declared it was the "duty of every Californian to employ all the white labor possible at this time." Editors opined that while the Chinese were "much better able to bear any depression in the labor market," the plight of "our own people... whose families form a permanent and desirable part of our population" was far more distressing and deserving of concern. Other writers privileged white male-headed households with dependent wives and children, mistakenly assuming that the Chinese in California had "no families" to support, when in fact most of them sent remittances to wives, children, and other family members in China."[105]

Claims that rural Chinese immigrants were bachelors who did not share the same provider responsibilities as white male household heads served to further distance the Chinese from the family farm ideal, cementing racial boundaries on the basis of gender roles and family structure. Confirming the transnational configuration of many Chinese immigrant families, records of the county coroner indicate that nearly three-quarters of the Chinese males whose deaths were investigated between 1891 and 1913 were married, though none of their wives appeared in the testimonies, since they were likely living in China. Chinese exclusion laws restricted the immigration of Chinese women by making the immigration status of women derivative of the male household heads. That is, the wives of Chinese laborers acquired their husbands' status and were barred from entry. Like most Chinese migrants, the Chinese farmers and farm laborers of the Santa Clara Valley could not relocate their wives and children to the United States but supported them and other members of the extended family in home villages with earnings from abroad. Overseas migration was one of multiple investment strategies designed to maintain the family line and to sustain economic viability and family prosperity.[106]

As a result, few Chinese women and children resided in rural Santa Clara Valley at the turn of the century. Those who did were rarely the immediate family members of farmers but affiliated with Chinese merchants based in Heinlenville Chinatown or in San Francisco, 50 miles north of San Jose (merchants were one of the exempt categories in exclusion laws). Of the Chinese residents in Santa Clara County in 1900, only 2 percent were female and 3.5 percent of the population under the age of eighteen.[107] When six-year-old Chin Sui Sum died of pneumonia on a Milpitas ranch run by her uncles and cousins, white neighbors were surprised because, being unaccustomed to seeing women and children among the Chinese farmers, they had not suspected her presence. John Costigan, a Milpitas farmer who lived nearby and also served as the town's constable, attended the inquest that followed the child's death. He testified that he was "around [the ranch that employed members of the Chin family] every once in a while" and "never saw no women around there, nor girls of any kind.... No Chinese women at all." As it turned out, Ching Lung, the child's father, a merchant who operated a grocery store on Sacramento Street in San Francisco, had taken his ailing daughter to the ranch where his brothers worked on shares for Henry Abel, hoping the change of climate "would do her good."[108] Ching Hoy, the girl's uncle, who had farmed on the Abel ranch in Milpitas for over five years, found his brother in tears over his daughter's death, which occurred before her mother Leong Shee and older sister arrived from San Francisco that very afternoon. Chin Sui Sum, born in the United States, was survived by her parents and five siblings. Nonetheless, Costigan's observations that there were "no women...nor girls of any kind" among his Chinese neighbors in Milpitas reflected the demographics of most agricultural districts in California, as the few settled Chinese families who lived on the mainland tended to reside in urban Chinatowns and seldom in rural areas.[109]

Ultimately, Santa Clara Valley growers did not decry the lack of Chinese families in America, as it confirmed the sojourning status of Chinese men. White farmers who employed or boarded Chinese only sought to mitigate what they believed were the vices that plagued a "bachelor" population living without the domesticating influence of families. Some Valley landholders became preoccupied with banning prostitution on their property, sometimes to the point of forbidding the presence of Chinese women altogether. Alice Younger Gally inserted a clause in her 1888 lease to Quong Deep, following instructions about washing the trees for scale and codlin moth, that read "no China women to live on or visit said premises," a clause repeated in an 1889 lease for additional acreage to be farmed by Quong. Not to be outdone, her sister Rosalie Younger prohibited "pig pens, Chinese women, opium dens or gambling" on her share of the family estate.[110] Most of the women of the Younger family continued to reside on the property they leased to Asian tenants. That they were not absentee landlords may help explain their fixation with maintaining the respectability of their domestic space.

Hiring Chinese immigrants as tenant farmers and agricultural laborers ultimately exposed the family farm ideal as fiction, and the practice was met at times with public criticism. In the fall of 1904, the *San Jose Evening News* published a series of investigative pieces on Everis "Red" Hayes, then a congressional nominee and publisher of the rival *San Jose Daily Mercury*, who had been trying to augment his anti-Chinese credentials by "declaring that he was in favor of sending back to their native lands all the Chinese and Japanese now in this country." The "dirt" on Hayes and the subject of controversy was that in the early 1890s he had employed numerous Chinese laborers on his ranch in Edenvale, about 6 miles southeast of San Jose, and had even forced white workers to share meals with them. Hayes and his brother, Jay Orley Hayes, also owned and operated several gold mines in California at the turn of the century, and their property in Edenvale totaled over 600 acres; 180 acres was devoted to orchard fruits, 375 acres reserved for general farming, and the rest was laid out in ornamental gardens.[111] According to the *Evening News*, George Osen, a San Jose automobile dealer who had been employed as a carpenter by

Hayes in Edenvale from 1891 to 1894, recalled several Chinese working there under the direction of an "imported gardener" who Osen thought to be an Englishman.[112]

In a follow-up article, the *Evening News* cited another source, San Jose hay dealer Manuel Perry, who informed reporters that Hayes had definitely employed "a Chinese to do the washing" and seated him at the table "where the white men were eating." This seating arrangement produced an outcry, and the white employees designated Charles Richmond to speak to Hayes about the matter. Although Hayes assured Richmond that the situation would be remedied, the Chinese worker again sat at the white men's table during the next meal, at which point Perry recounted, "all of us, excepting Whipple, left the table and went to the stables, where we had our sleeping quarters." Hayes followed the protesters to the stables, where Perry informed him that they "were Californians; that [they] were not accustomed to eating with a Chinese and that [they] did not intend to do it." Perry could not recall Hayes's "exact words," but the latter allegedly "said something to the effect that a Chinese is just as good as a white man," which angered Perry "almost to the point of striking him." Perry told reporters he and the other offended white workers immediately "quit our employment and returned to San Jose."[113]

In the backdrop of a contentious election in an area supposedly inhabited by small orchards operated by white families "independent" of Chinese workers, the uproar over hiring practices on the Hayes ranch dating over a decade ago demonstrated how the family farm ideal had permeated the political culture of the Valley by the 1900s. Reporters highlighted the desire of white hired men like Perry to maintain their identities as "Californians" separate from Asiatic foreigners. To these men, Hayes had betrayed their implicit bond of whiteness, a bond that reassured white workers of their racial superiority, regardless of their wealth or class status.[114] As demonstrated by his cavalier dismissal of his white employees' complaints of being made to eat with a Chinese, Hayes, a wealthy, powerful San Jose rancher, businessman, and politician, apparently did not have qualms about hiring Chinese workers until it became damaging to his political career. George A. Whipple, the only former Hayes employee interviewed by the paper who became an orchardist, was also the lone white man who Perry observed did not stalk off in disgust over the dining arrangements. Whipple, then an aspiring fruit grower, may have understood, and thus was more sympathetic to the reality of a Santa Clara Valley rancher needing to hire Chinese workers on his property. Though he admitted to being employed at Edenvale during the years in question, Whipple in 1904 refused to comment on "the matter of the Chinese laborers," rationalizing: "I am trying to make an honest living, and I do not care to injure myself by telling anything about the Chinese business."[115] Whipple's actions indicated he believed a man engaged in the "honest living" of fruit growing should not be lambasted for employing Chinese laborers, a regular practice among Valley growers.

With its crews of native and foreign-born hired white men and probable employment of Chinese immigrants, the Hayes ranch in Edenvale did not remotely resemble the family-run orchard depicted in the lore of promotional literature. Then again, neither did Andrea Malovos's Light-house Farm, William Edwards's Alviso farm, John Pyle's Berryessa ranch, or the Younger clan's property planted in orchard fruit and berries. Nevertheless, as long as they were not working alongside or seated with Chinese, Hayes's white laborers could still believe that the family farm ideal held true, and by dint of their hard work and whiteness, they were the "right kind of men" sought by boosters to settle the prosperous valley. Whipple's neutrality suggested his acceptance of the reality that Asian labor was integral to horticulture in the Valley. Whether because Whipple's pragmatic attitude was widespread or because of the damage control undertaken by the *Mercury*, the controversy over the "Chinks at Hayes' Ranch" in the end did not hurt the politician at all. Local voters elected Hayes to the first of his seven terms in the U.S. House of Representatives in 1905.[116] That December, Hayes made the first ever anti-Japanese speech in the House of Representatives. In 1912, the *San Francisco Labor Clarion* quoted the president of the American Federation of Labor, Samuel Gompers, as having applauded "Red" Hayes for being an "indefatigable" friend of labor, apparently unaware that Hayes had been under fire just a few years prior for questionable hiring practices.

Hayes was not the only prominent, openly anti-Asian politician with Santa Clara Valley ties who privately employed Chinese on his property. In 1892, James Phelan, who would eventually become mayor of San Francisco and a U.S. senator, leased a large parcel of his San Jose property, almost 157 acres, to Chin Quong Dip, Chin Quong Gin, and Richard Healy for ten years at the annual rent of $2,000 for "purposes of cultivation."[117]

If the goal of Santa Clara Valley growers and promoters was to be "independent" of Chinese labor, they failed miserably. Living in an exceptionally fertile region that excelled in the cultivation of orchard fruits, berries, vegetables, and garden seed alike, white growers drew on the diversified nature of the Santa Clara Valley agricultural economy to relegate the Chinese to certain crops and tedious forms of agricultural labor, calling it "exacting work" not suitable for white men, women, and children. Despite the variety and complexity of labor on Valley farms, the status of the Chinese as nonwhite men without visible families facilitated the ideological racialization of agricultural labor. In practice, however, Valley farmers made little distinction between hiring Chinese immigrants to grow and harvest prunes or strawberries, and these immigrants occupied a central place in the region's agricultural landscape. Furthermore, even as they demarcated racial

boundaries by crop, many white growers valued the specialized knowledge associated with Chinese horticultural labor.

Thus within an economy stratified by race and gender, Chinese farmers had
carved out a place for themselves as highly skilled, thoroughly resourceful businessmen who secured and negotiated contracts that allowed them not only to
survive in America but sometimes to thrive on the land. In the Valley and across
the state, while some growers accepted their dependence on Asian labor as a fact
of agricultural life, the presence of Chinese farmers and farm laborers made
others insist on the family farm ideal even more fervently. The arrival of Japanese
immigrants in the first decades of the twentieth century provided growers with
another source of skilled agricultural labor, as well as new challenges to the white
family farm ideal.

2

Transplanted

The World of Early Issei Farmers

When Katsusaburo Kawahara arrived in San Jose from Shimane prefecture as a child to join his immigrant parents in 1911, he had distinct impressions of the Japanese population in his new home: "It seemed the Japanese [who] gathered in San Jose were all hard working young people in their thirties. I didn't see any old people. There were mostly single men who had no families—they all came because Santa Clara was a 'garden valley.'"[1] Indeed, the youthfulness of the early Japanese immigrants, or Issei, in California stood out in contrast to their Chinese counterparts in the Valley who labored in the region's thriving horticultural industry. By 1910, as a result of exclusionary immigration legislation, anti-Chinese violence, and attrition due to old age, the Chinese population in Santa Clara County had dwindled to barely over one thousand, just a third of what it had been in the 1880s and 1890s. With the declining availability of Chinese laborers and tenant farmers in the 1900s, many white residents of the Santa Clara Valley turned to newly arrived Japanese immigrants for help on their ranches, signaling a relatively smooth transition from the employment of Chinese to Japanese laborers, though the process was gradual and varied by crop. In the early twentieth century, the subordinate place of Japanese workers in Valley agriculture, similar to that of the Chinese, assured most white residents that these new immigrants from Asia did not pose a significant economic threat.

In the years prior to the 1913 California Alien Land Act, Japanese immigrants fit into the economic niches Chinese agriculturists had already established, continuing the racialized patterns of labor defined and accepted by white growers in the Valley. Indeed, they became a far larger and more enduring presence. Despite their often menial positions in the agricultural economy, the Japanese who farmed and sharecropped for countless Valley growers were far from passive, subservient laborers, but became capable and shrewd agricultural entrepreneurs who made crucial contributions to the region's horticultural prowess and asserted their rights in the legal system. Furthermore, in this period of transition from Chinese to Japanese labor, interethnic relations in the realm of agriculture flourished. The Bayside Canning Company epitomized the presence of an ethnic economy not entirely dependent on whites, offering a glimpse into the ways in which Chinese and Japanese residents continued to shape how white residents and growers defined themselves and their livelihoods in the "Valley of Heart's Delight."

"Yellow-Skinned Pickers"

Within the first decade of the twentieth century, California saw a fourfold increase in its Japanese population: from 10,151 in 1900 to 41,356 in 1910, and 85 percent were male. According to the 1900 census, about 40 percent of Japanese in Santa Clara County worked in agriculture, 95 percent of them as laborers (in comparison, 61 percent of the county's Chinese worked in agriculture in 1900, 89 percent as laborers).[2] At the peak of their dominance as farm laborers in California, about 30,000 Japanese made up 42 percent of the state's total farm labor population.[3] By 1915, scholars estimated that between 50 and 65 percent of all Japanese immigrants in the United States were engaged in agricultural industries. "Japanese take to farms like ducks to water," historian Yamato Ichihashi explained in a book published in 1915, noting that the immigrants involved in farm labor "were almost exclusively drawn from the agricultural classes of Japan." Social scientists' findings corroborate the results of the 1910 and 1920 U.S. Censuses, which classified 55 and 54 percent of the Japanese population in California as rural. By 1925, over half of the Japanese in Santa Clara County lived on farms and were considered part of the area's farm population.[4]

Japanese immigrants first arrived in the Santa Clara Valley as migrant agricultural laborers during the late 1880s. The first official documentation of Japanese in Santa Clara County appeared in the 1890 census, which recorded twenty-seven Japanese residing there. These figures corresponded with Ichihashi's findings that in the late 1880s, two groups of about thirty Japanese left San Francisco, one headed for the Sacramento Valley and the other to the Santa Clara Valley, where Japanese laborers likely cultivated strawberries from April through June, harvested apricots, pears, and prunes during July and August, and left in the late summer to pick grapes in Fresno.[5] Census figures show that the bulk of Japanese settlers came to Santa Clara County in the first decade of the twentieth century, with the county recording a Japanese population of 2,299 in 1910, compared to only 284 in 1900. Santa Clara County ranked sixth among California counties in terms of the number of Japanese residing there, and Japanese made up almost

4 percent of the county population, the fourth highest proportion among the 58 counties of the state. Only Sacramento, Yolo, and San Joaquin Counties boasted higher percentages of Japanese.[6]

The vast majority of Japanese trans-Pacific migrants were of rural origin, and early immigrants fell into two categories: contract laborers bound for Hawaii from 1885 to 1894, numbering around 70,000 total, who tended to be destitute at the time of migration, and the approximately 130,000 free laborers who left rural Japan for the continental United States and Hawaii between 1895 and 1908. In the case of contract laborers, the rural depression and drastic deflationary measures of the Meiji state during the 1880s formed the backdrop for their emigration to Hawaii, as a majority of these emigrants came from landless or small landowning families, which suffered most during the economic downturn. They came from a limited geographical area of Japan, with 38 percent hailing from Hiroshima in southwestern Honshu and 36 percent from neighboring Yamaguchi prefecture. These two prefectures, along with Kumamoto and Fukuoka in Kyushu, combined to make up 96 percent of all contract laborers. The prefectures boasting the highest numbers of emigrants represented some of the principal agricultural regions of Japan. Hiroshima, the prefecture with the smallest average amount of farmland owned per capita, produced the highest number of emigrants.[7] In contrast to contract laborers, the average free emigrant, who tended to be unmarried or migrated without his wife, came from slightly more prosperous households, had some immediate family connection overseas, or had once been a *dekasegi* (sojourning laborer). They were men who saw labor migration as an investment in future earning potential rather than a sheer necessity. With the termination of contract labor in 1894, the phenomenon of free emigration spread from southwestern Japan to other parts of the country. In addition to the aforementioned emigrant prefectures, Wakayama, Niigata, Okayama, and Okinawa ranked among the most common origins of Japanese in the continental United States and Hawaii after 1894.[8] In Santa Clara County, at least 15 percent of Japanese residents in 1910 had migrated first to Hawaii before arriving in California, though it is difficult to discern exactly how many had been contract laborers versus free emigrants.[9]

As they settled in the Santa Clara Valley at the turn of the twentieth century, Japanese immigrants, 95 percent of whom were men in 1900, became steeped in the agricultural industry at all levels as laborers, sharecroppers, tenant farmers, contractors, and foremen. White landowners hired Japanese day laborers to do seasonal work on their property, just as they had employed Chinese immigrants before exclusionary legislation shrunk that population. The 1900 census enumerated 95 percent of Japanese men in agriculture in Santa Clara County as laborers and only 5 percent as farmers, compared to 89 percent of Chinese men employed in the farming industry who were counted as laborers and over 10 percent as farmers. But while the proportion of Chinese laborers to farmers remained constant during the 1900s, the percentage of Japanese farmers in the county grew to 20.5 percent in 1910, decreasing the corresponding percentage of Japanese agricultural laborers to roughly 79 percent, according to census figures.[10] Even though Asian farm laborers vastly outnumbered farmers in the early twentieth century, census takers likely overcounted the former by assuming that any Chinese or Japanese working on a farm was a menial laborer.

White growers employed both Chinese and Japanese farm laborers in the 1900s through the early 1910s in a period of transition, with many increasingly favoring Japanese workers over the physically and numerically declining Chinese. In the seed industry, Valley growers at first attempted to retain as many Chinese workers as possible, believing they were more skillful in the meticulous work of caring for seed stock. When labor shortages forced seed farm proprietors to seek other employees, they hired some Portuguese and Italian laborers, but more commonly, it was the Japanese who had "practically displaced the white men doing hand work and made good the diminishing number of Chinese." In the orchard fruit industry, Japanese labored on nearly all of the ranches investigated by the federal Immigration Commission in the 1908 harvest season, picking, cutting, packing fruit, and performing general farm work.[11] When it came to choosing between Chinese and Japanese farmhands in the 1900s, the age of workers along with availability likely had greater influence on white growers' evolving ethnic hiring preferences. With few new arrivals in the wake of exclusion laws, the Chinese population in Santa Clara County was much older than the Japanese one: in 1900 the average age of Chinese men eighteen and over was forty-five, and only twenty-seven for Japanese men. A decade later, the age differential held steady, with forty-nine the average age of Chinese adult men and thirty-three for Japanese men.[12]

The presence of Chinese contractors who employed Japanese laborers in the early 1900s shows the overlap of the two ethnic groups within the Valley's agricultural economy and the contest to define new patterns of labor relations. As Japanese immigrants entered the Santa Clara Valley's agricultural sector as laborers during the first decade of the twentieth century, some local Chinese alleged the Japanese were "making a systematic effort to displace Chinamen" already employed on Valley ranches by offering to work for much lower wages and then petitioning to employers to hire their countrymen to take the places of Chinese.[13] With fewer of their own countrymen available for work, however, established Chinese contractors also recruited incoming Japanese immigrants, many of whom boarded in the new Nihonmachi, or Japantown, which had emerged in San Jose by 1902, conveniently located adjoining Chinatown on Sixth Street. These arrangements sometimes went awry.

A Chinese labor contractor named Young Kow, also known as Ah Kow, employed a group of Japanese laborers in Alviso to work in the 1903 strawberry harvest (he likely had a sharecropping or lease arrangement with a white landowner). The contractor was to divide the proceeds from the sale of the season's berry crop with the Japanese ranch hands. But Young failed to pay his employees the wages and fled. According to the San Francisco–based Chinese-language daily *Chung Sai Yat Po*, one of the Japanese men who worked for Young initially thought the Chinese contractor might have been robbed on his way back to Alviso from San Francisco, where he had collected the money from the commission merchant. Upon inquiry with the company, however, the Japanese man learned that Young had cashed a check for over $600 (approximately $14,000 today). The aggrieved Japanese worker proceeded to file a complaint charging Young with felony embezzlement, and officials attempted unsuccessfully to procure his arrest upon landing in Hong Kong or Yokahama.[14]

In another case of a Chinese contractor not paying his Japanese employee's wages, in 1908 T. Nakashiki sued Fook Lee for "work, labor and service" the plaintiff provided in the "cultivating and farming of land and crops for the defendant" for the past year in Gilroy. As new Japanese immigrants began to establish themselves in the Valley's vast agricultural labor market, a few Chinese contractors attempted to take advantage of the changing state of affairs.[15]

With some reluctance, the Valley's white growers slowly acknowledged that the diminishing supply of Chinese workers meant that they would have to meet their seasonal labor needs with Japanese immigrants. But this did not happen immediately, the Immigration Commission reported, as ranchers attempted to fill the "deficiency in the labor supply due to the disappearance of the Chinese" in the 1900s with white men, women, and children. In 1906, the San Jose Chamber of Commerce announced a "gigantic advertising scheme" designed to draw five thousand white families to the area from eastern and Midwestern states to "take the places of hundreds of Japanese," thus reducing fruit growers' reliance on "yellow-skinned pickers."[16] A White Labor Committee formed around the same time under the auspices of the Santa Clara County Farmers' Union to publicize agricultural employment opportunities for white families in California. The committee mailed letters and informational literature to school boards, requesting that principals adjust summer vacations "to suit local ripening periods." In addition, the group extended its outreach efforts to San Francisco newspapers and unions. At a mass meeting of the Valley's prune growers in the summer of 1911, participants made a declaration "against the employment of Japanese or any other than white labor to harvest the crop."[17] Though the *California Fruit Grower* reported that two thousand white women and children arrived for work in Campbell in 1911, there is no evidence that county growers found white labor a consistently reliable solution for their labor needs. "The question of obtaining satisfactory labor for harvesting," according to the trade journal, continued to cause farmers "some considerable anxiety in certain sections of the State," including the Santa Clara Valley. When Campbell prune grower and White Labor Committee chair Homer Craig died suddenly in December 1911, ambitious attempts to recruit white help to the Valley petered out and visions of supplanting Japanese labor evaporated.[18]

Moreover, many other local growers readily accepted Japanese laborers, who, unlike white women and children, could be recruited in gangs, cheaply and easily, at boardinghouses in San Jose Japantown and other labor camps, including some in Sunnyvale.[19] When U.S. Congressman Everis Hayes, accused of using Chinese labor on his Edenvale ranch just a few years earlier, presented to orchardists in Saratoga and Cupertino his plan to push for Japanese exclusion in October 1906, those constituents "firmly combated" his arguments. Farmers reliant on the Japanese to harvest and process deciduous fruits told Hayes that "to exclude the Japanese would be equivalent to pauperizing them [the farmers]."[20] Between late 1907 and early 1908, however, President Theodore Roosevelt, acted in response to organized labor's anti-Japanese agitation centered in San Francisco. It was during this period that Roosevelt extracted an understanding from Japan to bar the emigration of laborers to the United States in a series of six diplomatic notes known collectively as the Gentlemen's Agreement. The agricultural community at this time opposed Japanese immigration restriction and criticized the president for his actions, though over the ensuing decade many growers soured on Japanese farm labor.[21]

As Japanese immigrants settled in rural California during the 1900s, they relied less and less on interethnic arrangements with Chinese middlemen and established their own extensive, efficient system of labor contracting. Japanese contractors, or *keiyaku-nin*, recruited workers in San Jose Japantown and by placing advertisements in the immigrant press, often making appeals based on prefecture connections, highlighting, for example, that a "boss" was "respected by people from Kumamoto." Recruitment notices included the name of the contractor or contracting firm and usually an address in Japantown where job seekers could apply.[22] Contractors handled room and board, transportation, and payment of labor crews, affording growers the convenience of simply paying one set price for all of their labor needs. In numerous specialty crop districts around the state during harvest time, federal investigators found that Japanese labor contractors wielded great influence over white growers, who often conceded to rates and terms contractors set before the season began and consented to paying competitive wages. As white growers' dependence on Japanese harvest labor intensified in the early twentieth century, Japanese contractors sometimes reneged on deals just as crops ripened and demanded a higher wage rate. They knew hard-pressed growers would agree to the new rate because it would be nearly impossible to secure enough Japanese pickers otherwise, given how rare it was for contractors to venture into one another's territory.[23] During the 1908 season, almost all of the Japanese laborers surveyed in Santa Clara County made $1.50 per ten-hour day (white farm laborers received $1.75). An exceptional case arose in 1910, when a scarcity of workers allowed contractors to negotiate a wage of $2 a day. That year, a shortage of prunes worldwide resulted in "the highest prices in the history of the prune business paid to growers" recorded to date. Many prune growers felt they had no option but to pay the higher rate Japanese contractors called for if they wanted the crop harvested, since "white men did not seek this work voluntarily." Nevertheless, the growers who conceded were able to recover the higher costs with excellent prices for their produce.[24]

Like the Chinese before them, Japanese farm laborers in the Santa Clara Valley and throughout California tended to concentrate in certain types of agricultural work deemed too menial for whites to perform, a trend that also mitigated fears of economic competition with white workers. Commenting on data culled from a report from the California Commissioner of Labor listing agricultural occupations by type and by number of whites and Japanese employed in them, economist H. A. Millis concluded that the Japanese engaged chiefly in "handwork, much of it of the 'stoop over' or 'squat' variety.... much of it dirty

Figure 2.1 Japanese pear pickers on a Santa Clara farm, c. 1900–1910.
Courtesy of California History Center.

and arduous." This work included weeding, thinning, hoeing, picking berries and grapes, pruning trees and vines, and topping and loading sugar beets. While native-born orchard fruit ranchers found Japanese acceptable as seasonal workers, they preferred to employ "'American labor,' i.e., white men other than Portuguese and Italians" as permanent farmhands; only occasionally did they place Japanese in year-round positions.[25] On John Francis Pyle's ranch in Berryessa during the 1907 season, teams of Japanese spent days hunched over the earth, digging everything from borers and drains to tree holes, beets, and ditches: "5 Japs dug borers forenoon 4 afternoon 2 dug drains in the 19 Acre lot"; "6 Japs worked all day digging tree holes and beets halling trash"; "3 Japs came afternoon. Dug ditch untill 6 o'clock." A few days later, some Japanese workers tried driving a team on Pyle's ranch for a change, "but got stuck and went to the tree holes," and returned to digging holes for prune and peach trees. In the spring, when there was no more digging to be done, Pyle reported that the Japanese "filled in ditches all day," plowed, and hoed in his orchard and on the property of his sister, Mary Overfelt.[26]

Some of the same white growers who found themselves relying on Japanese immigrants for seasonal work also leveled protests against them. Santa Clara rancher and fruit dryer Samuel S. Haines employed a few Japanese laborers on his farm in 1906, but his journal entries conveyed growing dissatisfaction and bitter, racially charged complaints. Before Japanese workers had finished stacking barley and wheat at his ranch in June 1906, Haines noted "Japs quit at noon" and the following week, "Japs do not come. Whether the yellow monkeys will keep their promise and come tomorrow we shall only know when the day comes." Never acknowledging any miscommunication on his part, Haines recorded in his journal that "Japs fail again" the next day and appeared to have given up hiring Japanese day laborers altogether thereafter because of his perception that they were capricious and did not "keep their promise."[27] The Immigration Commission found a marked rise in ranchers' complaints regarding dealings with Japanese laborers in the mid-1900s. Like Haines, white growers said the Japanese were undependable, "less accommodating and do less work in a day," as well as "very independent and hard to deal with," noting that they had secured higher wages through strikes and threats to strike. Others lamented that Japanese on day wages "shirk work and are slow" but required "constant supervision" when they were on a piece rate since they were prone to work "extremely fast.... careless and wasteful in their eagerness to make large earnings."[28] Instead of viewing Japanese farm laborers as typical wage earners who behaved according to their own interests, growers attributed the actions they deplored to inherent "Japanese" characteristics.

Negative views of Japanese farm labor led many California growers to adopt a nostalgic image of the Chinese as ideal workers. The consensus of opinion in the state's agricultural districts that had employed Chinese farm workers in the nineteenth century was that the Chinese were "skillful and painstaking and strictly honest as to contracts," and "much preferred to the Japanese." Above all, white growers perceived the Chinese to be less ambitious about acquiring land and engaging in business, noting that fewer Chinese rose to "higher economic positions than that of the laborer" and commenting on an "absence of a desire on their part to associate with others on equal terms."[29]

Reports of Japanese labor unrest on Hawaiian sugar plantations in the early twentieth century undoubtedly weighed on the minds of California growers beginning to experiment with Japanese workers. In the seminal 1909 Oahu strike, 7,000 Japanese laborers in all of the island's plantations abandoned the cane fields for three months just before harvest, resulting in collective bargaining on an unprecedented scale. For the first time strikers called for abolition of racial discrimination in treatment of workers and demanded wage increases to improve living conditions. Whites in Hawaii and on the mainland decried the strike and viewed such labor activity as indicative of Japanese conspiracy. Sugar planters expressed preferences for Chinese over Japanese workers and the desire to re-import excluded Chinese labor, reflecting beliefs that "the Jap is as unpopular in Hawaii as the Chinaman is well liked." Californians were gradually arriving at the same conclusion and felt validated by the experience of sugar planters in Hawaii, noting "the Hawaiian has experimented with both [Chinese and Japanese laborers], and such is his verdict."[30] The demand for farm labor and increased food production during World War I also prompted discussion among California growers to import Chinese labor, though opinions remained divided and such schemes, considered "physically, politically, and legally impossible," never materialized.[31]

William A. Z. Edwards, the faithful diarist and Alviso farmer who had employed Chinese immigrants extensively as farm laborers in the late nineteenth century, may have been influenced by some of these prevailing views of the Japanese. Though his farm was located in an area of the Santa Clara Valley where numerous Japanese laborers resided, he never recorded in his journals any instance of having hired them. Instead, in the years preceding his death in 1908, Edwards continued to employ Chinese workers whenever possible, though the infrequent mentions of them compared to previous years attested to their declining availability. In fact, after 1905, Edwards appeared to have had trouble keeping reliable help on his property, and his diary entries chronicled his encounters with Antonio Silva, a Portuguese man he had hired who was later arrested for stealing a bicycle ("Toney being in jail, Frank and Will milked the cows."), "Oscar the Swede" who quit and proceeded to a better paying job at the farm of a Mr. Powell, and a succession of "Darkeys" (likely southern or eastern European immigrants) he obtained from the Garden City Employment Office to milk cows and hoe beets.[32] None of these arrangements resulted in the steady, long-term help Edwards had when he boarded Chinese farm laborers in the cabin on his property. For odd jobs on his ranch, diarist Haines also sought out Italian and eastern European men (his journals named laborers with last names "Talio," "Svilich," and "Valko") over Japanese workers after his 1906 experience. Though he recounted frequent frustrations with his permanent hired hand James Dearing, Haines would entrust this position only to a white native-born man. That he tolerated what seemed to be indolence and alcoholism from Dearing (who is referred to in the diary as "D_") is indicated by such entries as "D_ tries to drown Frank [a horse] am not quite sure but think he is sucking a whisky bottle"; "D_ appears slower than molases [sic] at these furrows not yet in short roes"; "D_ is drunk as a fool and more than a fool."[33]

In the absence of Chinese employees, Edwards was willing to experiment with an assortment of ethnic European immigrant workers, but he never hired a Japanese. The only mention of an encounter with a Japanese in his diaries involved a search for tomato plants in mid-May of 1906, about a month after the San Francisco earthquake and fire. Edwards found none, but reported that his sister-in-law Myra "went to Seeley's where a Jap gave her some 2 doz. Plants which we planted in the garden."[34] An ailing rancher in his late seventies and early eighties during the 1900s, Edwards had spent his entire adult life in the Valley hiring Chinese workers to help run his farm and felt comfortable dealing with them. While he must have been aware of the growing Japanese presence in the Valley and surely knew that many ranchers were beginning to use them in lieu of the Chinese, Edwards chose to pay an erratic, motley crew of European farm laborers over trying out one Japanese worker.

In contrast, Edwards's acquaintance John Pyle, who lived nearby in Berryessa and was twenty-two years younger than Edwards, expressed no qualms about hiring Japanese. His crisp, matter-of-fact diary entries detailing his ranch and canning operations in the early twentieth century suggest a generational divide in white growers' acceptance of Japanese labor in that period. A skilled farmer and entrepreneur, Pyle raised tomatoes, rhubarb, beans, peas, peaches, plums, and apricots, processing most of his fruits and vegetables either at his cannery, J. F. Pyle & Sons, established in 1895, or in his vast dry yard. During the 1890s and through the 1902 season, Pyle was a frequent employer of Chinese day laborers. But beginning in the summer of 1903, Pyle's diaries bore few mentions of Chinese working on his ranch, and in their place, Japanese workers arrived. Pyle noted buying supplies for the "Japs," including thirty-five boxes of tea in October 1903, and his workers lived in what he called "the Japs Boarding house," which may have been the same "China house" he recorded setting up to accommodate Chinese boarders in 1895.[35] On occasion, especially during tomato planting season, Pyle had as many as twelve Japanese working for him at one time. Pyle also hired at least one Japanese man on a permanent basis. Charley, first mentioned on March 27, 1908, was employed as a full-time gardener, turning up in Pyle's diary entries mainly working in the flower garden and on the lawn, though he, referred to as "Charley the Jap" or "Jap Charley," also hoed berries and tended tomatoes when Pyle needed extra help. In Pyle's time book, Charley appeared in a separate category from the other Japanese laborers, who usually received an hourly wage. Though he recorded dismissing several unsuitable white hired hands and related personnel difficulties ("I fired Al and Frank Conrad paid them off and let them go brought out a man but the job did not suit him afternoon looked after another man but did not find him"), Pyle did not note any management problems with his Japanese workers.[36] As much as some white growers pined for the days of Chinese labor, many quickly accepted Japanese laborers as apt replacements for their agricultural needs in the Santa Clara Valley.

"Prune, Clean, Harrow and Cultivate"

Though frequently relegated to menial seasonal labor, Japanese immigrants also used sharecropping and the rental of farmland to create opportunities to farm in the Santa Clara Valley prior to the 1913 passage of the California Alien Land Act. From 1900 to 1912, white landowners and Japanese farmers filed a total of 75 lease agreements at the Santa Clara County recorder's office, covering well over 3,000 acres of county agricultural property. Parcels of leased land ranged from 3.4 to 520 acres, averaging 42.6 acres per lease. Of these leases, 88 percent stipulated cash rentals for farmland, while sharecropping arrangements made up 11 percent.[37] Lease statistics, however, give only a partial picture of the extent of Japanese agriculture in the Valley, since many white growers did not record the farming arrangements they made with Japanese, as with Chinese immigrants. Crop and chattel mortgages filed with the county recorder in the same period provide information on additional leases that were not recorded but are implied in mortgage transactions, bringing the estimate of the total acres of agricultural land operated by Japanese prior to the 1913 California Alien Land Act to approximately 5,000–6,000 acres, or at least 3 percent of the total acreage of improved farmland in Santa Clara County.[38] In the first decade of the twentieth century, numerous Japanese immigrants thus made clear inroads in Santa Clara County's agricultural scene, farming for themselves and not working only as day laborers.[39]

Japanese cultivators' ability to transfer farming skills and experience from their homeland in part accounted for their tremendous productivity in California, which was often noted by whites in the first decades of the twentieth century. Southwest Honshu and northern Kyushu, considered the agricultural heartland of Japan, include the emigrant prefectures of Yamaguchi, Hiroshima, Okayama, Hyogo, and Fukuoka, known for highly diversified agriculture, cash crops, and double-cropped paddies, with rice, vegetables, fruit, tea, and wheat being the most important crops.[40] While Japanese rice production on a national level showed a steady increase in the period from 1885 to 1930 amounting to 23 percent of crops farmed, the growth of paddy rice was rather negligible in southwestern Japan, the original home of many immigrants, suggesting that those who eventually settled in California also had experience with fruit and vegetable crops.[41] Japanese agriculture tended to be "intensive in every sense of the word," in terms of the copious amount of human labor involved, fertilizing methods, number of crops planted in a field per year, and output. Multiple cropping, the use of one field to support more than a single harvest, and intercropping, sowing alternate rows of different crops at the same time, took advantage of the limited supply of farmland and a relatively mild climate.[42] Japanese immigrant farmers immediately put these practices to use when they arrived in the Santa Clara Valley.

Cash tenancy was the most common method through which Japanese acquired farmland in Santa Clara County in the early twentieth century, with written terms of agreements tending to benefit white growers more than Japanese lessees. In his 1915 study, Yamato Ichihashi classified Japanese cash leasing practices as either simple leasing or quasi-leasing. In the latter case, the lessor had "absolute control over the management of the industry as well as over the disposition of the crops." This was not "leasing" in the strict sense, according to Ichihashi, but a system "initiated by white farmers for their own convenience" to secure their own economic gains. By renting farmland to Japanese, white landowners guaranteed themselves a ready supply of labor to cultivate and harvest their crops during a time when labor shortages plagued many California growers.[43] Through white landlords' firm grip on the growing and sale of crops, many cash leasing terms "virtually nullified the significance of the 'autonomy' in marketing on the part of the tenant."[44] This was the typical arrangement in the Santa Clara Valley, as exemplified by one of the first recorded cash tenancy leases between a white landowner and Japanese lessees in the county, signed in May 1902 by Romeo Mauvais and F. T. Kuranaga and H. T. Gishi, for a 181-acre farm owned by Mauvais near Guadalupe Creek on the Santa Clara–Alviso Road. The terms fit Ichihashi's description of "quasi-leasing," as evident from the agreement that Mauvais "may manage and control said crops and dispose of the same in his own name and sell the same." Since lessees usually paid yearly rent in two installments, the first due when the lease was signed and the second after harvest, cash leasing required the most capital next to the purchasing of land; leasing, however, gave Japanese farmers more independence than farm labor or sharecropping arrangements.[45]

Beginning in the early twentieth century, many white landowners who had previously leased their property to Chinese farmers transitioned to Japanese tenants. The Younger family of San Jose, who recorded their first lease with Chinese tenants in 1879 to plant pear orchards, continued through the 1890s to lease the family ranch to Chinese for berry and vegetable cultivation. After the death of their father in 1890, the three Younger sisters, Alice, Rosalie, and Augusta, signed multiple leases with Chinese farmers to farm their respective inherited parcels. By 1903, all the leases the Youngers made with Chinese tenants in the 1880s and 1890s had expired with no recorded renewals, creating an opening for recently arrived Japanese immigrants. The Japanese quickly overtook the Chinese population in numbers during the 1900s, so by 1910 there were twice as many Japanese as Chinese residents of the county. In 1905, unmarried daughter Augusta Younger leased nearly 19 acres of her inherited property to two Japanese tenants, becoming the first in the family to replace Chinese lessees with Japanese ones. Her mother and her brother followed with their own leases to separate groups of Japanese farmers in 1907.[46]

Not far from the Younger property, the Cropleys of Berryessa also made the transition from Chinese to Japanese tenancy in the same time period. By 1900, Charles Cropley had died, leaving the management of two ranches to his widow, Henrietta. One ranch was cultivated in berries and vegetables by a Chinese tenant in Alviso, and the other was the family's residence on Capitol Avenue, where Henrietta Cropley lived with her four teenage sons and two white farm laborers. When all four sons were of age in 1910, she deeded them the 119 acre-ranch between Alviso and Milpitas (including the land her husband had leased to Ah Wah in 1887), which they appear to have rented out and not farmed themselves, though no official leases appear on record.[47] At that point, Henrietta Cropley began using Japanese farm labor to intensify production on her San Jose home ranch, which was for the most part still in hay and grain. In the 1910 census, no workers lived there except for a longtime hired hand.[48] After that ranch became her only property, Cropley likely determined it would be more profitable to grow specialty crops and in 1910 signed a seven-year lease with four Japanese farmers to cultivate nearly all of her property in prunes and cherries. Other Japanese tenants were already farming berries and vegetables on the remaining acreage.[49]

In 1913, after the passage of the state's first alien land law, which barred land ownership and limited leases to "aliens ineligible to citizenship" to three years, Henrietta Cropley signed a series of three-year leases with various Japanese tenants. By 1920, there were at least eight Japanese families renting land on the Cropley ranch; a total of thirty-two people lived on 45 acres.[50] None of the four Cropley sons chose farming as a career, which may have contributed to their widowed mother's decision to rely on Japanese tenants to manage her ranch and thus ensure a steady income for herself. Three of the brothers moved out of Santa Clara County and worked for oil, tire and rubber, and steamship companies, industries that boomed in California by the 1920s, while the fourth, James Cropley, stayed in San Jose, engaged as a presser in the cleaning and dyeing business.[51] The Youngers and Cropleys had leased their land to Chinese tenants for berry growing well before wives and daughters inherited the property, but the frequency of leases with Chinese and Japanese tenants increased when women became solely responsible for managing the ranches.

While Japanese farmers succeeded their Chinese counterparts without any documented overlap on the Youngers' and Cropleys' farms, the shift to sole Japanese tenancy was more gradual on the Malovos family's Light-house Farm in Alviso. Though purported in promotional literature to employ "none but white labor," the proprietors of Light-house Farm continued to engage Chinese laborers and tenant farmers in its operations at least through 1909, which marked the end of the term of the asparagus sharecropping arrangement Maria Malovos had made with Hi Loy.[52] The Malovos clan recorded its first Japanese lease in 1906 with R. Shiraishi, who leased approximately 50 acres of Light-house Farm and vastly expanded his rental to 235 acres several years later, farming tomatoes, potatoes, and other vegetables, as well as hay. Shiraishi also mortgaged his crops to his lessors on several occasions for small loans.[53]

In 1908, the Andrea Malovos Company, a corporation run by Maria Malovos and several of her sons after the death of Andrea, leased 20 more acres to three Japanese tenants for six years and another 30 acres to a pair of Japanese farmers. Since the two tracts were adjacent, the five lessees were to share the water from two wells on the property, with the landowners providing an engine and pump if that amount of water became insufficient for irrigation. The corporation agreed to furnish construction materials for the lessees to build a cabin on the property to live in while they farmed the tracts.[54] Just a few years later, in 1911, the state forfeited the charter of the company for its failure to pay the annual license tax. As a means of "settling their affairs," the directors of the corporation began selling off its land to various buyers, including Japanese farmer Chozaburo Kumagai, who purchased 27.13 acres of what had been Light-house Farm in November 1912.[55] Andrew J. Malovos, one of the directors and a local real estate agent, assumed some of the company's obligations after its dissolution, including the chattel mortgage the company had made with Shiraishi in 1911.[56]

In the early twentieth century, many Japanese leased farmland not far from Light-house Farm, the Malovos property. The acreage lay in the northern part of the Santa Clara Valley, between San Jose and the southern end of the San Francisco Bay, where Chinese immigrants had begun raising berries as early as the mid-1860s. Chinese settlement had centered around Alviso and Agnew, small towns located about 8 and 6 miles from San Jose, respectively, in the fertile crescent extending from Milpitas and Berryessa to the east and Santa Clara to the west, on land early white settlers found undesirable because of frequent flooding, saltwater seepage into the freshwater supply, and refuse that washed ashore from San Jose and the Valley.

In Alviso, Immigration Commission investigators found five "colonies" and 44 individual farmers leasing a total of 273 acres of land in 1908. In each colony, the first of which had been established in 1901, land was usually rented as one tract and subdivided among members, with houses built in a cluster in the midst of the tracts, sectioned off with irrigation ditches. Regarding Alviso farming arrangements, the federal investigator noted that "cooperative effort in plowing and other work" was common among the Japanese farmers, some of whom worked with a business agent who purchased supplies for them and shipped and marketed their crops. South of Alviso, in nearby Agnew, one-third as many farmers leased about half as many acres of land as the settlers in Alviso.[57]

Government officials documenting the Japanese colony in Alviso may have visited the 34 acres of land leased to Iwataro Zenihiro by Frank Zanker, whose German immigrant family owned substantial property along the Alviso-Milpitas Road. The lease, signed in October 1903 for a term of eight years, included 3 acres already planted in strawberry and blackberry vines and stipulated that the lessees use the remaining acreage "for farming or for the purpose of growing berries or fruit." In 1905, Zenihiro, who had emigrated from Japan in 1894, used his blackberry crop on Zanker's property to obtain a loan for $100 (equivalent to roughly $2,400 today).[58] About a year later, at the age of twenty-nine, Zenihiro sent for a bride from Japan, whose occupation census enumerator listed as a "farm laborer" on a "home farm" in 1910. Under Japanese government regulations, farmers, considered stable and settled immigrants, were eligible to bring over wives.[59] The Japanese settlement in Alviso also included land belonging to Zanker's neighbor to the east, Edmund B. Farney, who in 1905 leased 20 acres for "general farming purposes" to U. Yamagami for a term of seven years at an annual rent of $315. As part of the agreement, Yamagami had the use of Farney's farm implements, 100 boxes, and a house to live in. A third neighbor, Paul Shearer, whose land bordered both Zanker's and Farney's properties, signed an agreement in May 1908 to lease 25 acres of his Alviso ranch to five Japanese farmers, H. E. Furuto, U. Tomimatsu, T. Honda, Y. Wemura, and Y. Hirata for an annual sum of $450.[60] Of the five names, only Honda's could be verified in the 1910 census. Enumerators listed Honda as a forty-five-year-old childless widower and "fruit farmer" in Alviso who had arrived in the United States in 1899.[61]

One of the largest parcels of Alviso farmland leased to Japanese settlers was the 157-acre property known as the McKiernan Ranch, just east of Shearer's and Zanker's holdings on the Alviso-Milpitas Road. In 1901, the McKiernan

sisters, Catherine McKiernan, Mary Colombet, and Nellie G. Bailey, leased the
entire ranch to farmers Yaichi Yamakawa and M. Shirachi. One year before,
census takers found the three sisters living with their sixty-nine-year-old widowed mother, Barbara, their brother James (Nellie's twin), Colombet's husband
and the couple's eight-year-old daughter, and a Swedish servant, all under one
roof on North Eighth Street in downtown San Jose. Not long after the census
was taken, Barbara McKiernan passed away and James McKiernan married and
moved from San Jose to Santa Cruz County, leaving his sisters to manage the
family's ranch in Alviso.[62] White women's decisions to lease to Japanese farmers,
which reflected a developing pattern in the area, in fact provided opportunities
for the growing number of immigrants from Japan newly arrived in Santa Clara
County. Moreover, the absence of an adult male in the household increased the
chances that many women would turn to Asian tenants. Though ostensibly
"family farms," these female-managed agricultural operations did not conform
to the labor ideal lauded in the promotional literature of the day, that of white
men, women, and children self-sufficiently farming orchard fruits. Yaichi
Yamakawa sub-leased 69.5 acres of the McKiernans' land to K. Hirano and
G. Kiyomura for a term of four years. To obtain necessary cash on several occasions, Yamakawa and Hirano mortgaged their crops, horses, and farm equipment to the McKiernan sisters, who readily loaned $800 at a time to the ten-
ants. Within one decade, at least eight Japanese tenant farmers had cycled
through the McKiernan ranch, providing steady income for the absentee
landowners. By 1907, Yamakawa had done so well as the McKiernans' tenant
that he left their engagement and purchased a fruit farm on McLaughlin Avenue
in east San Jose. In 1910, he was living on his own ranch with his new wife,
Kazu, brother Hiromu, and six Japanese boarders who likely worked for him.[63]

Japanese farmers' achievements occurred within the racialized and segmented
structure of the Santa Clara Valley's horticultural industry. Even though they
lived in what the *Pacific Rural Press* called "the greatest orchard area of California,"
Japanese growers remained chiefly in berry and vegetable cultivation.[64] Echoing
the heavy presence of Chinese immigrants in berry farming during the late
nineteenth century, beginning in the 1900s, the Japanese in the Santa Clara
Valley established themselves as the county's leading growers of strawberries.
Due in large part to the acreage the Japanese devoted to strawberries, the San
Jose district ranked fourth in California as a producer of that crop, behind Florin
in Sacramento County, Los Angeles, and Watsonville.[65] Compared to deciduous
fruit and even vegetables, labor-intensive berries required less land to grow and
bore fruit quickly, making them an attractive start-up crop for new Japanese
immigrants with little capital, just as they had been for Chinese farmers. Under
the restrictive clauses of some agricultural leases, Asian farmers could not grow
deciduous fruits even if they had the means. In a 1908 agreement, for example,

Alviso landowner Paul Shearer stressed that his Japanese lessees were to plant only strawberries on his land, likely intercropped, while Shearer reserved "the right to plant fruit trees on said premises" and claimed the fruit of those trees to be his "exclusive property." Other leases mandated the specific distance from fruit trees Japanese tenants had to cultivate their berries and vegetables without hindering the growth of the trees. In these agreements, Japanese farmers leased a limited portion of the white landowner's property, commonly the space between deciduous fruit trees, an arrangement particularly beneficial for growers with young orchards, since it offered an opportunity to profit from renting out unused land even before the trees bore fruit.[66]

While Alviso, Agnew, and parts of San Jose became centers of Japanese berry growing in the early twentieth century, the rural vicinity of Mountain View and Sunnyvale emerged as a major site of Japanese vegetable cultivation. An example of one early agreement was between Sunnyvale grocer Louis Zolezzi and J. Fukuda and H. Ogawa, who were to plant 17 acres of onions, 8 acres of tomatoes, and 3 acres of pie pumpkins in the 1905 season, and to deliver the harvest to Zolezzi in Sunnyvale.[67] The grocer was to market the vegetable harvest, paying the lessees between 60 to 65 percent of the net proceeds depending on the type of produce. Although Zolezzi officially recorded his sharecropping arrangements with Fukuda and Ogawa, many landowners did not use such documents, relying instead on informal oral agreements. During the 1908 and 1909 growing seasons, J. K. Oda made a series of signed and verbal contracts with the Laughlin Seed Company to plant 27 acres of onions in San Jose with seed the company provided. Oda was to receive 65 cents per sack of onions once he had delivered the harvest to a designated shipping point. Similarly, Tiga Ishida entered an oral agreement with the John Heinlen Company in 1909 to grow a potato crop in Edenvale for half the gross returns on the harvest.[68] Sharecropping allowed Japanese farmers to gain access to land for cultivation without outlays of capital for rent and made sense for crops that did not take long to mature, such as berries and vegetables.

Under Japanese tenancy, Mountain View became a center for tomato cultivation, with up to half of the Santa Clara Valley's vegetable acreage planted in tomatoes and an abundance of canneries on hand to process them. In 1912, Marguerite Stierlin, daughter of Swiss-born forty-niner-turned-gunsmith-turned farmer C. C. Stierlin, signed an unrecorded lease with a Japanese farming partnership, renting 55 acres of her ranch in Mountain View. The partnership, calling itself T.M.T.O., included four Japanese immigrants, M. Tachibana, Masataro Matsushita, Naosuke Tsumura, and Yasutaro Oku. Tsumura and Oku immigrated from Japan in 1903; as early as 1909 they were farming near San Jose Japantown, and in 1910 were living together in a Japanese rooming house. The daughter of an early pioneer settler with large landholdings, Stierlin turned to

Japanese tenancy in order to profit from the intensification of crops on her property, previously planted in just hay and grain. Like many female landowners who
left the operation of their ranches to Japanese tenants, Stierlin did not live on
site. By 1910, she had made her residence in a home on The Alameda, between
the city limits of Santa Clara and San Jose.[69] In November 1911, the T.M.T.O.
partnership signed a ten-year lease to farm 65 acres of the James Center ranch,
which bordered the Stierlin ranch in Mountain View. As their fitting acronym
implied, the T.M.T.O. partners grew primarily tomatoes on the Center and Stierlin ranches, along with corn and hay.[70] By 1920, in addition to berries, Japanese
farmers had a firm grasp on the region's production of vegetable crops, supplying
60 percent of the tomatoes, 82 percent of the spinach, and 100 percent of "other
vegetables" delivered to canneries in the Santa Clara Valley district.[71]

When it came to deciduous fruits, the county's most celebrated and lucrative
crop, Japanese farmers were not key players, furnishing a mere 3 percent of the
peaches, pears, apricots, plums, and cherries that were canned in the Santa Clara
Valley. Moreover, in comparison to the Valley's acclaimed orchard fruits, the
berries and vegetables that Japanese immigrants tended to farm made up a small
fraction of the agricultural wealth of the region while requiring vast amounts of
manual labor. A 1908 report of the California State Agricultural Society showed
that deciduous fruit, whether green (unprocessed), dried, or canned, comprised
almost two-thirds of Santa Clara County's total value in farm and dairy products, while the value of berries and vegetables combined was only 13.8 percent
of the total.[72] Some Japanese farm families eventually came to operate orchards,
but in the fields of the Santa Clara Valley at the turn of the twentieth century,
Japanese farmers raised less profitable and more labor-intensive crops, a trend
that continued well into the 1920s. Even after they had been established for
almost two decades, about 50 percent of Japanese farm families cultivated
berries, vegetables, and garden seed, while only 18 percent reportedly worked
on "fruit farms" or orchards.[73]

Nevertheless, a few Japanese immigrants did make inroads in cultivating
orchard fruit in the early twentieth century, sometimes starting out with sharecropping agreements like the ones used for berry and vegetable farming. Sharecroppers depended on what landowners provided and usually had the incentive
to be productive, since the size of their set share was relative to the crop they
produced.[74] In some cases, however, lessors made adjustments so that
they would reap more benefits from a larger crop than their tenants. In May
1904, Caroline Henning drew up a contract with Frank Shimizu, J. Hawa, and
S. Homasaki in which the lessees agreed to pay $300 for the privilege of culti-
vating 32 acres of her orchard on Foxworthy Road in San Jose, with the use of
two horses and a variety of farm implements; in exchange, the tenants were to
receive half the crop, plus a cash amount that depended on how much green

fruit, likely prunes or apricots, the Japanese harvested each season. In addition to the $300 already paid, if the crop amounted to as much as 105 tons green, the lessees would pay Henning an additional $100, and an additional $200 if the harvest was 125 tons.[75] In November 1908, Henning's brother, sixty-one-year-old George W. Theuerkauf, who was retired from active farming, arranged for Fudetaro Horio to grow prunes on 14 acres of orchard land also on Foxworthy Road in exchange for half the crop. This property adjoined Georgia McBride's orchard in Willow Glen (in fact, McBride had purchased nearly 12 acres in 1882 and 5.5 acres in 1888 from Frederick and Catherine Theuerkauf, parents of George Theuerkauf and Caroline Henning), where McBride claimed to employ no Asian labor, a practice that would have differed markedly from her neighbors'. George Theuerkauf also contracted with Horio to cure and dry the landowner's portion of the prunes "at the going price." A well-to-do landowner who had run a 578-acre grain and stock ranch in Monterey County before settling in San Jose in 1893, Theuerkauf placed Horio in charge of his entire prune orchard on Foxworthy Road, located several miles from his San Jose residence.[76]

Reflecting the intertwined web of Japanese tenants and white landowners in the Valley, Horio had also signed a lease with the Hennings to cultivate 20 acres of "Mrs. Henning's Orchard" for five years, from 1907 to 1912. Here, the parties made a cash rental arrangement, with Horio paying a premium $1,000 yearly rent.[77] In part because he was able to secure farming arrangements involving prunes, a far more lucrative crop than the berries and vegetables most local Japanese grew, Horio eventually accumulated enough capital to purchase his own orchard on Foxworthy Road with his older brother Seijiro, heralded in a 1922 Japanese American directory as a "role model" in managing fruit orchards and "a success among Japanese immigrants in the county." Before the passage of the 1913 alien land law, the brothers bought adjacent tracts of land in San Jose, which they farmed together with their growing families.[78]

Taken together, Japanese immigrants in the Santa Clara Valley comprised an integral part of the area's agricultural economy in the early twentieth century and were represented at all levels of the farm ladder, from laborers to tenant farmers and a tiny number of landowners. Many Japanese farmers attained stable, profitable farming arrangements, negotiating long-term contracts and frequently adding acreage to what they were already farming.[79] The distribution described also suggests a growing bifurcation between men who worked as seasonal laborers for white landowners and those who had accumulated enough capital to rent or purchase farmland and even hire their countrymen to work for them. Most of these farmers, however, cultivated less remunerative crops that did not come close to yielding the profits brought in by the famous orchard fruits of the Santa Clara Valley. Given a horticultural economy in which crops were informally segregated by race, even if class fissures were taking shape within the rural

Japanese community, the gap between farmers and laborers was not insurmountable at this time.

Japanese Immigrant Farmers and the Legal System

Even as new immigrants with limited command of English, Japanese farmers
held onto the economic gains they made in part through litigation to protect
and advance themselves in the agricultural sector. Whether they had misunder-
stood terms of their contracts or white landowners had attempted to exploit the
immigrants, records of the Santa Clara County Superior Court show that on a
number of occasions, Japanese sharecroppers and tenant farmers took white
growers to court for violating terms of set farming agreements. In 1911 potato
farmer Tiga Ishida sued the John Heinlen Company for the $92.50 he claimed
he should have received for approximately 340 sacks of potatoes of two different grades. When the Justice's Court of San Jose Township found in favor of
Ishida, members of the Heinlen family appealed the decision to the Santa Clara
County Superior Court. After a barrage of answers, counterclaims, and motions,
the court likely dismissed the appeal, as no judgment was recorded.[80] Like
Ishida, San Jose farmer J. K. Oda had engaged in a vegetable sharecropping
arrangement and sued for an unpaid harvest, though the damages he sought
totaled more than $4,000 and included interest on the balance for which he
alleged the Laughlin Seed Company had failed to compensate him. Oda's complaint featured numerous convoluted details of multiple contracts, including
unrecorded oral ones, to plant acres of onions and deliver them in sacks to the
nearest shipping point in the San Joaquin Delta.[81] Due to the high volume of
the harvest described, Oda may have been a labor contractor. Though he possessed some facility with English, he appeared to be plagued by miscommunication over the terms of labor and payment, a theme that persisted in numerous
Japanese farming cases.[82]

In an intensively farmed region, access to well water for irrigation was crucial,
and Japanese tenants readily took legal action when they believed white landowners were depriving them of their right to obtain water for their crops.
M. Shirachi's 1913 lawsuit charging F. C. Sloan with violating the terms of their
lease centered on the contention that Sloan did not supply wells as promised.
Shirachi, who had partnered with Yaichi Yamakawa to lease the McKiernan
sisters' ranch in Alviso in 1901, found a new farming opportunity in 1912 when
he began renting a tract of over 162 acres from F. C. Sloan for a ten-year term.
Likely because Shirachi could not afford to pay all rental costs in cash, he mortgaged his crops, livestock, and farm equipment to Sloan as security for the lease.
For his part, Sloan agreed to construct a barn for Shirachi's horses and sink two

wells for irrigation.[83] Shirachi's complaint to the county Superior Court alleged that the plaintiff had planted vegetables and other crops during the spring and summer of 1913, but those crops did not "mature or ripen" because of Sloan's failure to construct the wells or "to furnish water for domestic use as agreed," leading to $6,000 in damage by Shirachi's estimate. The complaint further stated that Sloan had seized the portion of the crop that could be harvested and sold it for approximately $3,000.

In another dispute over irrigation, tenants of the Younger family sued for damages to the strawberry and raspberry crop they said had occurred when the landowners tampered with an underground water pipe. In April 1913, Jenzaburo Inouye had laid this pipe from a well he had dug across the San Jose property of Edward and Sarah Younger. Asserting their right to the use of this water for the berry crop, Inouye and his two co-plaintiffs alleged that the Youngers had destroyed a portion of the pipe and threatened to tear down the remainder. Incomplete court records do not indicate whether the Japanese tenants received the injunction they sought to restrain the Youngers from taking further action on the pipe, but it is clear that access to water was a perpetual source of consternation for Japanese farmers in the Valley.[84] Shirachi was so incensed by the turn of events concerning his irrigation arrangements that a few days prior to filing the lawsuit in December 1913, he rescinded his contract with Sloan, just over a year after the signing of the lease and mortgage, and demanded that Sloan pay him for the harvested crop along with damages for what had failed to ripen, allegedly as a result of Sloan's failure to provide adequate irrigation.[85] Existing evidence shows that Shirachi's understanding of the rent schedule was incomplete, with the result that he was not aware that according to the terms of the lease, he should have paid the balance of his rent by August 1, 1913. The Superior Court judge thus found Sloan's cross-complaint valid and ordered Shirachi to pay over $1,500 in overdue rent but mentioned neither the actual value of the crop Shirachi claimed Sloan had seized nor whether that amount could have been applied to the disputed rent.[86]

While Japanese immigrant farmers initiated a sizable number of lawsuits against their white landlords in the county, the reverse occurred far less frequently, suggesting a high degree of satisfaction among the county's white landowners with their Japanese tenants. In a rare case in which a white landowner became displeased with the agricultural methods of her Japanese tenants, the court eventually sided with the defendants. In 1912, Lila Peterson sued Japanese lessees Charley Chakuno and Frank Furuya ("Charlie" and "Frank" were the most common English first names Japanese immigrant men took) for "negligently, carelessly and improperly" caring for her 50-acre orchard on Boyter Road in San Jose. Peterson also objected to the common Japanese practice of intercropping strawberries, tomatoes, and other vegetables between the prune and peach trees, claiming that "their policy of planting vines between the trees is impoverishing the soil to the detriment of the trees." Her disapproval echoed prevailing stereotypes that Japanese farmers' intensive planting methods, while productive, had the effect of overworking and ruining farmland. The defense declared that contrary to Peterson's allegations, Chakuno and Furuya had pruned, cultivated, and irrigated the existing trees using "every precaution.... that ingenuity and horticulture could suggest," but some of the trees were "old, past their usefulness as orchard trees" and required removal and replacement. As for the tomatoes and other plants intercropped, the defendants denied having caused "any damage or injury" to the fruit trees and pointed out that the lease contained no prohibition of intercropping. Furuya stated that he was "an experienced orchardist" who utilized "first class up to date methods of husbandry" and as a result, Peterson's orchard was "in a far better state of cultivation" than when he had taken possession it, estimating the property was "now worth more by several thousand of dollars" because of his care and diligence.[87]

The defense skewered Peterson, a young woman transplanted from Calaveras County who had taken possession of the orchard just before the lawsuit, intimating she knew almost nothing about the cultivation of fruit trees. Indeed, the defendants had had to inform her that the leaves on her trees were turning brown not from lack of care, but because it was "the time of year when the leaves of deciduous trees turn brown and fall." At the trial, she came off as a naive woman incapable of operating her own farm, in contrast to the two Japanese men, who appeared to be thoroughly qualified and adept agriculturists. Believing Peterson needed a primer on the life span of fruit trees, the defense also suggested she did not understand that some of her peach trees, approximately thirty years old, were deteriorating "on account of extreme age," not from the lessees' negligence.[88] This particular legal action aside, white residents for the most part were inclined to believe the Japanese were competent, skilled farmers. Ruling in favor of Chakuno and Furuya, the county superior court adjudicated that the Japanese lessees had indeed "cared for the said orchard and trees in a first class manner," fulfilling the conditions stipulated in the lease, thus entitling Peterson to no damages "on account of any neglect or want of care."[89]

In addition to settling disagreements with white landowners, county court cases involving Japanese agriculturalists further reveal a strategy of turning to the legal system to resolve business disputes they could not mediate within their own ethnic community. A series of Superior Court cases from 1909 to 1915 involving an absconded, insolvent tenant farmer named J. Takano and his litigious creditors (multiple Japanese farmers and a Chinese merchant) reflect intra-ethnic conflict endemic to the burgeoning Issei farming community and show how immigrants from the two countries vied against each other to legitimate their claims in the eyes of white authorities. In 1907, Takano began renting three adjacent parcels of farmland located along the Guadalupe River in the Orchard District of San Jose, where numerous white landowners had lease arrangements with Japanese tenant farmers (at the time, R. Shiraishi was farming for the Andrea Malovos Company just north of Takano's tracts). In 1908, fellow farmer Jennosuke Sumida invested in Takano's farming venture by providing a cash loan and labor amounting to over $1,000. Takano drafted a "deed of loan" to Sumida in Japanese, which also gave Sumida permission to use all of his farming equipment and livestock until October 31, 1909, by which time the season's crops would be harvested and sold, and Takano presumably could pay Sumida.[90] At the beginning of June 1909, Takano left the Santa Clara Valley for an unknown destination to the chagrin of two additional creditors: Yasukachi (K. Y.) Toda, who had loaned Takano more than $400 in cash, and Leong Yim of the Tuck Wo Company, from whom Takano purchased approximately $400 worth of goods on credit and obtained a small cash advance. On June 25, 1909, realizing that Takano was nowhere to be found, Toda filed suit against Takano in the Santa Clara County Superior Court for the unpaid loan plus interest. Three days later, Leong also filed a suit for repayment of his loan to Takano. In answer to these lawsuits, Sheriff Arthur B. Langford made an unsuccessful search and inquiry after Takano and seized what he believed was Takano's personal property.[91]

On July 6, 1909, Sumida filed a lawsuit against Langford, claiming that the seized property was rightfully his. Sumida produced the "deed of loan" Takano had signed along with a translation of the Japanese into English by G. S. Okamoto, president of the Japanese Association of San Jose. With the sheriff questioning the legitimacy of the translation, the document did not convince the court, which found in favor of Langford. The decision prompted Sumida to file a new suit for nonpayment, similar to the ones Toda and Leong had already entered with the court. On September 1, 1909, the court ordered Takano's seized property, leasehold interests, and growing crops be sold at public auction. At the auction that took place one week later, Sumida purchased Takano's livestock, leasehold interest, crops, and nearly all of his farming equipment for $1,000.50. The situation became even more complicated when two other Japanese farmers leasing nearby tracts, Shiraishi of Light-house Farm and T. Fugisaki, proceeded to sue Sumida and Leong Yim, alleging that Toda had accepted Takano's property, including the crops and leases Sumida had just bought, as repayment for his loan. Toda had then sold those same crops and leases to Shiraishi and Fugisaki for $500. Sumida protested vehemently and maintained his right to the crop, part of which was in ripening tomatoes that he said needed to be picked daily. Sheriff Langford testified he had no knowledge that Shiraishi and Fugisaki laid any claim to Takano's property in June when he seized it. He supported Sumida's assertion that landowner R. H. Powell was to hold Takano's property and that

Sumida was permitted to care for it. The judge dismissed the case on September 17. Still attempting to recover their rights to Takano's crops, Shiraishi and Fugisaki filed subsequent suits against landowners Mary J. Powell, R. H. Powell, and B. J. Horn, to no avail.[92]

When heated disputes over business matters surfaced among Japanese immigrant farmers and they could not reconcile the issues within the community, their ultimate recourse was to take their adversaries and countrymen to court, even if this meant putting themselves at the mercy of white men who did not consider Japanese-language documents valid. Perhaps if he had officially recorded a contract with Takano in English, Sumida would have saved himself not only a great deal of subsequent litigation, but also the need to pay for equipment and livestock he appeared already entitled to use. Whether Toda deliberately deceived Shiraishi and Fugisaki regarding his legitimate claim to Takano's crops, or possibly also misled the white landlords, the documentary record cannot say. When intra-ethnic conflict arose in the agricultural arena, Japanese immigrants had to stake their investments and losses on the decisions of a legal system foreign to them, though they were quick to learn and navigate its intricacies.

"The Employment of Asiatics"

By 1920, Japanese immigrants had undeniably replaced the Chinese as the Santa Clara Valley's dominant nonwhite group in agriculture. But the first decades of the early twentieth century represented a unique period of overlap for the two immigrant populations. Although Chinese and Japanese residents of San Jose maintained separate ethnic neighborhoods (as the *San Jose Mercury* observed in 1908, "no Japs live in Chinatown, and no Chinese reside among the Japs"), they often mingled in business transactions. Katsusaburo Kawahara, the *yobiyose* (child of Issei immigrants left behind in Japan until old enough to work) who was reunited with his parents in San Jose in 1911, recalled congenial relations with Chinese immigrants there. Kawahara remarked that he "always had support" from his Chinese friends and as an adult, encouraged his Japanese compatriots to support Chinese stores and businesses. A number of Nisei who grew up on Valley farms recalled dining in Chinese restaurants in San Jose as an end-of-the-week treat for the family. By 1909 there were 79 Japanese businesses in San Jose, most located in San Jose Nihonmachi, which developed in the vicinity of Chinatown, along North Sixth and Jackson Streets. As the Japanese population continued to grow in the 1920s and 1930s while the Chinese population numbered only in the hundreds, Nihonmachi gradually replaced the older Chinatown.[93]

While regular interactions between Chinese and Japanese residents at places of business in Chinatown and Nihonmachi were the norm, on occasion international tensions incited conflict among the local Asian population. In mid-June 1908, Japanese residents of San Jose implemented a boycott against Chinese-run businesses in protest against the seizure by Chinese authorities of a Japanese ship in Chinese waters. According to San Jose merchant G. S. Okamoto, the local Japanese community was actually responding to a Chinese boycott of Japanese goods and steamships that Chinese residents of San Francisco had observed for some time. It was the recent Chinese action against a Japanese vessel that galvanized San Jose Issei to express their grievances. In the first decade of the twentieth century, Japanese customers were normally frequent patrons of Chinese establishments in San Jose, and their absence as a result of the 1908 boycott was "very noticeable."[94] Elite leaders of the Japanese community reportedly tried to exert their influence to extend the boycott for as long as possible in order to address one of their key concerns: the problem of gambling among Issei men, which many considered to be instigated by the Chinese, who owned the vast majority of gambling places Japanese visited. To reformers' satisfaction, as long as the boycott was in place, Japanese would-be gamblers would not dare enter Chinese gambling houses in San Jose.[95]

In the early twentieth century, the Bayside Canning Company in Alviso emerged as an unparalleled example of interethnic relations between Chinese and Japanese residents of Santa Clara County. At its peak, the successful cannery employed Chinese, Japanese, and Filipino workers, providing a place in which Asian immigrants were most likely to cross paths, as well as indicating the presence of a vibrant local ethnic economy. Bayside offers a window into the ways in which Chinese immigrants navigated the changing ethnic composition in the Valley's agricultural sector and shows how Chinese and Japanese shared similar challenges from continued white racism.

Chinese immigrant Yen Chew founded the Precita Canning Company in the late 1890s and his son, the remarkable businessman Thomas Foon Chew, took over operations in 1906 after most of Precita was destroyed in the earthquake. The younger Chew rebuilt the business, renamed it the Bayside Canning Company, and turned it into a thriving enterprise in Alviso. Chew, widely known as Tom Foon, was considered "well Americanized" in attire and mannerism; he was active in the local Masonic order and the San Jose chapter of the Scottish Rite. In an effort to find relief for his chronic asthma, he moved his wife and seven children from Alviso to a home in Los Gatos, located in the Valley's scenic western foothills, where he was regarded as a "respected resident."[96] Savvy and fluent in English, Chew invested in the most up-to-date canning equipment and worked closely with white agents and distributors, who often represented him in business dealings.

Bayside initially packed only tomatoes, but later branched out into other fruits and vegetables, including its specialty, green asparagus, for which Thomas

Foon Chew earned his title "Asparagus King." With income from his cannery business, Chew purchased and leased property in northern California through the Thomas Foon Ranch Company, which at one time owned approximately 8,000 acres in the Sacramento Delta region and hundreds more in the Central Valley. By 1920, Bayside had become the third largest cannery in the United States after Del Monte and Libby, with other branches throughout the county and in the San Francisco Bay region. When Chew died in 1931, three Santa Clara County farms, totaling 57 acres, remained in the name of his corporation, thus circumventing alien land laws.[97]

While most Valley canneries employed only white workers, Bayside was notable for hiring mostly Asians, a succession and combination of Chinese, Japanese, and Filipinos, along with some Mexican and European immigrants. In contrast to harvest and field labor, white workers dominated the fruit packing and processing trades in the Santa Clara Valley. Federal investigators in 1908 reported that whites, including many women and children, outnumbered Chinese and Japanese in fruit cutting and packing by a margin of three to one, and three out of the four large county fruit packing houses surveyed employed white men and women only—no "Asiatics." "Native whites" predominated among the employees, followed by a small number of immigrant Italians and a "still smaller number of other foreign-born white races." Whites expressed a preference for cannery over orchard work.[98]

Many Japanese men and women worked at Chew's Alviso cannery, and their earnings from cannery work, in conjunction with sharecropping and receiving

Figure 2.2 Thomas Foon Chew with two foremen at Bayside Canning Company, Alviso. Courtesy of Gloria Hom.

"liberal credit from Chinese, Japanese, and white storekeepers," helped some become tenant farmers within a couple years of their arrival in the country. The company constructed cabins and boarding houses for its hundreds of laborers on land surrounding the cannery buildings. In addition, Chew provided numerous loans to Japanese immigrants in the form of crop and chattel mortgages during the 1910s and 1920s. R. Shiraishi, the same farmer who leased portions of the Malovos family's Light-house Farm in 1906, was farming multiple parcels in the San Jose area by 1912 when he mortgaged his entire tomato crop growing on 83 acres to Thomas Foon Chew for a loan of $1,500. The two parties arranged another loan for the same amount the following year, expanded to crops of "fruit, vegetables, seeds" in addition to tomatoes farmed on Shiraishi's leased property.[99] From 1912 to 1922, Chew recorded 16 loans to Japanese farmers in the form of crop or chattel mortgages. In the face of dwindling numbers of his own countrymen, Chew maintained longstanding business relationships with Japanese farmers, making repeated loans and hiring them as foremen and ranch managers to oversee the extensive farmland held under the name of the Thomas Foon Ranch Company.[100]

Some local white residents, including a few employed at Bayside, resented Chew's ties with fellow Asians and accused the cannery of reverse racial discrimination. Insinuating the existence of preferential treatment for Asian over white employees, white workers in the vicinity of Alviso protested the hiring practices at Bayside Canning Company, exhibiting "strong feeling. . . . against the employment of Asiatics."[101] In the summer of 1908, a particularly robust harvest season in which growers faced a scarcity of help, all the cannery's white employees went on strike, "claiming that it was impossible any longer to stand the abuses the Orientals in charge of the place heaped upon American women and girls." White female workers complained of "smoke from Chinese cigars" permeating the establishment and "Chinese bosses" throwing rotten fruit and cursing at them in "pigeon English." These same bosses, the women further alleged, assigned Japanese laborers to "high tables" while white workers "were given tables so low they had to stoop."[102] For white residents of the Valley whose racial identity was intimately bound up with fruit growing and processing, the presence of a Chinese-run cannery was an affront to their ideas of agricultural work, just as the presence of Japanese-operated family farms eventually provided another flashpoint of conflict in the subsequent decade.

Because Chew's Alviso cannery employees were a racially diverse mix, Valley boosters and nearby competing canneries, playing to contemporary white prejudices, emphasized the racial purity of their establishments. One writer described the Flickinger Cannery near Berryessa, one of the county's first fruit canneries, as a place where "the fruit is all packed by white men and women, who are required to exercise care that neatness and cleanliness shall characterize all their

work." Whiteness denoted the "neatness and cleanliness" of the workers as well
as the cannery itself: "The drying ground is kept clean and neat and the fruit is
dried on clean white pine trays. Everything about the place, in fact, is kept perfectly neat and clean."[103] L. F. Graham, president of the Flickinger Cannery and
son-in-law of company founder Joseph Flickinger, earnestly supported the
efforts of the San Jose Chamber of Commerce to recruit white families to the
Valley, providing anecdotal evidence to the *San Jose Mercury* that families working
at Flickinger earned enough in the summer to support themselves in the winter
while children attended local schools.[104] Widespread concern over the race of
fruit canning and processing employees resulted in a 1905 state bill requiring a
package of fruit to be labeled showing "whether the fruit was packed by Chinese,
Japanese or white labor." Aware of the fruit industry's general reliance on Asian
labor, the *California Fruit Grower* firmly opposed the label law, which never
passed, calling it "vicious" and defended a man's right to "employ yellow labor in
the packing of his fruit" without being placed "at a disadvantage on account of
exercising that right."[105] Still, some canneries like Flickinger attempted to leverage
claims to an all-white labor force to their advantage, assuring customers that only
white hands had touched their food. Because of its geographic proximity to its
rival, the decidedly non-white Bayside, the proprietors of Flickinger Cannery
were keen to portray their establishment as managed and operated exclusively
by whites.

The paths of Bayside and Flickinger intersected in December of 1909 when
Chew began leasing over 100 acres of land that the Flickinger operations had
purchased in 1892 at Lawrence Station in what is now Sunnyvale, several miles
west of Flickinger's Berryessa orchards and cannery. The Flickinger Company
was in the process of selling this parcel, pending litigation that would correct
some imperfections in the title; the prospective buyer, Rizziero Tognazzini, was
the son of an Italian-Swiss dairyman who had immigrated to California in the
1860s.[106] According to the 1909 lease between Chew and Tognazzini, Chew
intended to farm a variety of vegetables, including tomatoes, potatoes, onions,
peas, beans, and lettuce, and to erect buildings, presumably to house workers
who would farm those crops. As the agreement also allowed for the planting
of "a small quantity of vegetables for the use of men employed on the said
premises," the lessor, Tognazzini, acknowledged that Chew would be setting up
a crew of farmers and farmhands, likely of Chinese and Japanese origin. Curi-
ously, the lease forbade Chew from planting "radish of any [k]ind" on the property, perhaps as a deterrence to the excessive employment of Japanese laborers.
The J. H. Flickinger Company, still the legal owners of the farm at the time this
lease was made, could have dictated these terms.[107] After Chew's sudden death
from pneumonia in 1931, Bayside declined quickly and shut down in 1936.

As they settled in the Santa Clara Valley at the beginning of the twentieth century, Issei men and women assumed the place of the dwindling numbers of Chinese in farm labor, sharecropping, and tenant farming arrangements. Though some Japanese farm families, capitalizing on their agricultural background from their homeland, would eventually operate orchards in the Valley, these early years were characterized by the segmentation of Japanese immigrants in the less profitable, more menial cultivation of berries and vegetables, even before the advent of alien land laws, along with the widespread employment of Japanese men as ranch and field hands. The establishment of Issei farmers in the Valley's horticultural industry involved constant complex negotiations with white land-owners, sometimes leading to heated conflict and legal battles, as well as alliances with longtime Chinese residents and entrepreneurs. The context of limited economic opportunity within the agricultural sector's racial structure not only had implications for Japanese-white relations, but it also immensely impacted community formation and intra-ethnic affairs, especially as intensified by gender imbalance among the early Issei population.

3

Pioneering Men and Women

Japanese Gender Relations in Rural California

On July 12, 1910, thirty-four-year-old Tomihei Hayakawa shot himself outside a barn on a ranch near Mountain View, where he had been picking apricots. Although in May 1910 a census enumerator listed him as a "servant" living with Charles and Mary Woog, Hayakawa, who had emigrated from Japan in 1902, had worked for Mary Woog as a foreman on her fruit ranch for at least two years. After he took a load of apricots to a nearby cannery and returned to the ranch that July day, Hayakawa reportedly summoned his friend and distant relative Matajiro Uchida to the barn and proceeded to say that he was going to die, that "the love between my wife and myself is not in a happy way." Hayakawa instructed Uchida, who hailed from Hayakawa's hometown in Yamanashi Prefecture in Japan, to take care of his body after his death. He then drew a pistol from his pocket. Uchida desperately struggled to pull the gun away, but Hayakawa managed to fire five shots at himself, the last of which fatally pierced his aorta and became lodged in his backbone.[1]

The suicide, initially investigated as a murder by the Santa Clara County coroner, generated over 50 pages of typewritten testimony from numerous Japanese and white witnesses, as well as substantial press coverage in local papers and the San Francisco–based Japanese-language newspaper *Shin Sekai* (New World Daily). The *Mountain View Leader-Register* reported that about 40 Japanese and 80 other local residents were present at the coroner's inquest. Of the Japanese spectators, only three were women, one the widow of Hayakawa, dressed in black, her face hidden by a heavy mourning veil.[2] At the trial, spectators learned that on the night before the suicide, about a dozen Japanese men came from farms and orchards scattered throughout the Santa Clara Valley to celebrate the arrival of Hayakawa's new wife, Masa, with rounds of beer and sake. Tomihei Hayakawa had been awaiting his wife's arrival excitedly and had planned the evening gathering to introduce and show her off to his friends. Sometime between picking her up in San Francisco and bringing her back to Mountain View, he ascertained that Masa did not want to be with him or was repulsed by him sexually (witnesses hinted that Hayakawa suffered from some type of disfiguring venereal disease, a "private sickness").[3] Several friends confirmed his despondence about his new wife and anxiety over the debt he had incurred to marry her, noting he had been "drinking a good deal" of late.[4]

On the surface, the Japanese immigrant community in the early twentieth century bore significant resemblance to the Chinese one that Santa Clara Valley residents had grown accustomed to from prior decades, especially in terms of their demographics and subordinate relations with white growers. Investigating Japanese immigrant gender relations, however, sheds a different light on this population, reflecting how the peculiar conditions of immigrant life in rural California produced new forms of intra-ethnic conflict, with surprising, occasionally tragic consequences for Japanese men and women. Tensions within Japanese immigrant society stemming from gender imbalance were widespread in the early twentieth century, exacerbated by racial marginalization, heavily circumscribed economic opportunity, and an increasingly polarized class structure within the Issei farming community.

"He Told Me to Be Very Careful Especially in America"

The historical record left in the wake of Hayakawa's death offers many clues about the nature of rural Japanese immigrant life in the early twentieth century. All the Japanese men who testified at the inquest were involved in some aspect of farming in the Santa Clara Valley, whether picking apricots and prunes or cultivating strawberries and vegetables; often the men worked for white landowners. Mary Woog, according to the *Shin Sekai*, found Hayakawa a "faithful worker" and readily approved of the arrangement he made to have Uchida take his place as foreman on her ranch while the former traveled to San Francisco to meet his new wife. Uchida had been working in this capacity for six and a half days before the suicide occurred.[5] That Hayakawa killed himself allegedly over soured relations with his bride highlights another salient characteristic of the Japanese immigrant community in its early years: the scarcity of women and their high value among Japanese men.

In the early twentieth century the Japanese immigrant community faced a lopsided gender ratio. The 1910 census recorded that in the state of California, there were 35,116 Japanese men and 6,240 Japanese women, meaning that 85 percent of the Japanese population consisted of men, who outnumbered their female counterparts with a ratio of 5.6 to 1. Since many Japanese men came to the country to work as field hands and farmers, they were also overwhelmingly young and in the prime of life, as Katsusaburo Kawahara had observed when he first arrived in San Jose as a boy. In 1910 almost 84 percent of Japanese men residing in California were between twenty and forty-four years of age, compared to only 47 percent of the state's total male population and 42 percent of native-born white men (Tomihei Hayakawa, who had immigrated at the age of twenty-six, was thirty-four when he died).[6] While the gender imbalance among Japanese immigrants in California was never as extreme as it was for the Chinese community, in which men outnumbered women 12 to one in 1900 and by 10 to one in 1910, Japanese women were still grossly underrepresented in rural settlements like the Santa Clara Valley, where more than 81 percent of the Japanese residents of Santa Clara County over the age of eighteen were men.

This would change gradually with the arrival of numerous female immigrants and the birth of second-generation children. For more than a decade after the Gentlemen's Agreement of 1908 banned the migration of Japanese laborers to the United States, women made up the bulk of Japanese immigrants.[7] In February 1920, however, under pressure from the U.S. State Department, the Japanese government abolished the picture bride practice, through which Japanese immigrant men married women in Japan by proxy and petitioned for them to come to the United States. Nevertheless, in the early years of the twentieth century, white residents of the Valley were far more accustomed to seeing large numbers of Japanese men congregating on their farms rather than units of Japanese men, women, and children. In contrast with the image of family-oriented community life, characterized by Japanese-language schools for children and festive celebrations and gatherings in the years before World War II, the pioneering Japanese immigrant society in California, made up of young laboring men like Tomihei Hayakawa, was far from settled.[8]

Further aggravating difficulties in the Japanese immigrant marriage market in California were cultural taboos within the ethnic community, which along with legal prohibitions on white-nonwhite marital unions, prevented Japanese men from seeking women outside the limited female population of their own race. An 1880 state law, which was declared unconstitutional in 1948, outlawed the marriage of a white person to a "Negro, mulatto or Mongolian." While miscegenation laws did not completely inhibit the formation of interracial sexual relationships between whites and Asians, there were very few instances of intermarriage in the Japanese American community during the early twentieth century. Rather, endogamous marriages prevailed until the postwar years.[9]

The paucity of women in early Japanese immigrant society had vital implications for gender relations, especially in the context of rural life, where possibilities for women's exploitation and agency appear in sharp relief. In the initial period of settlement in America, unique forms of gender conflict emerged within the Japanese immigrant population. Historian Yuji Ichioka noted that the Japanese vernacular press frequently reported marital scandals called *kakeochi*, cases of married Japanese farm women deserting their husbands to elope with other Japanese men. The deserted husbands posted printed notices containing physical descriptions of the fleeing wife and her "scoundrel" lover along with offers of monetary reward for information on their whereabouts. Sometimes deserted husbands reported *kakeochi* incidents as kidnappings or abductions of their wives, but in most cases women likely went missing of their own volition.[10] What has not been considered is how *kakeochi* functioned as part of a greater nexus of new relationship possibilities between Japanese men and women, many of whom exhibited nonstandard patterns of behavior and interaction with each other upon immigration to California.

The Santa Clara County coroner's inquest files provide a detailed glimpse into the lives of rural Japanese immigrants—working on farms, performing chores, caring for children at home, exchanging greetings with white neighbors and bosses, frequenting general stores, and dining at restaurants operated by their compatriots in San Jose—until a death interrupted the flow of everyday life. The testimonies, when corroborated with other sources and information on Japanese immigrant life, also reveal the striking intricacies of gender relations among Issei men and women. In charge of holding inquests over individuals who were murdered, had committed suicide, or had died suddenly of unknown causes, the county coroner was authorized to convene a jury to hear a case, subpoena witnesses, and issue arrest warrants (or, as in the Hayakawa case, once a jury had determined that suicide was the cause of death, the coroner could order the release of suspects who had been taken into custody). At the inquest, a proceeding often held at a funeral parlor where the corpse was viewed, the coroner presided, with a jury of 9 to 15 men charged with returning a written verdict stating the cause of death. Typically picked from voter lists, all jurors were male and had to be at least twenty-one years of age, U.S. citizens, residents of California and the county, and property owners assessed on the county roll; jurors were also required to have "ordinary intelligence" and to be able to understand English.[11] From 1900 through 1913, the Santa Clara County coroner investigated 42 Japanese deaths; of those, he and the jury determined that 12 were suicides and 3 were murders; 3 fatalities had resulted from self-defense, and the rest were due to accidental, natural, or unknown causes. In the more than 60 inquests of Chinese deaths from the same period, there were no comparable signs of conflict between men and women.[12]

Coroner's inquests offer a rich source for details about life and death in any community. Whenever the Santa Clara County coroner's office investigated the death of an individual, it filed a report that consisted of testimonies by witnesses, family members, friends, neighbors, business partners, physicians, law enforcement officials, and anyone ascertained to have had a connection to the deceased immediately preceding the death.[13] Therefore, inquests into the deaths of the county's Japanese residents include rare recordings of rural Japanese men and women speaking in their own words, albeit often mediated through an interpreter, usually a fellow countryman who was not always fluent in English, and guided by the interrogation procedures of the coroner's jury. The reports also show the racial attitudes and prejudices of white residents of the county, as white witnesses, the coroner's office staff, and jury members candidly expressed assumptions about Japanese immigrant life during the course of the investigations.[14]

Several inquests demonstrate that faced with a lack of female companionship, some Japanese men resorted to desperate measures to consort with Japanese women, who experienced unwanted advances as part of their daily lives in America. In July 1908, the coroner held an inquest into the death of Hisagi Yamamoto, a thirty-two-year-old contractor (also identified as a "gambler" in the coroner's report) fatally shot by S. Sakata in the latter's San Jose home adjoining Midori-tei, his restaurant on North Fifth Street. Sakata had recently married Hagime Ishizaka, who worked as a waitress at the restaurant. The bride of three months testified that she had known the deceased for over three years and that Yamamoto had been in the habit of hassling, perhaps even propositioning, her: "He often used to come to me and saying some annoying things and just I right along refused him."

On the evening of July 24, 1908, Yamamoto arrived at the newlywed couple's home as they were about to eat dinner. Again he harassed Ishizaka, who said he "asked me that if I wouldn't live with him he might do something against me." According to other witnesses, including the young woman's father, Yamamoto demanded that she go with him or he would kill her and her husband. As the threats escalated, Sakata shot and killed Yamamoto. The coroner's jury decided that Sakata had acted in self-defense and was not guilty of murder.[15] The *San Jose Daily Mercury* initially reported the incident as a quarrel between "two lovers" over the "possession of a Japanese girl," who remained unnamed in all of the paper's coverage of the case. In a series of articles on the shooting, the *Shin Sekai* portrayed Yamamoto as the "victim" of the manipulative seductress Hagime Ishizaka. The paper reported that Ishizaka had been involved with Yamamoto and may have been pregnant with his child even though she was married to Sakata. On the day of the shooting, Yamamoto sought out a *Shin Sekai* reporter in San Jose and gave him his own version of the story.[16] None of these details emerged in the inquest testimony or any other accounts. More likely, Yamamoto had attempted to court Ishizaka for several years and had developed an obsession with her that continued even after she had married another man. Ishizaka's marriage to Sakata several months before the shooting perhaps propelled Yamamoto into deep despair, driving him to terrorize Ishizaka and her family.

Inquests also provide evidence of attempted rape by Japanese men who took advantage of the isolation of farms in the Santa Clara Valley, where immigrant wives were often at home alone with small children. On the night of September 20, 1912, Kamekichi Kojima, a laborer who worked for tenant farmer and contractor Yasujiro Yoshida in Sunnyvale, assaulted and tried to rape Yoshida's wife while her husband was out running an errand. Both men hailed from Wakayama Prefecture and were reported to have been good friends. In addition to farming tomatoes and other vegetables, Yoshida worked as a foreman and labor contractor for Albert Bessey, a well-to-do manufacturer of poultry incubators and owner of the Jubilee Incubator Company in Sunnyvale.[17]

At the time of the assault, Yoshida, his wife, Tsuneno, and fifteen-month-old son, George, were living in a four-room house located on company property on Sunnyvale Avenue.[18] That evening, Kamekichi Kojima, Yasujiro Yoshida, and another laborer named Kunibe were at the Yoshida home talking informally about business matters. Yasujiro Yoshida drafted Kojima a check for $75, presumably his wages for work at Yoshida's tomato ranch. Upon leaving, Kojima said he was going to the post office to drop off the check. Yasujiro Yoshida, who testified that he had some business to attend to at the ranch, left with Kojima and waited at the crossroads while the laborer supposedly mailed his check, thinking the two could walk over to the ranch together afterward, since Kojima boarded at the laborers' camp there. As it turned out, Kojima did not go the post office at all but returned to the Yoshida house, knowing that Tsuneno was alone with her child.[19]

Through an interpreter, twenty-eight-year-old Tsuneno Yoshida gave graphic, terrifying testimony of how, as she was putting the baby to bed, "Kojima came in, and after he came in he grabbed me here (indicating in the neck). He grabbed me here, and therefore I screamed, but he overpowers me, and he hold up my skirts with his feet, and he tried to push his organ to mine." As they struggled, Yasujiro Yoshida, having surmised that Kojima had not gone to the post office and fearing foul play, returned to his house to discover Kojima assaulting his wife. After a protracted altercation, Yasujiro Yoshida shot and killed the assailant. County investigators reported that no semen was found at the scene.

In further testimony, Tsuneno Yoshida stated that just ten days before the shooting, Kojima had approached her in a suspicious manner while she was washing clothes, and she was relieved when "just as I leave outside other men came so I was saved." She recalled her husband's telling response when she relayed the incident to him that night: "He told me to be very careful especially in America."[20] Conscious that the yearning for female companionship could drive male laborers to violence, Yasujiro Yoshida feared for his wife's safety. Perhaps for this reason and with some unexplained premonition, he had cleaned and oiled his pistol on the day of Kojima's attack, and it lay conveniently on the bureau in the bedroom. He was taken into custody for the shooting, but the coroner's jury declared a verdict of justifiable homicide and immediately acquitted him. Despite his legal exoneration, the *Nichibei Shimbun* noted that Yoshida was quite traumatized by the incident and spent his days "in a depressed mood," unable to concentrate on his work.[21]

Japanese husbands and wives in the United States indeed learned to be "very careful" and on guard against the actions of male laborers, often close acquaintances who worked for Japanese tenant farmers and boarded in their homes, as Kojima once had boarded with the Yoshidas. Assailants were rarely known criminals and were sometimes even close friends with the husband of their victim, as in the 1913 case of Fukumatsu Kitaura, who farmed with Hisakichi (Harry) Handa on the Edenvale ranch of Herman Renzel. With notable parallels to the Kojima case, the forty-year-old Kitaura timed his assault on Rei Handa to coincide with her husband's absence, knowing that his business partner had gone to Renzel's house to use the telephone. Rei Handa testified that after her husband had left and she had just given her infant son a bath, Kitaura entered her home and grabbed her, saying, "I know your papa went out, and I want to have with you, sexual intercourse." At some point during the violent attack, Rei Handa reached over the bed for a .38-caliber revolver and fired three times at Kitaura, killing him with what the *Mercury Herald* called "two well directed shots" that pierced through the center of his forehead and chest. Kitaura died instantly.[22]

Guns were not uncommon possessions in Japanese farm homes, and women like Handa were adept at using them, attesting to an awareness among Japanese immigrant families of the need for self-defense. According a 1908 account in the *Daily Mercury*, a San Jose resident investigating Japanese agricultural camps in the vicinity found "large collections of shotguns, rifles, and pistols, anything capable of shooting" and said that local Japanese men regularly carried revolvers. The newspaper frequently reported shootings in the Japanese community, enthralling readers with sensational stories of Japanese killed over gender conflict. Nonfatal shootings were included as well, like one that took place on a ranch in Milpitas in 1912 in which Shinchi Hamada fired shots at his estranged lover Kiku Kato and fled through a berry patch.[23]

When Hisakichi Handa heard gunshots while he was at Renzel's house on the night of December 19, 1913, he rushed back home to find his wife running toward him screaming. Unlike Yasujiro Yoshida, Hisakichi Handa had never suspected that Kitaura, a married man with a wife and two children in Japan, would entertain and execute sordid designs on Rei. As he told the coroner's jury, "We were very friendly with each other." The Handas and Kitaura had all emigrated from Wakayama Prefecture, and Kitaura came to the Handa home often because of their farming partnership. Handa confirmed that he and the deceased had never had any trouble up to that fatal night. The sympathetic jury was quick to pardon Rei Handa, stating that she had acted in self-defense and should be exonerated "from all blame."[24]

Japanese immigrant wives in rural California often lived isolated on farms and in neighborhoods surrounded by men. Women became skilled at recognizing potential menaces and devised strategies to protect themselves. Although violent incidents resulting in official investigations occurred only sporadically, Japanese women experienced recurrent harassment from their countrymen. The men would start out by "saying some annoying things," as Hagime Ishizaka had testified, becoming more aggressive and increasingly agitated by women's refusals. Japanese women learned to be adamant and repetitive in their rejections as a matter of survival in America. Ishikaza related to the coroner's jury that the man her husband eventually shot, Hisagi Yamamoto, had approached her "so many times" with questionable motives. On each occasion, Ishizaka recalled, "so stubbornly I refused." Rei Handa insisted multiple times that she had never shown her attacker any sexual interest.

Similarly, when Tsuneno Yoshida was asked at Kamekichi Kojima's inquest whether she did "ever at any time give him any encouragement," the young woman likewise testified emphatically, "I never give him anything." She declared that she had known Kojima for about five years, the entire length of time she had been in California after her arrival as a picture bride in 1908. She had already seen signs of shady behavior and had fled from Kojima as he approached her while she was doing laundry: "he told me to come in so I run away," "saved" when other men also arrived. As historian Sharon Block found in her study of rape in early America, harassment in the form of "daily nonviolent social interactions" or initial attempts to replicate "consensual social and sexual relationships" often preceded rapes, a pattern that occurred in Issei farming communities as well.[25]

The Japanese men who preyed on women tended to be less affluent than the settled married couples described in the inquests, suggesting that feelings of jealousy and emasculation may have driven men to pathological behavior. As scholars of rape have shown, an imbalanced sex ratio does not automatically explain incidents of rape, nor does it make sexual violence biologically inevitable. Studies in psychology, anthropology, and sociology have debunked the view of rape as a product of "sexual arousal that has no other opportunity for gratification," emphasizing instead how rape involves affirming manhood and power through conquest and intimidation.[26] Historian Albert Hurtado has used psychological theories to help explain the prevalence of rape of Indian women by white men in nineteenth-century California, arguing that conditions producing "extraordinary stress" during the gold rush era led men to compensate for feelings of inadequacy. Specifically, Hurtado linked miners' frustrations with their inability to get rich quick when surrounded by "the constant possibility of fabulous wealth."[27]

Kojima had been in the country for twelve years at the time of his death, Kitaura for about nine years. Kojima worked mainly as a day laborer, while Kitaura had entered what appeared to be a tenant farming or sharecropping arrangement just a year earlier, indicating that he was not a particularly prosperous farmer. Kitaura likely worked under Handa, though the terms of their business relationship are not entirely clear. Both Kojima and Kitaura were married, with wives in Japan, but they had seen their spouses infrequently while they were in California and could not afford to send for them.[28] Disheartened by their economic prospects in rural California, these men possibly sought to assert their masculinity and power through the subjugation of women—women who happened to be the wives of the more nominally successful immigrant men they encountered daily.

Questions of class complicated gender relations among early Japanese immigrants. Historian Eiichiro Azuma has traced the efforts of elite, educated Issei leaders to respond to the early twentieth-century anti-Japanese movement by enacting social control and reform movements on the immigrant masses in hopes of curbing "immoral activities" in rural settlements across California and instilling bourgeois values into ordinary Japanese.[29] Yet there were further, more subtle class divides among the Issei than these. A closer look at the lives of Yasujiro Yoshida and Kamekichi Kojima and their respective socioeconomic positions reveals emergent class distinctions within the Japanese community and the growing frustration of men who may have felt "left behind" by the promise of wealth in America. In 1912 Yoshida and Kojima had much in common: the two men were in their thirties; both had arrived in the United States from Wakayama Prefecture around 1900; both worked in farming and at the same incubator factory; and both were married with children. But they led completely divergent lives and held different positions of status in the community. On one hand, after a sojourn in the United States of more than a decade, Yasujiro Yoshida had attained the position of Japanese foreman at a thriving manufacturing plant, supervising dozens of his fellow countrymen. He gave his testimony to the coroner's jury in English without an interpreter, demonstrating language competency that allowed him to communicate with his white American employer. In the years before the 1913 California Alien Land Act, he had also managed to amass enough cash to rent a tomato ranch, and he ran a farming business to augment his income from Bessey's factory.

Kojima, on the other hand, in the same length of time had failed to find a stable source of income. Tsuneno Yoshida recalled Kojima's irregular labor patterns, that he would work at Jubilee Incubator in Sunnyvale with her husband, then "sometimes he go out, out to the country, and working on the farms, and in the winter time he came back to the Incubator." Tsunekichi Kojima, brother of the deceased, confirmed that Kamekichi Kojima engaged in various pursuits to earn a living: "Sometimes he done fishing, and sometimes he worked in the ranch as a farm hand." According to the *Nichibei Shimbun*, Kojima caught salmon in Monterey most summers and reportedly had a "good catch of fish" in the previous year. What became of the income he earned from that catch, however, remained a mystery.[30]

There were yet more differences between the two men. Five years prior to the attempted rape incident, Yasujiro Yoshida, confident that he had the means to provide for a family, sent for his wife, and they lived in a modest but roomy house on Bessey's property. The *Nichibei Shimbun* stated that Yoshida had been a contractor for Bessey for a dozen years or so and as a result, the couple had achieved notable status and savings.[31] In 1912, Tsuneno gave birth to the couple's first child, a son who was followed by four younger siblings over the next decade.

Meanwhile, at the time of his death, family life and reliable work in America still eluded Kamekichi Kojima. After having been in the United States for over ten years, he still had not brought his wife and children out of Wakayama-ken to the Santa Clara Valley. Following Kojima's death, both the *Nichibei Shimbun* and *Shin Sekai* reported that his estate was estimated to be worth about $5,000 (equivalent to approximately $115,000 today). Despite investigations at several bank branches, the money was never found.[32] A Japanese immigrant man who possessed such savings would have been able to bring his wife over from Japan, but signs indicated that Kojima lacked these means. For many Japanese immigrant men in the early twentieth century, no wives in America meant a peripatetic existence and no permanent home. Tsuneno Yoshida testified that Kojima had roomed two nights at her house two weeks prior to the assault, and "after that he was sleeping in the other camp," in reference to a Japanese camp set up for itinerant workers at the Yoshidas' tomato ranch near the incubator company grounds.[33]

When Kamekichi Kojima attempted to rape Tsuneno Yoshida in 1912, the Yoshidas were a family on the rise. By 1920, the Yoshidas had three children and had moved from Sunnyvale to Mayfield, currently part of the City of Palo Alto, where they farmed not far from the Stanford University campus. Ten years later, the family included two sons and three daughters, ranging in age from six to seventeen, and lived in Los Altos, just south of Palo Alto. According to census takers, Yasujiro Yoshida ran a goldfish hatchery, a business he engaged in up until World War II, when the family was incarcerated in Heart Mountain, Wyoming.[34]

The Yoshidas followed a pattern typical of many rural Japanese families in the Santa Clara Valley and throughout California: that is, in the prewar years they became established not in the region's famed orchard fruit industry, but in niche enterprises. For example, the Oku family of Mountain View ran a flower nursery, the Yonemotos of Sunnyvale specialized in chrysanthemums, and numerous Japanese farm families in the San Jose and Palo Alto area formed a celery growers' association. Their lives were characterized by hard work, the contributions of all family members, and an ongoing search for better economic opportunities.[35] Whether Kamekichi Kojima, had he lived, would have eventually joined the ranks of these Valley families, is uncertain.

Female Virtue and "Immoral Business"

What emerges clearly is that the Yoshidas' lives would have taken a very different course if Yasujiro Yoshida had been prosecuted for killing Kojima in 1912. But the Yoshidas, like the Handas, benefited during their inquest trials from stereotypes of Japanese women, which reveal as much about white perceptions of the Japanese living in their midst as they illuminate fissures within the immigrant community. Throughout investigations of Japanese deaths, police officers, the coroner and his staff, and members of the all-white, all-male jury disclosed preconceived notions of Japanese women as either ultra-protective of their sexual purity or as "immoral," loose women. In the Kitaura inquest, the jury added its own sociological interpretation of Japanese gender mores, concluding that Rei Handa killed Kitaura "to protect her own honor. That was all. As we understand it, the Japanese women, especially, after they are married, are very particular of their virtue, very careful." For the members of the jury, women being "particular of their virtue," even to the point of murder, was not completely out of line with white middle-class values in the early twentieth century.[36]

The contrasting image of Japanese womanhood ingrained in the minds of white Santa Clara County residents was that of the promiscuous woman, who capitalized on the gender imbalance in the Japanese community to lure lonely, sex-hungry Japanese men for personal gain. In the 1903 investigation of the shooting death of Kiku Tabuchi, identified as a married housewife who lived in San Jose Chinatown, officials and jurors pointed to "immoral business" to explain her murder and implied that the deceased might have been a prostitute. In the late nineteenth century, before the arrival of large numbers of picture brides and women in family units, prostitutes did comprise the majority of the female Japanese population on the West Coast. Even so, white Americans tended to sensationalize the presence of prostitutes and assumed that most urban Japanese women were prostitutes.[37]

Using widely held notions of Oriental inscrutability to excuse what appears to have been sloppy police work on the Tabuchi case, San Jose police detective George Pickering declared, "Well the Japanese as a rule they are like a Chinaman, it's very hard to find out anything." He noted that a man in Chinatown named Kudo, whom "nobody seemed to know," had killed Tabuchi and himself; the gunman had also shot Tabuchi's husband, who was in critical condition at a local hospital and was reported to have uttered "Kudo, Kudo" as he lay bleeding. Night watchman George Kilvington commented, "it is almost an impossibility for a man to explain" the ways of the Japanese, but he speculated that Kudo "was infatuated perhaps with this woman, and hadn't seen her for some time." In Kilvington's opinion, Kudo "belongs to a class of people that ain't first class I don't think. At least his associates ain't what I should consider respectable Japanese." U. Yamakami, a cousin of Kiku Tabuchi who was picking prunes when the homicide occurred, testified that Kudo was a farmer on Brokaw Road just north of downtown San Jose, an occupation that did not seem to merit Kilvington's disapproval, unless Kudo was perhaps a known frequenter of prostitutes. Although even Kilvington said the Tabuchi house was "quite respectable" and sounded more like a boardinghouse than a brothel, once interpreter H. T. Oishi conjectured there was some "immoral business" going on there, investigators seemed satisfied that the case involved the murder-suicide of a Japanese prostitute and her client and closed the inquest, ignoring the numerous questions that remained.[38]

Some county investigators thought "immoral business" was so common among the Japanese that they made interrogations along these lines even when there was no evidence to support the assumption. At the inquest following the death of twenty-eight-year-old Kinsaku Kuraoka in February 1905, officials immediately launched into questions about the sexual decorum of the wife of the deceased upon learning that she worked at a Japanese restaurant owned by her brother in San Jose. They asked physician J. D. Fukui muddled questions like "Well what I mean is was she true to her husband?" and "Was she a Geishi girl?" to which the perplexed doctor responded, "Do you mean beautiful?" The interrogator replied he meant "Did the other boys go with her?" Fukui said, "Oh no" and answered in the affirmative when asked, "She is a good woman, good morals?" As it turned out, the death of young Kuraoka, who had been picking olives at the Mount Hamilton Vineyard in San Jose and succumbed to food poisoning of some sort, probably had nothing to do with his wife's sexuality or behavior.[39] Yet the jury persisted in questioning witnesses about whether "other men wanted his wife" and might have poisoned Kuraoka out of jealousy.

Genzaburo Yamamoto, who had lived and worked with the deceased at the vineyard for over a month and was the "boss" of the crew, dismissed this theory and instead gave intriguing details about camp life—what the men ate ("eight boys" helped with the cooking and made "rice and macaroni"), the work they did ("All the time working, picking olives"), and how they spent their leisure time (the men were learning English and held a "Jiu Jitsu wrestling" match on the day Kuraoka died; he was purportedly "the strongest in the camp").[40] The coroner's office never summoned the widow Kuraoka to testify but did not hesitate to suspect her of being a "Geishi girl" who drove other men to poison her husband.

Although Japanese women were vulnerable to attacks from scheming countrymen and subject to facile characterizations by whites, as rare and valued members of the immigrant community, they also wielded significant power during the early years of immigration. In particular, women managed to exercise substantial control over a major aspect of their lives, marriage. While marriages very often were prearranged by families and matchmakers according to Japanese custom, once Japanese women were in America, they experienced a unique freedom in carrying out those arrangements and, in some cases, making new ones.

Under the picture bride practice, parents or relatives selected wives for single immigrant men, who furnished photographs and information about their lives in America for negotiations with families of prospective brides. Even though grooms were absent from wedding ceremonies in Japan, the marriages were legal as long as wives' names were entered in their husbands' family registries. Perhaps not surprisingly, many picture brides were shocked when they met their husbands in the United States, finding that photographs were either old or altered, and "suave, handsome-looking gentlemen proved to be pockmarked country bumpkins."[41] Masa Hayakawa, who saw her husband, Tomihei, in California for only four days before he committed suicide, may have been one of these shocked, disappointed picture brides. As witnesses at the inquest testified, she did not conceal her dissatisfaction with him upon her arrival in San Francisco. Her noticeable lack of affection led him to lament to his friends that "He don't love his wife or his wife doesn't love him," and they got no "satisfaction" out of one another. Masa's cousin Toshiharu Takei, who lived in San Francisco and met with the couple before they headed to Mountain View, observed that something was awry: "Yes, he go to the hotel every night with her, but it looks very funny.... They were not happy. Very funny."[42]

Testimony confirmed that Tomihei Hayakawa had made extensive arrangements and gone into considerable debt to marry Masa. He had happily anticipated her arrival and had spoken eagerly of his fiancée to his friends. Existing evidence cannot prove whether it was physical unattractiveness, lack of sexual satisfaction, or the disclosure of venereal disease that repelled his new wife, though all were implied at some point during the trial and in Japanese newspaper accounts. In any case, while she probably could not have imagined the tragedy that ensued, Masa Hayakawa had made her dislike of her new husband clear, and she may have even entertained plans to extricate herself from the marriage. The *Mountain View Register-Leader* noted at the coroner's inquest that she appeared "very nervous and did not seem to know what was going on or what it was all about." But she knew enough to attempt to ward off accusations that she indirectly drove her new husband to suicide. Through an interpreter, she spoke at length about her own speculation that news she brought regarding her husband's family's financial distress in Japan caused him worry and he killed himself as "blood atonement" to wipe out family disgrace in accordance with Japanese custom.[43] No other witness mentioned this possibility, but Masa Hayakawa made certain her account was on the record.

For some Issei men like Tomihei Hayakawa, who equated success and status in their community with being economically viable as farmers and having a wife and children in the United States, feelings of failure, despair, and depression resulted from the inability to achieve that dream and sometimes drove them to drastic measures. Meanwhile, Japanese women like Masa Hayakawa, many of whom arrived in California as picture brides, faced a different scenario. In America, the presence of so many Japanese immigrant men and so few women meant that Japanese wives were highly valued and respected by their husbands and by the rest of the immigrant community. According to the *Shin Sekai*, following the coroner's inquest, Masa Hayakawa stayed with her cousin in San Francisco while determining what to do next. The newspaper reported that she was "ashamed" for her parents and did not want to return to Japan.[44] She may well have realized after just a few days in California that the United States was full of eligible Japanese bachelors, and widows did not remain unmarried for long. Tabulations from the 1910 manuscript census supported this analysis: more than 95 percent of Japanese women in Santa Clara County over the age of eighteen were married, compared to only 40 percent of Japanese men over eighteen. In Japan, laws and customary practices would have discouraged widows like Masa Hayakawa from remarrying, but immigration to America opened up entirely different opportunities.[45] Even if her husband had not died suddenly, based on her disgruntled state and the fact that other men looking for wives were readily available, Masa Hayakawa would have found it relatively easy to negotiate new arrangements. Indeed, married Japanese women whose husbands were living also explored new relationship possibilities.

"Great Humiliation and Mental Distress"

Given a gender ratio in which Japanese men far outnumbered women and the prevalence of *kakeochi*, or desertions of husbands, the picture of Japanese marital relations becomes even more complex and suggests considerable female agency. County divorce records involving Japanese litigants in the early twentieth century bear this out. From the scant research on divorce in the Japanese immigrant community, it appears that unlike their white counterparts, few Issei sued for divorce in California courts. The *San Jose Mercury Herald* remarked that

"Japanese [seldom] come into courts seeking freedom from an irksome marital yoke" and thus the paper considered the divorce proceedings of local couple Shirohei and Chiyono Ando in 1912 newsworthy.[46] As Harry Kitano has observed in his sociological study of the Issei, "The disillusionment was there, but not the divorce.... Expectations of marriage lay not in the traditional American reverence for love and romance, but in a conception of duty and obligation."[47] Evidence from the early twentieth century, however, indicates that Japanese men and women did not always feel bound by "duty and obligation." Divorces in Meiji Japan were common and relatively easy to obtain without official court proceedings. The Japanese nuptial and family system traditionally considered failed marriages the result of mismatch, not personal moral failure, and for the most part did not suggest that divorce should be prevented. Remarriage was also commonly accepted in rural Japan.[48] While only a small number of Japanese couples initiated divorce proceedings that can be traced in court records, many others separated informally and led lives with new partners.

Among the Japanese divorces filed at the Santa Clara County Superior Court between 1900 and 1917, women were plaintiffs in approximately 43 percent of cases, even though they represented only 20 to 25 percent of the county's Japanese population during that period.[49] Japanese women sued for divorce on various grounds, including cruelty, physical abuse, and failure to provide, indicating the use of the legal system by women seeking to leave their marriages or abusive situations. Machi Matsushita sued for divorce in 1912 after reporting that her husband had been in the habit of "striking and beating her, cursing and swearing at her" for two years.[50] Hisae Kubo detailed the domestic violence she experienced since marrying her husband in San Francisco in May 1915, noting that he had thrown her to the ground, beaten her, locked her out of the house for hours, and threatened to kill her. Kubo left her husband to reside with her brother and sister in San Jose. In March 1917, Kubo retained attorney Robert Wright of San Jose to represent her. On the requisite documents filed in the superior court, she signed her name in English with painstaking block script. Her husband, Kanematsu Kubo, then living in Sacramento County, responded to the summons by hiring his own lawyer, demanding a change of venue (since he was no longer a resident of Santa Clara County), and denying all the allegations in his wife's original complaint. After some back and forth, he withdrew his motions and eventually the divorce was granted.[51]

Even when Japanese immigrant women did not sue for divorce, they found other avenues to end their marriages, often by abandoning their husbands. Japanese immigrants appeared to fit the trend of high desertion rates in the American West, but in reverse. The vast majority of desertions in the West involved husbands leaving wives; in contrast, most Japanese deserters were wives.[52] Married Japanese women from Santa Clara County, like Kimi Matuzaka, who disappeared from a Milpitas farm labor camp in 1911, were the subjects of a fair share of runaway wife notices and desertion stories published in the San Francisco–based *Shin Sekai*. One notice described Matuzaka as a "shady woman" with "grim-looking" eyes. Occasionally a husband whose wife had left him filed for a legal dissolution of the marriage.

In the Santa Clara County Superior Court, when Japanese husbands brought suits for divorce, the cause was nearly always desertion by the wife. This mirrored divorce trends among white California couples in the late nineteenth century: indeed, one study found white women charged with desertion in almost two-thirds of proceedings filed by men, while men were charged with desertion in just under 40 percent of suits brought by women (in Santa Clara County, about half of the Japanese women who filed for divorce cited desertion as the principal reason).[53] Referring to the large number of deserted husbands in Issei society, a Japanese writer lamented, "the entire newspaper pages are not enough to report unrevealed scandals."[54] Contrary to images of deserters as social outcasts who fled their communities in shame, the Japanese wives accused of desertion in divorce cases rarely went far. In eleven divorces cases alleging that wives had deserted their husbands, all except three wives received their summons in Santa Clara County; one was served in San Francisco and two had reportedly returned to Japan. For the most part, after they abandoned their husbands, Japanese women were not afraid to remain in the community.[55]

In the five cases featuring husbands who had deserted, however, authorities served summons to only one husband in Santa Clara County, while the other men could not be located. In one case, summons were sent to a deserting husband in Kumamoto, Japan, with no response. Wives had to prove in court that they had searched for missing husbands with due diligence and had investigated all leads regarding the whereabouts of the deserter. In a detailed affidavit filed in 1912, Toyo Kobayashi deposed that upon learning that her missing husband, Kido, was living in Sacramento, she promptly traveled to that city and "visited all Japanese hotels and boarding places and enquired of many Japanese" to no avail. She also described her unsuccessful attempts to find him through the Japanese consul and from published directories of Japanese immigrants in California. Similarly, Nat Ogawa of Sunnyvale conducted a futile search for her husband, who had last been heard of in Oregon City, Oregon, by making numerous inquiries among friends of her husband in Portland, Gilroy, and San Jose.[56] Given the gender imbalance in the immigrant population, Japanese men may have had a much easier time eluding detection by assuming a new identity in a different community and blending in with scores of other male laborers.

In over a third of divorce cases brought by Japanese men citing desertion as the main ground, complaints included allegations of infidelity on the part of women. None of the lawsuits initiated by wives suggested that spousal infidelity had taken place. Sunnyvale farmer Tatsukei Hirano declared that less than two years after he had married in San Francisco, his wife, Koiki, began a relationship with a man named S. Shimada, whom she accompanied on a three-month sojourn to Lodi, a farming town in San Joaquin County. The betrayed husband may have entertained the possibility of a reconciliation when Koiki returned to Sunnyvale in November 1914 and temporarily resumed residence at his home. Those hopes were dashed, however, when one night she "abruptly left the bed of plaintiff and refused to sleep in the same room with him," proceeding to remain "in company of S. Shimada all night." On Christmas day that year, the Hiranos commenced their separation permanently, and three days later, Tatsukei Hirano filed for divorce.[57]

Kino Tsuruda, the twenty-two-year-old wife of Tatsuji Tsuruda, a forty-six-year-old man she had married as a picture bride in San Francisco in 1912, also openly spoke of her disdain for her husband and her feelings for another man. According to divorce proceedings, before she left for Sacramento in November of 1914, presumably with her lover, a man named Kuwada, she told the plaintiff that she "never cared for him, that he was too old, that she would not live with him, and would never return to him." The superior court granted Tatsuji Tsuruda a divorce in March 1915 but did not make a ruling regarding custody of the couple's infant daughter.[58]

Japanese men expressed indignation not just over their wives' actions, but at their own tarnished image in the community. Hirano complained that his wife's repeated statements to numerous mutual friends that she did not want to live with him or have children with him and "did not want the advice or counsel of her husband but wanted S. Shimada for her guardian," had become "a source of common gossip among the Japanese residents near the Town of Sunnyvale," causing him "grievous mental suffering."[59]

Women's brazen declarations shamed Japanese men in the eyes of their compatriots. In 1913, the marriage of Iwataro and Shina Zenihiro unraveled quite publicly over allegations of infidelity. Iwataro Zenihiro, an established Alviso tenant farmer who had resided in California for nearly twenty years, relayed in his court complaint the "great humiliation and mental distress" he suffered when his wife "openly and publicly declared...in the presence of friends and countrymen" that she no longer loved him and "her affection was all for...Umekichi Furuya." (This was the same man as tenant farmer Frank Furuya, sued unsuccessfully in 1912 by landowner Lila Peterson for poor upkeep of her San Jose orchard.) Iwataro Zenihiro's tremendous embarrassment turned into the desire to seek his own public forum to shame his wife and Furuya. He paid for a personal advertisement in a Japanese-language newspaper, proclaiming Furuya as "the great immoral one" who had subjected Zenihiro's wife to "such an insult that she cannot face the world again." The notice also insinuated that Furuya had a history of committing adultery. Refusing to keep the matter to himself, the cuckolded Zenihiro felt compelled to share this news with the public "not only for my own benefit," he claimed, "but also for the sake of humanity."[60]

Shina Zenihiro, however, chose to refute her husband's charges, thus becoming one of the only female defendants in the extant Japanese divorce cases filed at the county superior court to retain an attorney in response to a lawsuit. One month after she received her court summons, she submitted a lengthy answer to Iwataro's allegations, denying everything he claimed she had done to inflict "extreme cruelty" on him. Furthermore, her statements about the treatment she received in her marriage indicated significant dissatisfaction with her life as an immigrant farm wife and illustrated how Japanese brides' expectations about life in America often were crushed.

The items on Shina Zenihiro's numbered list of "inflictions" included being compelled "to work in the fields upon agricultural land in Santa Clara County and elsewhere and do the work of a man," deprivation of her earnings by her husband, described as a "stingy and penurious" spouse who "would only purchase for her second hand hats and second hand wearing apparel" and chastised her in the presence of friends "for not having children born to them." Shina Zenihiro countered that it was she, not her husband, who had suffered "great humiliation and mental distress" without cause in their marriage.[61]

Perhaps the young woman had come from a more prosperous family in Japan and was unaccustomed to and unprepared for the vast amount of field labor required of immigrant farm women in California. Or perhaps in her dreams of life in America she had imagined herself as a stylish, impeccably dressed wife and mother who devoted her days to keeping a home, not spending long hours engaged in backbreaking farm labor. Clear in her cross-complaint to the court was Zenihiro's sense of her identity as a woman being assaulted by the realities of Japanese immigrant rural life in California, and for this she blamed her husband. One can speculate that Furuya, who had arrived in the United States in 1900 and was an orchard foreman at the time of the divorce filing, may have wooed Shina Zenihiro with promises of fine clothing and hats and a life of no farm work.

But ultimately Zenihiro's goal in pursuing her own course of legal action was practical: her cross-complaint concluded with a statement that during their marriage she and her husband had accumulated community property valued at approximately $3,000, of which she believed she deserved an "equitable and just portion." She feared her husband would dispose of the money and "defraud" her unless the court properly restrained him. Predictably, Iwataro Zenihiro denied all of his wife's charges, except to acknowledge that she did work "in the fields on agricultural lands," but stated this was "the custom of women of her race in her station" and not objectionable to her. As an immigrant who had been in the

country since 1894, he found it natural that his Issei wife would perform agricultural labor and probably had counted on her contribution to his farming
enterprise in Alviso when he sent for her from Japan in 1905.[62] Zenihiro likely
deemed his wife's contrary assumption confounding.

The judge agreed with the plaintiff and declared Shina Zenihiro's charges of
cruel treatment untrue, while ruling that her affair with Furuya constituted
"extreme cruelty" toward her husband, entitling him to a divorce. On the issue of
community property, the court took Iwataro Zenihiro's word that the sum
claimed by the woman did not exist. After the divorce, both parties remarried. In
1922, the Japanese American directory listed Umekichi Furuya as a San Jose
tomato and berry grower farming an impressive 160 acres, residing with his wife,
Shinako, and their son, Yoshisada. In February 1916, in Santa Clara County, Iwataro Zenihiro married a woman named Yei Mukai.[63]

Given these patterns of divorce and desertion, it is not surprising that the
Japanese community developed a paradoxical view of women's position in
America. On one hand, Issei commentators blamed women for committing
adultery and using the uneven gender ratio to their own advantage. As a *Shin
Sekai* writer asserted in 1908: "In our colony settlement where there are many
men but fewer women, women are not behaving themselves well." He chided
immigrant women for taking in "the air of American individualism" to disrupt
marital relations. Bemoaning the rash of "miserable missing persons advertisements" published in the immigrant press, the author further faulted Japanese
wives for falling "under the spell of a devil," which caused each one to neglect her
duty to her family.[64] On the other hand, many in the community were also well
aware of women's vulnerability and implored women to protect themselves from
predatory men. Belying depictions of women as scheming adulterers were the
concerns of some that Japanese women were too "reserved" and lacked "the
nerve to firmly resist men's insult." Another observer went so far as to say that
Japanese women tended "to be passively raped by pressure" and did not acknowledge "their dignity and the importance of personal rights."[65] Issei thus viewed
women in Japanese immigrant society as both victims and instigators.

"She Asked Me to Marry"

The unsolved murder of Kume Emoto illuminates both the precarious position
of Japanese women in California and the power they gained in an overwhelmingly male immigrant society. Her journey, as related by her husband and other
witnesses, revealed an astute, independent spirit who balked at Japanese gender
conventions but could not escape them entirely. Kume Emoto was found shot to
death at the Japanese restaurant she and her husband ran on Sixth Street in San

Jose. On the night of February 13, 1910, she was preparing pickled *daikon* (Japanese radish) in the kitchen when three bullets hit her from behind. Not long after, a would-be diner received no answer when he called repeatedly for service around 8:30 p.m. When he ventured into the kitchen, he discovered the blood-covered body of the thirty-two-year-old restaurant proprietress on the floor.[66]

Kume Emoto's husband, Ichisaburo Okumura, testified that the couple had been married in Sacramento five years earlier. Shortly after, they moved to Santa Clara County, where Emoto worked as a cook for a Mrs. Silva in Los Gatos; next, she and Okumura cooked for a family in San Jose for several years. Thirteen months before the murder, they opened their restaurant, Hatsuhi-tei.[67] The coroner's inquest identified the victim's husband as "I. Okumura" and never referred to Kume Emoto by her husband's last name. In contrast, the *Shin Sekai* spoke only of "Kume Okumura" and made no mention of the fact that she went by the name Emoto.

Fixated on the different surnames used by husband and wife, interrogators at the inquest drilled Okumura about Japanese marriage customs, skeptical that they constituted valid marriages. Investigators asked about licenses, ceremonies, and finally "What is the custom with reference to marriage among the Japanese?" Okumura explained, "Well after both agree to marry we notify the friends, and have a party for it." Doubting that this could be a legitimate practice, the interrogator chided, "You merely agree to marry, and then call in friends and announce it to your friends, and then they have a friend to consummate it? And ... according to Japanese customs, that is sufficient to be a sufficient marriage, is it?" Still incredulous, he called on the Japanese interpreter to verify that couples who had gone through this procedure were officially recognized as married in Japan.[68]

As the questioning continued, the interest of the cross-examiner and jury was further piqued by the revelation that Kume Emoto had been married once before in Japan, to Hakutaro Emoto, whose surname she retained. Kume and Hakutaro Emoto had immigrated to Hawaii together around 1902 and eventually moved to Sacramento, where she divorced him three months before she married Okumura. Questions directed at Okumura about the timing and propriety of their actions persisted:

> Did you ask her to [seek] this divorce so that you could marry her?
>> She asked me to marry.
> Before she was divorced?
>> After the divorce....
> You did not speak of marriage to her, nor she to you, until after she was divorced, is that right?
>> Never asked before.

Okumura testified that he did not know why his deceased wife divorced her first husband, who he believed still resided in Sacramento, "farming, milking, or something." Given rising divorce rates in the United States at the beginning of the twentieth century, questions about the sanctity of marriage and the validity of divorce were very much on the minds of Americans like the cross-examiner.[69]

Although Kume Emoto's voice could not be heard at this trial, her actions, as divulged by her husband, spoke loudly. A young bride in her mid-twenties when she emigrated to Hawaii and then to California, she divorced her first husband seemingly of her own accord and proposed to another man three months later. Perhaps she and Okumura had had an affair, perhaps she sought an escape from the drudgery of being a farmer's wife in the hot Sacramento Delta, or perhaps there was another explanation. Choices and opportunities opened up to Kume in the early immigrant society of California, and, unencumbered by parental or other traditional forms of social control, she seized them freely. Married to a man she had selected, Emoto found she could make a good living as a cook and eventually opened a restaurant to serve her fellow Japanese in San Jose, work she might have found less isolating and more autonomous than domestic service.

That was when a mysterious man named Koike, a gambler and laborer who frequented Hatsuhi-tei, entered her life. F. M. Murakami, the court interpreter who also ate often at the deceased's restaurant, intimated that Koike was more than Emoto's customer: "I believe that she and this man Koike had some connection, sexual intercourse, something like that I think." His suspicion was aroused when, about a month and a half before her death, he saw "both of them coming out from the bed room, from her bed room," which adjoined the restaurant. Okumura admitted that his wife might not have been faithful in their marriage, stating, "I have some suspicion of it, but I am not positive." At that point, jury members and spectators probably assumed they understood the kind of woman Kume Emoto had been: unfaithful, promiscuous, and easily lured by new men whom she found more interesting than her current husband.

But as the interrogation continued, it became clear Emoto was not as well in control of her destiny with men as she appeared. Okumura testified that about two months earlier, while he was "in Chinatown at To Qua's store my wife came in and told me that Koike frightened me [i.e., Emoto] so you had better come back right away." Asked whether Koike "frightened or insulted her," Okumura said "Insulting and frightening I think both.... she told me that Koike asked her to have sexual intercourse," and she pleaded with her husband to "tell to Koike that he must stop that," for "Koike was always trying to tell my wife to go away with [him]."[70] Okumura's description of Koike's repeated sexual propositions and threats echoed the experiences reported by other Japanese women at county coroners' inquests. Also familiar was Kume Emoto's attempt to seek protection from Koike by telling her husband of a particularly "insulting and frightening" incident, though to no avail.

From then on, the testimony uncovered only more questions. Koike had absconded, and no one had seen him since the night of the murder. Had Kume Emoto eventually given in to Koike's advances a month and a half before when Murakami purportedly saw them emerging from her bedroom, or was she forced against her will? If she was forced, why did she not report the incident, and why did she and Koike appear to be "all talking very friendly" at the restaurant even just minutes before she was found dead? While circumstantial evidence pointed to Koike as the murderer (he was the last person Emoto was seen with, he sometimes carried a revolver, and .38-caliber cartridges were found in his room), what was his motive? Did he become enraged when he asked her to go away with him and she again refused? Deputy Sheriff Thomas Mulhall, the last person to testify in the investigation, pointed out that there was no indication of a struggle at the crime scene, and though a .38-caliber handgun was found under a pillow in the bedroom, it had not been recently discharged.

In addition, Mulhall testified that he had noticed Okumura's "demeanor changed very quickly after we entered the place. He was apparently wailing and carrying on, and all of a sudden he got very sober, and he seemed to readily talk," consulting friends whenever police asked questions that "would throw any suspicion on him at all" and still failing to account for where he had been for over a half hour on that fateful night. Just when all the evidence seemed to point to Koike as the killer, the possibility surfaced that Okumura may have killed his wife out of jealousy or revenge for infidelity, attempting to frame Koike for the crime. Mulhall concluded, "I have heard a good many stories in connection with the thing, and as near as I can get at it this Koike evidently is mixed up in it some way. I think the husband knows a great deal more though than what he has told.... The same applies to the Interpreter."[71]

During the first decade of the twentieth century, Kume Emoto had migrated from Japan to Hawaii, then to Sacramento, and finally to the Santa Clara Valley, where her life ended tragically. As one of few Japanese female immigrants at the time, Emoto developed increased courage and independence to make choices about marriage, work, and where she would settle. Although she came to reside in a prosperous agricultural region and likely interacted with many Japanese farmers and farm laborers as a cook and restauranteur, Kume Emoto managed to escape the lot of many Issei women of the period who lived on isolated farms and faced grueling agricultural labor, household, and child-rearing responsibilities in often primitive rural conditions. While she was able to defy many cultural conventions of her time, Emoto's identity as a Japanese female immigrant ultimately made her vulnerable to unscrupulous men, including possibly her own husband, without much recourse for protection.

Besides providing rare glimpses into the daily lives and long-term hopes of Japanese immigrants in an important agricultural center, county inquest records and court cases reveal the remarkable instability and contested nature of immigrant gender relations on multiple levels at the start of the twentieth century. This period of early settlement offered to Japanese women in rural California both new opportunities and new perils, which they would not have encountered in traditional Japanese society. They experienced harassment and aggression from their countrymen and were subject to demeaning representations by whites, but also gained some measure of power in a predominantly male immigrant society. There was a heightened awareness among immigrants that encounters between men and women were different in the United States than in Japan. Yasujiro Yoshida summed up this common understanding when he warned his wife Tsuneno to "be very careful especially in America" after she informed him of Kamekichi Kojima's shifty behavior around her. The immigrant press exhorted women to resist advances and protect themselves from fellow immigrant men with sinister motives.

Incidents of fatal violence toward women occurred with enough frequency that many white Californians had come to assume that most crimes involving Japanese were related in some way to disputes over women or other forms of gender conflict.[72] A *Shin Sekai* editorial writer in 1909 pointed to a larger crisis of "public morals ... corrupted in our Japanese society," from men's harassment of women and violence between the sexes to "scandals based on lack of virtue or marital infidelity." The inescapable fact at the root of these phenomena, he felt, was demographic: "we all recognize that the number of men and women is remarkably unbalanced."[73]

The writer's assessment was not far off the mark. As the sex ratio began to even out—by 1920, women comprised 37 percent of the Japanese population in California, as opposed to only 15 percent in 1910—fewer incidents of gender strife appeared in the historical record. By 1930 the ratio of Japanese men to women had almost reached parity, as women made up 42 percent of Japanese residents in California.[74] From 1914 to 1930, the Santa Clara County coroner investigated more than 70 Japanese deaths, but among those, no inquests suggested attempted rape, suicide, or homicide relating to conflict between Japanese men and women. There was instead a marked increase in fatalities involving children, coinciding with the rise of the Nisei.[75] The first dozen or so years in the early twentieth century thus represented a unique demographic window featuring unusual patterns of behavior between Japanese immigrant men and women.

These patterns also point to another form of intra-ethnic conflict that historians have only recently begun to explore: class fissures within the community and the divide between increasingly affluent tenant farmers with families in

America and Japanese men who remained day laborers. Cases from the Santa Clara County coroner's office bring into view the contrasting lives of these settled farmers and the itinerant laborers on the economic margins. Some laborers demonstrated tremendous frustration with their inability to achieve the status of the tenant farmers who often employed them, and they took their frustration out on women, including the wives of their bosses and more established countrymen.

Furthermore, the internal community turmoil among the pioneering Issei indicates the presence of a distinctive form of the "American dream" for Japanese immigrants that at its core placed a high premium on family life, not unlike the white family farm ideal of the time. For Japanese men, success in America meant achieving both financial security and stability as farmers and being able to bring over wives and raise children in America. Kyutaro Abiko, the longtime publisher of the *Nichibei Shimbun* and a respected businessman, implored male immigrants to summon wives from Japan. He promulgated an agrarian version of the Japanese immigrant dream predicated on family farming. This goal resonated deeply with his immigrant countrymen, including those in Santa Clara County, one of whom in 1912 called the increase in the number of married men in Mountain View a "pleasing sign."[76] One man who aspired to Abiko's vision but also illustrated its dark side was Tomihei Hayakawa. Employed in a stable position as an orchard foreman in Mountain View and united with his newly arrived bride, he came close to achieving this dream, only to see his hopes dashed by a dissatisfied, uncooperative wife and the possibility that he might be physically unable to father children. Despite his success in agriculture, all of his efforts to establish a family in America appeared to be in vain, and he saw no other option than to take his own life.[77]

Migration across the Pacific Ocean had disruptive effects on the lives of many Japanese who settled in the rural Santa Clara Valley during the early twentieth century. Gender conflict, along with emergent class conflict, fractured ethnic solidarity in the early stages of the Japanese community's settlement, but it also reflected the processes through which ordinary men and women acted in unexpected ways to claim and carve out new lives for themselves in an unfamiliar land. In this early period of community formation, characterized by gender imbalance and limited socioeconomic mobility, punctuated by gun battles over women, the Japanese of the Santa Clara Valley stayed relatively insulated from the anti-Japanese movement. Ironically, the most virulent agitation and legislative discrimination did not occur until almost two decades after their arrival, by which time Japanese immigrants had become established as resident farmers and workers in California. This trend can be traced directly to the visibility of Japanese women and children.

4

Defending the "American Farm Home"

Japanese Farm Families and the Anti-Japanese Movement

In 1919, the California legislature ordered an investigation of Japanese land-holding in the state. The result was *California and the Oriental*, a 231-page document that warned readers of the dangers of the Japanese immigrant presence, in particular that of Japanese farmers. Governor William M. Stephens prefaced the June 1920 report with a letter to Secretary of State Bainbridge Colby outlining what he considered the most alarming findings of the investigation. Stephens highlighted the "strong trend to land ownership and land control" and went on to attribute Japanese success to none other than "their use of economic standards impossible to our white ideals," namely, "the employment of their wives and their very children in the arduous toil of the soil." Stephens then conveyed his distress over the Japanese birthrate, a subject that also troubled many immigration exclusionists, claiming the "fecundity of the Japanese race far exceeds that of any other people that we have in our midst."[1] Though claiming to be an objective work of the State Board of Control, the report could easily be seen as an attempt to sway potential voters to support the 1920 initiative that would enact an even more severe alien land law targeting the Japanese. According to the *Mountain View Register-Leader*, after reading Stephens's letter and the "exhaustive" report, hundreds of Santa Clara Valley residents who had been indifferent to the Japanese question "changed their attitude" and promptly added their names to anti-Japanese landholding initiative petitions circulating in the county.[2]

The assessment linking Japanese agricultural prowess to their family values and practices pervaded exclusionist propaganda by 1920 and represented a shifting emphasis in the anti-Japanese movement. New concerns about the Japanese in California reflected the changing demographics of the Japanese immigrant community, which during the decade of the 1910s experienced a transformation from a pioneering, overwhelmingly male society to one that consisted of more settled young families. As Japanese immigration coincided with the ascendance of Japan as a foreign power, white Americans increasingly viewed the arrival of Japanese immigrants with alarm, the transition from sojourners to settlers as an extension of Japan's imperial designs. In 1910, only 6,240 Japanese women resided in California, making up 15 percent of the state's total Japanese population. By 1920, the number of Japanese women had more than quadrupled to 26,538, close to 37 percent of the Japanese population. With the arrival of women came the birth of the Nisei, or second generation. In 1910, only 13.5 percent of the state's Japanese were under twenty years of age and a mere 8.5 percent were under fifteen. The Japanese Association of American in 1918 counted nearly 15,000 Japanese boys and girls under sixteen in California, comprising 22 percent of the state's Japanese, while the 1920 census estimated almost 25,000 Japanese under twenty-one in California, corresponding to 34 percent of the total Japanese population. In Santa Clara County, where 38 percent of Japanese residents in 1920 were female and individuals under twenty-one represented nearly 41 percent of the Japanese population, the Japanese community closely mirrored statewide demographic trends toward gender ratio parity and the rise of a sizable American-born second generation.[3]

Whereas standard interpretations of the anti-Japanese movement attribute the agitation for a more stringent alien land law and other exclusionist legislation to mounting racism, fears of economic competition and Japanese military prowess, and the political power of California propagandists, white Californians' fervent fixation with the American family and "home life," specifically as related to farm families, must also be taken into account.[4] Family structure and gender roles within the farm family became markers of race, the means through which whites asserted their racial and national identity. This perspective suggests a new periodization of the anti-Japanese movement, distinguishing the outcry over Japanese in the 1900s to early 1910s that resulted in the passage of the 1913 alien land law from new agitation beginning in 1919. The earlier phase, which originated with the labor movement in San Francisco, rarely mentioned the presence of Japanese families. Moreover, white farmers in agricultural regions like the Santa Clara Valley, who demonstrated little interest in barring Japanese from emigrating to or farming in California, largely declined to participate. Not until the second wave of anti-Japanese sentiment that resurged after World War I did white Californians begin using descriptions of Japanese families to construct racial difference between whites and "Orientals." The specter of Japanese farm families fueled white fears about Japanese agricultural dominance and resulted in a new anti-Japanese movement that intensified long after the arrival of the first Japanese immigrants.

The Case of the "Missing" Japanese

Robert Newton Lynch had been a member of the California Immigration Commission, part of the federal team that completed an extensive study of the immigrant presence in America in 1912. Writing for *Sunset* magazine in 1913, he commented on the remarkable contributions immigrants had made to California agriculture. Lynch applauded the North Italians who were cultivating vineyards and wineries throughout California with their "capable hands," noting also how the "hills and valleys of San Francisco's rural southern side," were "checkered with their year-round gardens." He went on to praise the Portuguese in Alameda County for their small vegetable and fruit farms, the German-Russians and Armenians farming around Fresno, the Finns engaged in lumbering and dairy farming on the northern California coast, and the Dalmatians (Croatians) in the apple orchards of the Pajaro Valley. To Lynch, these European farmers, with their "intimate knowledge of the soil" and impressive intensive farming skills, were "uniformly a blessing" to the state, and their presence catapulted California "to the fore as the home of the successful small farmer."[5]

One group of immigrant farmers, also of rural origin and marked horticultural skill, was conspicuously missing from Lynch's list. Though by the end of 1918 they owned and leased 365,826 acres of farmland in California and produced almost 92 percent of the state's berries, 89 percent of the celery crop, two-thirds of California tomatoes, and over three-quarters of the state's asparagus, onion, and garden seed crops, and cultivated significant amounts of other fruits and vegetables, the Japanese failed to appear at all in Lynch's article on immigrant contributions to California agriculture.[6] In the few years following their arrival at the turn of the century, the Japanese had established themselves as a formidable presence in the state's agricultural sector, and yet a former government expert on immigration failed to acknowledge either their presence or their contribution.

With the passage of California's first alien land law in 1913, just six months before the publication of his article, Lynch may have believed Japanese agricultural prowess would soon decline to irrelevance, and the state's fields would become the domain of whites only, Europeans of all nationalities included. Beginning in 1907, the California legislature had repeatedly discussed bills designed to deny ownership of land to "aliens ineligible to citizenship," clearly targeting Japanese immigrant farmers, even though legislators asserted that the draft was couched in neutral language. Passed in 1913 with overwhelming support in the state senate and assembly, the California Alien Land Law denied Asian immigrants the right to buy land and stipulated that they could lease farmland for terms of no more than three years, seeking to deal a sizable blow to

Japanese farmers in the state just as they were establishing farms.[7] In the aftermath of the law's enactment, perhaps Lynch saw no reason to believe the Japanese could remain solvent in agriculture for much longer.

For the most part, California farmers did not pay much attention to the first alien land law, even though it was ostensibly designed to assist them. Trade journals like the *California Fruit Grower* and the *Pacific Rural Press* devoted scant space to the proposed law in 1913; the latter published a long editorial and letter to the editor providing general "impressions" of the Japanese, a convoluted jumble of positive and negative characterizations. Minutes and proceedings of the state's fruit grower conventions during 1913 made no mention of alien land laws, pro or con, though whites in rural regions like the Central Valley, where agricultural competition was more direct than in the Santa Clara Valley, rallied their legislators to pass the law.[8] In Santa Clara County, however, few growers vehemently pushed for its passage or organized opposition with a view to protecting their agricultural interests. Since a significant portion of white growers employed or contracted with Japanese, it was not in their interest to be strong backers of a law limiting Japanese farming. At the same time, growers did not want to risk being exposed as utterly dependent on the Japanese, and so by and large, like Robert Lynch, they turned a blind eye to the subject, hoping no one would call their labor practices into question.

White proprietors of local laundries, not farmers, headed up the county's first anti-Japanese league in April 1912 and organized a "campaign against the interloper," appealing for a boycott of Japanese laundries, which they blamed for forcing whites to "cut wages of their employees or get out of the laundry business and abandon the field to the Orientals."[9] The organization, bolstered by the Asiatic Exclusion League, eventually broadened its platform. Paving the way for its support of the 1913 alien land law, the league vowed to "not only seek to have the laundries operated by white labor, but strive to have the Japanese employees in the orchards and those engaged in domestic service displaced." Without backing from the county's farmers, members of the anti-Asian group inserted themselves into the debate over control of California's agricultural lands. In July 1912, the league sent a letter to the "real estate men of San Jose" to discourage them from selling farmland to Japanese, noting that since the mid-1890s, the Japanese had displaced white farm laborers, along with the Chinese, "by the simple method of underbidding," or accepting "impossible prices" for their labor. Drawing on a classic argument for the protection of white labor against Asian "cheap labor" and claiming that Japanese competition in laundries and agriculture was comparable, the letter closed by posing a question to the San Jose realtors: "If this is allowed to continue, how long will it be before you find yourselves in the same position as the laundrymen, with the same gigantic struggle confronting you?"[10]

Throughout the spring of 1913, before Governor Hiram Johnson signed the Alien Land Law on May 19, the *San Jose Daily Mercury* and other local papers gave consistent coverage to the progress of the bill in the state legislature, as well as to reactions from the Japanese government, and attempts by the administration of Woodrow Wilson to persuade California to soften the bill's terms. Though most editorials favored passage, the papers reported no local action or gatherings to rally around the cause of anti-alien legislation. Even more surprisingly, in the middle of its almost daily coverage of events related to the bill, the *Mercury* ran a celebratory article on the new Japanese Methodist Episcopal Church building in San Jose. The cornerstone was laid at a ceremony attended by the city's Methodist ministers, Japanese clergy and congregants, and the Reverend Herbert B. Johnson, superintendent of the denomination's Pacific Coast Japanese missions. Johnson dedicated the new church with a fitting Bible verse from Paul's letter to the Ephesians that may have hinted at his awareness of the predictable unfairness of the bill for the Japanese: "Now ye are therefore no more strangers and foreigners, but fellow citizens with the saints, and the house of God." The *Mercury*'s editors, however, seemed to have missed Johnson's subtle pleading for whites to view the Japanese, or at least Japanese Christians, as "no more strangers and foreigners" and the following day printed its most vitriolic editorial to date, declaring, "California cannot afford to be made the dumping ground for peoples whose traditions and habits of life are so greatly vary from our own. Let the floodgates loose and instantly a horde from the coolie sections of the Orient would be upon us, buying our land, underselling our labor, and generally rendering life less desirable."[11] Reminiscent of nineteenth-century attacks on Chinese "hordes" and "coolies" and calls for exclusion, the *Mercury* drew on familiar tropes of Asian invasion and labor conflict.[12]

Though the editorialist claimed "no prejudice against the Japanese in this State" and cited protection of economic interests as the primary reason for his support of the land bill, racist rhetoric permeated the piece: "What, for example, would land in Santa Clara County be worth if ranches were commonly owned by Japanese? There are good Japanese, it is true, law-abiding citizens, but they are not white people in the sense that Europeans are white, nor are they as assimilable."[13] In editorials and in opinion pieces, the paper went on to praise the state legislature for taking "so aggressive a position" on the Japanese landholding issue, returning to economic interests, "the fear that so much of the revenue-producing fruit and grain lands would fall into their hands as to practically discourage more desirable investment." At the end of April, the *San Jose Daily Mercury* drew another racial comparison, this time contrasting the Japanese with "the negro," who editorialists professed to be "one of us." Styling itself as a progressive proponent of equality, the paper, owned by the ardently Republican Hayes brothers, Everis and Jay, derided the federal government's hypocrisy in "bowing" to pressure from Japan by sending Secretary of State William Jennings Bryan to Sacramento in an effort to warn state legislators of diplomatic ramifications, while it "uttered no protest" over the South's disenfranchisement of blacks. For Californians, debates over the status of African Americans were not meaningfully influenced by everyday interactions with blacks, who made up less than one percent of the state's population in 1910.[14]

Anti-Japanese forces pushing for the support of the 1913 law, also known as the Webb-Heney Act or simply as the Webb Act, espoused insipid arguments highlighting the alleged inferiority of immigrants from "the Orient." In a July 1913 article, Stanford history professor Yamato Ichihashi summarized the trite rhetoric of Carlos Kelly McClatchy, Washington correspondent of the rabidly anti-Japanese *Sacramento Bee* and nephew of emerging Asian exclusionist powerhouse Valentine S. McClatchy. The historian scored the attacks as an elaboration of the tired racist diatribe that "Japanese cannot be assimilated and are objectionable principally because they are of an entirely different and antagonistic race, with customs, habits and mental and moral traits opposed to ours." James Duval Phelan, who made his debut as a fervent opponent of Japanese immigration while mayor of San Francisco in 1900 and owned extensive property in the Valley, including his opulent estate Villa Montalvo in Saratoga, pronounced the Japanese "a blight on our civilization, destructive of the home life of the people." A chief California supporter of Woodrow Wilson's presidential campaign in 1912, Phelan asked the candidate rhetorically whether the Japanese should be allowed to lower standards of living for "members of the white race, who stand for home life, Republican Government and Western Civilization," foreshadowing the emphasis on families that became the mainstay of anti-Japanese arguments by the end of the decade.[15]

With some exceptions, white farmers in Santa Clara County in 1913 remained relatively silent on the subject of the pending land bill. In trade journals, local growers discussed the nuisance posed by thrips and peach tree borers in the Santa Clara Valley, their fears about the lack of February and March rains, and crop reports that estimated disappointing harvests for apricots, pears, peaches, and prunes in their region. They made no reference, however, to the proposed law.[16] Up until April 1913, the main activities of the county's Farmers' Union, with active locals in Campbell, Saratoga, and Morgan Hill, revolved around educating farmers on "the latest things in agricultural science" and forming effective marketing cooperatives. Under pressure to take a stance in support of the alien land bill, the Farmers' Union adopted a resolution favoring a law to prohibit Japanese from owning land but did not comment on lease limits. Indeed, many growers preferred a version of the bill that allowed them to keep their arrangements with Japanese tenants and at the same time join their voices with popular sentiment against the Japanese.[17] In a telegraphed statement to Governor Johnson, the organization said its members recognized "the danger of land ownership by Orientals ineligible to citizenship" but approved "all diplomatic efforts to avoid international complications" and attempts to ensure that California law would "harmonize with existing treaties." The latter statement concurred with the Wilson administration's cautious stance as it tried to induce the California legislature to draft a law that would not spark a diplomatic crisis with Japan. Meanwhile, Johnson and hard-line Progressive Republicans, including the Hayes brothers, took the point of view that Washington had no right to interfere with California legislation at all, much less to encourage state residents to cave in to fears of Japanese ire.[18] Speculating on the results of Secretary of State Bryan's visit to discuss the alien land law with legislators in Sacramento, the *Mercury* lamented that "a yellow race dominates our legislation by appeal to Federal authority, and we, cowed into submission, calmly yield. That is what the world will say if Mr. Bryan's move for delay succeeds." Governor Johnson also deflected accusations that the state sought to enact discriminatory measures. He maintained that the United States had already "decreed certain races, among whom are the Japanese, are not eligible to citizenship" and thus if California followed "the line marked out by the federal government, the United States and not California should be accused of discrimination."[19]

As the governor finally prepared to sign the bill into law, the *Mercury* applauded his leadership and unwavering stance toward Washington and Japan alike. The paper commended Johnson for handling the situation "with good judgment and superb tact, at no time forgetting the relations of the State and Federal Governments," and for calmly ignoring dispatches informing him of mass meetings in Tokyo and Japanese threats of war if the bill passed.[20] Despite its continuing coverage of the negative Japanese response to the Webb Act, the *Mercury* expressed confidence that the law was in the best interest of the state and would adequately address the problems stemming from the Japanese immigrant presence. Like Robert Lynch, the immigration expert who may have felt so certain the Japanese would make their exit from the fields that he omitted them from his account of immigrant contributions to California agriculture in 1913, many residents of the state concluded legislation had banished Japanese farmers from agricultural dominance for good.

If in the minds of most Californians the 1913 alien land law supposedly "laid the ghost of the Japanese question" to rest, why did the anti-Japanese movement return with greater intensity and vigor by 1919?[21] One reason is that the law did not have much effect, since Japanese farmers were able to use certain loopholes to their advantage. One method of circumventing the alien land law involved the establishment of land companies in which a majority of the stock was held by Japanese. The *Pacific Rural Press* reported that 400 Japanese farmers in 19 California counties formed a total of 99 incorporated companies to acquire agricultural holdings in just several months following the passage of the alien land law.[22] Furthermore, Japanese farmers with sufficient capital to own land avoided the alien land law's restrictions by purchasing property in the names of their American-born children.[23]

For example, Chozaburo Kumagai bought slightly more than 27 acres of land along the San Jose–Alviso Road from the directors of the Andrea Malovos Company in 1912, before Issei landownership was prohibited. Kumagai had arrived in the United States around 1900, followed by his wife Hatsuno in 1906. When preparing to move on to a new farming opportunity in 1916, however, he could not purchase additional land himself but recognized his sons, both born in Santa Clara County and thus American citizens, could be legal landowners. Lacking birth certificates, to obtain official documentation that the boys, Toyotsugu and Iwao, were in fact born in the United States, Chozaburo Kumagai filed two petitions in the Santa Clara County Superior Court in 1916 certifying that the children were born in rural areas of the county "without attendance of physician or midwife." In late October of 1916, Chozaburo and Hatsuno Kumagai sold their acreage in Alviso and several months later utilized the names of their two young sons to purchase 30 acres of orchard property along Embarcadero Road in Palo Alto. In addition to farming this new ranch, Chozaburo Kumagai entered into a three-year lease on 55 acres of farmland in Mountain View belonging to Marguerite Stierlin. A biographical directory of Japanese immigrants published in 1922 listed Chozaburo Kumagai as a fruit farmer who owned a pear orchard in Palo Alto along with two cars and four horses.[24] Despite the loophole in the 1913 law allowing property to be held under the names of American-born minors, few Japanese families had the means to purchase farmland as the Kumagais had done. By 1920, Japanese residents owned a mere 843 acres of farmland in Santa Clara County or 1.7 percent of the county's total irrigated acreage (statewide, Japanese owned 1.9 percent of the state's irrigated farmland and 0.2 percent of total farmland).[25]

Though Japanese landownership remained negligible because the Webb Act permitted the practice of leasing for up to three years, Japanese agricultural landholdings actually grew between 1914 and 1920, with dramatic increases in the acreage of leased land.[26] In direct response to the law, nearly all of the Japanese–white leases signed in Santa Clara County between 1913 and 1921 were for terms of exactly three years or less. The three-year lease term limit also reinforced the relegation of Japanese farmers to berries and vegetables, discouraging many from cultivating orchard fruit or other crops that required a longer commitment of time and resources. Some Japanese farmers evaded the three-year-lease limitation through other means. For example, if three farmers undertook joint farming, each could sign a separate three-year contract, allowing the partners to lease land for up to nine years.

Though the ineffectiveness of the 1913 Webb Act was apparent, the law was not enforced. During World War I in particular, officials, recognizing the need for maximum food production, did not want to jeopardize Japanese agricultural contributions to the war effort. Growers across the state rejoiced as prices for California specialty crops climbed steadily. The outbreak of the war and the fact that Japan, like the United States, was also at war with Germany, further explained the lack of widespread anti-Japanese agitation between 1913 and 1919.[27]

When the anti-Japanese movement regrouped in 1919 to address the deficiencies of the 1913 law, it developed a new fixation on Japanese farm families and their control of California agricultural lands, which culminated in a state initiative in 1920 to amend the alien land law to prevent Asian aliens from leasing agricultural land at all or from acquiring land under the names of American-born minors and through corporations. Another amendment in 1923 made it illegal for aliens ineligible for naturalized citizenship to "acquire, possess, enjoy, use, cultivate, occupy, and transfer real property." While Japanese farm families were present in 1913, their numbers were not sufficient to capture the attention of white Californians. By 1919, however, the growth of the Japanese population propelled these Asian immigrants and their children to the center of public debates over landholding, immigration policy, and citizenship.

From Berry and Truck Farms to Orchards

Japanese immigrants to rural California brought with them a history and tradition of family farming from their homeland. In Japan, the transition from large communal holdings farmed by dependents and servants to tenant cultivation in small family units had occurred in many regions by the mid-nineteenth century with the development of trade and industry. As large landholders became enmeshed in trade and finance, they gradually withdrew from farming and began entrusting more and more land to tenant farmers in exchange for rent in kind. By the time Japanese immigrants arrived in California, family farming had been established firmly in Japan. All members of the family, including women and children, contributed to the enterprise, which employed little outside labor.[28]

Ironically, not unlike vocal white opponents of Japanese agricultural domination who believed family life and farming were at the heart of American identity, Japanese immigrant community leader Kyutaro Abiko regarded agriculture as the foundation of the ideal Japanese immigrant society. He founded Yamato Colony in the San Joaquin Valley in 1906 to encourage laborers to settle on small farms, summon wives from Japan, and develop an economic and social stake in American society. By the time Abiko established Cortez Colony nearby in 1919, thousands of Japanese family farms were in operation throughout the state, including nearly 400 counted in the 1920 census of Santa Clara County. Never-theless, Abiko's strategy of populating the United States with stable, prosperous Japanese immigrant farms ultimately clashed with the white family farm ideal and sparked the ire of California nativists.[29]

Unlike their Chinese farming predecessors, by the mid-1910s, Japanese immi-grants in the Santa Clara Valley were more likely to settle as families or to begin the process of family formation in the United States. In 1910, men comprised 96 percent of Chinese residents in Santa Clara County age eighteen and over, compared to 81 percent of Japanese residents. Ten years later, the percentage of adult Chinese males remained fairly constant at 92 percent, but the proportion of Japanese men eighteen and over dropped to two-thirds, indicating the migra-tion of Japanese women. The emigration of picture brides, which peaked during the 1910s, also facilitated the formation of Japanese farm families in the Santa Clara Valley and throughout the Pacific coast. While there were only 410 mar-ried women in Japanese immigrant society in 1900, the number had increased to 5,581 by 1910 and had jumped to 22,193 by 1920. Because few bachelors could afford the time and expense of returning to Japan to seek a bride, and in any event returnees faced possible military induction, many resorted to the so-called picture bride practice, in which household heads selected marriage partners for family members through intermediaries.[30]

In 1916, three years after his first wife, Natsuye, died of typhoid fever at O'Connor Sanitarium in San Jose, forty-one-year-old Alviso farmer Umejiro Inouye sent for a new bride, whom he married by proxy. Toshiye Inouye was twenty-one years old in 1916 and hailed from Kumamoto prefecture. In a note to the Immigration and Naturalization Service solicited by Umejiro Inouye to prove his status to immigration officials, Santa Clara County resident Miles Hol-lister certified that Inouye had lived in the vicinity for the past ten years (he could have been one of the Japanese male farmers interviewed by the Immigra-tion Commission in 1908) and was leasing farm land from Edmund Farney. Hollister called Inouye "a successful man in that business and is a quiet and peaceable inhabitant of good report."[31] By 1920, the Inouyes had moved a few miles southwest to a farm in Sunnyvale on Evelyn Avenue. Another picture bride from Kumamoto, Nobuye Hashizume, arrived in June 1916 to meet her hus-band, Mototaro, in Sunnyvale, where he was leasing farmland on Maude Avenue, not far from where the Inouyes eventually settled. Mototaro had enlisted real estate and insurance agent W. L. Atkinson of San Jose to write a letter to the appropriate federal agency, which at the time was the Immigration and Natural-ization Service, attesting that the Japanese immigrant was "honest, capable and industrious and able to support any one who might be dependent on him."[32]

No longer the sparsely settled, male-dominated community it had been in the first decade of the twentieth century, the Japanese population of Santa Clara

County increased by 30 percent between 1910 and 1920, with women and children accounting for a substantial portion of the growth. The number of Japanese women over eighteen more than doubled from 1910 to 1920, from 15 percent of the county's Japanese population to one third. Individuals eighteen years of age and younger made up 17 percent of Japanese residents in the county in 1910 and over 42 percent a decade later. As early as 1915, there was a critical mass of Japanese children in the vicinity of Mountain View, warranting the establishment of a Japanese school, which selected the Fourth of July as its opening day. By 1925, about a third of the Japanese farm population in the county was under ten years of age.[33] Taken together, the number of Japanese farm families in the county grew by approximately 75 percent from 1910 to 1920; on the average, each family in 1920 had 2.4 children.[34]

Yaichi Yamakawa, the tenant farmer who began his career renting the McKiernan ranch in Alviso, exemplified a common pattern of family settlement. Two years after arriving in California in 1899 as a young man of eighteen, Yamakawa and a business partner leased from the three McKiernan sisters a 157-acre parcel of land on Alviso-Milpitas road. Yamakawa's wife, Kazu, probably a picture bride, arrived in the Santa Clara Valley in 1909, along with his younger brother Hiromu, barely eighteen years old, the same age Yaichi was when he emigrated from Japan. Yaichi and Kazu had three children before she passed away in 1917. In or around 1921 Yamakawa married a twenty-three-year-old woman named Yoshiko, and the family remained on their San Jose farm on McLaughlin Road, which Yaichi had purchased in 1907, up until their World War II incarceration. His brother Hiromu sent for his wife, Chika, in 1914, and by 1920, the couple had two young sons. They lived with Yaichi on his McLaughlin Road farm in San Jose, along with another brother, Ishijuro, who was three years older than Yaichi. By 1930, Hiromu Yamakawa, having lived in the Santa Clara Valley for over twenty years, had moved with his wife and four children to a Japanese farming cluster in Gilroy.[35]

By 1920, a growing number of Japanese immigrant families who had started out farming berries and vegetables shifted to more lucrative agricultural opportunities in the Valley. In 1920, Japanese farmers occupied about 5,000 acres of land in the county, owning 843 and leasing 4,284 acres, thus farming about 10 percent of the total irrigated land in Santa Clara County even as they represented scarcely 3 percent of the county's population. Although defenders of Japanese immigrants, responding to anti-Japanese agitation and white concerns over Japanese agricultural domination in California, held that Japanese specialized only in berry, celery, asparagus, and other vegetable crops that had to be cultivated and harvested in a "stooping posture" and were universally "shunned by white farmers," this was no longer the case for some Japanese farm families in the Santa Clara Valley. The 1920 census showed 18 percent of Japanese enumerated as farmers grew deciduous fruit, while 31 percent cultivated vegetables, 13 percent berries, and 8 percent seeds. Another 22 percent of Japanese farmers were listed as operating "general" or "home" farms with no crop specified.[36] Matagoro and Naka Kurasaki, who were about the same age as Yaichi Yamakawa, exemplified the transition to orchard fruits that had occurred by 1920. The Kurasakis had first settled in Alviso in 1906, surrounded by many newly arrived countrymen. They had emigrated in 1894 from Japan to Hawaii, where their eldest child was born in 1900. The family moved to the Henrietta Cropley ranch on Capitol Avenue in San Jose in 1912, where they farmed garden crops with numerous other Japanese tenants. Cropley officially recorded a total of nine leases with ten different Japanese tenants from 1910 to 1916 and eventually leased 10.5 acres of her ranch to Matagoro Kurasaki for three years at a time.[37] In 1919, the family, which included two daughters and three sons, purchased 11 acres of a prune orchard in west San Jose on Williams Road, where many of their neighbors were ethnic Europeans: Italians, Portuguese, and Swedes. One of the sons, Henry, was named for Henrietta Cropley. The Kurasakis successfully moved from farming vegetables for a white landowner to owning their own orchard in the coveted West Side of the Valley, though they could do so only by placing the land in the name of their American-born children before the 1920 amendment to the alien land act erased that possibility for Japanese farmers.[38]

The case of the Araki family of San Jose also reflected the possibility for upward mobility among Japanese farmers in the Valley who worked closely with white landowners and advanced to orchard fruit cultivation prior to 1920. In 1900, at age twenty-nine, Suyetaro Araki migrated from Hiroshima to Hawaii; several years later he moved to Sacramento and eventually to San Jose. He worked for R. D. Fox, proprietor of Fox Nurseries on Milpitas Road, one of the largest nurseries on the West Coast in the late nineteenth century, and subsequently began farming on the Fox ranch, near the former home of the Kurasakis in Alviso. In December 1908, Julia Fox, wife of R. D. Fox, signed an eight-year lease of 10 acres planted in deciduous fruit trees at Wayne Station by Coyote Creek to Araki and a partner by the name of Nishimura. In the 1910s, Araki made four more lease agreements that were recorded in county official records for land in the San Jose area, two of which explicitly listed orchard fruit as crops planted.[39] In 1920, Suyetaro Araki, his wife, Chiyo, and seven children under seventeen years of age, lived on a farm on Hostetter Road in San Jose. The family prospered as fruit growers: on the eve of World War II, they owned 55 acres of the old Hostetter ranch in Berryessa and leased a total of 130 acres of property on farms located in Milpitas, Wayne Station, and across from their home ranch. While interned at Heart Mountain, the family lost the Berryessa farm when the white manager to whom the Arakis had entrusted their ranch transferred the property title to himself.[40]

Figure 4.1. Araki family farm on Hostetter Road, San Jose, 1922.
Courtesy of Japanese American Museum of San Jose.

Despite the economic mobility of numerous Japanese farm families during the 1910s, the vast majority of Japanese in agriculture in Santa Clara County worked as farm laborers, not as tenants and farm owners, or even sharecroppers. Only 30 percent of Japanese men over eighteen in the county listed by the 1920 census as employed in the agricultural industry were farmers, while 69 percent were enumerated as farm laborers. A key determinant that separated farmers from laborers was marital status. In the early 1910s there were hints of an emergent divide in the Japanese immigrant community between single male laborers (or men who were married but could not afford to bring their wives from Japan) and better-off married immigrant farmers with wives and small children in America, like the Yoshidas and Handas. By 1920, this divide was even more pronounced: 89 percent of Japanese men who had risen to the status of "farmer" were married, while single men made up only 10 percent of Japanese farmers in the county. Being married did not necessarily mean that a Japanese man would be a farmer, since two-thirds of married men in agriculture remained farm laborers in 1920. But the odds were that any Japanese man who entered the elite farmer minority in the community was married. Thus Japanese farm families, being able to draw on the agricultural and domestic labor of women and children, were indeed more successful in agriculture than single immigrant men, and statistical confirmation of this intuitive notion convinced many white residents in California that a new Japanese threat had appeared in their midst.

"Working the Women and Children in the Fields"

Japanese immigrant women undeniably made vital contributions to their rural households and were instrumental in supporting the family through their agricultural and wage labor, which white observers relayed as proof of deviant Japanese gender norms. As early as 1908, nearly all the Japanese wives interviewed by the Immigration Commission in Alviso and Agnew found some type of regular employment, either laboring in the fields, providing room and board for their single countrymen, or working at the Bayside Canning Company in Alviso. Women at the cannery earned more than a dollar a day on a piecework basis. Wives of Japanese tenant farmers and sharecroppers commonly worked for wages for a few years while their families developed farms and berry patches.[41] Women who joined their husbands in the 1910s followed a similar pattern.

The busy domestic and work lives of Japanese women captured the attention of white observers in the Santa Clara Valley, including Stanford economics student Ruth Miriam Fowler, who undertook extensive field research on the standard of living among the county's Japanese in the early 1920s. In Berryessa, just east of Alviso, Fowler observed, "The women do the washing on Sunday and in many cases work in the field during the week. In most cases the mother has not been here long enough to have a large family and what she has is young— between one and from five to ten." In one household she visited, Fowler met an eighteen-year-old Japanese girl, the daughter of a berry farmer whose wife was in Japan with two other children. In the absence of her mother, this young woman, who spoke some English, functioned as the household caretaker. Fowler noted that "although she liked school, she had to give it up for work." During Fowler's visit, the young woman was preparing the noon meal and was also keeping an eye on some children belonging to neighbor women who "were spending their morning (Sunday) weeding the strawberries." Saddled with cooking and child-care responsibilities for other laboring women's children, the girl could spare "but a few minutes" and, in the end, told Fowler "if I had no further questions, and [since] she could not tell me anything about their income or expenditures, she would leave me as she was very busy." As Fowler prepared to depart, the pre-occupied young woman "hurried to the garden for some large beats [sic], carrots, and turnips."[42]

Fowler's firsthand observations exposed the strenuous nature of rural life for Japanese immigrant women in California as they faced long days of labor at home and in the fields. Though all members of the family did farmwork, for the most part, women alone performed domestic tasks. Japanese wives often rose before sunrise, did morning chores, spent an average of 10 hours on farm labor, up to 16 hours during harvest time, and returned to their homes to prepare dinner for their families and often other male laborers who worked and boarded with them. Women made cooking fires, hauled water from wells, did laundry, and tended to other household duties, including childcare.[43] In this context, Shina Zenihiro's 1913 complaint in divorce proceedings that her husband "inflicted" on her the burden of working "in the fields upon agricultural land in Santa Clara County... [doing] the work of a man" was not shocking. Asked if she ever felt free while she was married, Misao Kondo, who arrived in California as a young bride in 1916 and gave birth to nine children while living in the Santa Clara and Salinas Valleys, answered immediately, "Never." She and her husband sharecropped in Sunnyvale and Mountain View before moving to Salinas in the 1920s. Seeing Kondo's poverty and distress, the Chinese manager of a fruit drying shed tried to persuade her to give up her newborn baby for adoption. She considered the proposal until a friend pointed out to her, "You have five fingers. Which would you cut off?"[44]

As a matter of economic survival, Japanese children were not exempt from labor on the family farm. A Nisei woman born and raised in Alviso recalled her arduous routine as a child picking strawberries and beans in the fields before and after school: "Yes, on the farm we had to work hard....I woke up early in the morning—before I went to school, I had to put all the baskets into the drawers of the chests [for strawberry picking]...and then I come home—sometimes I go to Japanese school after three o'clock and sometimes I have to come home and pick strawberries." Harry Nishiura, who arrived in the Santa Clara Valley as a twelve-year-old, recalled a similar existence on his family's Mountain View strawberry farm: "Before you go to school, you have to get up at six o'clock every morning and help to pick strawberry until about seven-thirty." His only full meal was one his mother cooked at night after she came home from the fields. The family schedule "revolved around work," which sometimes took precedence over schooling, as older Nisei stayed home to contribute necessary labor.[45]

While most women adapted and endured, some found the isolation of farm life and exhausting labor too much to bear. In Santa Clara County, three Japanese women, all of whom resided on farms, were reported by the coroner's office to have committed suicide between 1910 and 1920, while ten Japanese men took their own lives. In two cases, inquests suggested that the women had suffered from unbearable pain stemming from health conditions for which they received inadequate treatment and no relief, a common cause of suicide at this time. For example, it appeared that Kimi Yanita, a thirty-nine-year-old woman who shot herself in August of 1913, suffered from a brain tumor that caused forgetfulness, headaches, and made her head "heavy." The Yanitas had been strawberry growers on Henry Abel's ranch in Milpitas for at least three years, and though Kimi complained of pains in her head, her husband Senmatsu reported that up to her death, "she was working continuously" in the berry patch.[46] The *Nichibei Shimbun*, which reported that the couple had been happily married for ten years, speculated that Kimi Yanita's frequent headaches may have caused her to "become insane and decide to die." Her husband was taken into police custody until the coroner's investigation confirmed suicide as the cause of her death.[47]

Masayo Ota was a twenty-seven-year-old wife and mother of three who drowned herself near her Coyote Creek residence. Mental illness, possibly brought on by the difficulty of life in America, appeared to have played a role in the suicide. Ota had arrived in the country in 1911, six years prior to her death, likely as a picture bride. Her husband, a tenant farmer named Teiichi Ota, identified by authorities only as S. Ota, lived and worked with his brother and sister-in-law on John Heinlen's ranch east of San Jose. Within a year of her emigration, Masayo Ota had her first child, who was followed by two more. At her inquest, her husband reported that the couple had three children, ages five and two, plus "a little one." He testified that his wife had tried to kill herself "so many times" for "pretty near three years," including an attempt several days before her death in Coyote Creek to drown herself in a large water tank and multiple attempts to slit her throat, "some days, four or five times, she get a knife and anything, some times she get the axe." The widower said that he, his brother, and his sister-in-law had watched Masayo constantly, and he was in perpetual fear and turmoil over his wife's unpredictable behavior: "I can't sleep at night. At night I wake all the time, and [she] change every minute, some times pretty good, some times looks pretty good, and after four or five minutes, she change right back."[48]

On the fateful morning of Masayo Ota's drowning, her husband had gone into town on an errand, leaving his sister-in-law to monitor his wife. Masayo said she "wanted to go to the toilet," likely an outhouse on the property, and her sister-in-law stepped into the farmhouse for a few minutes, only to find that her charge had disappeared. A call was placed to the Japanese Association in San Jose to locate Teiichi Ota, while family members proceeded to search the house and ranch in vain. That afternoon, neighbor C. T. O'Connell, who was driving cattle at a nearby ranch, noticed a body in the creek and fished it out with some boards. It was soon identified as the missing woman's.

The only clues to explain Masayo Ota's suicide came from the testimony at the coroner's inquest, which revealed a woman who became deeply depressed and suicidal several years after her arrival from Japan.[49] Possibly contributing to Ota's decision to drown herself were the monotonous, grueling pace of farm life coupled with childbearing and the weariness of caring for three young children, and the lack of treatment for a mental illness her family did not understand or know how to deal with. The suicides of Japanese women in rural California provide a window into the daunting challenges and pressures faced by female immigrants who spent years laboring in fields and homes.

The difficulties rural women like Ota endured did not escape the attention of anti-Japanese agitators, who, far from being sympathetic to their plights, gathered evidence of women and children being overworked to make the case for Japanese deviance from American gender and family ideals. Critics of Japanese family labor practices voiced their concerns in the context of Progressive Era campaigns to improve the welfare of working women and children, operating from "a deep fear that current employment conditions would destroy the health, family life, morality, and stability of the working class and therefore harm the nation as a whole."[50] Reformers in California led the nation in spearheading protective labor legislation for women and children and in 1911 successfully advocated for the passage of a law mandating an eight-hour day for wage-earning women, one of the first of its kind (women employed in canneries were specifically excluded from the law). The law also mandated the establishment of the California Industrial Welfare Commission in 1913 to regulate wages and working conditions for women and children.[51]

Although protective labor laws in California and other states targeted urban laborers in factories and mills, they reflected many white Americans' concerns about safeguarding the home and preserving the moral integrity of the American family. The fact that nearly all Japanese women and children performed agricultural labor to support the household offended some white Californians' sensibilities about proper family roles and fed into anti-Japanese sentiment by the late 1910s. In September of 1920, exclusionists came together under the leadership of the vocal and tireless Valentine S. McClatchy, publisher of the *Sacramento Bee*, and the newly formed Japanese Exclusion League of California. Supporters of the league included the Native Sons of the Golden West, the American Legion, the California State Federation of Labor, and the California Federation of Women's Clubs, along with major California farm organizations, the state Grange, and the Farm Bureau. In contrast to their indifference to the Webb Act in 1913, California farmers united behind the exclusionist program and overwhelmingly supported the 1920 alien land law.[52]

Citing several state commission reports, an author for the 1920 report by the state Board of Control complained that white Americans could not compete with Japanese labor strategies: "The Japanese farmers and every member in the family, physically able to do so, including the wife and little children, work in the field long hours, practically from daylight to dark, on Sundays and holidays." Claiming such practices caused gender confusion, Valentine McClatchy decried the importation of Japanese picture brides who "performed a man's work in field or shop."[53] The *Mountain View Register-Leader* quoted a Sacramento farmer who surmised that Japanese men sent for picture brides so that they "could save paying wages by putting their wives to work," thus circumventing the terms of the Gentlemen's Agreement barring the immigration of laborers from Japan. Cora Woodbridge of the Native Daughters of the Golden West, an influential pressure group, called the Japanese mother a "beast of burden up to the time of the birth of her child," forced to resume her field labor "within a day or two at most... from twelve to sixteen hours a day." These women were likely to be found "on their hands and knees in the fields, or wading in the mud, with babies in baskets near them."[54] Such customs suggested to agitators that the Japanese callously neglected gender distinctions to the point of treating pregnant women and those who had just given birth like "beasts of burden," and not women at all.

With over 87 percent of Santa Clara County farms in 1920 smaller than 100 acres and a majority of farms between 10 and 50 acres, it was unlikely that one man could provide the sole labor to operate a farm. Oral histories and recollections by white residents who lived on fruit ranches in the Valley during the 1920s and 1930s confirm that white women and children regularly performed farm labor.[55] While it seemed unusual for white Americans to assume that only the male household head should do farm labor on a family farm, by the 1920s, this was precisely the model agricultural experts prescribed for the nation's farmers. The modern depiction of rural gender roles held that the farmer should act as manager or businessman, employing efficient, capital-intensive methods and the latest technology, and the farmer's wife was to be solely a homemaker who raised her family to a middle-class level of refinement and consumption. In this idealized vision, women who performed physical labor on the farm were "drudges," burdened, overworked, married to "an oafish, and probably inefficient man who did not respect his wife."[56]

Accusations that Japanese men worked their wives like common field hands, or even worse, like domestic animals, added a racial dimension to the charge that laboring women were "drudges." Furthermore, according to anti-Japanese arguments, through their distorted gender roles, Japanese families hindered the ability of upstanding white farm families to earn a livelihood. Opponents of Japanese immigration alleged that Japanese farmers were creating "impossible competition" by tainting the "American principles so universally approved in America," which included most importantly, "refraining from working the women and children in the fields."[57]

Aware of the charges against Japanese farm families, elite Issei leaders attempted to uplift the rural immigrant masses and established programs to "teach" Japanese women domestic and child-rearing skills, admonishing them to "demonstrate the true virtue of Japanese women and compel [white] Americans to admit them as first-rate women in the world." Community leaders instructed immigrant women to discourage "unsavory conduct and foul speech" in their homes along with gambling, drinking, and smoking. The Japanese Association of America sponsored educational meetings and lectures on "general social betterment" and published reference materials aimed at women titled "Camp Sanitation" and "Mother's Guide." Touring rural communities in California, Bryn Mawr College–educated Michi Kawai, who became the head of Japan's YWCA and developed programs for Japanese immigrant women, found wives and mothers unaware of basic sanitation and child-rearing practices. Other Issei women leaders in local Christian associations offered new immigrants lessons in American housekeeping, child care methods, and English language, sometimes with the support of white Protestant women espousing racial uplift and missionary agendas.[58] The attempts by elite Japanese to improve the image of the immigrant community in California reflected continuing class fissures as well as strategies designed to counter external attacks on Japanese domesticity.

Recognizing the increasing importance of the white public's perception of the Japanese family, defenders of the Japanese by 1920 argued against prevailing perceptions of Japanese women as "beasts of burden." Writing in 1920, Japanese community leaders acknowledged that while it was true that women and children worked in the fields, they did "trivial work" not requiring "undue physical exertion." Young children, they argued, were "usually allowed to play in the fields around their parents while the parents work," but anti-Japanese forces erroneously represented this image as "compelling children of tender age to engage in 'arduous toil.'"[59] John P. Irish addressed the state fruit growers' convention in 1919 on the "present vituperative discussion of the question of the Oriental people in California" by focusing on elevating the image of Japanese immigrant women. Irish, who made no mention Japanese women and children when debates over the alien land law raged in 1913, now went on at length about them, attempting to disabuse his audience of the idea that Japanese women were "held as the common property of the men," calling it "an outrageous falsehood." He claimed that to the contrary, Japanese women guarded "their virtue as holy and rigidly as any women married under our law," and as "a housekeeper and a mother...cherishes her children and honors her pledges to her husband in marriage." Perhaps stretching the truth even as he knew it, for the sake of opposing anti-Japanese agitators' contentions that Japanese women worked in the fields just as men did, Irish maintained that "They attend to the housekeeping interests and Japanese women never work out."[60] Irish, who owned thousands of acres in the Sacramento Delta and leased to numerous Japanese tenants, could not have avoided seeing Japanese women working outside the home, whether in the fields or in the canneries. Nonetheless, his exaggeration attempted to reassure whites of Japanese adherence to prevailing domestic norms.

Aside from the concerns over Japanese women, gender roles within farm families, and the division of household labor, much discussion emerged over the allegedly staggering Japanese birthrate and maniacal Japanese designs to populate the state, claims frequently used after 1919 to bolster the anti-Japanese movement. McClatchy wrote extensively on Japanese birthrates, asserting that such "extraordinary" statistics would soon assure "the inundation of the white population in this country by the yellow race." In 1920, the *San Jose Mercury Herald* published English translations of several articles that purportedly originated in a San Francisco Japanese-language newspaper, in which the Japanese author called on readers to "Beget!" children who would be "treasures more valuable...than hundreds of millions of gold." The San Jose paper's translation also included remarks that endorsed unconventional methods of family formation and chain migration: "Let those who live in separate houses immediately live together in one house. Let newly married people at once adopt sons and have them registered. Let married people without children, all the more immediately adopt sons and bring them to America. Then immediately give a lovely bride to the adopted son. And let everyone who has dependent relatives immediately send for them and bring them over."[61] Questions about article's origins and its translation aside, these lines must have startled the readers of the *Mercury Herald* as they pondered the distressing calls for nonmarital cohabitation, immigration law violation, and twisted adoption practices.

Alarm over the Japanese birthrate promulgated further anxieties about the presence of numerous American-born Japanese children. In January 1920, to kick off his "Keep California White" Senate reelection campaign, James D. Phelan issued a resolution to alter the Fourteenth Amendment to prohibit Japanese born in the United States from obtaining citizenship. Manipulating figures published by the state Board of Health, Phelan surmised that one-third of California's rural population was "substantially Japanese" and called on "all thinking men and women" to recognize the assault on American national identity, since the "rural population is the backbone of every country." Local farmers like J. J. McDonald, president of the county's Farm Operators' Association, backed Phelan's proposal to eliminate birthright citizenship for Japanese American children, in addition to recommending the cancellation of the Gentlemen's Agreement and ending the immigration of picture brides.[62] McClatchy put forth the latter suggestion, claiming that Japanese women were "being used for breeding purposes in carrying out Japan's clearly defined policy of 'peacefully penetrating' the United States." He quoted reports that showed that the Japanese birthrate in 1918 was four times as great as that of whites and remained three times greater in 1919 (Phelan favored another version of these statistics, citing the increase in Japanese births in the previous ten years to be 3,000 percent, compared to white births, which had decreased by 9 percent). In response to the second-generation flood, McClatchy also supported the amendment forbidding the automatic citizenship of American-born Japanese children.[63]

However unfounded, anxieties about the presence of Japanese women and the frantic breeding of Japanese children demonstrated the centrality of family formation in the debate over the "Oriental question." *California and the Oriental* applied the birthrate concern specifically to the state's "rich agricultural counties," where the average births of Japanese were said to have risen from 3.2 percent of total births in 1910 to 12.3 percent in 1919, with certain rural parts of Sacramento County registering a shocking 49.7 percent. McClatchy concluded that in the 18 "rich agricultural counties" covered by the study, the average number of Japanese births had quadrupled in the period from 1910 to 1919.[64] In Santa Clara County, 58 percent of rural Japanese families had one or two children in 1920 (42 percent had three or more), and the average number of individuals in each household was 3.8, suggesting that birthrates along the lines of McClatchy's claims were unlikely. *California and the Oriental* reported that in Santa Clara

County, the Japanese birthrate reached a high of 17 percent in 1917. Given the number of Japanese children who were born between 1910 and 1920 in Santa Clara County, a Japanese woman over the age of eighteen would have given birth to an average of 1.27 children in that period, hardly an astonishing birthrate.[65]

Whereas white fruit growers were relatively quiet on the issue of the 1913 alien land law, which received scant attention at state growers' conventions, they became more vocal beginning in 1919, influenced by exclusionists to support a more severe law by connecting issues of Japanese birthrates, marriages, and land acquisition. Attendees of the 1919 Convention of Fruit Growers and Farmers held in Chico heartily applauded Sherman A. Reynolds's welcome address. The keynoter gravely pointed out "the unfortunate ownership of property by Asiatics in California," surmising that the Japanese did not believe in the "sanctity of marriage" and were willing to "consummate it with a photograph." Nor did the Japanese understand the "sanctity of motherhood," he added, choosing instead to procreate merely "for the purpose of acquiring the land in the name of what to us are more or less illegitimate children."[66] He assumed that Japanese family formation occurred under completely fraudulent circumstances and questioned the validity of picture marriages to the point of declaring the children born of those unions to be "illegitimate." Reynolds suggested that Americans, who did "hold sacred" the institutions of marriage and family, should rightly take offense at these violations of decent family values, especially since the Japanese allegedly neglected them for selfish gain, "in order to obtain possession of this land." Despite some impassioned discussion on the Japanese question, however, the *California Fruit News* reported that "nothing concrete developed," and the conventioneers did not move to pass any resolution, "being largely content with suggesting that there is a problem and that it appears important."[67]

In response to charges of high Japanese birthrates, immigrant leaders and intellectuals argued for more impartial comparisons between population groups as well as class factors. In 1921, Kiyoshi (also known as K.K.) Kawakami, chief publicist for the Japanese consul in San Francisco, pointed to a study by the California Bureau of Vital Statistics, which showed the Japanese birthrate to be higher than the Caucasian birthrate up to four births, but that the latter birthrate exceeded the former from five to nine births, thus scientifically demonstrating that "Caucasian fecundity exceeds Japanese fecundity."

Also writing in 1921, Kiichi Kanzaki, author of *California and the Japanese*, called on the public to examine more objectively the basis of comparison used in the exaggerated statistics cited by exclusionists like McClatchy and Phelan. "For the sake of justice," Kanzaki declared, the Japanese immigrant birthrate should be compared to that of "other immigrant races or that among the whites with similar income groups, intellectual status, age-groups and social environment." Noting similarities between southern and eastern Europeans, Kanzaki stated that the birthrate among Italians and Poles was "quite as high, if not higher, than among the Japanese," who should not be matched up against "the old white population whose make-up is entirely different and whose birth rate is necessarily low." In an elitist, apologetic tone, Kanzaki added that the high birthrate among the "first generation of immigrant laborers in a strange land" was not a Japanese racial trait, but instead reflected "their limited social and economic condition and less advanced intellectual status," for the "uncultured always suffer from high birth rate...[but] as they advance in their culture their fecundity declines."[68] Though it is unclear whether Kanzaki was citing scientific theory or his own cultural observations, he evidently believed that deeming his immigrant countrymen "uncultured" provided compelling explanation for high birthrates.

In the context of the uproar over Japanese farm families, women, children, and birthrates, a 1920 proposition designed to plug loopholes in the Alien Land Law of 1913 passed in a landslide, with 75 percent of California voters casting ballots for the initiative. A proposal presented to the public for popular vote, rather than a bill drafted by the state legislature, the 1920 initiative banned "aliens ineligible to citizenship" from leasing land and stated that those who financed land purchases and placed the ownership of property in names other than their own were liable to be prosecuted for violating the new alien land law. In Santa Clara County, where the 1920 measure held the unwavering support of two influential local politicians, Senator James Phelan and Representative Everis A. Hayes, more than 70 percent of voters approved the proposition. The county's American Legion post also mobilized forces to "restrain the feverish aggression of the Japanese" through the proposed law and kept a blacklist of individuals and firms that sold or leased real estate to Japanese.[69]

Nevertheless, confirming white growers' continued and desired reliance on Japanese tenants, some Valley farmers resisted the amendment. One grower from Mountain View who did not succumb to anti-Japanese rhetoric praised the Japanese farmers he knew, saying they were "first to raise the Stars and Stripes, first in fruits and vegetables...first to buy Liberty bonds...first to get to work in the morning and the last to go to bed at night." J. J. McDonald, president of the county farm owners' association, called on politicians to keep their "hands off the Japanese question," which McDonald claimed was a "grower's problem" meant for growers to resolve. He declared the Japanese were "good workers and highly productive....No one will deny that." He noted, in addition, that the Japanese worked "more than 385,000 of the most fertile and productive soil in California" that "supplies almost unbelievable amounts of foodstuff."[70] Having experienced strong harvest seasons in 1919 and 1920 with record prices for Santa Clara Valley fruit, local growers may have hesitated to vote for legislation that would alter their labor and tenancy arrangements. McDonald's delicately constructed stance on behalf of farmers, which maintained that Japanese were "good workers and highly productive," supported the importation of Chinese laborers "under bond and for limited periods," and fought for a law to take away citizenship rights from American-born Japanese children all at the same time, reflected the ambiguous position white growers continued to espouse regarding the use of Asian labor in agriculture.[71] It was this enduring ambiguity that in 1923 propelled one white grower and his Japanese sharecropper from the Santa Clara Valley all the way to the U.S. Supreme Court.

Cropping Contracts and the "American Farm Home"

The 1920 amendment to the 1913 Webb Act closed the loopholes that had allowed the growth of Japanese agriculture in California. While the new law did not trigger the complete demise of Japanese farming, it made many Japanese families dependent on white landowners, leaving "a legacy of stagnation and powerlessness." The California law, along with similar measures passed by state legislatures throughout the American West, historian Nayan Shah argues, had the effect of establishing a "racial cartel in the agricultural property and contract market" that denied Asian immigrants economic rights and prevented "everyday interracial association and intimacy."[72] Under the 1920 law, aliens ineligible for naturalized citizenship could not lease agricultural land at all, nor could they acquire land under the names of American-born minors or land corporations. As a result, between 1920 and 1925, the amount of land Japanese owned in California dropped from close to 75,000 acres to about 42,000 acres, and Japanese-leased lands declined from 192,150 acres to just over 76,000 acres. In contrast to the Alien Land Law of 1913, the 1920 legislation produced a significant decline in Japanese American farming. San Jose farmer Katsusaburo Kawahara noted that the 1920 law "hurt us all the way through.... That was just like [being] in a barrel—you can't stretch no more."[73]

Although the steady demand for California produce that developed rapidly during World War I continued through the 1920s, Japanese farmers in the Santa Clara Valley and elsewhere ultimately could not capitalize on promising market conditions. From 1918 on, the region saw a boom in new canneries to handle the Valley's increasing output of fruits and vegetables. In 1919, the *California Fruit News* predicted that the Santa Clara Valley would be responsible for one-quarter of the state's canned fruits and vegetables, aided by several large new cannery projects, including the Richmond-Chase Company and the Herbert Packing Company, regarded to be the "most modern and well equipped."[74]

In 1922, the Santa Clara Valley was home to 40 canneries and 30 packing houses, one of the highest concentrations in the world, and by 1930, the region processed 30 percent of California's annual pack of fruits and vegetables.[75] Aware of the lucrative climate for canning produce in the area, the Mountain View–based Japanese farming partnership known as T.M.T.O. ramped up entrepreneurial efforts to build a new cannery, only to be stymied by an adverse business climate for Japanese immigrants. In the fall of 1918, T.M.T.O. partners Yasutaro Oku and newlyweds Masa and Naosuke Tsumura purchased the equipment and stock of the Mountain View Canning Company in preparation for their entry into the canning business. They signed a lease for the property the following spring, while continuing to farm raspberries, strawberries, and tomatoes on the nearby James Center ranch, which the partnership was also leasing.[76] Under Oku and the Tsumuras, the Mountain View Canning Company operated from 1919 to 1921, canning crops of tomatoes and berries the partners purchased from Japanese farmers based in Mountain View and Sunnyvale, including former T.M.T.O. partner Masataro Matsushita.[77]

T.M.T.O.'s lease on the Center ranch expired on November 1, 1921, with no legal option for renewal under the new land law, and thereafter the fortunes of the partnership and its cannery took a turn for the worse. According to county records, in May 1922 the Mountain View Canning Company merged with Tsunetaro Sutow's Foothill Canning Company of San Mateo County, with Oku mortgaging his cannery to Sutow for $25,000 (approximately $340,000 today). The following year, Sutow and Oku mortgaged their cannery equipment to the Fontana-Hollywood Company.[78] There is no evidence showing that the cannery purchased any crops from local farmers in 1923 and 1924, indicating it was not in operation. On May 22, 1925, Yasutaro Oku sold the site of the Mountain View Canning Company and was subsequently sued by R. G. Fontana, who held the mortgage on the Japanese entrepreneurs' equipment.[79]

It is uncertain whether the demise of the first and only Japanese-owned cannery in the Santa Clara Valley resulted from poor business decisions of the T.M.T.O. partners in launching and financing their canning endeavor or for other reasons. Clearly their entry into the industry came at a particularly inauspicious moment when the local Japanese farmers whose produce they relied on confronted new restrictions designed to drive them out of farming altogether. Oku's and the Tsumuras' longstanding tenant farming arrangements with Mountain View landowners terminated as well, leaving the partners without their primary source of income. Moreover, the new land law may have posed further obstacles to the validity of the three Japanese owners' title and may have called into question the legality of their status as a farming corporation involved in handling crops for canning.

The rise and fall of the Mountain View Canning Company paralleled the fate of Japanese farmers who had gained a foothold in the Valley's agricultural economy by the late 1910s, attempted to improve their circumstances through cooperative endeavors, and found themselves unable to maintain traction. By

1920, like their white orchardist counterparts, numerous Japanese farmers had begun to form marketing cooperatives to secure advantages for their crops, but their participation in these associations was short-lived as they faced setbacks with the renewed alien land law and restricted opportunities for farming.

In 1916, with the assistance of Nihonmachi businessmen, Japanese berry farmers in the Santa Clara Valley began a marketing cooperative, the Bushberry Growers Association. Yaichi Yamakawa, the farmer who had purchased a ranch in San Jose in 1907 after leasing a large tract from the McKiernan sisters in Alviso, led this undertaking. About 30 members paid a percentage of their sales to the cooperative, which owned a market in San Jose Japantown for farmers to sell their berries to fruit merchants from San Francisco and Oakland. The association also hired a secretary to keep track of market conditions and accounts. Although it had been a beneficial arrangement for members, the cooperative dissolved by the early 1920s as farmers could no longer lease agricultural property legally. As a whole, observed Stanford graduate student Yoshio Ichikawa in 1925, Japanese cooperative associations were "seriously handicapped by the passage of the Alien Land Law of 1920."[80]

Some Japanese farmers who had joined agricultural marketing cooperatives with mixed membership also withdrew from them in the aftermath of tightened alien land laws. The California Pear Growers Association, organized in 1917 with the practical agenda of promoting pear production and marketing for growers, drew numerous Santa Clara Valley growers, both white and Asian. Listings of members by county in 1919 included Ah Cho, S. Yoneji, and T. Yamada of Santa Clara County, along with white growers, and meeting minutes contained multiple mentions of the Chinese-operated Bayside Canning Company of Alviso, which prepared to can 1,800 tons of pears in 1922. At two of the association's annual meetings, in 1922 and 1925, no Japanese members were present in person or by proxy.[81]

Another organization comprising white and Asian growers was the San Francisco–based Central California Berry Growers Association, formed in San Jose in 1917 under the leadership of the Japanese Agricultural Association in collaboration with local Japanese associations. At its first meeting, held in Gilroy in late March 1917, members elected five Japanese and five white directors. Though Japanese farmers had spearheaded the founding of this cooperative, which claimed sales of approximately $1 million, by 1924 the Japanese made up less than a quarter of the membership, many having been forced out of the strawberry industry by the 1920 alien land law.

Other Japanese cooperative marking associations were "compelled to disband because ineligible aliens have no title to the crop."[82] Local Japanese farmers who remained in agriculture continued to join cooperatives, including the Peninsular Co-operative Growers' Association, which spanned from Menlo Park (in San Mateo County, bordering northwestern Santa Clara County) to San Jose, formed in 1922 as "an organization of white men and Japanese" to eliminate duplicate haulings of fruits and vegetables to San Francisco commission houses. Area farmers brought their produce to a trucking company yard on Hope Street in Mountain View, where it was picked up daily and expedited to San Francisco.[83]

In the meantime, to remain in agriculture after 1920, many Japanese farmers relied on white landowners to hire them through sharecropping contracts, generally considered employment agreements, which paid the "employee" farmer (technically not a "lessee") a share of the crops as a salary.[84] This specific practice eventually became the subject of *Webb v. O'Brien*, the case initiated in 1921 by Santa Clara County plaintiffs and decided by the Supreme Court in 1923.

Jeremiah J. O'Brien, owner of a large holding on Brokaw Road in San Jose, catered to Japanese farm families with this new form of land tenure that blurred the boundaries and semantics of wage labor, sharecropping, and tenant farming. In the early 1920s, 35 Japanese families lived on his property, each farming its assigned parcel of land. O'Brien arranged for the Japanese farmers to send their produce to commission houses in San Francisco under his name. He received payment for the crops directly and deducted his share, 50 percent plus a "silent commission" amounting to 5 percent of gross sales, before distributing the remainder to the Japanese sharecroppers, ostensibly as "wages" for their services. None of O'Brien's arrangements with Japanese farmers appear in county records. The only document at the county recorder's office in which O'Brien's name is listed with Japanese lessees was an August 1913 agreement to lease a small piece of land on Milpitas Road for the installation of a motor and water pump. The lease was for seven years at the monthly rent of $5, increased to $10 beginning August 1, 1915.[85]

Jenzaburo Inouye, a sharecropper on O'Brien's property in the early 1920s, gained notoriety through the legal proceedings associated with the 1923 U.S. Supreme Court case *Webb v. O'Brien*. The case reflected the culmination of white Californians' prevailing fears about Japanese dominance of agricultural lands in their state and specifically highlighted the central concern over family farm ideology. What began as a test case of the 1920 Alien Land Law, in which the parties differed on what should be legal definitions of sharecropping contracts and land tenure, turned into a debate about the nature of American farming and identity, in which gender and family issues were at the forefront.

In the fall of 1921, Japanese farmers in northern California convened emergency meetings under the auspices of the Japanese Agricultural Association and organized extensively to initiate several test cases contesting the 1920 Alien Land Law. They established a land litigation committee to file a bill of complaint in Santa Clara County on behalf of O'Brien and Inouye.[86] Court records stated that O'Brien was the owner of 10 acres of land in Santa Clara County, "particularly adapted" to the raising of strawberries, loganberries, raspberries, and vegetables. Documents never mentioned the cultivation of orchard fruits. Following a practice that had been common in the area for decades, O'Brien entered into a sharecropping contract with a man identified in court records only as J. Inouye. The 1920 census confirms that the sharecropper was Jenzaburo Inouye, who with his wife Isono and four California-born children resided on O'Brien's property on Rock Avenue.[87] No stranger to the legal system, Inouye was one of the three Japanese plaintiffs who sued Edward and Sarah Younger in Santa Clara County Superior Court in 1913 over access to a water pipe Inouye had laid across part of the Youngers' ranch, not far from O'Brien's property in the Orchard District of San Jose. Coincidentally, the 10-acre parcel Inouye farmed under O'Brien had previously belonged to Valley pioneer Coleman Younger, father of Edward Younger.[88]

In 1921, attorneys for O'Brien and Inouye filed a motion for a temporary injunction against California attorney general Ulysses S. Webb and Santa Clara County district attorney C. C. Coolidge. Their goal was to prevent the enforcement of the 1920 Alien Land Law in the matter of the sharecropping agreement between O'Brien and Inouye. The plaintiffs contended that the law violated the Fourteenth Amendment of the Constitution by depriving them of property without due process of law and also by denying them equal protection of the law. On December 20, 1921, the U.S. District Court of Northern California granted

Figure 4.2. Inouye children and their cousins at Inouye farm on Rock Avenue, San Jose, 1932.
Courtesy of the Inouye family.

an interlocutory injunction, and Webb appealed, arguing that the state had an interest in preventing a sharecropping agreement and that in the present case a person who was ineligible for citizenship actually enjoyed the possession and dominion of land, which was against the plain intent of the 1920 Alien Land Law. The plaintiffs insisted that a sharecropping agreement was a contract for the performance of labor and entailed an employer–employee relationship, hence not constituting a conveyance of land. In November 1923, the U.S. Supreme Court ruled in Webb's favor. In May of the same year, moreover, the California state legislature had amended the land law specifically to ban the type of Japanese employment agreements in question, which were in effect equivalent to share-cropping leases.[89]

Justice Pierce Butler, speaking for the Court, held that the 1920 law evidenced "legislative intention" to prohibit sharecropping agreements because it stipulated that ineligible aliens should not be allowed to use land for agricultural purposes. O'Brien's contract led to the "practical result" of a Japanese sharecropper having rights "substantially similar to that granted to a lessee." Ultimately, the Court ruled invalid arguments claiming that alien land laws violated equal protection under the Fourteenth Amendment. As a commentator on *Webb v. O'Brien* and other land cases pointed out in the 1923–1924 volume of the *Harvard Law Review*, "The equal protection clause forbids neither distinctions between citizens and aliens nor distinctions between classes of aliens, provided the classification be supported by reasonable considerations of public policy."[90] The government could and did classify the Japanese as "aliens ineligible to citizenship" as a matter of "public policy," and the California law was based on this particular "distinction."

The attorneys for O'Brien emphasized the constitutional right of individuals to earn a living and to enter into contracts. Attorney Louis Marshall described Jenzaburo Inouye as a law-abiding, diligent resident of Santa Clara County who earned his livelihood engaging in "legitimate agricultural labor" as a "capable farmer, in all respects a desirable and competent person to farm such realty." If the court kept the plaintiffs from executing this proposed contract, Marshall argued, Inouye would be "deprived of his right to earn a living in the business for which he is best fitted and which he understands." His manhood and capacity as a breadwinner for his household would be threatened, as Inouye became "seriously embarrassed in his efforts to earn a living for himself." The Japanese Association may have chosen Inouye to be a plaintiff in its test case precisely because, as a thirty-six-year-old married man with four young children, he fit the profile of a stable family man.[91]

Still, Justice Butler contended that contracts like the one between O'Brien and Inouye could lead to an undesirable change in the character of American farming, to the point that "the population living on and cultivating the farmlands

Figure 4.3. Wedding of Della Inouye (daughter of Jenzaburo Inouye) and Toshio Santo, Fifth Street Buddhist Church, San Jose, c. 1931–1932. Jenzaburo Inouye in front row, first from left, holding daughter Elsie, next to wife, Isono Inouye.
Courtesy of the Inouye family.

might come to be made up largely of ineligible aliens."[92] Presuming these Japanese "aliens" to be loyal not to the United States, but to Japan, and thus posing a threat to the security of the nation, the justice continued: "The allegiance of the farmers to the state directly affects its strength and safety." It is unclear what Butler had in mind as to the specific types of subversive activities berry and vegetable growing farmers like Inouye might engage in to undermine the state. His arguments could have been lifted from the writings of anti-Japanese agitators like Everis Hayes, who were convinced that the Japanese were "steadily absorbing the best agricultural lands" and if not stopped, would become "masters of agricultural California." According to Hayes, it was "as tillers of the soil" that the Japanese stood to do the most harm to the nation.[93] For Butler and Hayes, control of California farmland defined white racial and national identity, and Japanese farmers threatened that very identity.

The legality of sharecropping arrangements and the threat of Japanese agricultural domination were not the only contested issues in *Webb v. O'Brien*. Webb, like Butler and some of his colleagues on the Court, showed a keen desire to keep this institution of the "American farm home," which Webb called "our

country's boast," from being tainted by an influx of Asians. In his lengthy appellants' brief for *Webb v. O'Brien*, Webb had laid out his assignment of errors,
pointing out where he believed the district court had erred in its decision in
favor of the plaintiffs, parsed the language of the California statute in relation to
cropping contracts, and argued for the state's interest in the dominion and possession of its agricultural lands. But Webb's conclusion to his brief was most
notable because technical legal issues had been eclipsed by the state attorney
general's decided focus on what he perceived to be the interrelated issues of race,
gender, family farming, and American identity. Returning to the reasoning
behind the passage of the amended 1920 alien land law, Webb reminded the justices that this legislative act was designed to protect the American family farm:
"It was drawn by those who know and in recognition of the established fact that
the American farm which is in competition with the Oriental farm will cease to
be cultivated, or will be cultivated by Orientals."

Attorney Louis Marshall, arguing for O'Brien, understood the threat of
competition Webb was referring to when he noted that the criticism made of
"Oriental" farmers was not that they were "incompetent, that they prevent
the land from being productive, that their methods of tilling the soil are inadequate or wasteful, that they are indolent or careless or negligent" but, ironically, "that they are too industrious, too intensive and too efficient, and that
they have increased the productivity of the land on which they are employed."[94] Whereas Webb had claimed that white American farmers needed
protection from "Oriental" competition, lest the former be forced out of
farming altogether, Marshall's position was that Japanese farmers should not
be penalized unduly for their success and constructive contributions to
California agriculture.

This unfair competition, Webb proposed in the climactic section of his brief,
was in large part due to deviant "Oriental habit and custom" of exploiting the
labor of "wives, widows and children." In the remainder of the brief, which di-
gressed from legal issues entirely, Webb called for keeping an "American" standard for gender roles within the family: "The American farm was not builded
[*sic*] upon the idea of wives and daughters tilling the soil."[95] In the face of Japanese
competition, "the members of the American farm home" would not be able to
continue "the activities which now ennoble farm life." These "activities," according
to Webb's conception of sex-segregated family roles, involved "wife and daughter"
keeping the home, "children of suitable age" enrolled in school, and "father and
son" tilling the farm, all of which Webb claimed would be impossible to maintain if the "American farm home" had to compete with Japanese farmers who
had no qualms about defying such conventions. The perception that Japanese
immigrants in California were successful farmers because they worked their
"wives and daughters" was an abomination, not only because this practice supposedly

led to "unfair competition" but, more important, because it violated white family ideals that many Americans were trying hard to uphold.

When the first Japanese seasonal harvest laborers arrived in the Santa Clara Valley during the late 1880s, they were unaware that their presence would lead to numerous pieces of legislation and, ultimately, to the *Webb* decision and other U.S. Supreme Court rulings designed to keep them out of farming. In the opening decades of the twentieth century, the settlement of Japanese immigrants who came to farm the fertile Valley transformed the region's agricultural arrangements. The Japanese replaced the departed Chinese in farm labor positions, as well as in berry and vegetable farming, and eventually established an impressive dominance of these areas in Santa Clara County, mirroring trends throughout the farming districts of the state.

In the Santa Clara Valley, opposition to the Japanese in agriculture did not develop when the Japanese immigrant community consisted mainly of itinerant men who did menial farm labor and occasionally became embroiled in disputes over the few Japanese women living there. While the sex ratio imbalance of the early twentieth century created new conditions and crises for Japanese immigrant men and women, during this time white agitators did not object to Japanese labor with the fervor that would consume them by 1920. Ironically, whites began to clamor against the Japanese community precisely as it became centered around family life. The Japanese, who seemed intent on settling permanently, bringing wives and having children, threatened the institution of the American family farm in the eyes of some whites in a way Chinese immigrants, a population almost entirely made up of men without families living in the United States, never did.

The formation of Japanese American families in large part explains why so many white Californians, from politicians and Supreme Court justices to labor union members and fruit growers, opposed the Japanese so relentlessly after they had been in the country for over two decades, eliciting cries that family farming must remain the pursuit of white Americans alone. Although only a minority of Japanese families made the leap from farm labor to operating their own farms, and an even smaller subset took on cultivating the area's prized orchard fruits, their presence posed a fundamental challenge to the white family farm ideal and forced its reconfiguration. Whereas late nineteenth-century boosters of the Santa Clara Valley marveled at the wholesome opportunities for women and children to engage in productive labor on orchards and farms, by 1920, anti-Japanese forces lambasted Japanese families for "working the women and children in the fields," now considered to be an un-American, aberrant practice.

After World War I, the contest over who should cultivate the fields of California produced a renewed anti-Japanese movement, one that lauded a distinctly racialized brand of American family ideology. White exclusionists set on preserving American agriculture and protecting the "American farm home" made direct connections between race, gender, and control of the state's farmland. When the Supreme Court affirmed California's alien land law and ruled against sharecropping contracts in *Webb v. O'Brien* in 1923, many residents felt that the decision had resolved not only the Japanese threat to white farmers, but the entire anti-Japanese movement that had occupied the political life of the state for over two decades. The *San Jose Mercury Herald* praised the Court for "completely wiping out the last remnants of the Japanese problem in America" with its decisive blow to Japanese "attempts at pseudo-ownership" and related forms of "alien land danger."[96] By the mid-1920s, the barrage of legislated discrimination that grew out of the clamor over Japanese family farmers ultimately contributed to a climate of tolerance from which emerged a new understanding of the "Oriental Problem."

5

From Menace to Model

Reshaping the "Oriental Problem"

In the aftermath of the anti-Japanese movement, which peaked in 1920 with the passage in California of an alien land law much more stringent than earlier legislation, sociologists who studied race and immigration concluded that an "Oriental Problem" existed in America and sought to understand its causes and manifestations. They observed that although Asians had resided in the United States since the mid-nineteenth century, whites continued to discriminate against them legally, economically, and socially. The decade of the 1920s featured numerous events underscoring the "Oriental Problem" for researchers. The Supreme Court unswervingly upheld the constitutionality of the California Alien Land Law of 1920 in cases that included Santa Clara County–based *Webb v. O'Brien*, in which the Court affirmed the 1920 law that prohibited Japanese sharecropping arrangements. In *Ozawa v. United States* (1922), the Supreme Court shut the door on the possibility of naturalized citizenship for the Japanese in America on the grounds that no matter how assimilated or Americanized, Japanese were "not Caucasian" and therefore not qualified to become citizens. Again labeling the Japanese "aliens ineligible to citizenship" to justify discrimination against them, the Johnson-Reed Act, or the Immigration Act of 1924 banned Japanese immigration entirely, completing the federal government's decades-long process of total exclusion of Asiatic immigrants as a matter of policy.[1] In this environment, social scientists and their allies formed the Survey of Race Relations, an extensive research project that set out to determine the attitudes behind the clamor over "Orientals" in America. They found Santa Clara County to be one of the best research sites on the West Coast.

What researchers discovered was a new racial climate in which tightened alien land laws and Japanese exclusion paradoxically had enabled a shift in white perceptions of the Japanese in America from menace to proto-model minority. Central to this transformation was an emerging comparative ethnic and racial framework that by the mid-1920s frequently considered Asian immigrants to be less problematic and more industrious than other new immigrant groups, namely, southern Europeans and Mexicans. Living in an ethnically and racially diverse region that provided ample opportunities for inter- and intragroup comparisons, Santa Clara Valley residents found it nearly impossible to confine their discussion of race relations to native-born whites versus "Orientals" when their communities encompassed a more complex set of relationships.

Further contradicting and complicating any simplistic notion of the "Oriental Problem" was the emergence of positive stereotypes of American-born Chinese and Japanese. During the 1920s, Santa Clara Valley fruit growers, schoolteachers, students, researchers, and others articulated glowing views of Asian American children in defiance of the decade's reigning nativist sentiment. These positive images operated in conjunction with negative depictions of southern Europeans and Mexicans, as Asians received praise for possessing the very attributes other groups seemed to lack. Even if the Japanese parents of these children were reported to be sometimes "tricky and sly" and unreliable laborers, many whites commented on the intelligence and commendable deportment of the American-born youngsters. By the late 1910s, the visible presence of Japanese American children in the area had alarmed white residents enough to mount a campaign to drive Japanese farm families out of agriculture. In the mid-1920s, however, locals took a new view of young Asian Americans in their midst.

The subordinate position of first-generation Japanese farmers in the Santa Clara Valley and throughout California played no small part in facilitating more benign opinions of them and their offspring. In the 1920s the Issei fought to maintain their foothold in California agriculture, coping through constantly evolving farming arrangements and looking to the second generation to realize the promise of economic mobility on both practical and ideological levels.[2] As the "Valley of Heart's Delight" basked in its command of the national and international market for deciduous fruits during the prosperous decade preceding economic depression, the continued marginalization of the Japanese in agriculture contributed to a more favorable image of the community, and of "Orientals" in general.[3]

Decline of Japanese Agriculture

After several unsuccessful attempts to contest the legality of the 1920 Alien Land Law in *Webb v. O'Brien* and other court actions, Japanese farmers significantly altered their farming arrangements and employed new tactics to maintain their livelihoods, with "extreme variations from one community to another."[4] Perhaps the most common replacement for sharecropping contracts rendered illegal after 1923 was a method known simply as the foreman system, through which Issei farmers worked for whites as salaried employees in the true sense, not as a front for sharecropping or tenant farming, which also increasingly occurred. In the Santa Clara Valley, white landowners continued to hire Japanese as foremen on their ranches, as they had done well before the passage of alien land laws. During the 1920s, others decided to capitalize on growing business and industrial opportunities in the Valley, leaving the day-to-day management of farms to Japanese. In 1924, Stanford researcher Ruth Fowler reported that the father of a local schoolteacher she interviewed had trained a young Japanese man to handle his ranch as a foreman, a position he "attended successfully even to the shipping of produce," thus allowing the farm owner to devote his time to his real estate business. As employees of white landowners, however, Japanese foremen faced limited job security and restricted autonomy as farmers.[5]

In an exceptional case of foreman arrangements in the late 1920s, Japanese farmers did not work for a white employer, but received their salary from Chinese cannery owner Thomas Foon Chew, born in San Francisco to Chinese immigrants and thus able to own and lease land under the law. In 1921, Chew signed a six-year lease to farm the San Jose fruit ranch belonging to Swedish immigrant and longtime Santa Clara County resident John P. Nilson. The property had been farmed by Tsunejiro Iwasaki since 1910. Iwasaki's lease with Nilson officially expired at the end of 1918, but he continued to reside on the ranch with his family and was enumerated as Nilson's farm tenant in the 1920 census. Given the passage of the revised 1920 Alien Land Law, it is likely that Nilson and Iwasaki decided to protect their farming arrangements from legal prosecution by bringing in Chew as a lessee and naming Iwasaki the ranch foreman. When Iwasaki died of a stroke in December 1927, Chew appointed Heikichi Ezaki foreman of the orchard, planted mainly in pear and apple trees.

According to Takeshi "Tom" Ezaki, Chew knew little about farming and frequently consulted Heikichi, Tom's father, on matters related to the operation of the ranch. Ezaki delivered his pear crop to Chew's cannery in Alviso, and Chew reportedly shipped the ranch's apple crop to Hawaii and China. During harvest time, Ezaki supervised as many as 40 laborers, comprising Filipino and Portuguese workers. In 1929, Chew purchased 50 acres on Mount Pleasant Road in San Jose and placed Masami Ezaki, Heikichi's eldest son, in charge of an apricot orchard there.[6] During the 1920s, the Bayside Canning Company in Alviso and Chew's associated agricultural operations continued to foster remarkably intertwined relations among Asians of distinct ethnicities in the region.

Outside of the foreman system, Japanese families that had American-born adult children and wished to remain in agriculture after 1923 could continue to lease land from white residents for farming. At first few could avail themselves of this option, since in 1920 the number of Nisei eighteen years of age and older in the county was tiny, about 2.5 percent of all Japanese residents born in California. As Japanese American children turned eighteen during the 1920s, however, they gained the legal right to secure agricultural land, and documents of the county recorder show them doing so on behalf of their families. In October 1926, eighteen-year-old Suetsugu Ishikawa leased a parcel of land in Mountain View for berry and vegetable farming from George and Kate Pejare. Called "a single man a native born citizen of the United States" in the agreement, Ishikawa, the oldest of five children, all born in California, likely acted on behalf of his father Asikichi, who had emigrated in 1904. Having farmed in the Santa Clara Valley for over twenty-five years, the Ishikawas, by 1930, had saved enough of the family's earnings to purchase a ranch at Homestead and Saratoga-Alviso Roads. As an "alien ineligible to citizenship," Asikichi Ishikawa could not buy land and so relied on his oldest son to make the transaction.

In 1930, Suetsugu Ishikawa and his wife, Tsugiyo, who lived with Suetsugu's parents and siblings, purchased 40 acres of farmland from George Glendenning for $46,500, mortgaging all of the crops that would grow on the property from 1930 through 1939.[7] Masami Ezaki purchased 14.5 acres from Charles Nelson, son of John Nilson (the Nilson siblings went by the surname Nelson as adults) in 1936; in early 1942, at the age of twenty-one, Masami's brother Tom bought another 13.5 acres from Emma Nelson just before internment was under way. Only a few acres of this land were in the pear orchard their father had managed as Chew's foreman. Instead, the Ezakis farmed mostly vegetables, a mix of celery, beans, tomatoes, and peppers.[8]

Issei farmers shut out of California agriculture by law continued to rely on their American-born offspring to secure farmland that would generate income to support the entire family. A Nisei faced with a family situation similar to the Ishikawas', eighteen-year-old George Masato Ikeda signed a lease with C. H. and Jean Simonds in 1927 to rent 12.5 acres of land in Alviso for $500 per year over a term of four years. Unlike Suetsugu Ishikawa, Ikeda was not the oldest child in the family, but his elder brother, Isami, was born in Hawaii and thus may not have qualified as a U.S. citizen eligible to lease agricultural land. In 1930, George Ikeda, his parents Kakutaro and Umeno, his newlywed brother Isami and sister-in-law Masako, and another younger brother, Dickie, all resided on Alviso-Milpitas Road, just down the street from grower Frederick (Frank) Zanker, who had leased farmland to Japanese tenants as early as 1903. Most of their other nearby neighbors were Portuguese dairy and fruit farmers from the Azores. The fathers of George Ikeda and Suetsugu Ishikawa were both in their late fifties when, out of necessity, they turned over the responsibility of acquiring land for their families to farm to their American-born adult sons; both the older Issei men had emigrated from Japan at the turn of the twentieth century and had raised their families in the Santa Clara Valley.[9]

Nisei who attained the age of majority in the 1920s found themselves leasing land not only for their own parents, but for other members of the community as well. Hatsu Kanemoto, whose family farmed on Trimble Road in San Jose, recalled her father subleasing their farm from a Nisei acquaintance (a young man whose brother later became her husband), who in turn leased the land from the *hakujin* owner: "That's how we were able to farm. And that was the only way, you know, 'cause we weren't old enough to lease it." Kanemoto, the oldest of twelve children, was born in 1916 and would not have been eligible to lease farmland for her family until the mid-1930s.[10] Considering that the 1910s was the primary decade of Japanese immigrant family formation, most families in the Valley did not have American-born children over the age of eighteen with legal rights to tenancy in the 1920s. Moreover, since 85 percent of California-born Japanese in Santa Clara County were under ten years of age in 1920, the children of the vast majority of families would not turn eighteen in the near future, though by the 1930s, as the number of adult Nisei rose, more Japanese farmers employed this method of circumventing the 1920 legislation.[11]

To lease from someone who was not a close relation without the ability to legally record the transaction left Issei farmers vulnerable and living in uncertainty. "You would have to take a risk... and hope everything worked out," said I. K. Ishimatsu, a San Jose produce broker in the 1920s. He noted that Japanese farmers engaged in such an arrangement kept a separate "set of books...for inspection by the state authorities" to prove that they were working for wages, not farming leased land as prohibited under the law. The middleman, who could be any American citizen, not necessarily an older Nisei, had to hire the Japanese farmer as a manager or foreman to avoid prosecution. The Japanese farmer generally paid a brokerage fee for this service, either a flat sum, a percentage of the farmer's net profit, or a percentage of each acre leased. Ishimatsu remembered the "uneasy feeling" among members of the agricultural community, informed that "the punishment for alien land law violation was condemnation of all the subject's property and imprisonment."[12]

In some cases, white landowners used unwritten agreements with Japanese tenants to defy the 1920 land law and subsequent court decisions related to it. Instead of making arrangements through a middleman, the landowner and Japanese farmer entered two separate agreements, one a written public agreement stating the latter was hired as a foreman or employee on the owner's property, and the other a private, verbal agreement based on an understanding that the Japanese grower would cultivate the property as a cash or share tenant. As with the middleman arrangement, the two parties maintained parallel accounts through the duration of their agreement.[13] In this manner, J .J. O'Brien, of the

1923 Supreme Court case *Webb v. O'Brien*, and his family continued until 1942 to lease to Japanese farmers extensive acreage comprising land the O'Briens owned and rented from white neighbors. In defiance of the Supreme Court decision, O'Brien kept sharecropping arrangements with Jenzaburo Inouye and in fact expanded the acreage Inouye farmed beyond the 10 acres contested in *Webb v. O'Brien*. Not only did Inouye and his family grow berries and vegetables as court documents indicated, but also pears and prunes on a total of 54 acres. After a debilitating accident left him partially paralyzed in 1930, Inouye increasingly relied on his oldest child, Shigeo (Fred), to run the farm and support the large family. In 1932, twenty-one-year-old Shigeo Inouye signed an official lease for the family's farm. Three years later, his father died following a stroke.[14]

Residing elsewhere on O'Brien's tract were Katsusaburo Kawahara and his family, who in 1921 had moved there from a nearby truck farm on Hostetter Road in north San Jose. In the 1920s, the Kawaharas and other Japanese families paid O'Brien $40 an acre for rent in addition to a silent commission ranging from 3 to 5 percent of gross sales. Accepting those terms, Kawahara, who went on to become a celery specialist, farmed 40 acres for O'Brien in 1921, expanded his lease to 80 acres in 1927, and then to 150 acres. At the outset of World War II, he rented a total of 225 acres. Kotaro and Fude Omori had a similar long-term arrangement with O'Brien from 1924 until the war, farming celery, berries, cauliflower, and beans with a half-dozen other Japanese American families on a 200-acre tract located on Alviso Road.[15]

J. J. O'Brien died in 1939, and his son Jerry M. O'Brien took over the business arrangements with Japanese tenants. The younger O'Brien realized, according to Kawahara, "how much profit could be reaped from the Issei farmers." Kawahara suggested that J. J. O'Brien, a county tax collector and school trustee, had not feared prosecution because he was well acquainted with such prominent local officials as the chief of police and the district attorney. Indeed, white landowners' ability to influence county law enforcement officials to condone these verbal agreements was critical and explained why, for Japanese farmers across the state, such arrangements were "not always satisfactory nor everywhere possible."[16] Still, by devising new methods and strategies both within the ethnic community and in collaboration with amenable white landowners, Issei farmers maintained an enduring presence in California agriculture. In doing so, they also recast dominant racial discourses and saw themselves as "pioneers" in America who overcame political and legal obstacles to achieve the Japanese version of the American dream. By the late 1920s, Issei historians confidently narrated this teleology in their writings and forged a distinct ethnic identity that encompassed their evolving experiences with white racism.[17]

"Higher" and "Lower" Types

At the same time that Japanese residents in the Santa Clara Valley faced increasing difficulty in remaining viable in agriculture and, by the mid-1920s were navigating new strategies in response to legal restrictions, their white neighbors began to espouse more positive views of them. No longer threatened by the specter of Japanese farm families dominating California agriculture or becoming more numerous, many whites developed a more neutral impression of Asians in general. Among Santa Clara County residents, researchers discovered these new attitudes, shaped largely through interactions with Japanese immigrants in agriculture, included distinctions by class, a comparative framework measuring Asian ethnic groups against each other, as well as against Europeans, Mexicans, and even blacks, reflecting deeply rooted racial notions and foreshadowing new racial tensions in succeeding decades. Although rabid exclusionists like *Sacramento Bee* owner Valentine S. McClatchy continued to categorically deem Asian immigrants a detriment to the nation, many white Californians did not hold such extreme views. This was especially true of those who knew and worked with "Orientals" in various daily contexts or were able to evaluate Chinese and Japanese Americans alongside other ethnic immigrant groups. When they considered the issue of race relations, white residents in the Santa Clara Valley, being accustomed to its relatively heterogeneous population, could not limit their frame of reference only to Asian Americans. Above all, the shift in white views of the Japanese in California from menace to "model" workers and students coincided with renewed alien land laws and Japanese exclusion through the 1924 Johnson-Reed Act. Such discriminatory legislation had an obvious impact on the Japanese immigrant community, but it also was influential in reshaping white racial ideology.

A close examination of white perceptions of Japanese and other Asians in the Santa Clara Valley during 1920s is possible because of a social science research project called the Survey of Race Relations, initiated in 1923 by the Institute of Social and Religious Research, a New York–based organization of Protestant ministers inspired by Social Gospel ideals. Seeking to finance scientific research projects that served social reform goals, the Survey of Race Relations brought together a group of missionaries, sociologists, and other researchers interested in investigating racial attitudes toward Asians on the Pacific coast. Its administrative director, sociologist J. Merle Davis, who had been a missionary in Japan, wrote that the Survey's goal was to "supply all the racial facts on the two thousand-mile Pacific frontier from which a complete picture of the Orientals and their relationship to the whites could be gained."[18]

This ambitious project, involving most of the major universities on the West Coast and numerous sociologists, graduate students, and local investigators, along with hundreds of human subjects, collected a prodigious amount of data in the form of questionnaires, personal interviews, observation reports, life histories, and statistics. By the fall of 1924, the central office had received 640 reports, manuscripts, and case histories gathered by 265 researchers on regional, county, and city committees, yielding a total of approximately 6,000 typewritten pages.

Santa Clara County was one of nine California counties with an active Survey of Race Relations committee, and Stanford University administrators, faculty, and students came to play key roles in the project. Ray Lyman Wilbur, the university's president, was involved in the organization of the Survey from its inception, having been elected in August 1923 to the Survey's Executive Council for the Northern California district.[19] Social scientists based at Stanford believed that the Santa Clara Valley, with its sizable Asian presence, agricultural importance, and history of interest in race issues, presented an ideal location to study the Oriental Problem. Stanford economics professor Eliot Grinnell Mears served as the Survey's executive secretary and eventually published *Resident Orientals on the American Pacific Coast* in 1928, presenting and interpreting the Survey's findings.

One of the first intellectuals of Asian ancestry in the United States and a pioneering scholar of Asian American history, Stanford professor Yamato Ichihashi participated extensively in research panels and spoke at a tentative findings conference held on campus in March 1925. His 1932 book, a comprehensive study of Japanese immigrants, *Japanese in the United States*, drew considerably from Survey research materials. Collaborating with colleagues like Mears, economist Harry Alvin Millis, psychologist Edward K. Strong, and education specialist Reginald Bell, Ichihashi helped establish Stanford as a leading center for research on Asians in America.[20] Through the efforts of academics there and at other leading West Coast universities, the findings of the Survey became the basis of many published and unpublished sociological works on race relations. The Survey dissolved in 1926, owing to lack of funding and ideological differences between the missionaries and sociologists who supervised the effort.[21]

When surveyed about the "Oriental Problem" in the 1920s, numerous white inhabitants of Santa Clara County conveyed an unexpectedly nuanced view of Asians involving distinctions rooted in ethnicity and class, based primarily on a range of experiences with Asians as farmers and workers. Although certain ethnic and racial classifications recurred, such as the labeling of the Japanese as "unreliable" and the Chinese as "docile," along with an expressed preference for educated, elite Japanese over common farmers, there was hardly a monolithic categorization of Chinese and Japanese as the "yellow peril" among native-born, white citizens of Santa Clara County, who were far from fervent anti-Asian agitators. Over two-thirds of San Jose questionnaire respondents reported that they espoused a "friendly feeling toward the Oriental," while only 9 percent admitted they did not, and the rest were neutral or qualified their answers with remarks like "Chinese only," "under proper conditions," or "at a distance."[22] "Friendly feeling," however, was a somewhat empty term and belied a host of other sentiments about Asians.

Even as land laws were further marginalizing Japanese immigrant farmers in the local economy by the mid-1920s, positive views emerged when white Valley residents were questioned specifically about how the Japanese fared as agriculturists. This was not surprising, given that even at the height of the anti-Japanese movement, whites had conceded that Japanese immigrants were capable, industrious farmers, perhaps to their own detriment. When asked if "Orientals" were good farmers, close to 81 percent of San Jose respondents who answered the question replied affirmatively. A YWCA investigator in San Jose concluded from her conversations with orchardists that they respected Japanese labor: "All I have talked to say they find the Japanese utterly dependable, thrifty, exceedingly cleanly and morally straight." She observed it was "not an uncommon thing at all in this section" to find Japanese foremen who had worked on one ranch for twenty or thirty years, attesting to their skill and dependability, for, as she asked rhetorically, "Would they be kept if they had not given satisfaction?" In its 1925 tentative findings report, Survey of Race Relations social scientists pointed out that even banks shared this positive reaction to Japanese farmers and considered them "superior risks," readily approving loans and providing lower rates of interest.[23]

Many Santa Clara County agriculturists saw Japanese skill as on par with and sometimes exceeding that attributed to white laborers. A Stanford student who had been a longtime resident of the Valley reported that his family occasionally employed Japanese for gardening and other work, finding that they worked "harder and better than the unskilled white laborer." Still, the student opined that the Japanese were "often impertinent and presumptuous and consequently very irritating," revealing an expedient attitude that was prejudiced against the Japanese but simultaneously accepting of them as competent laborers. Another respondent who had worked with Japanese in orchards was less critical, noting that "except in certain cases of labor which demands excessive height and strength," he found Japanese workers "fully the equal of white labor." Extolling the virtues of Japanese agricultural labor, Stanford's Eliot Mears quoted a state chamber of commerce official who called the Japanese "undoubtedly...the best class of labor that ever reached America...obedient, energetic, careful to the minutest detail."[24]

Nevertheless, echoing attorney Louis Marshall's legal arguments in *Webb v. O'Brien* that Japanese farmers incurred ire for being "too industrious, too intensive and too efficient," some white growers continued to criticize Japanese agricultural methods as overly aggressive. Though most of the Santa Clara

County residents surveyed thought Asians were "good farmers," those who qualified their answers or responded negatively all held similarly dubious views
about Asian productivity: one said "yes, but they work the land very hard,"
others, "no, get good results but overwork the soil," and "no, overtax the land."
Santa Clara County growers agreed that Japanese and Chinese farmers produced
"more from the soil than any other race," but believed the downside of this
immense output was "how soon the land is depleted." A field investigator remarked that this was not true when Japanese owned the land they farmed and
suggested that they would "soon learn to rotate crops and work according to
approved methods."[25] But because alien land laws prohibited Japanese ownership of farmland, some of those consigned to leasing or sharecropping land did
not always see it as in their interest to preserve it.

White residents' positive opinions of Asians in agriculture carried over to
other forms of employment and business dealings. The Survey of Race Relations
found, from its San Jose questionnaire, that 41 of 121 respondents had employed
"Orientals," in reference mainly to Japanese, in some capacity, generally as farm
laborers, cooks, laundrymen, and domestics. Thirty-eight of those 41 employers
responded to a follow-up question asking "What sort of workman are they?"
Twenty-seven of the 38, or 71 percent, gave some variation of a positive answer,
such as "very good and dependable," "loyal and conscientious," and "as a rule
good." Two employers of Asians concluded there were "all sorts" and "good and
bad" workers. Of the respondents who had not employed Asians, almost 85 percent had a favorable impression of "Orientals" as workmen.[26]

For the most part, then, survey respondents who had employed Asians found
them to be "in housework, very good," "fine always," "good imitators," and "clean
and orderly" prune pickers. Unlike most residents who favored Chinese workers,
the manager of the Lyndon Hotel in Los Gatos expressed a preference for the
Japanese, giving the example of Boyson, a Japanese man who ran the furnace and
had helped with baggage. He had worked "longest and…steadiest" and had
taken only one vacation in seven years, spending one week in the summer "in a
peculiar way," helping a widower friend care for his two children." The hotel
manager, having showed measured admiration for Boyson's meticulous work
ethic and wholesome routine, was also struck by his Japanese worker's loyalty to
a friend in need.[27]

Despite vast improvement in white opinion of Japanese residents by the mid-
1920s, the Chinese still ranked higher in favorability. At a time when the Chinese
population of the county hovered at under 1,000 or about 0.5 percent of the
total residents and dropped with each decade until the 1960s, white respondents
answered as if they frequently employed and interacted with Chinese and could
vouch confidently for their superiority over the Japanese. Though San Jose police
chief J. N. Black declared to Survey of Race Relations interviewers that he

despised Chinese and Japanese alike and would like "mighty well to see San Jose rid of all Orientals as they are a source of trouble from the minute they arrive until they depart," the majority of questionnaire respondents expressed a marked preference for the Chinese over the Japanese in their midst. Eighty-seven individuals answered the question "Is there any distinction in the feeling between the Chinese and Japanese?" Of these respondents, 55 percent said they favored the Chinese, while only 5 or 6 percent preferred the Japanese. The rest did not believe there was a distinction between the ethnicities or did not specify which group they favored. Reiterating the nostalgic views of the Chinese in the wake of their population decline in the Valley, many described the Chinese as "more dependable," "more trustworthy," "honest," "reliable," and "better characters."

One of few respondents who acknowledged that not many Chinese were available for work in the 1920s wrote she had "always favored Chinese rather than Japanese, tho I now employ Japanese." Summing up the reasons for whites' overwhelming partiality for the Chinese, Fred Hanchett, a respondent who stated his support of "restrictive immigration," also conjectured "we have less to say about Chinese because there are not so many and are not as agressive [*sic*] as the Jap."[28] For residents like Hanchett and many others, absence did make the heart grow fonder as they pined for "honorable," subservient Chinese workers even when there were hardly any Chinese left in the Valley to hire.

While local whites generally had favorable impressions of Japanese residents as farmers and laborers, some leveled complaints against them that directly contrasted with the compliments paid to the Chinese and echoed criticisms expressed in the 1900s when Japanese first settled in the region. A Valley employer of Asians found "Chinese slow but diligent. Japanese working per diem need close watching. Contractors tricky." Among some white growers, Japanese laborers in the Santa Clara Valley developed a reputation for being "tricky and sly" and meeting obligations only as long as they were "receiving immediate benefits."

One Stanford student gave a bitter account of his family's experience with Japanese agricultural laborers: "At first they were good help and tried to please. Later at times when they were being relied on and they knew it they would take advantage of it and prove unsatisfactory and unreliable." Whites who had negative perceptions of Japanese laborers often grumbled about the duplicitous nature of these employees, who violated employers' trust presumably for selfish personal gain. Since the first off-putting incident, the student's family had hired Japanese for contract work, but again in those cases, "they will not live up to their bargain." He classified this behavior as racial, concluding, "Always a Jap no matter how long they have been in America."[29] Testifying to the dependence of Valley growers on Asian labor, even after several negative episodes with Japanese workers, the student's family continued to hire them to work on their ranch over a period of fifteen years.

Along these lines, some white employers were constantly frustrated by what they saw as Japanese workers' inherent inability to honor contracts in the "American" way. Another student recalled a time his family rented a cottage to a Japanese family for a year, but the Japanese household head "very soon after decided to move to a better cottage across the way." The student's family arranged for another Japanese to pick their almonds, but this worker "soon became discouraged and broke his contract." The same young respondent observed that these were common occurrences, and there were "many persons in the neighborhood who have had similar experiences with Japanese."[30]

A local teacher interviewed in November 1924 admitted with "considerable feeling" that his view of the Japanese was colored by his negative experiences with them as an employer. About twenty years ago, he had hired some Japanese on contracts to harvest prunes and concluded they were "untrustworthy workmen, sneaking out of work." Although this teacher found Japanese children to be "clean, obedient, and good students," the two-decades-old episode with "untrustworthy" Japanese prune pickers had so infuriated him that he "expressed a definite dislike" for "all Japanese other than children as pupils."[31] The violation of contracts strongly soured white residents' opinion of the Japanese, leading to ethnic stereotypes of Japanese as unreliable and deceitful.[32]

For the most part, these disapproving impressions of the Japanese were confined to the arena of agriculture and reflected a conspicuous class bias. Survey of Race Relations researchers found that Santa Clara County white residents distinguished between the Japanese they considered to be of a "higher class" and those of the lower class, usually associated with Japanese farmers. Survey participants and interviewees brought up the case of a young Japanese woman "who was reared in an American home in the county and married a Japanese," speaking of her "with the highest regard." They were referring to Misa Seki Okamoto, a Japanese woman adopted as a small child by the Whitneys, a well-to-do San Francisco merchant family who settled in the affluent western Santa Clara Valley town of Saratoga. Okamoto was reportedly liked by her neighbors and "exceedingly attractive to look upon or to talk with" to the point that "All who meet her are charmed and usually say, 'if only all [Japanese] were so attractive.' "[33] Okamoto was raised by white parents, educated at Bryn Mawr College, and studied music in Europe, all factors that set her far apart from the mass of Japanese residing in the Valley.

Some of those who answered the Survey of Race Relations' "Public Opinion of the Oriental in San Jose" questionnaire articulated this class distinction in their responses to the question of whether they would mind "living in such close proximity" to "Orientals." A minister from San Jose replied, "No if they were cultured, educated and intelligent. Yes (triple underline) if they were ignorant or shiftless," plainly contrasting "higher class" Japanese like Misa Okamoto with common laborers. Others expressed similar class biases in considering whether they would accept Asian neighbors: a Mrs. L. Chandler said she would "not prefer to," but "if necessary would not object to those of the educated class," while another survey respondent presented a similar view, writing, "yes and no. If higher type, no. If lower type, yes."[34] For these residents, vague notions of class status trumped exclusionary sentiments based solely on race.

The results of the questionnaire researcher Ruth Fowler administered to Stanford students further revealed the class distinction that existed in the minds of white residents and indeed produced "classification difficulties": rather than viewing Japanese Californians as a monolithic bloc, respondents consistently spoke in terms of "two outstanding classes of Japanese in Santa Clara County, the working group and the cultured class." Thus when asked their opinion of the Japanese, some residents called to mind "the dwellings of the farming Japanese seen in the valley," and others referred to contacts with "fellow students and pro-fessors." At least two students spoke from their experience with a Japanese fac-ulty member at Stanford, likely referring to history professor Yamato Ichihashi. One recounted that a Japanese professor "has been a most unselfish friend and advisor to me. He is an example of what education and culture can do for many of our Japanese." A female student mentioned having contact with "a Professor [Japanese], and his wife, attending his classes, and meeting them at dinner in the home," and reported to Fowler that "they are people of refinement and culture, and their relationship with us could be nothing but favorable," again pointing to the acceptance of elite Japanese in the Valley. The respondent stressed she answered the survey questions about race relations with the professor and his wife in mind, "and not the class of Japanese who with our own Americans main-tain a lower status of living conditions." Fowler concluded that "thought of one group alone brought one response, thought of both tended to confuse the answer." Overall, survey respondents expressed the desire to maintain dis-tance from rural Japanese in the Valley, the "skilled intensive farmers living in humble cottages or shacks."[35]

Beyond class distinctions, many Santa Clara County residents in the mid-1920s frequently compared Japanese immigrants with southern Europeans, with a significant number stating an explicit partiality toward the Japanese and against Europeans. Even though the Survey's San Jose questionnaire sought to elicit res-idents' opinions about "the Oriental," responses were peppered with comments about Italians, Portuguese, and Slavic immigrants. Concurring with the prevail-ing sentiment that the Japanese were respectable agricultural workers, one Survey respondent who had worked with some Japanese in the Valley's orchards wrote that he would "much prefer having Japanese for orchard and farm work than I would Southern Europeans who have immigrated recently." One resident who bought fruits and vegetables from Japanese vendors claimed they were "much more honest than the Mediterranean nationalities." Another expressed an even stronger, anti-Semitic preference for Asians over European immigrants, characterizing the Japanese as "always polite, amicable, and pleasant to do business with," and telling his interviewer, "In our family we always patronize Japanese fruit stands in preference to those run by dirty, cheating Jews."[36]

The passage of the Johnson-Reed Act in May 1924 kept the topic of immigration on the minds of many local white citizens and predisposed them to intergroup comparisons, as the law severely reduced the numbers of southern and eastern Europeans allowed to enter the United States and excluded Japanese immigrants entirely. Editors of the *Daily Palo Alto Times* celebrated President Coolidge's signing of the federal immigration bill, proclaiming the desirability of "Northern Europeans" as immigrants "rather than the Mediterranean peoples" who would be restricted by quotas.[37] Though the *Times* editors also lauded the exclusion of "Asiatics" under the law, some county residents did not find Asians as objectionable as Italians. One female resident ranked Asians above Italians, calling the former "industrious and honest, much more than the Italian," while another respondent stated that Asians' "standard of living, sanitation, etc. are not on a level with ours," but followed with the remark, "However—they are no more undesirable than Italians!" These responses reflected two common attitudes of Valley residents who made the European vs. Oriental comparison: some found Asians preferable to Italians, Jews, and other recent European immigrants, while other nativist types judged the groups to be equally undesirable.[38]

Just as Santa Clara County residents and researchers in the 1920s tended to measure Asians against southern Europeans, they also made comparisons of Asians and Mexicans with increasing regularity. In this case, however, the unanimous opinion was that "Orientals" far outranked Mexicans, who were viewed as an impending racial and social menace despite possessing the legal status of "white."[39] Hundreds of thousands fled Mexico after the outbreak of Mexican Revolution in 1910, many ending up in agricultural regions with seasonal labor demands, like the Santa Clara Valley. Between 2,689 and 4,239 Mexicans and Mexican Americans resided in San Jose in 1930, comprising 4.7–7.4 percent of the city's total population. The abandoned, infertile East Side of San Jose became the demographic center of Mexicans in the Valley beginning in the 1920s, though new arrivals found "few longstanding Mexican American residents, no established Mexican American middle class, and no identifiable Mexican neighborhood."[40]

White growers in the Valley were first to express their revulsion at the prospects of Mexican farm laborers replacing Asians on their ranches. In 1920, J. J. McDonald, president of the Santa Clara County Farm Owners' and Operators' Association, spoke on behalf of the area's farmers when he criticized the U.S. government for "bringing into this country car load after car load of Mexican labor to replace the

Japanese," claiming with exasperation that Mexicans were "the poorest class of labor on the face of the earth."[41] McDonald was not alone in conveying his disgust for Mexican workers, who elicited far more ire than southern Europeans among county residents. Survey of Race Relations interviewer Ida Case learned that when Valley orchardists and berry growers imagined the day that Mexicans would replace the Japanese in the fields if the latter left California (presumably because of alien land laws and other exclusionary legislation), they "raise their hands in horror and say 'Then may the Lord preserve us for we'd rather have ten thousand Japs any day that [*sic*] one thousand Mexicans.'"[42]

Social scientists' positive racial construction of Asian immigrants, the Japanese in particular, evolved in tandem with their disparaging views of Mexicans in California. Although most whites continued to consider both Asians and Mexicans to be foreign and inferior, by the mid-1920s, nativist concerns about the Japanese presence in California had been assuaged through legislation curbing their immigration, circumscribing their livelihood in agriculture, and reaffirming their ineligibility for U.S. citizenship. Meanwhile, the Johnson-Reed Act conceded to Southwestern growers by enacting no numerical quotas on Mexican immigration, even as the construction of Mexicans as consummate illegal aliens was cemented in border enforcement policy and popular discourse.[43]

In his report on Santa Clara County schools, William C. Allen underscored the superiority of Asians over other "alien peoples" in California. Allen, a Quaker civic leader from San Jose, had been recruited by the Survey to conduct field research in the Valley's public schools. On the drive from Alviso to Milpitas, Allen's chauffeur pointed out "5 Mexicans lying in the field, while near to them one man was working, whom he declared apparently was a Japanese although he was not sure."[44] Allen, though, was fairly sure that this picture was worth a thousand words, or at least supported his disdain for idle Mexicans and admiration for the hard-working Japanese. Grower J. J. McDonald expressed his views without ambiguity: "Give a Mexican $5 and he is through work, ready to gamble and lay off until it is spent." Allen and his chauffeur likely would have agreed with this condescending characterization, easily imagining that the five Mexicans lying in the field were "through work" and looked forward to gambling away their earnings or engaging in some other vice. Summarizing the opinions of the growers she interviewed, Ida Case stated the established view among them: "The Japs are law abiding, polite, courteous, thrifty and industrious but the Mexicans obey no laws and are mentally, morally and physically inferior to all Orientals." The racialization of labor kept ethnic Mexicans out of key industries in San Jose, including canneries, solidifying their low-ranking position as construction workers and seasonal farm laborers during the 1920s.[45]

While sociologists frequently commended the Chinese and Japanese, by the mid-1920s they also displayed a palpable racial bias against Mexicans, proclaiming them to be an inferior people who threatened to create problems for California and other western states on the scale of upheaval that the importation and continued enslavement of Africans had ultimately wrought in America. The published findings report of the Survey did not attempt to hide researchers' contempt for Mexicans when contrasting them with "Orientals": "The Mexican, on the other hand, is one of the most disorderly of immigrant population[s] and has only the most primitive organizations for mutual aid and protection." Survey of Race Relations director and famed University of Chicago sociologist Robert Park called "these people," referring to Mexicans, "not so ambitious."[46] Social scientists spoke admiringly, however, of self-sufficient "Oriental" communities and Asians' absence from the rolls of those requiring social services. J. Merle Davis, the Survey's administrative director, stated that the roster of the Santa Clara County Poorhouse for the five-year period ending in June 1924 "contained the name of no Japanese and but one Chinese," and the sheriff had informed him that no Japanese had ever been admitted to the poorhouse in forty years, reflecting advanced forms of "mutual aid and protection" purportedly absent from Mexican communities.

In a proposal to the California Development Association in 1924, Robert Park also called Mexicans a "primitive people," warning that importing them into a "highly organized society" would result in a "penalty" for that society. He made an intriguing historical analogy, likening the Pacific coast to the antebellum South in the age of slavery: "[African slaves] seemed to be at the time an economic necessity, but they created a social problem."[47] Social scientists like Park in essence felt that Mexican immigrants represented a backward, "primitive," population not unlike African American slaves had been, and the "importation" of Mexicans for labor might prove as costly a mistake as the slave trade had been for the nation.

Such discussion generated an unusual slippage in racial stereotypes, with Mexicans and "negroes" viewed as similarly inferior and equally problematic for California, even when the latter group did not populate the state in any significant numbers.[48] The Survey interviewer Ida Case commented that the people of the Santa Clara Valley were beginning to realize that if the Japanese left, "a much inferior type of labor will take his place." Based on the negative comments Case elicited from growers regarding Mexicans, readers would naturally assume she was speaking of them as the "much inferior" labor. Yet without much basis for the statement, she cautioned, "The Japanese is taking the place of the negro in the cotton fields of the south and the result is that the negro is coming here to take the place of the Jap."[49]

But African American sharecroppers did not figure in the perceived "race problem" of California, since few blacks migrated to Santa Clara County or anywhere else in California prior to World War II. Nor did Japanese move to the

American South in droves to work in cotton fields. Case's worst-case scenario of "inferior" labor overtaking her home region to replace the departing Japanese, however, reflected a common racial fear that lumped blacks and Mexicans together as undesirables. The fear of these more objectionable nonwhites arriving in California made some whites embrace Asians as an "acceptable" minority group.

The report of the Survey's tentative findings concluded that the social costs of Mexican immigration in terms of poverty, disease, and crime were too high and that Mexican farm laborers did not compensate for the trouble they caused to California and its citizens.[50] William C. Allen, who had surveyed the public schools in the Valley, complained that Mexicans in California made "trouble and expense for the state because they are constantly getting into jail and the hospital." Native-born whites had a long history of blaming immigrants for tracking a host of diseases into the country, and beginning in the 1920s, they focused on Mexicans, who were supposedly "bringing disease into every city where they are stationed."[51] Whereas in the nineteenth century, Chinese immigrants and Chinatown had been the targets of San Francisco health authorities' campaigns, by the 1920s, sociologists concurred with public officials who homed in on Mexicans as purveyors of disease, asserting that Chinese and Japanese rarely suffered from "nervous diseases" and "circulatory diseases." Allen reminded readers that a recent outbreak of "the bubonic plague in Los Angeles...was in the Mexican quarter," and that Mexicans had introduced a smallpox epidemic into Oakland and were also bringing trachoma into California.[52]

In the process of making such anti-Mexican claims, social scientists and other commentators pointed to Asians, particularly Japanese, as a more tolerable, even desirable, nonwhite group, with vast agricultural skills and experience, and a perceived lack of social problems in their communities, indeed a "model minority" in the making. Valley whites' distinctive racialized characterizations of "Orientals" became more layered and refined as interactions increased, predicated on ethnic and class distinctions. The historical record left by Survey of Race Relations sociologists and researchers reveals that in the mid-1920s, white residents and intellectuals mutually constructed new ethnic and racial stereotypes of Asians that were strikingly different from blatant anti-Asian attitudes of the past.[53] The presence of American-born Japanese children, who began to come of age in the 1920s, would further solidify the growing positive view of Asians in the Santa Clara Valley and throughout California.

From Race Menace to Model Students

Speaking of her grade school days in San Jose during the 1920s, Hatsu Kanemoto called to mind the reputation she and her Nisei peers developed among whites:

"I remember we were respected by the *hakujin*, as hard working, industrious, studious, and some of the cleanest kids in school." Just as the image of their parents shifted from socioeconomic threat to acceptable, even ideal immigrant residents by the mid-1920s, the American-born sons and daughters of Japanese farmers and agricultural laborers became viewed as model schoolchildren in academics and deportment. Researchers cited a plethora of observations and opinions about Japanese pupils in Santa Clara County schools, with "desirable behavior patterns...reported in almost all cases," while county teachers describing their Japanese charges as "'sweet, clean, little children' who were studious, bright, courteous, and kind."[54] The county supervisor of schools declared that there were no cases of truancy among the Japanese and Chinese, and that these students gave her the "least trouble" of all children.

At San Jose High School, where the only male honor student in 1925 was reportedly a Japanese American, a geometry problem stumped all students "except a Japanese boy who finally mastered it." Educators expressed their amazement at the impressive combination of intellect and obedience to authority displayed by Nisei students. Teachers at a segregated, heavily Japanese school near Agnew were "most enthusiastic about the Japanese and say they would not exchange places with another teacher any where." One respondent to Fowler's questionnaire also spoke from her experiences as a schoolteacher to deduce that Japanese were "almost invariably earnest, serious-minded and studious, ungentlemanly conduct was most rare and was learned from their American playmates."[55] The discussion surrounding the second generation in the 1920s represented an early historical incarnation of the Asian "model minority" stereotype, made possible in part by the legislative exclusion and economic marginalization of the Japanese in America.

As with general observations about the local Issei population, white residents of the Santa Clara Valley formed their impressions of second-generation Japanese Americans in a comparative ethnic context, building on triangulated comparisons of Asians with southern Europeans and Mexicans. When asked how they felt about "Oriental children being in school with your children," a number of questionnaire respondents made negative allusions to Europeans. One man from San Jose replied that for his children, racially integrated schools would be no worse "than having the scum of Southern Europe in school with them." Resident Phineas Lyon made a similar comment more euphemistically, saying, "It would be as satisfactory as association with the children of certain classes of Europeans." A childless woman who responded to a survey answered that if she had children, she would not object to them being in school with Asians, because she found "other classes of foreigners much more objectionable."[56] The non-Asian "foreigners" she had in mind were likely Italians, who comprised the largest foreign-born population in San Jose during the 1920s.

When William C. Allen visited several integrated Santa Clara County schools with diverse immigrant populations in the spring of 1925, his overwhelming impression was of Japanese and Chinese schoolchildren as bright, model students, while Portuguese, Spanish, and other European immigrant children lagged behind, some on the verge of delinquency. His methodology consisted of tabulating the ethnic composition of student bodies and soliciting commentary from teachers and principals. At Midway School, about 5 miles from San Jose, a teacher told Allen the Japanese were "the most obedient and controllable in and out of school" and got along "wonderfully" because "they apply themselves well." Allen learned that of the six Slavonian students (individuals of Croatian or Serbian background from the southern part of what was then Yugoslavia), only "one is good"; he was further told that the Portuguese were "not so very bright," and the Spanish were "backward." Except for two Spanish children, all the students at Midway were believed to be native born.[57]

Allen proceeded to visit a school in Alviso, which Bayside Canning Company owner Thomas Foon Chew had opened to educate the children of his cannery workers, most of whom were Chinese and Japanese. The Alviso school had an enrollment of 91 students: "29 Japanese, 20 Chinese, 16 Spanish and Mexicans, 15 Portuguese, 4 English or Canadian descent, 3 Mexicans, 3 Scandinavians, 1 Irish-Spanish."[58] In the primary class, where Allen was charmed by a teacher he called "an American girl of delightful personality," there were 13 Chinese and 10 Japanese students and smaller numbers of children of other ethnicities. The teacher ranked the Asians as doing "the best work" and reported that they "give the least trouble, they have good home control, they dress well, have good rubber boots and warm clothing in winter."

The correlation between family life and student performance reappeared in commentary by educators and social science researchers, who praised Asian "home control" and simultaneously derided southern European parenting skills. An English youngster came "next to the Orientals as to the above attributes," followed by a Scandinavian, a Spanish-American, and some Mexican students. The Portuguese, who many educators unfailingly characterized as poor students, ranked last in this class. Observations of the intermediate class at Alviso confirmed the same hierarchy "as far as racial comparisons could be made."[59]

The inferiority of Portuguese children as students, and the converse superiority of "Oriental," namely, Japanese children, remained consistent themes as Allen trekked to Milpitas School, north of San Jose. Portuguese children comprised 100 of the 150 students enrolled, reflecting the significant population in Santa Clara County of Portuguese engaged primarily in farming fruits and vegetables for the San Francisco market on the outskirts of San Jose. Portuguese immigration to Santa Clara County rose most dramatically in the 1910s and 1920s, with many farmers eventually becoming major landowners. The San

Francisco Bay Area was home to 55 percent of the state's Portuguese population in 1910, and Santa Clara County was the only California county that did not experience a decline in its Portuguese foreign-born population from 1880 to 1930.[60] Of the 50 non-Portuguese students at Milpitas School, there were 20 Japanese, and a hodgepodge of "mixed Spanish and Mexicans," Italians, French, Filipinos, Puerto Ricans, Irish, English, a Canadian, and just one child of "old American stock."

To Allen's question, "Are the Japanese keener than the others?" the principal responded, "Absolutely." When asked if they were obedient, the principal made the same reply, adding that "The Japanese children let nothing detract their attention from the work at hand.... They have the power of concentration." A young teacher remarked of the Japanese at Milpitas, "To tell the truth they are far ahead of the others." One Japanese boy was reportedly two years ahead of his class. The consensus among educators was that Japanese students displayed an almost uncanny academic ability that put them far above others, especially those of certain European nationalities.

In contrast, schoolteachers and administrators deemed the Portuguese at Milpitas School totally lacking in motivation and discipline. The principal informed Allen that a dismal 6 percent of the Portuguese went on to high school, and worse yet, "many of the children of the higher grades spend their evenings in Milpitas up to 10 or 11 o'clock playing cards and pool." Even though he could have guessed the answer, Allen asked the principal whether Japanese children did this. Predictably, the principal replied no.[61]

Aside from the Portuguese, Italian children were often singled out as a "burden" to the schools and to the county in general, contrasted with model Japanese students (incidentally, because Allen visited schools in the vicinity of San Jose but not within city limits, he encountered few Italian students.) During the 1920s, residents believed that organized crime was on the rise and blamed Italians, long viewed as perpetrators of violence and lawlessness.[62] In San Jose and Santa Clara County, observers tried to discern a pattern of criminality among Italian youth, often through ethnic comparisons. San Jose was the fourth largest center of Italian settlement in California during the early twentieth century. The number of Italians in Santa Clara County tripled between 1900 and 1910, the decade of the greatest growth in the total number of Italians in California.[63]

Ruth Thayer Wilson, a candidate for a master's degree at Stanford, researched the records of the San Jose Juvenile Court from 1928 to 1932, attempting to correlate the city's neighborhoods with rates of delinquency. Her implicit hypothesis suggested that foreigners or children of foreign-born parents were more likely to be delinquents. In the course of her research, Wilson made a specific case for *Italian* delinquency, not foreign-born delinquency in general. Wilson, who completed her thesis in 1934, discovered that although only 11 percent of the general population of San Jose was of "Italian parentage," 23.5 percent of delinquents were. She concluded that Italian children were more prone to criminality than children of other ethnicities.[64]

At the same time, Survey administrator J. Merle Davis provided a counterpoint about Asian children sounding very much like a precursor to the "model minority" image of Asians that would emerge in mainstream culture several decades later. Davis recounted an examination of the books of the Probation Office of Santa Clara County from 1920 to 1924. The records revealed that among hundreds of cases of delinquency involving children under eighteen, "not a child of Oriental parentage was listed."[65] In the midst of the Valley's farms and orchards, a picture of smart and well-behaved Asian children emerged during the 1920s alongside one of law-breaking Italian kids on the road to lives of crime.

From all they heard and observed about cards-and-pool-playing Portuguese teenagers, Italian juvenile delinquents, and studious, law-abiding Japanese students, researchers concluded that the behavior of children was naturally linked to their parents. Chicago School sociologists in the 1920s believed that ultimately, "social conditions, not racial traits, produced criminals," concluding as sociologist John Landesco did in his 1928 book *Organized Crime in Chicago*, "the gangster is the product of his surroundings in the same way in which a good citizen is a product of his environment." Parents, then, were a crucial part of those social conditions and surroundings.

William C. Allen found patterns of what he considered to be poor parenting "duplicated in many other schools, especially where the parentage of the children has been foreign." At Milpitas School, for example, the principal said in regard to the "slacker" Portuguese, "One of the things we are up against is the home life. The parents do almost nothing for the children and pass them over to us."[66] According to this view, parental negligence explained why Portuguese teens frequented pool halls in Milpitas instead of studying. Walter Bachrodt, superintendent of the San Jose schools in the 1920s, also highlighted the problem of absent, neglectful parents among some "foreign" families, noting how a social worker who surveyed Italian neighborhoods in San Jose discovered that parents employed at the canneries had left their children "at home or to run the streets and within a limited space," and hundreds of local children had "no supervision of any kind." Fortunately for the neglected Italian kids, "a few energetic and wide awake women attacked this problem" and implemented a successful program of "supervised play" during the summer of 1921 at Grant School, one of the poor-performing, overwhelmingly Italian schools in the San Jose district.[67]

Even though her research found that delinquent children did not generally come from families with divorced parents, Stanford researcher Wilson posited that the "home situation" for many of the crime-prone Italian youth "might be extremely unpleasant and yet there be no hint of it in the data which we are dealing" because two-thirds of the foreign-born fathers of this delinquent group were "Italians and Catholics," and thus unlikely to divorce.[68] Social scientists concurred that the dysfunctionality of southern European immigrant families, whether the specific culprit was inattentive parenting or unpleasant "home life," accounted for the lackluster performance of the American-born children at school and led to more serious social problems.

Unlike Japanese exclusionists of the early 1920s, who blasted Japanese family life and Issei farm families in particular, social science researchers praised the family system and values of "Orientals" in producing obedient and studious children. In stark contrast to the perceived negligence of Italian and Portuguese parents, Case noticed that "parental devotion" was a "marked characteristic of the Japanese. The care and attention given the children is wonderful. Rarely does one find insubordination cropping out in Japanese homes."[69] Feeding a different stereotype of Japanese families than anti-Japanese agitators, sociologists in the 1920s presented to the public an image of orderly, structured families made up of attentive parents and well-behaved children who were hardly ever "insubordinate." The implication was that Japanese parents would never allow their children to run amok unsupervised, like the Italians, or leave them to play cards and pool on school nights, like the Portuguese.

Figure 5.1. Grant School, San Jose, seventh grade class, 1925, including students of Chinese, Japanese, and Italian ancestry.
Courtesy of Connie Young Yu.

The rhetoric of family values continued to mark racial difference, whether negative or positive. Fowler also took a comparative view of parental control, stating that it was "greater among the Chinese and Japanese in the county than among other immigrant groups." Of course, there were always exceptions. One of Stanford doctoral candidate Charles N. Reynolds's survey respondents, a young man acquainted with a Chinese student who played on his rival high school's football team, reported that his Chinese friend's home life as "terrible" because his parents were florists who "worked in the store all day," leaving their son to play "about the street since his babyhood."[70] Speaking from direct personal contact and not as a theorizing social scientist, this respondent provided a frank perspective that countered the emerging construction of model Asian families.

J. Merle Davis, who found the lack of Asian juvenile delinquents in Santa Clara County especially impressive, hypothesized further that the culture of the "Oriental immigrant," which imparted social control and self-discipline, led to these notable results. Doctorate-wielding sociologists saw higher education attainment as a mark of success and were fixated on the high proportion of college-bound "Oriental" children, which Davis attributed to Asian immigrant parents' belief that education "must be had at all costs for their children." In an undisguised jab at certain Europeans and perhaps Mexicans, Davis declared that taken together, Asian parental discipline, social control, and emphasis on education offered "a striking contrast to the experience of the Pacific Slope in dealing with other immigrant groups with which the Oriental has lived side by side."[71]

The investigation of the "Oriental Problem" during the 1920s frequently devolved into a comparative discussion of "other" immigrants, replete with derogatory characterizations of southern Europeans. It came full circle to laud Asians for their academic prowess and exemplary families, ironically contrasting with inflammatory nativist rhetoric focusing on the deviance of Japanese immigrant families that had pervaded California just a few years before.

Indicative of the chasm between the vitriol of the anti-Japanese movement and the ensuing tremendously positive perception of Japanese American children, sociologists researching the "Oriental Problem" in the 1920s identified a related issue that both intrigued and vexed them: the so-called second-generation problem. Linked to Robert Park's "marginal man" theory, which saw the children of immigrants as caught between the Old and New Worlds, researchers roughly defined this problem as the situation of American-born Asians who were unjustly treated for "all intents and purposes, as if they were alien Orientals." As sociologist William Carlson Smith of the University of Southern California pointed out in 1925, this characterization was unjust because these young people "are Oriental in appearance but not in reality . . . [they] speak the best of English and betray not the slightest foreign accent; they can use the latest slang and make humorous plays upon English words. . . . These persons have the ideas, ideals, sentiments and attitudes of the American and not of the Oriental."[72] The second-generation children of Asian immigrants, sociologists felt, had taken on American ways to an admirable extent, yet they faced constant discrimination in unenlightened white society. Frustrated that white native-born Americans seemed oblivious to the plight of several thousand Japanese and Chinese boys and girls who were American citizens, the researchers saw their job as bringing the situation to the general public's attention and sharing the results of their investigation of "the most interesting and fascinating problem of any racial group."[73]

The "second-generation problem" surfaced in white residents' observations of social distance between the races, even among those who praised the Japanese as students, as reflected in Fowler's and Reynolds's extensive interviews and surveys of white young adults in the county. Reynolds spoke with a young man who noted the integrity and academic aptitude of the Japanese boys he knew from school, saying, "All the Japs I have known have been very decent fellows. They have been very bright in school and have usually run very high in the class standing." Notwithstanding these compliments, he preferred to "like and admire" the Japanese "from a distance" and found them "tricky but not very unsanitary."[74] Similarly, a female respondent expressed positive but guarded attitudes toward the Japanese, noting that she had always found the ones in her classes "conscientious, brilliant, and not at all presuming." Although they had "never been more than polite" and she had "nothing against them," this young woman would not accept the Japanese "on an absolute place of equality."

Fowler, who taught at Santa Clara Union High School for a number of years in the 1920s and 1930s while working on her master's thesis, observed that white students respected their Japanese peers academically, but when it came to "social activities," the Japanese were "thoughtlessly forgotten," even as they were sought "as study companions in a comradie-fashion." Her experience with Japanese students bore out William Carlson Smith's observation that despite American-born Asians' adaptation to their surroundings, "the young people are not given full entrée into the white group."[75]

Nonetheless, recollections of friendships between whites and Asians as children and teenagers revealed significant degrees of closeness. A woman whose children had attended the predominantly Japanese Jefferson School near Agnew for several years and had a daughter who was "absolutely devoted to her Japanese playmates" told Case that when her little girl transferred to a school in town, "she cried and cried and when asked what the matter was replied—'Oh why won't they let me go back to school with my friends.'" This mother, who also employed a number of Japanese laborers and foremen to run her ranch, appeared to be quite open to her children's contact with Japanese friends, who she characterized as "keen as whips and eager to learn everything possible," in addition to being kind, considerate playmates. She recalled that she "never saw such care as was given to her children by the Japanese" on the playground at Jefferson.[76]

As children grew older, however, interracial friendships tended to become more complicated and circumscribed. At the high school where she taught, Fowler noted quite frequently a Japanese boy or girl became "a fairly close friend of some of the Caucasian students, (always of their own sex) but not with the socially ambitious, of course."[77] Reynolds interviewed one young man who in his high school years befriended a fellow football player who happened to be Chinese, expressing tremendous respect for "the clean way of playing he had, and the good sportsmanship he displayed at all times," but appeared to have held his Chinese friend at arm's length. One Stanford student who responded to Fowler's survey recalled being friends with two Japanese boys in high school, who "mingled with other boys freely, ate lunch with them, played tennis, and so on." Despite these friendly interactions, the white student commented that the Japanese were "rather shy about getting into things socially as, I think, all of them are."[78]

Concerns about "amalgamation" came to the fore in these discussions of white-Japanese relations in the county's schools, as Japanese boys in particular understood that there was an unspoken rule restricting contact with white female peers. At Santa Clara Union High School, Fowler observed of the 10 or more Japanese boys and girls there (out of a total enrollment of 350), "none ever joined in the dancing except Japanese girl with Japanese girl." One of these girls served punch during a dance given by her class, and her family even came to watch, but it seemed that she did not actually take part in the dancing. Japanese boys, from a variety of comments, for the most part did not attend the dances at all. One student from a small town in the Valley recalled that a Japanese boy took part "in everything except dances, as the [white] girls' parents draw the line at that." Another Stanford student wrote of a popular Japanese high school boy who "was treated exactly as if he were 'white.'" The student said tellingly, "Although he talked and joked with the girls, he never appeared at dances, and I do not think the girls would have cared to dance with him if he had. He was not an exception. There were two other Japanese of the same type in the school."[79] To avoid both conflict and embarrassment relating to the intermixing taboo, these Japanese boys chose not to participate in school dances, though some were involved in all other aspects of school life.

Despite the many positive characteristics attached to second-generation Chinese and Japanese of Santa Clara County, for most white residents, the prospect of intermarriage or sexual contact between whites and Asians was consistently met with repulsion.[80] Fowler found that all but one of the participants in her survey who answered questions on "amalgamation" opposed it. Reynolds interviewed a white male who expressed his concerns over gender and race boundaries more explicitly, stating he would not care "to have the Chinaman mix socially with the women members of my family.... I abhor the idea of intermarriage between them and members of my own race. Whenever I read of the marriage of a white with a member of a race of another color, I have a feeling of sickening disgust." The same respondent, however, also said that "in strictly masculine company," he could consider "the Chinaman as my social equal."[81] This delineation partly explained the presence of numerous same-gender friendships between whites and Asians in school, but the lack of any interracial male-female relationships. The arrival of Filipino laborers in the Valley and their alleged tendencies to seek out white women kept the issue of miscegenation in the public eye during the 1930s, though attention no longer focused on Chinese and Japanese.

The presence of mixed-race Asian-white children posed a concern for a number of residents who adhered to the intermarriage taboo. Fowler interviewed a teacher who told her that some mixed-race children attending the school who "looked neither Japanese nor Nordic" were universally "shunned by American and Japanese children," though she knew "no actual facts" about the parentage of these children. A prominent white farmer in the Valley confirmed that biracial children would be ostracized by both races. "Children from such marriages would have no standing with whites or Japs.... California is a white man's country at present," he said. "Let's keep it as such."[82]

Although Survey sociologists did no extensive research on intermarriage and "hybrid" children in Santa Clara County, Davis, Park, and others focused on this question elsewhere. Documents relating to sex between Asians and whites made up about 10 percent of the approximately 400 life histories and interviews collected, as sociologists believed the examination of these relationships was "of great consequence for the future of American society." The products of these contacts were children who were both "American" and "Oriental" in culture, suggesting that intermarriage could be the ultimate solution to racial conflict in America.[83] Nevertheless, as the examples from Santa Clara County show, public reaction to the issue proved to be so inflammatory in the 1920s that sociologists could hardly advocate such a view.

The 1920s marked a period of transition in racial perceptions in the Santa Clara Valley. Through decades of interaction with local Chinese and Japanese populations, white residents on the whole had become more accepting and even admiring of Asians as laborers and farmers. The small numbers of Asian residents in the Valley, as well as the systematic barrage of legislation that denied citizenship to foreign-born Asians, tightened landholding prohibitions, and the ban on further Japanese immigration by 1924, neutralized any residual anti-Asian sentiment spawned by the exclusion movement. Furthermore, the presence of southern European and Mexican immigrants led local whites to extol Asians as the most hardworking, least burdensome "alien" group in the Valley.

Coming from residents and social scientists alike, positive commentary on assimilated, educated "higher class" Japanese residents, attentive Japanese parents and their academically accomplished, disciplined American-born children suggested the rise of more progressive racial attitudes. Indeed, during the late 1920s, many sociologists, including Stanford economist Eliot Mears, believed that hostility toward Asians in the American West had "either disappeared or is quiescent."[84] But the strong taboo against Asian-white race mixing pointed to the persistence of racialized hierarchies and proved that holding Asians up as a "model minority" group did not facilitate their entrance into the mainstream majority and underscored continued notions of racial difference.

When the Great Depression hit the region in the 1930s and devastated the agricultural economy, ideas about race, gender, and family took another turn as the plight of dislocated white farm families and the rise of Filipino and Mexican migrant labor practically erased the presence of nonwhite farm families like the Japanese from public discourse.

"Reds, Communists, and Fruit Strikers"

Filipinos and the Great Depression

On October 4, 1933, shortly after midnight, dynamite exploded under a bunk-house on the Hennessey ranch in Gilroy, where 50 Filipino laborers were sleeping. All of them narrowly escaped. The ranch cook later found two sticks of dynamite in the oven as he was about to light the fire for the day. Shaken, the Filipinos prepared to leave the southern Santa Clara Valley ranch, but foremen who promised to protect the premises with armed guards persuaded them to continue working there. On the same night as the Gilroy explosion, vigilante action broke out across the Central Valley in Modesto and Lodi, with whites harassing Filipinos at their camps and intimidating purported "reds, communists, and fruit strikers" with tear gas, clubs, and fire hoses. A spokes-man for the vigilantes declared that "The farmers of Central California have decided to clean house of agitators, radicals and undesirables, and they have gone back to the vigilante system, which is quick, effective and thorough." Despite conflicting accounts over who was responsible for the blast in Gilroy and its connection to the Central Valley events, the intent to equate Filipino workers and labor radicalism was clear.[1] Though some growers decried the ter-rorizing tactics, many white residents felt that battling "Communism" justified the violence.

During the spring and summer of 1933, Filipinos had participated in a string of strikes organized by the Communist-led Cannery and Agricultural Workers Industrial Union (CAWIU), disrupting the harvest of fruit and vegetable crops in the Santa Clara Valley and inciting new anti-Asian agitation. At a time when labor organizing soared in nearly all other industries, opposition to unionizing in agriculture remained fierce, making it natural for white residents to view non-white farm laborers like Filipinos as red-sympathizing foreigners whose labor militancy smacked of anti-Americanism. In the Santa Clara Valley, many whites associated union activity in the agricultural sector with radical agitators, Filipinos, and Mexicans, blaming the farm labor movement and its alleged communistic elements for undermining growers trying to preserve their family farms amidst the turmoil of the Great Depression.

The racialization of Filipinos as labor radicals eclipsed nearly all attention on other Asian ethnic groups during the Depression. For decades, public discourse and media coverage had spotlighted the Chinese and Japanese in the Santa Clara Valley, along with movements to exclude them. By the 1930s, mentions of "Orientals" had nearly disappeared. With the Chinese population barely hovering at half a percent of the total county population and numbering in the hundreds, the lack of attention was expected. But the Valley's Japanese population grew by 45 percent during the 1920s and numbered over 4,300 residents in 1930, representing 3 percent of the county population, its highest proportion in the Valley's history to that date. Yet from reading the county's newspapers and periodicals, one would hardly know the Japanese lived there, except that they sponsored entertaining Christmas programs, played baseball, and built new churches, benignly assimilating and attracting little note. The positive depictions of Nisei schoolchildren from the 1920s evolved into sporadic accounts praising second-generation Japanese American young adults in the Depression era.[2] The fact that many Japanese farm families employed Filipino workers and shared white growers' concerns about maintaining a tractable, inexpensive labor force in difficult economic times strengthened ties between Japanese and white farmers in the Valley, often against Filipino migrants.

Under the pressures of economic depression, internal migration, and an emergent farm labor movement, the dynamics of race, gender, and agriculture shifted significantly during the 1930s. The attempt by white Californians to hold onto the family farm ideal, even as it became vastly untenable, required defining themselves in opposition to Filipinos, a migratory population of almost entirely young, single men engaged in farm labor struggles. With its national reputation as a premier region for fruit growing and processing, the Santa Clara Valley became a center for CAWIU organizing efforts and home to some of the most vicious attempts at repressing labor radicalism in California. Filipinos had become targets of racial violence initially because of their tabooed involvement with white women. It was their quest to secure dignity and equality as American workers, however, that appeared to be a more serious threat to white growers in the Santa Clara Valley, whose association of agricultural strikes with dangerous radicalism intensified their animosity toward Filipinos during the Depression era.

"The Filipino Is Being Exploited by the Japanese Farmer, the American Grower, and His Own Countrymen"

Filipino immigrants entered the public spotlight and became immersed in labor struggles in the midst of the Great Depression. California experienced the dire effects of the nation's economic downturn beginning in the early 1930s, with businesses failing, thousands of mortgage foreclosures, more than 700,000 Californians (29 percent of the workforce) unemployed by 1933, and one-fifth of Californians dependent on public relief by 1934. Unemployment in the state continued to hover just below the national average until the end of the 1930s. By 1932 farm income in California had fallen to less than half of what it had been in 1929, while farm wages also dropped by more than 50 percent between 1929 and 1933. A surplus of agricultural workers, about 142 for every 100 jobs, further exacerbated the crisis. Following a decade of record profits and expanding operations, distressed growers and processors in the orchard fruit industry faced a sharp decline in prices and dismal domestic and international markets. Unlike staple foods, products like canned and dried fruits could be eliminated readily from Americans' diets.

Even more ruinous for California fruit growers was the loss of the German market, a result of the trade policies of the newly installed Nazi regime. After World War I, many growers had expanded their production to meet German demand, which accounted for up to half of annual state output. The excess supply of prunes, apricots, and peaches kept prices down during the 1930s, but growers responded by producing even larger crops in attempts to offset their lowered incomes, perpetuating a vicious cycle. Depression conditions forced the California canning industry to reduce its total output by one-third. In 1932, San Jose experienced an unemployment rate of over 20 percent. The devastation of the fruit industry during the 1930s reverberated throughout the Valley, saved only through massive federal aid in the form of extended loans, the government purchase of nearly 97 million pounds of prunes, and ultimately wartime demand for processed fruit.[3]

Nevertheless, California's diversified economy made it one of the country's more prosperous states, and even during the worst years of the Depression, from 1930 to 1934, per capita income in California totaled approximately 40 percent more than the national average.[4] Thus the state continued to draw hard-pressed, unemployed migrants, especially those from the Great Plains and the Southwest. The decade of the 1930s saw 350,000 white Americans from the drought-stricken states of Texas, Arkansas, Kansas, Missouri, and Oklahoma arrive in California. While the Depression hit farmers across the country with falling prices and disappearing markets for agricultural commodities, farmers in the Great Plains also experienced horrific drought conditions, compounded by severe wind erosion and dust storms in the region that became known as the Dust Bowl. Contrary to popular perceptions, however, dust storms devastated relatively few farms, and fewer than 16,000 migrants arrived in California directly from the Dust Bowl, just 6 percent of the total from southwestern states.[5] The internal migration of whites as a consequence of drought and dust followed a wave of Filipino migration from across the Pacific, and the two streams collided in California during the Depression.

The United States had acquired the Philippines in 1898, after its victory in the Spanish-American War, and a massive colonization program followed. The process, aimed at Americanizing the islands, included fighting a bloody guerrilla war to subdue the Filipino forces resisting their new American overlords. With U.S. sovereignty established by the early twentieth century, American sugar planters' labor recruitment efforts in the Philippines to counter striking Japanese plantation workers led to the arrival of 24,000 Filipinos in Hawaii in the period from 1907 to 1919; an additional 48,000 Filipinos landed between 1920 and 1929. Filipino emigration to the mainland gradually increased during the 1910s but did not rise significantly until after Congress passed the Immigration Act of 1924, with its ban on Japanese immigration. Growers on the Pacific coast subsequently relied on Filipinos and Mexicans for farm labor.

From 1920 to 1929, more than 14,000 Filipinos left Hawaii for the U.S. mainland, nearly three-quarters of them during the latter half of the decade, while another 37,600 arrived on the mainland directly from the Philippines.[6] Scores of Filipino immigrants on the Pacific coast and in Santa Clara County worked in agriculture during the late 1920s and 1930s, providing labor that was badly needed once Chinese, Japanese, Korean, and Asian Indian workers had been excluded; many Filipinos also found work as domestics and in the service industry. Most Filipinos in the United States were born in the Ilocano provinces in northern Luzon, some of the most densely populated areas of the Philippines, where farmers struggled to eke out a living under an oppressive land tenancy system. Others hailed from the Cebuano provinces in the center section of the Philippine archipelago, where residents were familiar with the cultivation of sugar because of plantations established by the Spanish and the Americans in the nineteenth and early twentieth centuries.[7]

Filipino migrants' status as "U.S. nationals" rendered them neither citizens nor aliens; they possessed the right to freedom of movement within the territorial jurisdiction of the United States but lacked such rights of citizenship as representation in Congress and trial by jury. Inundated with images and rhetoric of American abundance and modernity, but perhaps unaware of the restrictions they would experience, many Filipino nationals decided to exercise this right of migration. American teachers in the islands presented "vivid pictures of the U.S.," said Leo Escalante, who ran a pool hall in San Jose for his Filipino countrymen in the 1930s. It was no surprise that young, impressionable Filipinos would desire "to come here and see it and live in it."[8]

Led by Filipino contractors who negotiated the terms of work with growers, crews of Filipino laborers followed crops as they ripened for harvest, landing in the Santa Clara Valley to pick orchard fruits and vegetables. By 1930, Filipinos accounted for almost 18 percent of the agricultural workforce of the north and central coasts and the Sacramento and San Joaquin Valleys of California. Census figures showed that in 1930, there were 45,000 Filipinos in the continental United States, more than 10 times the number present in 1920. As a cohort of brown-skinned, young, unmarried men, they fell well outside the bounds of the white family farm ideal. About 85 percent of this population was under thirty years of age, 93 percent of it male, and 77 percent single.[9]

In 1930, over 30,000 Filipinos resided in California, where patterns of seasonal migration made it difficult to determine their exact populations by county. Berkeley researcher James Earl Wood estimated there were 45 Filipinos in Santa Clara County in 1920 and 857 in 1930.[10] The latter figure, just 0.5 percent of the county population, swelled to thousands at various points in the growing season. In a sample of 780 Filipinos residing in Santa Clara County enumerated by the federal census in 1930, 97 percent were male, and 78 percent of those men were between eighteen and thirty years of age. Among Filipino males who were at least eighteen, the average age was twenty-seven, far younger than the average age of Chinese and Japanese men in the county: thirty-seven and forty, respectively. Closely following statewide trends, 80 percent of Filipino men in Santa Clara County were single, compared to 48 percent of Chinese and 39 percent of Japanese men there. Only 17 percent of married Filipino men actually resided with their wives in the States. Of those, two-thirds had Filipina wives, while the rest were married to white, Mexican, or Japanese women. With an average age of thirty-three in 1930, Filipino husbands tended to be older than their bachelor counterparts, who averaged just twenty-five years of age.[11]

California growers' opinions of Filipino workers were for the most part positive though not effusive, tending to emphasize the convenience of obtaining them as a labor force. An April 1930 article from the *San Francisco Examiner* claimed that many local employers preferred Filipinos to white workers, considering the former "steadier, more tractable and more willing to put up with longer hours, poor board and worse lodging facilities."[12] Residents of the Santa Clara Valley registered similar sentiments. In Mountain View, conducting fieldwork in Santa Clara County in 1930, Berkeley researcher Wood interviewed a young woman who declared, "The Filipinos do their work well, collect their money, and bother no one—that is why the growers like them." George Becker, who operated a Sunnyvale ranch where a Filipino laborer died in an arson fire in August 1930, expressed his disdain for socializing with Filipinos but complained about the unreliability of white labor: "The less you mingle with them [Filipinos], the better off you are.... But if a man has a crop of peas or any other crop like that and is depending on white men to do the work he is just out of luck. All they do is loaf and talk about the dark skins who are doing the work. I'm not anti-American, but that's the situation." Local white growers' disapproval of white farm laborers became even more magnified in the Depression era with the arrival of Dust Bowl migrants.[13]

More favorable opinions of Filipino immigrants around Santa Clara County came from white employers in the service industry, who often spoke approvingly of the laborers and lauded their docility and conscientiousness in subservient positions. An estimated 25 percent of Filipinos in the continental United States in 1930 were service workers laboring as janitors, valets, kitchen helpers, dishwashers, busboys, bellhops, and elevator boys. In Santa Clara County close to 17 percent of Filipino residents worked in those occupations, while an additional 9 percent engaged in domestic service in private homes. Hotel managers, including Phil Riley of the St. Claire Hotel in San Jose, uniformly praised Filipino employees as "neat, clean, careful with the equipment," producing "hardly any turnover." A supervisor at the upscale St. James Hotel in San Jose reported the employment of five Filipinos in elevator, bellboy, and busboy jobs, earning two dollars per day and tips: "These Filipinos are always courteous and polite. They give the best of service even when there is no tip and give it to all alike." At the St. James, hotel management had had "a hell of a time" with white bellhops who smuggled in contraband alcohol during Prohibition and "would bring in liquor for the guests because of the big tips." That Filipino bellhops "never had to be cautioned about this" contributed to the supervisor's conclusion that "the Filipino is a wonderful servant and far superior to the white."[14]

University of Chicago–trained sociologist Emory Bogardus, noted for his work on race relations and the concept of "social distance," postulated that favorable reports of "the Filipino as being a splendid worker" tended to come from white Americans who employed Filipinos individually and not in large numbers, thus leaving out farmers who usually hired groups of Filipino workers through a contractor. Bogardus offered this tentative correlation: "When numbers work together, then unrest and organized requests for higher wages are likely to ensue." Confirming the impressions of San Jose service employers, the sociologist wrote that many Americans whose encounters with Filipinos employed "as elevator boys, as bell boys, and in cafes" were impressed with their "neat, well-groomed appearance, and courteous manners."[15] Filipino agricultural laborers did not develop the same reputations for docility and impeccable etiquette.

The fact that many Filipino domestic and service workers also happened to be students helped garner the approval of their employers. Called "pensionados," "fountain-pen boys," or "schoolboys" among themselves, small numbers of Filipino students attended American schools on Philippine government fellowships and pensions or were self-supporting, expecting to return to the islands after completing their education. Between 1920 and 1925, about 2,000 Filipinos attended U.S. colleges and universities. Tuition hikes and Depression conditions decreased their numbers to 800 in 1932, 500 in 1935, and only 300 in 1939.[16]

Mariano Catolico, who arrived in California from Ilocos Sur in 1928 at the age of nineteen and eventually settled in Mountain View, worked as a houseboy and farm laborer while intermittently attending high school and college. He went on to receive a master's degree in history and political science from the University of California, Berkeley, in 1937. Though he aspired to return to the Philippines and find employment as a teacher, Catolico remained in the States, working primarily as a seasonal farm laborer in California and Arizona before World War II.[17] The St. James hotel manager who said he would hate to replace Filipinos with whites at his establishment seems to have employed young men like Catolico: he acknowledged that a number of Filipino workers went to school and were so committed to obtaining an education that friends helped each other with their shifts if hours at school interfered with work schedules. On Filipino students contributing to a positive image of the immigrants, Bogardus wrote, "These educational ambitions and the attempts of Filipinos to get ahead bring them many friends in the United States."[18]

The vast majority of Filipino immigrants in the Santa Clara Valley, however, were not students and did not work in the service industry but labored in agriculture. Over 56 percent of Filipino men in the county at least eighteen years of age in 1930 were farm laborers, compared to 39 percent of Japanese adult males who held the same occupation.[19] As in the case of Chinese and Japanese communities in rural California, ethnic labor contractors played a key role in recruiting men and securing work from Valley growers. At Max Watson's Agnew ranch, a Filipino contractor traveled all around California and the Pacific Northwest to obtain workers, and in August 1930, he returned from a trip to Seattle with 14 new recruits. Filipino contractors generally did not receive a fee for their work; rather, they made their profits by charging laborers for room, board, and transportation, as well as arranging credit by drawing directly from their laborers' wages. Sometimes contractors paid the workers in full regularly, while in other cases, they paid the balance at the end of the season and deducted incurred expenses.

Robert Liuanag, a Filipino contractor who shuttled between Sunnyvale and Stockton, a growing center of Filipino population in California, informed Wood of his practice of meeting with growers to make verbal contracts, deciding on wage rates, the number of men who would do the job, and other details. Given the economic downturn and falling crop prices, Liuanag said he was lenient with growers when he knew they were not making money: "Last year one of the growers was paying 42½ cents an hour; it happened that he made no money on his crop. This year I told him that I wanted his work and that the price would be lowered to 40 cents. He appreciated that, he was glad to do business with me, and I'll probably have his account for a long time." But showing benevolence toward hard-pressed growers also had negative consequences for Filipino contractors, and Liuanag confirmed the common practice of having to pay laborers out of his own pocket before he received money from the grower, lamenting "Too many times I have to pay my men and wait on the grower—many times!" Watson said he had witnessed this custom in the Valley and cited a Filipino contractor he knew who had $2,300 outstanding from having paid his laborers before receiving his balance from the grower.[20]

White growers were not the only ones to rely on Filipino farm labor in the 1930s. Because they continued to grow labor-intensive berry and vegetable crops, Japanese farmers, particularly those with more established operations, commonly turned to Filipino contractors to supply them with hired help. Joe (Jitsuo) Nishida, a young Nisei berry and truck farmer who managed ranches in Santa Clara and Campbell, employed more than 30 Filipino laborers during summer and fall harvests in the mid-1930s, paying them 30 cents an hour. The workers typically put in 10 hours a day.[21]

Since the 1924 immigration act ended the possibility of obtaining new supplies of labor from Japan, numerous Japanese farmers came to depend on Filipino laborers as replacements, even if they did not warmly welcome the prospect. As a Valley Japanese farmer by the name of Oku (most likely deter-mined not to be Mountain View tomato farmer Yasutaro Oku) told James Wood, "I don't like Filipinos, but I have to use them. I can get them in [a] large enough group, they do good work, and they are single men. These Mexicans and Span-iards bring their families with them and I have to fix up houses," he said laugh-ingly, "but I can put a hundred Filipinos in that barn," pointing to what Wood assessed as "a large firetrap." By World War I, the supply of unattached Mexican immigrant men available for agricultural labor had dropped, and Mexican workers in large family units took their place. In the Santa Clara Valley during the 1930s, Mexican families who found abundant work picking peas and spinach beginning in March then returned to harvest fruit in the summer, the peak of their migration coinciding with the prune harvest in August. To meet their year-round demand for picking and packing labor, southern California citrus growers constructed new residences to house Mexican families. Specialty crop growers in northern California, including some Japanese farmers, did likewise, but also determined that Filipino migrants were an adequate seasonal labor force for their smaller scale operations. Filipinos' status as "single men" was an asset for Oku that justified putting them in substandard housing. Oku said he hired Mexicans "for the heavier work—driving tractors, and like that," but employed Filipinos to do all "stoop labor" because "[t]hey are small and work fast." On his farm, Mexicans were paid 40 cents an hour and Filipinos 35 cents.[22]

The employment of Filipino farmhands enabled Valley Japanese farmers to survive the Depression by continuing to cultivate crops considered less presti-gious than orchard fruits. On the vegetable farm he rented from J. J. O'Brien,

Katsusaburo Kawahara hired about a dozen Filipino men during harvest season in the late 1920s and 1930s at upward of 25 cents an hour. Like his white and Japanese counterparts, Kawahara provided the laborers with bunkhouses and left them in charge of meals.[23] Suyetaro Araki, the San Jose farmer who had purchased a ranch in the names of his American-born twin sons just before the passage of the Alien Land Law of 1913, maintained the orchards that had been planted on the property when he bought it, but also intercropped berries and vegetables between the young trees. His son Harry Araki recalled that the family was able to "barely break even" during the Depression because his father had diversified the crops. Japanese families mainly sharecropped berries on the Araki property, while "bachelor men," numerous Filipinos along with Japanese laborers, cultivated vegetables. Araki constructed cottages for the families and bunkhouses for the men, with separate accommodations for Japanese and for Filipinos.[24]

Like the Chinese and Japanese ranch hands who preceded them, most Filipino farm laborers boarded at camps run by contractors, often through arrangements with growers on their property. In 1930 there was even discussion among Santa Clara County Japanese growers and Filipino contractors about collaboration to construct a new camp, with the condition that the Japanese could set up a gambling house on the premises, an ironic proposal considering how Issei community leaders had leveled bitter complaints against Chinese gambling establishments and their corrupting effect on Japanese laborers just a couple decades before. It is not clear whether this camp was ever built. Max Watson maintained a large camp for Filipino workers on his ranch in Agnew, charging 10 cents a day for room and 75 cents for board (50 cents in winter), which Filipino labor contractor Thomas Flores provided. Considering that Filipino farm laborers earned an average of 20–40 cents an hour during the 1930s, Watson's prices for his accommodations were high, even if not prohibitive.[25]

Not a typical grower, Watson had a background in forestry and water conservation and was named Santa Clara County's first adult probation officer in 1927, a post he held for over two decades. Prior to establishing the Filipino camp on his property in Agnew, Watson had been in the business of placing unemployed men in jobs in forestry and agriculture; his position as the county probation officer gave him ample opportunity to find work for those who needed gainful employment to complete their probation terms. Running a labor camp for Filipino migrants may have been a profitable side business for Watson, who already had extensive experience in related fields. He proudly noted that some Filipinos resided at his camp year-round, working in the vicinity up to 10 miles away.[26]

If Watson did not fit the profile of a conventional Santa Clara Valley grower, neither was Flores representative of Filipino immigrants and contractors. In

1930, at age thirty-seven, Flores was older than most of his male counterparts, and he also was married with seven children under the age of fifteen. The province of Negros Occidental, where Flores was born, was an area of the Philippines with a long history of sugar cultivation under the Spanish and Americans; it had been targeted by the Hawaiian Sugar Planters Association's labor recruitment efforts in the early twentieth century. Flores and his wife, Vivianie, were part of the first wave of approximately 24,000 Filipinos who emigrated to Hawaii from 1907 to 1919 and labored on sugar plantations, as well as the 14,000 Filipinos who relocated from Hawaii to the mainland between 1920 and 1929, joining over 37,000 others who arrived on the West Coast directly from the Philippines in the same period. In 1926, the Flores family, consisting of the couple and five children, left Hawaii for San Francisco and eventually settled in the Santa Clara Valley. Max Watson, who lived in San Jose, not at the location of his Agnew camp, likely took into account the need for a reliable contractor with considerable fluency in English to put in charge of his on-site operations. A stable family man like Flores, unusual among the Filipino population, must have appeared a wise choice for Watson. During his trip to Santa Clara County in August 1930, Wood investigated the Watson camp and noted that the Flores children played "in overalls and romper suits (which are kept clean) and are like those worn by American children."[27]

According to Wood's observations, Watson's facilities in Agnew included a bunkhouse containing eight large rooms, each comfortably filled with 10 single beds. Scrawled on the door to the house was the greeting "Wellcome!!" Though there were 60 men occupying the rooms at the time of Wood's visit, 168 reportedly had lived there the previous year, 21 to a room. Wood found the bunkhouse "in comparatively good order," with beds made, clothing and towels hung up, floor recently swept, and "only a few odd things are to be seen strewn around between and under the beds." In the common room Wood took note of a neglected, out-of-tune piano, a phonograph, old records, a long mess table, benches, and spider webs, while the kitchen smelled of fish and cabbage and was full of flies. A young Filipino man who had attended the Teacher's College in San Jose (now San Jose State University) for a year was in charge of the cooking. He did not hesitate to confide to Wood, "I hate the job." A white facilities manager Wood spoke to remarked that the Filipinos were "certainly clean" and would shower immediately after returning from the fields, "and then they dress up—they like to do that." Watson's camp featured modern toilets and a shower room with hot and cold water, unlike other rural camps which only had metal bathtubs for men to wash in, requiring the water to be changed and heated every few uses, a process that often took hours.[28]

Contractor disputes occasionally erupted among Filipino agricultural workers and galvanized Filipino labor organizers to call for their countrymen to unionize.

In December 1933, writing for *The Agricultural Worker*, the short-lived newsletter of the CAWIU published in San Jose, Rufino Deogracias called readers' attention to the exploitative tactics of Filipino labor contractors, who he claimed helped "the bosses keep us divided by even dividing the Filipinos into castes and setting one group against the other." As a result, Deogracias alleged, "When we work under the contractors we are not having the full pay for our labor. Most of it goes to their pockets and the smallest part of it in our stomachs."[29] Another CAWIU member dubbed "Salinas Comrade" castigated a Filipino contractor named P. M. Olivetta, claiming that he had cheated laborers out of wages and issued "rubber checks" from a bank where for three years he had had no account. Writing in *The Nation*, which he later edited, Carey McWilliams declared it "impossible to verify just how much the average Filipino field worker is bilked by the contractor."[30] Having handled numerous complaints filed by Filipino agricultural workers, Santa Clara County deputy labor commissioner George Moody commented on the rampant exploitation by Filipino contractors who misled and manipulated laborers. In one pending case, a contractor boarded 90 men at his camp though he had jobs only for 32. Escalante, the San Jose pool hall operator, also regretted the way certain compatriots took advantage of newly arrived Filipinos by "promising them a job...keeping them green, keep them owing for board and room," but added that one could not rely solely on the testimonies of disgruntled workers: "Of course not everything said about a contractor, by men who have quit him, is true." Reports of shady contractor practices among Filipino laborers and other observers confirmed the presence of abuses during the 1930s, though upstanding contractors did not receive the same attention.[31]

Increased interaction between Japanese and Filipinos in the agricultural sector also gave rise to conflict, reflecting the complexities of intra-Asian relations in Depression-era California. Historian Eiichiro Azuma argues that Issei in the Sacramento Delta developed a "Japanese consciousness" rooted in localized American social relations and in their identity as overseas representatives of the Japanese state. In the 1930s Japanese ethnic identity formation revolved around campaigns to unite the community across class lines against the "racial menace" of Filipinos, a group Issei perceived as threats to both the economic position and racial purity of the Japanese (instances of intermarriage between Filipino men and Nisei women convinced many Issei that the "contamination" of their bloodline was at stake). Japanese farmers in the Delta, beholden to the small handful of white landlords who employed them, established a simplistic three-tiered race and class hierarchy: white landowners on top, then Japanese, and Filipino laborers at the bottom. In the Santa Clara Valley, Japanese may have ranked Mexican families even below Filipinos. Though the framework assumed no diversity within racial groups, it allowed Japanese to express their ethnic nationalism, as well as to appropriate white racism to exploit another racial minority for survival.[32]

Instances of Japanese farmers withholding wages from Filipino laborers emerged with some regularity during the 1930s. County labor commissioner Moody observed to Wood, "The Jap has always been a great agricultural gambler. He makes advances to these Filipinos and promises balance at the end of the season. If the crop fails, as it often does, he just tells them that he can't pay. Sometimes he issues 'due bills' [promises to pay] or writes out a check without funds. These are held until the money is deposited—if ever." Leo Cinco, former president of the Filipino Contractors and Labor Association, stated that Filipino farm laborers and contractors had "frequently been fooled by the Japanese farmers, who often fail to pay wages for several months." These farmers, Cinco contended, proceeded to declare bankruptcy after they had sold "all their goods and property," making it impossible for Filipinos to recover lost pay. Such practices were not confined to Japanese growers, and Moody noted "the same thing happens in the case of the American grower. He pays if the crop is successful. If it isn't he says 'I can't pay; what are you going to do about it?' "

From his observations of employment practices in the Santa Clara Valley, Moody summarized his opinion on the unfortunate predicament of the Filipino farm laborer: "The Filipino is being exploited by the Japanese farmer, the American grower, and his own countrymen."[33] The labor commissioner's bleak conclusion explains why many Filipinos were drawn to the Depression-era farm workers' movement and union leaders' message of justice and dignity for workers regardless of race.

"We Cannot Be Equals"

Their mistreatment within the agricultural industry aside, Filipinos throughout California and the West Coast faced still other tribulations. Clamor over Filipino men partnering with white women accounted for outbreaks of racial violence against Filipinos beginning in the late 1920s, peaking in the year 1930. It was then, with the onset of the Depression, that the basis of anti-Filipino sentiment gradually shifted from miscegenation fears to concerns of economic competition. The specter of race mixing evinced a set of dynamics different from that seen in earlier movements for Chinese and Japanese exclusion. Whereas sexual relations between white women and Chinese and Japanese immigrant men appeared only in occasional headlines, nativists railed against the alleged tendencies of Filipino men to go after white women and condemned the rise of taxi dance halls as community menaces. At these zones of "commercialized and sexualized leisure," which also served as sites of respite and identity formation for

Filipino migrants, Filipino men paid for dances with young white female dance hall employees by purchasing tickets at 10 cents each.[34]

Thus it was in January 1930, less than 50 miles south of San Jose, that the Pajaro Valley farming community of Watsonville became the scene of the most intense anti-Filipino riots to date. After the opening of a new Filipino taxi dance hall on the outskirts of town, hundreds of local whites gathered there, fueled by inflammatory press coverage in the *Evening Pajaronian*. During five days of rioting from January 19 to 23, mobs of 200–700 attacked Filipinos in the dance hall, on the streets, and at nearby labor camps. The mobs broke into smaller bands of assailants, who proceeded to raid Filipino residences and severely beat occupants until police arrived.[35] The *San Jose Mercury Herald* reported that between 60 and 70 carloads of Filipinos from the Santa Clara and Salinas Valleys rushed to defend their countrymen in Watsonville, many arming themselves with knives and guns. Filipinos fleeing the violence in the Pajaro Valley also flooded the southern Santa Clara County town of Gilroy, less than 20 miles northeast of Watsonville. On January 22, one mob of young men fired indiscriminate shots on a Filipino bunkhouse east of Watsonville, killing twenty-two-year-old Fermin Tobera with a bullet through the heart.[36]

Just one day after Tobera's death in Watsonville, anti-Filipino violence spread to San Jose, where white men beat two Filipino employees of the St. Claire Hotel. Two automobiles pulled up alongside Vincent Sabio and Denny Chavriano as they were crossing Market Street to retire to their nearby lodging house for the night. Sabio heard men in one car "shout something about 'Watsonville' and 'Filipinos'" as five men jumped out of the second car and attacked Sabio and Chavriano. Sabio received multiple blows with brass knuckles and was hospitalized. Later that night in the same vicinity, a group of white men followed Pedro Ventura and Leonard Santiago as the two Filipinos were leaving the Garden City Billiard Parlor in downtown San Jose. Ventura and Santiago stated to police they were unaware that anyone was behind them until they were struck down in front of the post office. In the midst of the attack, an unidentified assailant stabbed twenty-two-year-old Alfred Johnson, a white bystander on the scene. Two days later a fire gutted the three-story building on San Fernando Street that housed the San Jose Hardware Store and the residential hotel where Ventura and Santiago rented rooms along with other Filipino boarders. Though officials deemed the cause of the fire unknown, the two Filipino victims' address had been printed in the *Mercury Herald*'s coverage of the attack, leaving open the possibility of arson.[37]

The assaults on Filipinos in San Jose concurrent with the Watsonville riots prompted local officials and Filipino residents to mobilize efforts to maintain order. The *Evening News* lamented the "exceedingly bad publicity" brought to San Jose from the attacks and called on "young San Jose men" to separate

"Filipinos living here" from those involved in the Watsonville fracas. Leo Escalante, proprietor of the Manila Pool Hall in San Jose and leader of a Filipino fraternal lodge, convened about a hundred fellow Filipinos at his business on the evening of January 24, 1930, urging them to avoid behavior that would incite further conflict. Trouble had arisen in Watsonville as a direct result of Filipinos "associating with white girls," Escalante said, and he exhorted his San Jose brethren to learn from the unfortunate consequences. He acknowledged while many Filipino migrants had been taught at home that they were "the equals of Americans" and learned "in the churches" that "all men were created equal," it was a mistake to believe this, declaring, "they are white and we are brown and we cannot be equals."

Yet despite his disillusionment, Escalante retained faith in local police forces and appealed to his audience to refrain from fighting back when provoked: "so long as we are under the Stars and Stripes we can look to the Americans for protection." He proceeded to introduce San Jose chief of police J. N. Black, who had made disparaging remarks about Chinese and Japanese residents to Survey of Race Relations researchers just a few years before, saying he preferred the city be "rid of all Orientals." Addressing the crowd at Manila Pool Hall, however, Black assured the Filipinos gathered that police would work on their behalf against "hoodlums." The next speaker was Max Watson, who in his capacity as county probation officer and informal broker to Filipino laborers made similar statements, as well as a hopeful promise that order would be restored soon. At the adjournment of the meeting, Escalante announced that his pool hall was closed for the night, and he would not open it in the evenings until tensions in San Jose subsided. The *San Jose Mercury Herald* praised Filipinos in the area for subjecting themselves to police authority and "their willingness to trust to our sense of justice."[38]

White reliance on Filipino labor in Santa Clara County's agricultural and service sectors motivated Filipino workers and white employers alike to ascertain that the primary cause of the Watsonville riots was "social, rather than economic," as the *Mercury* editorialized. Determined not to follow the path of Watsonville and Santa Cruz County, white residents of the Santa Clara Valley expressed support of local Filipinos as long as they steered clear of relations with white women, deducing that social tensions had ignited the violent clashes. The newspaper went so far as to castigate the white women working at taxi dance halls, saying "public indignation might better have been directed" toward them instead of Filipinos.

Reflecting the belief that white women were to blame for the turmoil, the dance hall near Watsonville, scene of the first anti-Filipino riot, planned to reopen with only Filipina and Mexican women employed as dance partners. Acting on rumors that five of the white female dance hall workers from

Figure 6.1 Leo Escalante's Manila Pool Hall, Jackson Street, San Jose, 1931.
Edith C. Smith Photograph Collection, Sourisseau Academy for State and Local History, San Jose
State University, San Jose, California.

Watsonville were on their way to Gilroy, police there ordered "every unemployed white man and woman and Filipino" out of the city, leading to a Filipino exodus north to San Jose.[39] Local officers' inclusion of unemployed whites in their efforts to prevent an anti-Filipino outbreak reflected concerns that idle, lower-class individuals were more likely to take part in rioting. Commenting on the Watsonville events months later, an official from the San Jose Chamber of Commerce declared it was "principally white trash" who were to blame for the violence.[40]

Filipino laborers continued to receive advice on avoiding contentious social interactions in the following months. After the attack on Sabio and Chavriano, hotel manager Phil Riley cautioned Filipino workers at the St. Claire to "lay low and avoid trouble" as he was loath to hire whites in their place.[41] Escalante also maintained the right of every Filipino migrant "to support himself by labor" and repeatedly advised his countrymen against jeopardizing their ability to earn a living by consorting with white women in public, which he deemed "one of the quickest ways to cause trouble." Referring to his fellow migrants, Escalante suggested that "If they want to see white girls they should do it in private" like anyone who wished to maintain an illicit relationship. For his part, as one of few Filipino males in California married to a Filipina, Escalante, who was twenty-nine in 1930, did not face the same trials as the young bachelors to whom he was dispensing advice. At the time of the Watsonville riots, he had been married to his wife Domisiana (Diana) for five years. The couple lived at their place of business on Jackson Street with their three-year-old son, born in California, and were expecting their second child.[42]

By the last week of January 1930, the rioting in Watsonville had ended and no new attacks on Filipinos were reported there or in San Jose, though scattered clashes between whites and Filipinos continued in San Francisco and Stockton. Not surprisingly, Santa Clara County Filipinos remained wary, and, some, despite admonitions from Chief Black, still carried weapons for protection. Two Filipino men from San Jose reportedly took off running when they spied whites of suspicious appearance in the vicinity. Police arrested a twenty-year-old white man named Leonard Bressette of San Jose for threatening Filipinos and plotting against them.[43]

By early February, law enforcement officials and white residents seemed largely satisfied that racial tensions were under control in the Valley. In Watsonville, white residents and police also hoped that the riots would fade quickly in the public memory and order would be restored. Few of the individuals involved in instigating the mob attacks on Filipinos were investigated, much less prosecuted.[44]

In part because of their reliance on Filipino labor, white residents of the Santa Clara Valley had complicated and paradoxical views on controlling Filipino male sexuality. Some condemned relationships between Filipino immigrant men and

Figure 6.2 Filipino and white residents gathered for funeral, San Jose, c. 1930s.
Courtesy of History San José.

white women to the point of blaming the Watsonville uprising and ensuing conflict solely on these controversial unions. But many whites also tolerated Filipino-white race mixing within limits and intervened only when encounters became too public. Just months after the Watsonville riots, Max Watson said he found that the Filipinos who worked for him were "pretty well disciplined sexually; and you never hear of [a Filipino] as a homosexual. Of course some of them get mixed up with a cheap grade of white girl, and some go to prostitutes—but what of it. That's perfectly natural." For Watson, sexual commerce was acceptable, even "natural," and Filipino male heterosexuality justified these interracial forays. He had personally witnessed such exchanges and felt "any group of single men would be the same way. It would be funny if they weren't." Even though boardinghouses, ranches, and labor camps like the one Watson operated were "borderland spaces" often associated with disordered, homosocial, and homosexual behavior among men, Watson vouched for the normative sexuality of his Filipino workers.[45]

In public venues, however, white employers exhibited more social control over Filipino men and their liaisons with white women. Owning up to his disapproval of interracial mixing, the proprietor of a San Jose restaurant called O'Brien's admitted having had to fire a few of his Filipino workers "because of their familiarity with the waitresses—something I don't like to see." The experience did not, however, keep him from viewing Filipinos as "very satisfactory," "clean cut and courteous" employees.[46] Filipina immigrant Frances Trimillos, whose husband, Emil, worked as a bartender and waiter at the San Jose Country Club during the 1930s, reported a more dramatic incident. When the club's management learned that two Filipino men were constantly fighting on the grounds over a white woman who was purportedly in love with both of them, all Filipino employees were fired. Rather than risk offending club members with drama stemming from the interracial love triangle and aware that such romances were not uncommon, the country club decided to eliminate this liability altogether.[47]

In another case, fraught with complexities, Sunnyvale postmaster Leo Vishoot informed Wood in 1930 that a local woman who caught her daughter and a Filipino man copulating in the backyard had failed to bring charges. A grand jury took up the matter only to have the judge rule that if the mother did not file a complaint, the court would go no further in investigation. Contractor Robert Liuanag, who had employed the Filipino man in question, offered a less scandalous version of events, affirming that the girl had frequented the Filipino camp quarters he maintained and was "on friendly terms with a number of other men but she liked this boy about the best." The girl's mother did not catch her daughter in the act, Liuanag stated. Instead, the girl confessed that she had had "intercourse with this Filipino boy" when her mother saw her come into the house with her coat dirty and asked what had happened.

As a contractor and male authority figure for many of his employees, Liuanag, anxious to avoid unwanted publicity and further complications, spoke with the girl's parents. The three worked out an agreement to send the daughter's lover, a fraternal lodge brother of Liuanag's, to southern California if the parents would keep the case out of court.[48] In the eyes of white residents, banishment to southern California or termination of employment for associating with white women seemed like reasonable measures to handle their discomfort with Filipino sexuality.

In this atmosphere, Filipino-white couples who wanted to marry were the victims of bigotry. Sensational images and stories of white women and Filipino men drove the movement for anti-miscegenation prohibitions barring intermarriage between whites and Asians. Despite Filipino attempts to contest laws on the basis of their racial status as "Malays" and not "Mongolians," nativist forces by the early 1930s closed legislative loopholes that allowed state-sanctioned Filipino-white unions.[49]

While white disapproval of Filipino-white sexual unions contributed to anti-Filipino sentiment in the Santa Clara Valley, fear of economic competition soon moved to the forefront of racial conflict. By the time of spring harvests in 1930, charges that Filipinos undermined white workers' jobs and wages were ubiquitous, bolstered by the start of the Depression, even though there was scant evidence that whites actually competed for the Filipino work in question, particularly in labor-intensive crops like lettuce and asparagus. Nevertheless, in the orchard fruit industry, long viewed as the realm of white families, accusations of labor competition, along with perceptions of Filipinos as a "third invasion" from Asia, sparked violent outbreaks in rural districts across northern California during the summer of 1930 prior to arriving in the Santa Clara Valley.[50] Since fruit picking was an occupation many whites were willing to engage in, they felt entitled to the work and incensed when growers hired Filipinos.

By late July, as unemployment soared and economic conditions worsened, white laborers rose up against Filipino fruit workers in the apple orchards of Sonoma County, forcing Filipinos in the Sebastopol district to apply for police protection. Protest subsequently spread northeast to Marysville in Yuba County. In Yuba City, whites circulated petitions demanding that growers give preference to them over Filipinos, complaining that auto camps were crowded with white families unable to obtain peach-picking jobs because Filipinos reportedly had taken all the available work. Police estimated more than a thousand Filipinos were residing in the Yuba-Sutter district and had established a new quarter in the Chinatown in Marysville.

Tensions subsided only when Filipinos left the orchard areas following the agitation.[51] In his study of Filipino immigration in 1931, writer and social worker Bruno Lasker observed that the employment of Filipinos in orchard work posed a more serious form of competition, especially "when the work is taken away from families with small farms of their own who need the seasonal work for wages on the larger holdings to eke out a meager livelihood." Lasker identified competition in orchard work as primarily responsible for some of the more violent attacks on Filipinos, particularly as white orchardists increasingly favored Asian workers."[52]

Anti-Filipino agitation broke out in the Santa Clara Valley just before the start of the August 1930 pear harvest, when fruit growers in Sunnyvale, Santa Clara, and Agnew were warned that if they employed Filipinos, they would face destruction of their orchards. The Libby, McNeill, & Libby cannery and the Joshua Hendy Iron Works factory, both located in Sunnyvale, also received threats, though the latter had never employed Filipinos.

In Agnew, Max Watson found a scrawled note in his mailbox reading, "Work no Filipinos or we'll destroy your crop and you too." A Filipino man named Jeledone reported to Wood that in one morning, 20 Filipinos had moved out of Watson's camp upon learning of the threats. Other messages, crudely lettered on note paper, read "Let go your Filipino help or we'll burn you out" and "You and yours will be destroyed if you don't stop employing Filipinos." Grower Lloyd Wilcox of Santa Clara, one of the first employers to discover a threatening note, collected several similar ones that had been placed in the mailboxes of his neighbors and turned them over to the Santa Clara post office. Federal investigators failed to uncover the identities of the blackmailers.[53]

On August 12, 1930, around the time the threatening notes were being distributed, a Filipino labor camp in Sunnyvale caught fire, killing a twenty-two-year-old Filipino laborer named Joaquin Somera, who had been recuperating from illness in a cabin. Fellow laborers testified that Somera had worked with them in the onion fields near Coyote, southeast of San Jose, and in Watsonville and Isleton prior to that, reflecting the seasonal migration paths common to Filipino farm workers.[54] Since the body found in the ashes of the destroyed cabin was charred beyond recognition, Filipino witnesses identified it as Somera's based on his failure to appear at his place of employment or at the friends' residence where he had been staying.

The fire that killed Somera also incinerated five cabins on the Sue Gallimore ranch, where ranch operator George Becker and another employee had noticed "strange men" on the property who asked to see the "boss Filipino" and immediately drove away when told that the Filipino foreman was out. A half-hour later, at 5:30 p.m., the first cabin burst into flames. Neighbor J. W. Gilman spotted the fire while he was herding turkeys and summoned an aged Japanese farmer from a nearby field to help throw water on the burning cabin. Despite circumstantial evidence of arson, police officers maintained that Somera had fallen asleep while smoking, causing his pipe to set fire to the bedding. The coroner's jury returned a verdict that Somera "accidentally burned to death."[55]

The fatal Sunnyvale blaze and anonymous warnings throughout the Santa Clara Valley in the summer of 1930 scared local employers into dismissing an estimated 200 Filipino laborers for fear of retribution. One Filipino labor contractor told county officials that employers canceled two contracts for 120 workers the day after the first threats came to light. A nervous Portuguese tomato sharecropper relayed to Wood: "You think there be trouble if I get Filipines [*sic*] to pick my tomatoes? I no want any trouble. Let the tomatoes rot where they are rather than have trouble." The farmer added that because prices were so low, fruit growers in the Valley were already letting pears rot on the ground or dumping them into sloughs. Upon receiving a blackmail note, the Wilcox Fruit Company on Kifer Road in Santa Clara immediately discharged 15 Filipinos rather than risk destruction of its property. Although superintendent William C. Baker of the Libby cannery in Sunnyvale acknowledged that Filipinos were "the best workers that we ever had in trucking," he did not hesitate to replace them with white laborers now that "plenty" were available. Since the warnings were issued, he no longer welcomed Filipinos on the cannery's premises: "when they hang around here I order them off of the place."[56]

Through 1930, incidents of anti-Filipino violence were based largely on fears of miscegenation and economic competition. As agricultural strikes mounted in the Santa Clara Valley and throughout California during the 1930s, white residents, including growers who had previously supported Filipino laborers, found a new reason to decry their presence. As Filipino immigrants came to play active roles in the movement to organize agricultural labor, racial violence escalated in rural districts under the guise of campaigns to root out dangerous leftist radicalism.

"All Workers in One Big Union"

In response to the rampant economic exploitation and the harassment they encountered regularly as farm laborers, scores of Filipinos participated in the movement to organize agricultural workers as it underwent unprecedented growth during the Great Depression. Filipino migrants demonstrated an astute awareness that their colonial status gave them grounds to assert their adherence to "the American most precious TRADITION" of equality, as protesting asparagus workers declared in 1928. Because many had also been members of unions in Hawaii and the Philippines, Filipino laborers arrived on the mainland with a consciousness of the possibilities for collective action. Growers quelled the sporadic outbreaks of Filipino labor militancy during the late 1920s, and it was not until the Depression brought new urgency, momentum, and organizational resources that Filipinos took on agricultural unionization on a significant scale.[57]

Filipino involvement in agricultural strikes resulted in a new form of racialization beyond the earlier characterizations as hypersexualized pursuers of white women and job-stealers who undercut white working men. Because white residents and corporate interests perennially associated "radicals" with the burgeoning farm labor movement, they also came to view Filipinos as un-American leftists. Aided by new national labor laws that sanctioned union activity, industrial labor participated in numerous effective strikes across industries during the 1930s, and union membership soared. But the unionization of agricultural workers was a different story, and labor militancy in the agricultural sector proved difficult for most Americans to accept.

Historians have placed part of the blame on New Deal policies that excluded farm workers from the protections of the National Labor Relations Act (NLRA) and thus separated them from industrial workers on an institutional level. In addition, agricultural strikes in California tended to involve people of color, especially Mexicans and Filipinos, which decreased mainstream public support. Moreover, unionists faced a host of obstacles to organizing white migrants, who were reluctant to join farm labor unions and, as former farmers, remained "loyal to the enterprise of their ancestors," finding it "hard not to identify with their employers."[58] These migrants sought recognition as members of the native-born white community and as voting citizens, choosing not to cast their lot with striking Filipino and Mexican farm workers. For many white migrants in California, race identification undermined class solidarity, and the 1930s farm labor movement moved forward largely without their participation.[59]

Awareness that white migrants were less likely to join unions contributed to the widespread perception that farm labor union activity was indeed the province of alienated nonwhites under the influence of Communists. Beginning in 1928, party organizers commenced efforts to unionize cannery and farm laborers in California, with a keen eye on opportunities in Santa Clara County. Activists from outside the Valley, including the young Dorothy Ray Healey, who eventually rose through the ranks to chair the Communist Party USA (CPUSA) in southern California, bolstered the efforts of local Communists to reach out to Mexican and Filipino workers. During one of the first significant cannery strikes in the Valley in July 1931, Communist Party members declared the establishment of the CAWIU, an effective even if short-lived organization that led strikes involving 40,000 California agricultural laborers in 1933 alone. Given the Valley's numerous orchards and large fruit processing plants, the radical CAWIU chose San Jose as its headquarters to launch organizing drives throughout the state, though the Central Valley eventually became its center of activism.[60]

In 1933, the CAWIU's peak year, strikes that began in the pea fields of the northern Santa Clara Valley in April followed the path of seasonal agricultural labor migration and continued through the harvests of berries, sugar beets, apricots, cherries, pears, peaches, lettuce, and grapes. CAWIU action culminated in the massive 27-day-long cotton pickers' strike that extended over 100 miles in the Central Valley and resulted in the deaths of three Mexican pickers.[61] That year, as farm prices reached their lowest point in the 1930s, the nation experienced a record 61 agricultural strikes; half of them took place in California. When the CAWIU led 2,000 Mexican, Filipino, and white pea pickers in Santa Clara and Alameda Counties in a strike for higher wages in mid-April 1933, law enforcement officials took the side of growers, as did the *San Jose Mercury Herald*, which called the strikers "pea field terrorists." Santa Clara County Sheriff William J. Emig arrested eight organizers in the Milpitas and Piedmont districts for "molesting the workers" and "making inflammatory talks" with pickers. Striking workers succeeded in tying up the pea harvest during the first several days, but as growers recruited large numbers of scabs to work in the fields under armed guards, the strike lost effectiveness. Recognizing the Santa Clara Valley's potential, prominent Communist organizers Caroline Decker and Pat Chambers arrived in San Jose soon after the pea strike to focus on developing CAWIU strategies.[62]

The pattern of police authorities defending growers' interests during labor uprisings continued in the Valley with the next major strike of 1933. In mid-June, about a thousand cherry pickers at 20 ranches in northern Santa Clara Valley struck for higher wages and contended with armed special deputies wielding pick handles and tear gas. Except for a few in the Santa Clara Valley, cherry growers throughout the state had suffered dismal losses in 1932 and set their sights on better prospects in 1933, deepening their resolve to put down any strike activity. Sheriff Emig, who again saw his duty as suppressing the workers, authorized deputies to control strikers.[63] A foreman on the Spaulding ranch, one of the largest in the area, approached Pat Callahan, the CAWIU's principal leader of the strike, as he was walking a picket line with others and offered to discuss a settlement with him. As soon as Callahan assented to the invitation, the foreman signaled a group of deputy sheriffs hiding in trees to attack the union organizer, as he was now a "trespasser." A deputy struck Callahan in the face with the butt of a shotgun, breaking his jaw, while other deputies beat him, along with the strikers who tried to rush to Callahan's aid. According to CAWIU minutes, one of the strikers beaten with Callahan in the cherry orchard episode was Mike Marvos, president of the Filipino Labor Council. The strikers ultimately won a 50 percent raise.[64]

Filipino workers employed in Santa Clara County became a primary target of CAWIU recruitment during its peak of militancy. In preparation for a pear pickers' strike in the Santa Clara Valley during August 1933, the CAWIU held an organizational meeting in San Jose. After opening with their union hymn "Hold the Fort," leaders acknowledged the need to recruit more Filipino and Mexican workers to support the cause. They cited problems from previous strikes in which "Americans were unable to communicate with the strikers" despite reports that "spirit was high and picketing militant." The union proceeded to translate conference speeches into Spanish. Freddie Manzanas, a CAWIU organizer stationed in Mountain View, reported that the apricot cutters there also encountered language barriers, which impeded solidarity: workers, he observed, "do not understand each other; no unity between Mexican and Filipino." Decker recognized the problems of interethnic solidarity and the emergence of "nationalistic unions" like the Mexican Confederation and the Filipino Labor Chamber, whose strikebreaking goals she believed undermined that of a "revolutionary union." Decker, who served as executive secretary of the CAWIU, observed that "Filipino fakers" in Salinas planned to call Filipino workers out to break a Mexican grape strike in the summer of 1933 "and so create race prejudice," which her union sought to overcome.[65]

To California business interests, the CAWIU's ideology sounded extremist indeed, though in reality the organization toned down much of its revolutionary rhetoric to focus on farm laborer issues. Pat Chambers, Caroline Decker, and Pat Callahan were devoted members of the Communist Party USA and among its most talented organizers. To appeal to farm workers, however, they eschewed overtly Communist rhetoric and emphasized issues of decent wages and working conditions, fair negotiations, equal pay for women, and racial equality. By the end of 1933, only an estimated 5 percent of the 20,000 members of the CAWIU were committed to the union's communist orientation. Farm workers welcomed the organization's effective leadership in strikes and unionization but fell short of adopting its ideological principles. Samuel Darcy, director of CPUSA District 13, which included California, encouraged CAWIU organizers to stay close to bread-and-butter issues because he realized their constituency was interested in little else.[66] Nonetheless, those basic issues encompassed the CAWIU's principle of unionizing across racial, ethnic, and gender lines, aptly illustrated by a promotional photo that ran in The Agricultural Worker of five farm workers of various ethnicities (Mexican, Filipino, Japanese, and white) standing in a field, arms on each other's shoulders. Captioned "Solidarity," the photo reflected the CAWIU's goal of organizing "all workers in one big union, solid in unity in answer to the attacks of the bosses upon the working class."[67] It was an appeal that resonated with numerous farm laborers, including many Filipinos who heeded the call to unionize.

The August 1933 pear pickers' strike in the Santa Clara Valley, one of the CAWIU's major victories, bore out the perception of labor strife linked with abhorrent, "un-American" activity and nonwhite militants. In a strike that lasted four days, a thousand pear pickers demanded an increase in their hourly wage from 20 to 30 cents, an eight-hour day, and growers' recognition of the CAWIU.

Representing the growers, who had endured what the California Fruit Exchange bemoaned as "disastrously low returns…starvation prices" for pears in the previous season, attorney Louis Oneal lashed out against the presence of incendiary "outsiders" who had descended on the Valley to harass struggling pear growers: "The question is, shall a few disinterested and irresponsible persons coming in from the outside disrupt our industries."[68] Claiming that union organizers were a "menace to labor," Oneal harangued them for preventing "honest men" from obtaining work through "fear of strikers and threats of bodily harm to themselves and their families." He called such behavior "un-American, illegal."[69] By August 18, the majority of pear growers in the Valley consented to raising wages to 25–27½ cents, but they refused to deal with strike leaders or accept mediation, which would amount to indirect recognition of the union. Still, the pear strike forced growers into the courts (after the strike began, a nearby county appellate court decided the strikers had the right to picket, countering growers' injunctions against a picket line). In addition, the California Bureau of Labor Statistics, if not local growers, recognized the CAWIU and sent a representative to the Valley to arbitrate the strike. Decker believed that the state-enforced arbitration "saved our lives. Instead of sending out vigilantes to break heads, the growers treated the union as a legitimate entity."[70] Defendants in the injunction suits consisted of an interracial coalition of Mexicans, Filipinos, and whites involved in the strike, including Filipino labor leader Mike Marvos, who chose to affiliate with the CAWIU struggle rather than the Salinas lettuce strike that engaged numerous Filipinos around the same time.

The growth of Filipino labor militancy in agriculture during the 1930s marked a broad class critique of the economic system that crossed racial lines. The CAWIU attracted a number of active Filipino members, including Rufino Deogracias, who wrote an impassioned full-page appeal in *The Agricultural Worker* to Filipino workers. He asked his countrymen to eschew a narrow view of racial discrimination that "blamed our fellow workers of other nationalities, particularly the white workers," and exhorted them instead to examine the situation carefully and realize that "race discrimination is not originated from the workers, but from the bosses! It has been taught by our enemies to the workers so that all workers would not unite and it will be easy for them to do whatever they want to oppress us." Deogracias cited an incident that had occurred during a pea pickers' strike in the Santa Clara Valley. A farmer whose Mexican laborers had walked out in response to the CAWIU's call for a general strike came to the Filipino labor camp in search of workers. Reportedly, the grower said, "The Mexicans are no good, come boys and drive them out, this is not their country and it is your duty to drive 'em for they are crowding you out." The Filipinos showed their union solidarity with the Mexicans, so the grower left "quietly and silently." When Mexican pea pickers arrived in the

Valley from southern California during the following season in early April of 1934, the *San Jose Mercury Herald* reported that "communist agitation" was negligible.[71]

Though not directly related to Valley race relations and the agricultural labor movement, an incident that took place in San Jose in November 1933 made national headlines and had injurious repercussions on labor activity in the Santa Clara Valley, setting the stage for public and even official acceptance of vigilantism. When two white men confessed to the kidnapping and murder of twenty-year-old Brooke Hart, the popular son of a wealthy department store owner in San Jose, rumors circulated that residents planned to lynch the murderers. Republican governor James Rolph announced that he would not take action to protect the accused men from mobs. Encouraged by the governor's sanction of vigilantism and the failure of local authorities to adopt measures to safeguard the men in custody, a mob broke into the county jail and hanged the two prisoners from trees at St. James Park in downtown San Jose. For many Valley residents, the lynching emerged as their formative memory of the period. Tacitly approved by officials and occurring just over a month after the dynamiting of the Filipino bunkhouse in Gilroy, the mob action contributed to the emergence of a "new, much chillier climate for labor in the Valley."[72]

Following the November 1933 hangings, the CAWIU's San Jose district office received "a note threatening to lynch any leader of the Union if the workers went on strike for higher wages." A writer for *The Agricultural Worker* made an ardent plea for all CAWIU locals to attend a meeting to address "lynch-terror" in San Jose, citing the forces that sought to suppress the working class: "The newspapers, the authorities, the WHOLE ROTTEN OUTFIT UPHOLDING A DECAYING ECONOMIC ORDER, are determined to save the profits of their masters, the rich growers and canners. Yes, they will even lynch workers when they dare to raise their voice in protest against their SLAVERY WAGES."[73] Such anticapitalist language undoubtedly alarmed the growers and canners of the Valley, already apt to blame those they considered extremist "outside" organizers. In light of local intimidation, the CAWIU did not lead a strike in San Jose or elsewhere in the Valley again after the pear strike of 1933.

Though the Santa Clara Valley did not see any major strike activity involving Filipino laborers during the 1934 growing season, labor militancy erupted in nearby regions, prompting unease among the area's farmers and a sustained wariness of Filipino workers and the Communists who organized them. In San Mateo County, which borders northeastern Santa Clara County, more than 200 Filipino spinach pickers refused to accept the prevailing hourly wage of 20 cents and went on strike in late January 1934, demanding 25 cents. Twenty Japanese arrived from another ranch to break the strike, only to leave when Filipino spokesmen warned them to "quit or expect violence." Law enforcement officials, fearing interethnic hostilities, deputized Pescadero citizens and prepared them with tear gas, but riots never materialized.

Filipino strikes continued in the Sacramento Delta region in March when 21 asparagus cutters, allegedly under the guidance of "Communist agitators" from the CAWIU, abandoned their work after a wage dispute. Even though the strike receded, Delta growers remained on edge as the asparagus crop awaited harvest by nearly 7,000 Filipinos reported to be in the vicinity.[74] In the summer of 1934, Filipino lettuce workers in Watsonville and Salinas, just south of Santa Clara County, staged a strike under the auspices of the Filipino Labor Union (FLU), formed in 1933 with the influence of radical organizer Pablo Manlapit. The *Union Gazette*, the official newspaper of the county's Central Labor Council, cited FLU president Damiano Marcuelo's statement that Filipino workers were "[d]epressed by a most deplorable living condition, arising out of hourly wage of 30 cents, and with an average of 4 or 5 hours a day, absolutely insufficient to maintain a decent living or a fair American standard of livelihood." At its peak in 1934, the FLU had seven locals and a membership of 2,000.[75]

The unionizing efforts and labor protest of Filipino farm workers not only incensed white residents, but also served to drive a deeper wedge in their relations with Japanese farmers. Japanese growers in the Santa Clara Valley knew about the militancy of Filipino farm laborers mostly from news of strikes in the Sacramento–San Joaquin Delta region and the Salinas Valley; occasionally they encountered Filipino strikes on their own ranches. For example, on William Tenaki's spinach ranch in Evergreen, east of San Jose, Mexican and Filipino workers went on strike in April 1937, demanding a raise of 5 cents. Though he initially told the laborers "to get out if they did not like the job," all the other workers threatened to leave as well. Tenaki then changed his mind and gave the strikers their desired rate of 35 cents an hour.[76] Japanese growers' hostility to organized farm labor put them on the same side as many white growers in the 1930s.

Partly because of Japanese antagonism toward Filipino labor militancy, Japanese immigrant labor activism floundered in the 1930s despite union efforts to reach out to Japanese laborers. Minutes of a union meeting in the summer of 1933 record that Mountain View CAWIU organizer Freddie Manzanas spoke bluntly about the unwillingness of the Japanese to unionize: "Japanese in south did not join strike; willing to scab. Their ranks full of stool-pigeons." The Issei emphasis on their superiority as members of the Japanese race over class solidarity in the 1930s posed an insurmountable barrier to union organizing as laboring Issei internalized a racial identity and were reluctant to take on one rooted in class struggle. Manzanas confirmed the ostracism of seven Japanese laborers who tried to organize and were expelled from their camp by their own countrymen. Issei leaders commonly fought attempts at boycotts and strikes and prevented Japanese agricultural workers from forming bonds with their fellow farm laborers across ethnic lines.[77]

Like the Japanese, Chinese laborers, who numbered fewer than 700 in the county during the 1930s, largely eschewed labor unionism, raising the ire of white workers. The Valley's Chinese made a rare appearance on the public radar in late 1934 when white unionists complained of being undercut by nonunion Chinese meat markets. The union's grievance was that Chinese butcher shops, which did not operate on the prevailing union salary scale, refused to hire journeymen butchers, a decision that disadvantaged not only the unemployed white journeymen of San Jose but the economy generally. One observer noted that the journeymen "would, if gainfully employed, spend a large sum of money every week" in "legitimate channels of trade," as opposed to the Chinese, who kept their money within their own community until it reached "the hands of the big Chinese syndicate," otherwise known as "some rich old Mandarin in China."[78] White workers equated the failure of Chinese butchers to join unions with lack of concern for the nation's economic recovery, a claim they never made in the agricultural sector, where unionism was frequently viewed as anti-American.

The *Union Gazette* reported that the San Jose Butchers' Union Local 506 for five years had "done everything possible to organize the Chinese meat market operators in San Jose in vain" and now were forced to place them on the "unfair list" of businesses to boycott. In mid-December 1934, unionized butchers protested by wearing large signs on their chests proclaiming "Chinese Markets Unfair." Beneficiaries of New Deal relief and labor policies, organized labor went so far as to admonish those who shopped at nonunion Chinese markets as unpatriotic ingrates, who by the act had shown "their total lack of appreciation" of the "relief the United States government is making possible."[79] The uproar over butcher shops continued well into 1935, when the federal government, represented by the National Recovery Administration, finally agreed to investigate the complaints filed. In June, the butchers' union was jubilant over the renovation in progress of a new union meat market that planned to open in the location vacated by a Chinese meat market shut down by creditors on South First Street in San Jose. It was unclear what had forced the closure: tough times caused by the Depression or, as the union suggested, being placed on the county labor council's "We Don't Patronize" list.[80]

Because Chinese opposition to the union cause occurred among the butchers, not in the Valley's agricultural industry, the stance was linked to the un-American economic practices of the butchers and their disloyalty to the state and national recovery efforts. Meanwhile, many whites associated the newest group of "Orientals," Filipinos, with labor strife, though not the kind deemed worthy of "American standards." Unlike the white San Jose butchers, who convinced the public that labor solidarity conveyed their patriotism, workers who protested conditions in the agricultural industry rarely managed the same feat.

In response to the growing farm labor movement, numerous white residents of the Santa Clara Valley established and joined organizations having the avowed purpose of rooting out radicalism. In July 1934, 300 citizens announced plans to drive communism from the Valley and subsequently ran a large advertisement for the Committee of Public Safety of Santa Clara County, urging all "good Americans" to sign an oath at the Chamber of Commerce. The proximate cause of this mobilization was a four-day general strike in San Francisco that had originated with longshoremen and spread to tens of thousands of other workers. Well-to-do San Jose prune grower Charles Derby, one of the initiators of the antiradical drive, spent the evening of July 16 in a meeting to form a committee "to handle the Communist Activities." On July 18, while also managing the harvest of his prunes, which were ripening and "dropping fast," Derby noted in his diary he was "sworn in as Deputy Sheriff with 200 others for anti-communist action."[81]

Citizens in the Valley towns of Los Gatos and Palo Alto also established "security leagues" for the purpose of combating communism; Sunnyvale passed an antipicketing ordinance. Local organizers who had been working out of Communist Party headquarters on Post Street in San Jose left the premises on the same day. But irate citizens were not satisfied and, the following day, armed with pick handles, they stormed three other known Communist "hot spots," seized "red literature," and beat "nine assorted radicals," creating for San Jose a reputation for brutal, reactionary vigilantism.[82] The San Jose events coincided with another grim development for the labor movement, as growers, politicians, and law enforcement under the banner of the Associated Farmers arrested Caroline Decker and 16 other CAWIU leaders in Sacramento on charges of criminal syndicalism. Decker and seven others, including Pat Chambers, were convicted on two counts after a prolonged, sensationalized trial, and sent to prison.[83]

The events of 1934 revealed a continuing connection between anti-Filipino violence and Filipino involvement in labor organizing. In the late summer of 1934, following a strike of several thousand white and Filipino lettuce pickers in the Salinas Valley, 30 armed vigilantes, all "farmers and Salinas business men," forced 500 Filipinos from their camp at gunpoint, while 300 more pickers packed their belongings and prepared to flee. The Filipinos who had been driven out of the Salinas area headed north for safety toward the San Joaquin and Santa Clara Valleys, as well as San Luis Obispo and Santa Barbara Counties to the south.

Given that San Jose was about 40 miles north of Salinas, Santa Clara County residents had reason to fear that unrest would soon come their way. The Salinas lettuce fields continued to be the site of explosive violence in September, as vigilantes raided another Filipino camp, run by Rufo Canete, the newly appointed head of the FLU. A Filipina living at the camp, which housed about 60 people, burned to death in the raid.[84] Santa Clara County officials, keenly aware of nearby strike activity and the FLU's ascendancy, tried to forestall Filipino labor militancy in the Valley by informing local Filipino leaders that "both the police department and the sheriff's office will be powerless if a mass mob attack is made on the Filipinos." In contrast to promises of police protection in the aftermath of the 1930 Watsonville riots, the San Jose district attorney, the chief of police, and the county sheriff in 1934 together conveyed a message against Filipino strike activity and managed to preclude Filipino uprisings in the area.[85]

White Californians alarmed by the specter of Filipino radicalism found some relief in the passage of congressional legislation aimed at Filipino exclusion. The Tydings-McDuffie Act, or the Philippines Independence Act of 1934, set a 10-year transition period for the Philippines to become "independent," though ostensibly still under commonwealth status. More significantly for exclusionists, the act also declared Filipino immigrants "aliens," since the Philippines would hence be considered a separate country, and set its annual immigration quota at 50 (under the 1924 Immigration Act, the minimum quota for all countries was 100).

In 1935, Republican congressman Richard Welch of San Jose introduced new legislation designed to repatriate Filipinos. Signed in July 1935, the Filipino Repatriation Act provided authorized transportation to send Filipinos in the United States to the Philippines at the federal government's expense on the condition that repatriates forfeit their right to reentry. The free ride home was open to some 46,000 Filipinos in the country, but between 1936 and 1941, just over 2,000 took advantage of the offer, far below the number projected by the Immigration and Naturalization Service, 10,000–15,000.[86] Carey McWilliams connected the strike activity of Filipino workers to calls for their repatriation, pointing out ironically how "after his brief but strenuous period of service to American capital, the Filipino faces deportation, as a fitting reward for his efforts."[87] Unambiguously outside the family farm ideal, being single men in America who lacked the capital to buy land and the legal right to own it, the Filipinos had become avid participants in struggles to improve their lot as agricultural workers. For that reason, they were further racialized according to their politics and ties to "radicals."

The loss of top leadership, along with the Communist Party's decision to dissolve independent unions, put the CAWIU out of business altogether by 1935 and ended both the era of overt participation by the CPUSA in the union movement and the CAWIU's dominance in California agriculture. Nevertheless, the ideas the CAWIU had introduced continued to gain power. Between January 1933 and June 1939, more than 90,000 harvest, packaging, and canning workers went on some 170 strikes. In the mid- to late 1930s, California accounted for at least a third and frequently all of the agricultural strikes occurring in the country at any given time. In 1937, the Congress of Industrial Organizations (CIO) established the United Cannery, Agricultural, Packing, and Allied Workers of America (UCAPAWA), which carried on the industry-organizing principles of the CAWIU and in 1939 became the seventh largest CIO affiliate. Dorothy Ray Healey, who had helped organize Filipino and Mexican workers in San Jose for one of the CAWIU's first cannery strikes in 1931, later became a national vice-president of the UCAPAWA by 1939 and led a dramatic, successful strike of mostly Mexican women at a large food processing plant in Los Angeles. The UCAPAWA ultimately exceeded the CAWIU in its commitment to civil rights activism for agricultural and cannery workers within and beyond the Santa Clara Valley, attracting a broad cross section of the state's multiethnic population and becoming the "heartbeat" of California union organizing in the late 1930s.[88]

Continuity, Change, and the "Transient Labor" Problem

In a few intense years, the repression of the CAWIU and leftist labor elements, along with exclusion and repatriation measures, neutralized the Filipino radical threat for most white Santa Clara Valley residents, who no longer saw Filipino men as either social or economic hazards. Reflecting shifting attitudes toward Filipinos, Valley residents and officials remained divided over the issue of taxi dance halls, but without the same level of panicked fervor that had incited the Watsonville violence in 1930. In Alviso, a hundred residents who in June 1935 petitioned for the city council to prohibit the dances on grounds that they were a "nuisance to the city" were challenged by another group of residents who contended that the dances were "an excellent source of revenue for the upkeep of municipal property and the payment of officials." Expressions of blatant disapproval of Filipino-white sexual unions were rare in this debate, perhaps assuaged by the inclusion of Filipinos in amended state miscegenation laws. Alviso dance hall operator Joseph Messina called the dances orderly and "respectable affairs" that provided not only income for the city but also employment for Alviso residents. Judge William Ortley defended the Alviso dance halls and even commended the white women who worked there because they helped "clean up the Filipino boys of their money," ensuring that the Filipinos returned to work promptly after each "pay day spree." The judge released twenty-two-year-old Bobbie Robinson, a female dance hall employee arrested on vagrancy charges, at the same time proclaiming himself to be in favor of "as many dances as could be run peaceably" by the city of Alviso. Fully aware that the dances prominently featured physical contact between Filipino men and white women, Ortley postulated that such interactions were harmless and served to keep Filipinos dependent, docile workers who spent all their earnings on cheap amusements with white women.[89] The judge, along with Valley residents who supported dance halls for pragmatic reasons like contributing to city coffers, showed that by the mid-1930s, white public opinion on Filipino interracial relationships had evolved from outrage and disgust to implicit acceptance.

If tensions between whites and Filipinos simmered down following anti-miscegenation and repatriation measures, interethnic conflict between Filipino and Japanese residents changed little in the latter half of the 1930s, which saw some notable criminal incidents. Some Filipinos, frustrated by actions of their Japanese employers, took matters into their own hands. In 1936, for example, several Filipino laborers forged a series of checks in the name of a Japanese farmer from Mountain View. With accomplices, Gaspar Acosta and Pascual Bagasol cashed forged checks in amounts totaling several hundred dollars before bank officials finally became suspicious and notified local police. The men were arrested and found guilty at a perfunctory trial in 1937.[90] During the same year, a more serious crime resulted from Filipino-Japanese animosity.

On October 24, 1936, a group of Filipino men stormed into farm manager Joe Nishida's kitchen and stole $1,300 from him at gunpoint. The thieves knew in advance that Nishida planned to pay out his employees at a designated time on his Campbell ranch. In the chaos that followed, a member of the Filipino group accidentally shot and killed one of his accomplices, Pedro Ancheta. The jury found six of the men involved guilty of first-degree robbery; five of them were also found guilty of first-degree murder and sentenced to life imprisonment.[91]

According to the prosecution, two men who had worked for Nishida during harvest season for three years, cousins Marcella and Fred Avelino, met up with five Filipino acquaintances from San Francisco at an Alviso dance hall one week before the robbery and proposed that the men carry out a plan to rob Nishida on the day he was to pay his workers' wages in cash. Nishida, twenty-eight years old in 1937, and his wife Kimiyo, twenty-seven, both born in California, lived on Eden Avenue in Campbell. Their extended household included their seven-year-old daughter, Naomi, Joe Nishida's parents, Yaichi and Tome, and at least one other relative, Sada Tokutomi, possibly Kimiyo's sister. Yaichi and Tome Nishida had arrived in California in 1906 and by 1910, they were berry and vegetable farmers on Milpitas Road in San Jose, neighbors of the Araki family as well as Jeremiah O'Brien.[92] Their son Jitsuo, who went by the name Joe, had taken over the family farming operation by 1930 when he was just twenty-one. At the time of the robbery six years later, he was managing multiple farms for West Land Farms Incorporated, likely one of many Japanese farming corporations formed to circumvent alien land laws. West Land owned a pea ranch on Homestead Road in Santa Clara, along with the Campbell ranch where the Nishidas resided.[93]

The bulk of the wide-ranging testimony in the murder and robbery trial focused on witness accounts of the sequence of events surrounding the shooting. The sworn statements also revealed hints of discord between Joe Nishida and his Filipino employees. Nishida, who was not seriously injured in the robbery, testified in the Santa Clara County Superior Court that earlier in the harvest season he had "a little trouble" with the Avelinos as they demanded "more money to pick berries" and had discharged Fred Avelino about three weeks before the robbery and shooting took place. Marcella Avelino and his crew of eight to nine men remained in Nishida's employ at the time of the incident, boarding in shacks at the pea ranch on Homestead Road. Nishida acknowledged that Marcella Avelino was a competent contractor who knew enough English to negotiate terms of labor. The Nisei farmer showed some contempt for the Filipino's after-work behavior, however, suggesting that he thought Avelino intended to spend his earnings as soon as he was paid because "he always goes out every night." Attorneys unsuccessfully moved to strike that statement from the record. The defense insinuated that Nishida failed to pay his Filipino employees in full on a regular basis, though no direct evidence emerged to back that claim.[94] Whether the promise of quick cash, a vendetta against a boss perceived as stingy and condescending, or simmering interethnic hostility motivated the armed robbery and incidental murder, court records do not unequivocally prove.

Even though they were relatively more prosperous and established than Filipino migrants in the 1930s, Japanese farmers remained heavily constricted by alien land laws, which in part relegated them to cultivating less lucrative crops (after thirty years in California, the Nishidas never transitioned from berry and vegetable farming to orchard fruit cultivation), resulting in the same socioeconomic patterns that had plagued them since their arrival in the 1900s. The Great Depression pitted these two marginalized Asian immigrant groups against each other in the realm of agriculture and stymied any mutual understanding. Filipino participation in strikes against white and Japanese growers fostered further mistrust between the two Asian communities. Some time in 1941 before the bombing of Pearl Harbor, three generations of the Nishida family uprooted themselves from Santa Clara County, where they had resided for about three decades, and moved to Fresno County. There they continued truck farming until they were forcibly removed to Poston War Relocation Center in Arizona in 1942. The family never returned to the Santa Clara Valley and after the war resettled in Fresno County.[95]

Filipino exclusion and repatriation did not allay all fears of labor unrest and Communist activity. As the Depression wore on, Charles Derby, the antiradical San Jose prune grower, became involved in forming a county unit of the Associated Farmers of California and was named vice president of the unit in March 1937. During the spring of 1937, Derby was consumed with attending meetings and recruiting members for the Associated Farmers, an organization that first emerged in 1934, funded primarily by corporate interests to combat farm labor unionizing and Communism. The delayed formation of a Santa Clara Valley branch in part reflected the lack of large industrial agricultural operations in the Valley compared to the Central Valley, though growers like Derby still were concerned that their economic position was being undermined by "radicals." On April 2, 1937, Derby wrote that he had "spent practically all day on Asso. Farmers business. We got machinery started to gather in membership faster as we have information that the Reds will move in on this county shortly. Had a commity [sic] from San Mateo County down to ask our advice in forming a unit in that county." Several days later, representing the Associated Farmers, he met with county supervisors and the sheriff, ostensibly to prepare for potential Communist agitation, "trying to get proper equipment so that the laws may be enforced and we in the country may be protected." Mainstream local organizations that supported business interests like the San Jose Chamber of Commerce, the Growers and Employers League, and the Merchants Association banded together with the newly formed branch of the Associated Farmers and held dinner meetings that Derby attended."[96] The sentiment that "Reds" posed a threat to fruit growers who lived "in the country," rural areas with crops maintained and harvested by laborers possibly receptive to leftist organizing, continued to pervade the minds of men like Derby during the Depression years.

By 1937, however, Santa Clara County growers mobilizing to defend themselves from "Reds" were no longer referring only to the disturbing collusion between radical instigators and mostly Filipino and Mexican laborers under the CAWIU. White refugees fleeing from the ravages of the drought in the Plains states were pouring into California in record numbers, complicating the racialized structure of the farm labor market, which had previously relied on Asians and Mexicans. There were clear signs that white farmers in the Santa Clara Valley, long accustomed to a nonwhite agricultural labor force, found the new white migrants less than ideal replacements at best, and burdensome social nuisances susceptible to leftist propaganda at worst. Fears of lawlessness among the unemployed plagued local residents, who made numerous reports of young white men engaging in public drunkenness, vandalism, burglary, and other crimes.[97]

In one particularly egregious incident during the summer of 1936, a group of white prune pickers, enraged over the wages they had received from management at the Blabon ranch in Cupertino, went on a destructive rampage there, smashing windows and stripping fruit from trees. When seventy-year-old Abbie Blabon tried to stop them, the "gang of malicious boys," as the Mercury Herald called them, struck her on the arm with a stick. She could not identify her assailants and likely did not have any direct interaction with the dozens of prune harvesters who worked on the ranch prior to the attack. Her husband J.D. (Joseph Dudley)

Blabon, also seventy, was a descendant of pioneers who had arrived in Santa Clara County before the gold rush. One of the largest prune growers in the county, J.D. Blabon resided on the family homestead in Cupertino with his wife; his brother William lived nearby in their parents' old home and owned another portion of the family farm, also devoted to prune orchards.[98] That vengeful white workers, purportedly "inflamed by liquor," would assault affluent, elderly fruit ranchers because of a wage dispute was immensely disconcerting to Valley growers, still facing low prices for their fruit. Such incidents, unheard of in the decades they had employed Chinese, Japanese, and Filipino ranch hands, made it difficult for local growers to accept as viable seasonal workers the Okies, new white migrants from the Midwest, despite the latter's increasingly positive portrayals in the press.[99]

The suffering of the impoverished Okies, which New Deal reformers were beginning to bring into focus, had garnered widespread national sympathy by the middle of the decade, but also prompted new concerns among local white farmers. In October 1936, the *San Francisco News* published a seven-part series called "The Harvest Gypsies" by John Steinbeck. These articles by the future author of *The Grapes of Wrath* exemplified the new spotlight on white migrant families, albeit at the expense of "equally suffering Mexican, Filipino, Japanese, Chinese, and Indian agricultural laborers."[100] Steinbeck's articles set up a curious dichotomy between what he considered the "old" type of migrant agricultural laborers, invariably nonwhite, and the "new migrants," white families who were the backbone of rural America, "descendants of men who crossed into the Midwest, who won their lands by fighting, who cultivated the prairies."

Rationalizing that Mexicans and Filipinos were "being deported and repatriated very rapidly" and thus would not constitute a social problem much longer, Steinbeck explained his singular focus on the new migrants, "resourceful and intelligent Americans" of "English, German and Scandinavian descent," with strong, wholesome names like "Munns, Holbrooks, Hansens, Schmidts." He argued it was a shame for white American families of "good stock" to be living so shabbily, precisely because they were not "peons."[101] Whereas "The Harvest Gypsies" referred to the presence of Japanese, Filipino, and Mexican farm laborers if only to set up the foil of "old migrants" versus the new strong-blooded white American migrants, *The Grapes of Wrath*, written in Los Gatos in the western foothills of Santa Clara County in 1938, focused solely on the plight of white migrant families and depicted no trace of nonwhites struggling for survival during the 1930s.[102]

Reflective of the turn in national sentiment by the late 1930s, the best-selling novel that became a Hollywood film sensation fostered the invisibility of nonwhite farm laborers. The *San Francisco News* editorialized in response to Steinbeck's 1936 series: "These newcomers are Americans of old-stock, self-reliant men and women.... They cannot long be handled as the Japanese, Mexicans and Filipinos who preceded them were handled. They expect to be treated like Americans, and they must be."[103] As historian Neil Foley observes about the dynamics of race in the 1930s, "Only when whites were reduced to living like Mexicans and blacks did the nation take notice.... Such a large army of migrant whites was unsettling to white America." To New Deal liberals like Steinbeck, photographer Dorothea Lange, and her husband, economist Paul Taylor, exploiting white compassion for the Okies was justified if it led to improved conditions for all farm laborers.[104]

But evidence from the Santa Clara Valley shows that the degree of empathy white native-born Californians exhibited toward Okie migrants depended on class status. On the one hand, organized labor increasingly linked the union cause to that of the displaced transient agricultural laborers. The Santa Clara County Labor Council expressed concern for white migrants and passed a resolution in 1937 that condemned the "deplorable conditions existing among transient and dust-bowl refugees" in California. The council declared the federal and state governments "criminally negligent about providing rehabilitation and care for ever increasing thousands of unemployed workers coming to California each year," constituting a "homeless army of some 100,000 workers and their families."[105] The *Union Gazette* chastised growers for being "quite satisfied with allowing the present uncharted and uncontrolled stream of labor to come in on the chance of getting work, and to round it up and run it across the county line when the labor supply suited the needs of the growers." Concurring that growers wanted to maintain an "oversupply of labor" and were not concerned with the living conditions of workers, labor representatives castigated Santa Clara County supervisors for bowing to the demands of growers and being in "hearty accord" with their policy.[106]

On the other hand, Santa Clara Valley growers, devoid of Steinbeck's New Deal liberalism, feared the embittered migrants, under the sway of communist recruiters, would turn against their employers. In the spring of 1937, the organizing board of the county labor council reached out to white migrants and invited them to join a union of fruit and vegetable pickers. The board distributed pamphlets targeting white household heads in particular, appealing to their diminished ability to provide for families: "Perhaps you used to farm for yourself in Texas, Oklahoma, Kansas or some other place before the drought ruined you, and the bankers or mortgage company grabbed your farm.... You can see the difference between the way your kids looked when you could feed them right, and give them milk, and clothes and shoes, and the way they look today when they are hungry half the time and running in rags." A family man, the flyer urged, would consider what "a union that could get you higher pay and better living conditions would mean for the kids."

Mounting pressure on local growers like Charles Derby to address the plight of the new migrants from the Midwest and Southwest sped the formation of the county branch of the Associated Farmers in 1937. Though there was no evidence that local white migrants responded by unionizing in any significant way, the prospect nonetheless worried growers, who began to speak out more forcefully on behalf of their own interests. At the San Francisco meeting of a federal farm tenancy committee in early 1937, Santa Clara Valley grower John Leonard defended the rights of his peers who were "paying taxes to support fellows who refuse to work [and those] trying to get something for nothing." Other farm owners said they were improving living conditions for laborers on their properties as quickly as possible, but they grumbled about their mortgage burdens and having to pay California farm wages, the highest in the nation. Leonard asserted it was "farmers rather than workers" who needed help from the government, specifically in the form of refinancing legislation.[107]

Valley growers' opposition to white "transient labor" was apparent as they balked at efforts to establish a Farm Security Administration (FSA) migratory labor camp during the late 1930s. W. S. Rice, head of the field department of the California Prune and Apricot Growers Association noted the local opposition to the presence of a camp: "People talked of getting a F.S.A. camp in the county last year. The idea failed because each person wanted the camp to be placed in some other man's territory." Growers' disdain for the FSA stemmed from what they perceived as government-sponsored programs that interfered with local labor markets by making white workers excessively demanding and unwilling to work for low wages.[108] Upon learning of FSA proposals to construct camp facilities in their neighborhood, Los Gatos growers banded together in protest. More than 20 growers calling themselves "farm owners upon whom will be laid the burden of supplying these people with work" signed a letter to the FSA deriding the planned camp for numerous reasons and identifying their area as one of small farms that did not require migrant labor. Furthermore, growers argued, the county already had "more migrants than it can employ," and those who were "making commendable efforts at establishing themselves in their own homes" would be "injured" by having to compete for jobs with newcomers attracted to a federal camp.

The Associated Farmers categorically opposed the federal migrant camp program and suspected that camps would become union organizing centers. Indeed, the Communist-led UCAPAWA had branch headquarters in at least one FSA migrant labor camp. The vast majority of Okies did not join unions, however, being too wedded to their white racial identity and leery of collective action to ally with Filipino and Mexican laborers. Valley growers were ultimately successful in barring the construction of a camp in Santa Clara County, and by July 1941, the FSA abandoned its plans of leasing or purchasing land to build one there altogether.[109] Elsewhere in California, the Resettlement Administration and its successor, the FSA, constructed 15 migrant labor camps, none in the vicinity of the Santa Clara Valley. The program was eliminated after World War II.

The attempt to open an FSA camp in the Valley generated a plethora of mail from objecting farmers, including a petition to the agency's San Francisco district office from residents on the West Side. The petitioners complained that a "transient labor camp" was unnecessary and would have a detrimental effect on property values. Among the signatories were upstanding citizens whose names grace local elementary schools, parks, and streets to this day: Regnart, Jollyman, Bollinger, and others. Also embedded in the dozens of signatures were those of Henry Kurasaki and Harry S. Kobayashi of Cupertino, and Frank P. Ogata of San Jose. Kurasaki was the son of Matagoro and Naka Kurasaki, who had farmed vegetables for Henrietta Cropley in the 1910s before purchasing a small prune orchard in West San Jose in 1919. After graduating from high school in 1933, Henry Kurasaki took over operation of the 11-acre orchard from his father.[110]

The West Side was known for prune and apricot orchards, so the Japanese who farmed there were an elite minority who grew the region's coveted crops, unlike the majority of their countrymen in berries and truck produce. Japanese immigrants and their families disappeared from public attention during the 1930s, for there was no place in the national narrative for nonwhite family farmers or people of color uninvolved in labor unrest. But by the end of the decade, the white neighbors of Japanese fruit growers in the Santa Clara Valley went so far as to usher them into the fold as fellow family farmers opposing the presence of "transient" laborers and other potentially disruptive elements.

Japanese growers, weary after enduring years of low prices and uncertain times, understood that weathering the Depression required distancing themselves from Filipinos and other nonwhites. Thus they focused on maintaining their reputation for quietly farming and not having to seek public assistance as the Okies did. The Japanese signatures on a petition to oppose an FSA migrant labor camp marked how racial dynamics in the "Valley of Heart's Delight" had changed from the early twentieth century. The tentative acceptance of local Japanese farmers by whites was exemplified informally in another surprising way: the growing popularity of baseball in the Japanese American community during the 1930s, coinciding with Nisei men coming of age as young adults and replacing older Issei players, who had formed teams and recreational leagues throughout the state beginning in the late 1910s. A spirit of friendly competition between white and Japanese teams in San Jose characterized games, covered frequently in the local press.

After a group of American League All-Stars that included Babe Ruth toured Japan in late 1934, the Tokyo Giants reciprocated with an American tour in 1935 and played the San Jose Asahi team in March before a crowd of 1,500 spectators.

The *San Jose News* proudly reported the local team's 3–2 victory over the Giants, "a team every baseball fan in the world has heard of," and celebrated the Asahi's pitcher, "weather-beaten farmer" Russell Hinaga, as the game's hero. Hinaga managed a truck farm on Trimble Road in San Jose, where he lived with his wife and children. His younger brother Chickayohsi "Chickie" Hinaga, the team's shortstop, also worked on the farm. Indeed, nearly all the Asahi's members and enthusiasts of the popular American pastime were Valley farmers and farm laborers. The team was funded by the Japanese community's more well-to-do growers, like brothers Fudetaro and Seijiro Horio, early Issei immigrants who had farmed for white landowners before purchasing prune orchards on Foxworthy Road prior to 1913. The Asahi was part of the Northern California Japanese Baseball League, but also played all-white local teams, and the Asahi Baseball Park in San Jose often hosted games in which both teams were white.[111]

During the Depression, the game of baseball, whether played by white or Japanese residents, provided a welcome diversion for demoralized farmers and became a symbol for the possibility of shared interests between the Valley's Japanese and white growers. By the 1930s, alien land laws had rendered most Japanese immigrant farmers dependent on white middlemen and the Nisei to procure farmland for them. Japanese exclusion ensured that the resident population would not expand with the arrival of new immigrants. The bulk of Japanese farm families who remained solvent in agriculture continued to cultivate less profitable vegetable and berry crops requiring copious amounts of hand labor, often provided by newcomers from the Philippines. Issei able to venture into orchard fruit production did not fare much better in the 1930s and struggled along with white growers in the vexing Depression-era market. Under these circumstances, the Japanese community posed no real or perceived threat to white hegemony, and in fact had a common goal of maintaining a compliant labor force. Just as white growers felt they had the right to suppress the Filipino, Mexican, and other farm laborers who dared to strike for higher wages and better conditions, threatening growers' already precarious livelihoods, petitioners protesting the construction of an FSA camp, both white and Japanese, refused to let government bureaucrats spoil what they had achieved. The Valley's white growers emerged from the 1930s hardened but with firm resolve that the family farm ideal was worth protecting as a most enlightened, American way of life. For the region's Japanese farmers, stability proved elusive as the harrowing events of World War II devastated their community and made the Japanese targets of white American racism all over again.

Epilogue

World War II initiated a series of extraordinary changes in the economy and society of the Santa Clara Valley, ushering in a new era when the "Garden of the World" would become "Silicon Valley." After the bombing of Pearl Harbor on December 7, 1941, Japanese residents of the Santa Clara Valley were no longer absent from public discourse, as they had been during the Great Depression. Though whites increasingly accepted the Japanese as family farmers, when the United States entered World War II, Japanese Americans found their loyalty questioned and their foreignness affirmed. In a matter of months, the government rounded up the approximately 4,000 residents of Japanese descent in Santa Clara County and sent them to assembly centers and ultimately internment camps, where they remained for at least three years. Numbering only in the hundreds on the eve of the war, the region's Chinese and Filipino populations found new opportunities just as their Japanese neighbors faced tragic circumstances. A host of second-generation Chinese Americans from the Santa Clara Valley joined the war effort, working in Bay Area shipyards, serving in combat units in Europe and Asia, and finding administrative and professional positions in the military.[1] Local Filipinos also served in the armed forces, though many remained in agriculture, often managing Japanese internees' farms. In 1942, upon receiving an induction notice while working as a ranch hand in San Jose, Mariano Catolico reported to the local draft board, only to be told that his current employment qualified him for a six-month exemption from military service. The woman at the office who granted him the deferment, Catolico recalled, declared that "you Filipinos are hard working; we can depend on you." His brother and most of his friends were already serving in the army at the time, and "they kept urging me to join," saying there was a good chance Catolico could become an officer because he had advanced degrees. He finally enlisted with the U.S. Merchant Marine and traveled to the Philippines in 1945.[2]

Leaving Santa Clara Valley

In the winter of 1941 and 1942, Japanese residents all along the Pacific coast found themselves scrutinized and uncertain of the future. Itsuo Uenaka, who was twelve years old when the bombing of Pearl Harbor occurred, recalled playing with his friends on his parents' strawberry ranch. Caucasian neighbors became suspicious and kept their distance from his parents. As Uenaka recounted, "It was not a good thing to be associated with Japanese when the war broke out.... It was very, very uncomfortable." Before being sent to Topaz, Utah, in May 1942, his parents destroyed their collection of Japanese records and mementos. Uenaka's family resettled in the Valley after the war .[3] Eiichi Sakauye was thirty years old, farming with his father in San Jose, when the family heard news of the Japanese attack on Pearl Harbor. The government froze their bank account, which prevented the Sakauyes from paying the twelve workers employed on their farm. As a result, most of the workers left. One evening, Sakauye was driving with his friend David T. Rayner, a county agricultural commissioner who had asked him to help with some farm inspections. Police stopped them on the road and officers arrested Sakauye for violating the 8 p.m. curfew imposed on "enemy aliens." Even obvious ties with a county official did not protect Sakauye from police enforcement of the curfew for anyone who appeared to be of Japanese descent.[4]

President Franklin D. Roosevelt signed Executive Order 9066 on February 19, 1942, authorizing the War Department to establish security zones from which designated persons were to be excluded. To avoid forced eviction, some 10,000 Japanese on the West Coast voluntarily moved inland, outside the sensitive military zone. The family of Shoji Takeda, who had been celery growers in the Santa Clara Valley, moved to Gridley in Butte County during the war and farmed tomatoes. Hatsu Kanemoto and her husband, Yoshito, then newlyweds, decided to leave San Jose and go to Colorado with her family, where they found poorly paid work as farm laborers and sharecroppers. She recalled the lack of autonomy: "You weren't running your own farm, working for yourself. You were working for someone else." Sharecropping onions and cabbage, the Kanemotos went steadily into debt, living a "hand-to-mouth existence." In Colorado, Hatsu joined her husband in the fields, keeping their children inside the car with the windows rolled down while they tended to the crops. Decades later, she concluded that incarceration might have been a better option: "If we had to do it all over again, we'd go to camp."[5]

Most of the Valley's Japanese stayed on their farms, waiting for events to unfold, not expecting the government to round up local, native-born Americans. Sakauye remembered his white friends and neighbors telling him, "You won't be relocated, you are a citizen—just like us." As it became clear that the government was forcing the Japanese to leave their homes and farms, Sakauye remained incredulous: "you're born, reared, and lived here, and worked as a family, and now we're going to have to leave tomorrow morning and go to the station in San Jose. Gosh, I don't know. I just—went mentally berserk. Mentally blank so to speak."[6] On March 27, the military rescinded the option of voluntary relocation inland for West Coast Japanese and ordered all persons of Japanese ancestry to remain in the restricted zone and await government evacuation. Acknowledging the important role of these "enemy aliens" as farmers, General John L. DeWitt, head of the Western Defense Command, warned that the army would consider any neglect of crops to be sabotage. At the same time, the Wartime Civil Control Administration (WCCA) administered the transfer of Japanese farms to non-Japanese operators. FSA field agent Charles Hearn reported that Santa Clara County Japanese were cooperating "absolutely 100 percent," quelling public fears of crop sabotage.[7]

In the spring of 1942, Japanese farmers in the Valley hurriedly made arrangements to dispose of all "personal and real property" as ordered by the WCCA. Because of alien land laws, few Japanese residents were landowners, but many rented farmland and faced the quandary of what to do with the crops they had already planted for the season. San Jose tenant farmer Katsusaburo Kawahara, by then in his early forties, was cultivating more than 200 acres at the time of the war. He sold his crops and farm equipment to former schoolmate Leo Garcillo, an Italian American, and his partner, Al Gomes, for a mere $3,000, far below actual value. Because he did not own the land, Kawahara assumed he had no other option: "I figured my farming career was over.... The land wasn't mine—it was just 'temporary' farming." Writing from a detention camp in Santa Fe, New Mexico, Hisajiro Inouye (no relation to Jenzaburo Inouye) thanked a Mrs. Weston of San Jose for overseeing the sale of farm equipment belonging to him and his siblings before they left the Valley in haste.[8]

As the evacuation proceeded, there were additional changes in the Valley. Filipino laborers, looked down upon by some Japanese immigrants in the 1930s, were now enlisted to run evacuees' farms. The expertise of his Filipino workers, according to Kawahara, helped Garcillo and Gomes turn a handsome profit in 1942. Another San Jose farmer, Yoshio Ando, who did own property, rented his land to a former Filipino employee, Johnny Ibarra, for a nominal amount that covered taxes and mortgage interest on the land. Masao and Leonard Oku, carnation growers in Mountain View, also employed Filipinos to look after their land, carrying on the business by telephone while interned in Colorado.[9]

Evacuation happened speedily and methodically in the Santa Clara Valley, as it did all along the West Coast. On May 21, 1942, the WCCA directed all Japanese in northern Santa Clara County to deposit their automobiles at its office in San

Jose. On May 24 and 25, at a WCCA control station set up in the men's gymna-
sium at San Jose State College, 2,847 Japanese registered with the civil control
agency.[10] Two days later, special trains, one per day, began departing from the
Southern Pacific station on North San Pedro Street in downtown San Jose, head-
ing to the Santa Anita racetrack outside Los Angeles and to a temporary facility
in Pomona, even though the nearest assembly center was the Tanforan racetrack
in San Bruno, only about 40 miles north of San Jose. Kawahara was stunned by
the speed with which the military rounded up the Japanese: "I never thought
they would put us all into a camp—it's such a big job. But they did. The army did
it."[11] Stanford history professor Yamato Ichihashi, his wife, Kei, and their son,
Woodrow, were among the 144 Japanese Americans from the Palo Alto area
taken to Santa Anita. Ichihashi described the grimy accommodations in his
diary, the only known comprehensive account of internment written by an
internee during the events: "A stable which housed a horse now houses from 5 to
6 humans.... These are not only unsanitary, but mentally and morally depres-
sive."[12]

Wayne Kanemoto (no relation to Hatsu), born in San Jose to Japanese immigrants from Hiroshima and a graduate of Santa Clara University Law School,
recalled being at Santa Anita when the state bar examination was administered
in the summer of 1942. For three days, a white official escorted Kanemoto, who
was not allowed to travel on his own, from the assembly center to the City Hall
of Los Angeles where the examination was being given, and back to Santa Anita
in the evening. Kanemoto and his family were sent to the Gila River Relocation
Center in Arizona, where he learned that he had passed the bar, though his
professional options remained severely limited: "I always jokingly tell my colleagues that I was sworn into the State Bar of California under the shade of a
saguaro cactus in the middle of the state of Arizona on an Indian reservation. But
the minute I was sworn in I could not practice law because my license was only
good in California, where I could not go." Kanemoto went on to become a judge
on the Santa Clara County Municipal Court in 1961, one of the first Japanese
American judges appointed.[13]

Most of Santa Clara County's Japanese (about 2,572) traveled from Santa
Anita and Pomona Assembly Centers to Heart Mountain Relocation Center in
northwest Wyoming. Some 800 residents of Gilroy and the southern third of the
county were confined at Salinas Assembly Center and eventually taken to a camp
in Poston, Arizona, officially called the Colorado River Relocation Center. By
November 1942, the military had forcibly removed from their homes more than
120,000 Japanese residents, two-thirds of whom were American citizens, and
sent them to one of ten "relocation camps." A native of Santa Clara County, Katie
Hironaka, who delivered her first child at Pomona Assembly Center while her
husband, Alvin Uchiyama, served in the military, expressed the dread she felt

arriving at Heart Mountain in August of 1942: "It's really hard to even describe how you really, really felt ... especially with the Isseis, I think, it was very heartbreaking for them to go from a home that they lived in ... to a place like that, with nothing there, but one big pot stove, and beds. Just imagine that. Just having nothing, but the beds and the big old stove."[14]

The peak population of Heart Mountain exceeded 10,700, with two-thirds of internees hailing from Los Angeles County and a quarter from Santa Clara County, while the remainder were from San Francisco and Yakima, Washington. The Japanese essentially ran the camp, serving as cooks, police, mess hall attendants, construction workers, maintenance supervisors, teachers, and health care providers. Kawahara recalled being paid $16 a month for running a boiler in the barracks.[15]

Decades later, the bitter Wyoming cold stood out in the memories of Japanese internees from the Santa Clara Valley. The climate was considered severe even by War Relocation Authority (WRA) standards.[16] Masuo Akizuki, who had lived in San Jose since 1912 when he was sixteen years old, recalled Heart Mountain being "so cold in winter, everything was frozen." His eldest son was playing football when he fell on the frozen ground and suffered a broken rib. Former San Jose resident Harry Nishiura, whose wife was ill, found himself washing diapers for his infant children in the wintertime: "When you wash the diaper and step outside, it becomes an icicle in two seconds. The temperature went down to thirty-one below zero." Sakauye, who worked with the weather bureau at Heart Mountain for over two years, confirmed that 12 degrees below zero was the average winter temperature, while the record low, on Christmas Day, 1942, was 35 degrees below zero. Windstorms and dust storms were common in the high elevation.[17]

The agricultural expertise of the West Coast Japanese played a significant part in making the desolate Wyoming landscape bloom. Japanese internees operated about 1,500 acres of land to grow vegetables and grain at Heart Mountain and welcomed the opportunity to farm. Sakauye said they were "tickled to get out in the field ... just like a bird left out of the cage" after being confined to the barracks. At harvest time, around 400 Japanese worked in the fields. As assistant farm superintendent of the camp, Sakauye proudly remembered how he and others transformed into farmland fields that had previously been used only for grazing and how they cultivated an abundance of radishes, turnips, peas, corn, celery, potatoes, and cabbage. Crops flourished because of the internees' agricultural skills and knowledge of which vegetables were suited to certain types of soil. Sakauye's job was to coordinate crop plantings for the camp's agricultural department, calculating how long it would take for vegetables to mature, factoring in the short growing season of 109 days, much different from that of the temperate Santa Clara Valley. Japanese growers from Washington State who

Figure 7.1. Internees weeding at Heart Mountain Relocation Center, where they cultivated 30 acres of cucumbers and melons. The little white domes, or caps, were designed to protect crops from frost damage.

Courtesy of Japanese American Museum of San Jose.

were more experienced with farming in a cold climate, Sakauye noted, shared their knowledge of using hothouses to start seedlings indoors to be set out when the danger of frost was over, which gave the vegetables a head start and took advantage of the truncated growing period.

The internees were so successful that there was a surplus of produce, prompting them to start a *tsukemono* factory to pickle vegetables as well as a canning operation outside the camp. Years later, when he made a trip to Heart Mountain with his son-in-law, Ernest Kazato, a local store owner recognized Sakauye and praised the efforts of the interned Japanese farmers: "You showed us what can be done with this land. You showed us how to grow food."[18]

Another resourceful Santa Clara Valley internee who utilized his farming and food processing background at Heart Mountain was former T.M.T.O. partner and cannery operator Yasutaro Oku. In the spring of 1945, camp officials discovered in his possession "five barrels of mash, each barrel equivalent to 15–20 gallons, plus 5 gallons of sake and paraphernalia for manufacturing sake." Oku pled guilty to charges of brewing sake in violation of the camp's criminal code and was ordered to spend 15 days in jail, but a judicial commission made up of fellow internees suspended the sentence.[19]

In the span of three years of confinement at Heart Mountain, morale progressively declined among the Japanese. According to Nishiura, in the first year, the internees were "full of spirit, working hard." As time passed, "their spirit and morals crack down." He said comparing pictures of the camp mess hall from first year to fourth showed the drastic decline in internees' effort. People scrambled and fought each other for government-issued items like coats and blankets. Some young men known as the "zoot suit group" formed a gang and committed petty crimes.[20] Adding to the tense, uneasy climate, Heart Mountain also became the site of organized draft resistance, a movement of Nisei men who refused to join the army unless their constitutional rights as citizens were restored. At a mass trial held in June 1944, the largest in Wyoming history, the 63 resisters, the majority of whom hailed from Santa Clara County, were sentenced to three-year prison terms.[21]

Starting Over

In early 1945, Japanese internees began a gradual return to the Santa Clara Valley, their numbers increasing throughout the year. The WRA, which established a San Jose office to facilitate Japanese resettlement, reported 60 Japanese in the county in March, 600 in June, and 2,500 in October. By January of 1946, there were almost 7,000 Japanese in Santa Clara County; the pre-war population had

Figure 7.2. Internees stacking *daikon* (Japanese radish) at Heart Mountain Relocation Center.
Courtesy of Japanese American Museum of San Jose.

been about 4,000. Sakauye said his was the first family to return to San Jose, though their homecoming was bittersweet: "We started over again. But...our great loss is something that is very difficult to measure in the monetary sense. I think we lost the best years of our lives."[22] Hironaka, who was in her mid-twenties when she left Heart Mountain, described the plight of the evacuees who traveled back to the Valley and had no place to live. Her parents initially stayed at the Buddhist church in San Jose that had been transformed into a hostel, while Hironaka lived with her in-laws, who had secured a barn in Mountain View for shelter. Looking back at the experience of returning after the war, she said, "that is the hardest thing, to come home and you have nothing. You're just, like homeless." To serve returnees, the hostel remained open until 1947, when it was converted back to its original use as a Buddhist church.[23]

In the postwar period, the Santa Clara Valley developed a reputation for being one of California's "bright spots of tolerance" where anti-Japanese violence and intimidation were minimal. As a result, Japanese internees hailing from elsewhere before the war decided to settle in the Valley when released from the camps, accounting for the county's high postwar Japanese population. Former U.S. congressman and transportation secretary Norman Mineta, who was ten years old when he was sent with his family from San Jose to Santa Anita and then Heart Mountain, noted that the Valley was considered a more hospitable place for Japanese Americans: "Many who were afraid to return elsewhere came here."[24] The warm welcome was no doubt in part due to the county's shortage of agricultural labor and the fact that many Japanese returned in time for harvest season. According to journalist Frank Taylor, after August 15, 1945, when the Japanese surrendered, the U.S. government lifted gasoline restrictions and the "Mexicans and Okies who had been the wartime farm workers gassed up and hit the highways, leaving the prune crop lying on the ground. An outcry came from farmers to save the fruit. The Japanese moved in and saved the crop."[25] Valley growers scrambled to hire Japanese returnees, skilled agriculturists in dire need of jobs. As political scientist Timothy Lukes and historian Gary Okihiro note, "The icy terrors directed against Japanese Americans during the winter and spring melted in the heat of the summer's harvest," as returning Japanese were credited with "saving" Valley crops in the summer of 1945.[26]

In addition to putting an end to the labor shortage in Santa Clara Valley upon their return, many Japanese resettlers took up strawberry growing, which also facilitated their acceptance by white residents. The old associations of race and crop that had linked Asians in the Valley with labor-intensive strawberries since the late nineteenth century reemerged during the postwar period. Strawberries called for copious care and labor but yielded fruit after only three months and sold for decent prices in the postwar years. Hatsu Kanemoto remembered the many "non-San Jose-ans," all former farmers, who arrived in the Valley and

became berry sharecroppers. Even the WRA acknowledged that because returning Japanese took up strawberry growing, they did not compete with whites,
who mostly cultivated orchard fruits, thus contributing to the reputation of
the Santa Clara Valley as a place where postwar reception was better than
elsewhere.[27]

After World War II, the Driscoll brothers, strawberry growers in Morgan Hill
in southern Santa Clara County, became one of the largest employers of Japanese
labor. To accommodate the newly enrolled Japanese American children, Burnett
School in Morgan Hill had to arrange for additional classroom facilities and hire
a new teacher.[28] Bunrei Utsunomiya moved from Santa Maria in Santa Barbara
County to the town of Coyote, located between San Jose and Morgan Hill, in the
early 1950s upon hearing it was "a good place for strawberries" and sharecropped
for four years until his wife said "she didn't want anymore" since "it was a very
hard job to grow strawberries." With their children grown and able to support
themselves, the Utsunomiyas had fewer expenses and no longer needed to
burden themselves with the difficult work of strawberry farming. The couple
bought a house in Santa Clara, where Bunrei became a gardener, like many Issei
men after the war.[29]

As much as strawberry growing was a viable option for returning Japanese
farmers, it nonetheless failed to provide a secure living. A thirty-two-year-old
Nisei in the Valley expressed his fears over the precarious nature of farm prices,
noting "It would be all right if the price of berries would stay the way it is now.
But if the price should slip a little, with production costs the way they are, we
could lose $3,000 to $4,000 easily. Then our capital would be gone." Another
Nisei, Henry Kurasaki, the farmer who had signed a petition to protest the
construction of an FSA transient labor camp on the West Side before the war,
did not grow prunes as his family had prior to internment. Instead, he concen-
trated on strawberries, both on his own farm and on the property off of Saratoga
Avenue, where he and other Japanese farmers sharecropped. Unable to make a
profit in the postwar years, Kurasaki supplemented his income with wage work
for white farmers, including some nearby Italian apricot growers.[30]

Rather than resume the backbreaking rigors of farming, some Japanese Americans opted for different careers after internment. Yoshijiro (George) Santo,
former San Jose farmer and brother-in-law of Jenzaburo Inouye, opened a grocery store in Japantown in 1946. Fred Inouye, Jenzaburo's eldest son, helped his
uncle establish Santo Market early on, but left to find a salaried job to support his
wife, Alice, and their three children, along with his stepmother and numerous
younger siblings who came to live with them. While he never returned to farming
after the war, Fred Inouye drew on his agricultural expertise to work as a field
representative and buyer for a San Jose produce processing company, and also
sold cuttings to local vegetable farmers.[31]

Although the WRA declared that Japanese resettlement in the Santa Clara Valley was "more favorable than in any other section of the west," the region was not immune to racial hostility. In March 1945, an arsonist set fire to the San Jose home of pear grower Joe Takeda while he and his family were sleeping. As family members fled and attempted to put out the fire, someone drove by and shot at them. Over forty years later, Phil Matsumura, who was twenty-eight years old and living with the Takedas, his in-laws, recalled the terrifying night, but affirmed it as an exception to the otherwise welcoming environment of the Santa Clara Valley. "There were some isolated cases like this," Matsumura said. "But somehow the climate here was better."[32] "Better" or not, on June 23, 1945, a gunman fired a shot at the San Jose home of James E. Edmiston, district supervisor of the WRA. Though the sheriff deemed the incident accidental, Edmiston, nicknamed

Figure 7.3. The Inouye family outside their new home in San Jose, 1945. Alice and Fred Inouye in back row, center, with their sons, Gerald and Melvin, seated in front; Fred's stepmother, Isono Inouye, back row, left; Fred's sisters Lilly (standing) and Ruth (seated). War Relocation Authority Photographs of Japanese-American Evacuation and Resettlement, The Bancroft Library, University of California, Berkeley.

"Suzuki" for his defense of Japanese returnees, was likely the target of local racists. In another threatening incident, reminiscent of the threats anti-Filipino agitators placed in the mailboxes of Valley fruit growers in 1930, on July 25, 1945, Sakauye found a placard in his mailbox that read "SEND ALL JAPS BACK TO JAPAN," signed "COMPLIMENTS OF EVERY RANCHER THIS SIDE OF THE BAYSHORE HIGHWAY YOU BASTARDS." Sakauye also reported to the WRA that some laborers on a neighboring farm had harassed him verbally and their foreman informed him "that he and his family were not wanted and that it would be healthier for them to leave California."[33]

Wartime incarceration had destroyed many Japanese farms in the Valley, and some Issei, who were advanced in age and lacked land to return to or family ties, could not start over. Sakauye summed up the plight of the elderly Japanese after the war: "Their ambitions are gone. Even if they had ambitions, they're too old to do anything anymore." Many languished at county institutions. Sakauye occasionally visited invalid Issei and tried to "cheer them up, tell them something about what's going on, but I'm too busy keeping up on my own farm." Seeing these former farmers reduced to hospital patients was painful, and he recalled how he "just walked out in tears to see what happened."[34]

Midori Kimura, whose husband, Toshio, had a stroke a month after the family returned to San Jose, said he fell sick "of worry" at Heart Mountain. He was sixty-two years old when he passed away within a week of his stroke, leaving Midori with seven children, the youngest eight years old. She worked as a domestic for the first time in her life, while her older children found farming jobs in the summer to put themselves through college.[35] Daughter June Kimura, a student at San Jose High School when the war started, said of her father: "He had heart trouble and a stroke, but I think he really died of a broken heart." Midori Kimura became one of four Japanese plaintiffs in San Jose involved in a Supreme Court lawsuit demanding redress and reparations for survivors of internment. In October 1990, at the age of ninety-three, Kimura received a check for $20,000 and an official letter of apology from President George H. W. Bush.[36]

Those who attempted to start over felt pressure to work quickly to make up for all they had lost. One Berryessa farmer said there was no use looking back, or he would "go crazy." All he could do, he reported, was "work like when first come to this country. Pick cherries, pick pears, pick apricots, pick tomatoes." He had to "start all over again like when come from Japan, but faster this time." A gardener who worked near Palo Alto after the war said all of the Japanese he knew were working constantly, "evenings, Sundays, all of the time" to the point that there was "practically no social life." WRA officials observed that in the Valley, whole families worked as farm laborers, pooling their income in hopes of purchasing a farm when they could afford it.[37]

Figure 7.4. Eiichi Sakauye at his pear orchard on Trimble Road in San Jose, 1945.
In addition to pears, he and his family grew celery and bell peppers after the war.
War Relocation Authority Photographs of Japanese-American Evacuation and Resettlement.
Courtesy of The Bancroft Library, University of California, Berkeley.

Landownership finally became an option for Japanese immigrants in 1952
when the California Supreme Court declared the 1913 Alien Land Act unconstitutional. The Japanese American Citizens League then lobbied for a measure to
repeal all existing alien land laws, which passed by popular vote in 1956. Despite
some gains in the postwar period, Isamu Kawamura, a dentist who resumed his
practice in San Jose Japantown after internment and retired in 1972, declared,
"There is no way to estimate the material and mental damages resulted from the
evacuation."[38]

Toward Silicon Valley

Japanese internees who returned to the Santa Clara Valley found it a different
place, no longer an area primarily known for its prunes and apricots. World War
II sparked the transformation of the economy of the Valley, which became home

to large defense contractors during the country's Cold War military buildup.[39] After the war, Santa Clara County led the state in growth and saw its population increase at a rate double that of California itself. In the 1950s, the population of the county was under 300,000. In 1980, it reached nearly 1.3 million, and by 2010, the population had increased to almost 1.8 million.

The shift from farming to high-tech originated at Stanford University, which had produced sociologists investigating the "Oriental Problem" in the 1920s. Stanford engineering students Bill Hewlett and David Packard first partnered during the late 1930s to develop resistance capacity audio oscillators, and their company, Hewlett-Packard, became one of the most important pioneering high-tech firms in the emerging Silicon Valley. When Lockheed Aircraft purchased 275 acres in Sunnyvale and leased an additional 22 acres in Palo Alto in 1955 to establish its new missile division, the defense industry cemented its presence in the Valley. Lockheed boasted nearly 19,000 employees by 1959. Unlike orchard managers in the fruit industry, defense contractors could employ only U.S. citizens, so new immigrants were excluded from these union-wage jobs. Around the same time, William Shockley, inventor of the transistor, returned to Mountain View where he was raised, there to set in motion the invention of the semiconductor, which permanently changed the landscape of the Santa Clara Valley.[40]

To meet the demands of the burgeoning new economy, developers paved over Santa Clara Valley farmland, long prided for being naturally rich and productive. Geographers who studied land trends in 1958 observed that asphalt covered much of the best soil, and "only crops producing highest returns have been able to survive. Soaring land values threaten to crowd out even those crops which grow better here than anywhere else." The geographers estimated that 257 acres of land had been converted from farmland to accommodate each population increase of 1,000.[41] Local historian Yvonne Jacobson estimates that 77,000 acres of prime farmland was lost within a span of thirty years. In 1982, about 20,000 acres of agricultural land remained on the Valley floor, and in 2001, fewer than 4,500 acres remained, mostly in the southern part of the county near Morgan Hill and Gilroy.[42] In the wake of the area's transition from horticulture to high tech, Mariano Catolico, who had worked on Santa Clara Valley ranches as a farmhand for years, began new employment in 1954. One of his brothers found him a job in landscape maintenance with the City of Palo Alto. A number of other Filipino men were similarly employed as gardeners, rather than as farm laborers, attesting to the declining availability of agricultural jobs in Santa Clara County by the 1960s. Another Catolico brother did remain a seasonal farm laborer; he worked in Castroville in the Salinas Valley and lived with relatives in Mountain View during the off season through the 1970s.[43]

As orchards were leveled and replaced with office parks and housing subdivisions, the Valley's residents lamented the passing of the "Garden of the World." In the early 1980s, Jacobson's aunt Elsie Olson Kay pronounced her distaste for the Valley's new moniker: "I hate the name 'Silicon.' It even sounds awful." Other longtime residents nostalgically recalled the postcard-perfect views of blooming orchards. Louis Paviso, whose family had farmed in the Valley since the early twentieth century, said, "I will never forget the way it looked in spring. The creamy white cherry blossoms, the yellow mustard for miles and miles."

Others mourned not only the loss of a beautiful landscape, but the passing of family farming itself. Paviso's sister Catherine Paviso Gasich reminisced about growing up with the family farm ideal as promoted by boosters of the late nineteenth century, commenting, "We had purpose, the children knew that they had to help, we all worked together." Jacobson added to the lore of family farming and virtuous, orchard-fruit-growing widows found in promotional literature from a century ago: "in the Paviso family the five children worked in the orchards,

Figure 7.5. Mariano Catolico with pruning shears at a Palo Alto park in 1962. He worked as a gardener for the City of Palo Alto for over twenty years. Courtesy of the Catolico family.

cutting apricots and picking prunes through the summer in order to help support their widowed mother and themselves through the winter."[44]

Farmland became more valuable as real estate than as orchards, so Valley growers who wanted to continue farming often sold their property and bought three times as much land for the same amount elsewhere in California. As Jacobson notes, "The serious farmer and the marginal farmer were the ones to sell first."[45] Eiichi Sakauye recalled that his father paid $300 an acre in 1907 when he bought the family's San Jose pear orchard, in an area later considered "prime" land in Silicon Valley. In the 1960s, farmers in the Valley stood to make $25,000 an acre from selling their property to developers. Land is now sold by square foot and runs about $2 million to $7 million an acre. Former grower families, like the DiNapolis, the McCarthys, and the Marianis, took advantage of booming land prices and turned their property into hotels, residential developments, strip malls, and offices. One branch of the Mariani family relocated their dried fruit and nut business to Vacaville and Winters in the Sacramento Valley, while other members built Apple Computer's headquarters on DeAnza Boulevard in Cupertino on what had been an apricot orchard. In 2011, Santa Clara County ranked as the seventeenth wealthiest county in the country by median household income.[46]

Hatsu Kanemoto, the oldest of 12 children born to Japanese sharecroppers in San Jose in 1916, spoke of the change in the Valley, as "little by little all the big orchards and everything became subdivisions." After the war, she and her husband leased land to farm in San Jose from white owners, who eventually sold the land to housing developers. In the 1960s and 1970s, San Jose built approximately 20,000 housing units per year. Because of poor planning, the city, now the nation's tenth most populous, developed a reputation for unsightly urban sprawl. As for the Trimble Road community of Japanese farmers where she grew up, Kanemoto said in 1998, "That's all industrial now. I wouldn't recognize it now." Members of her family also shifted from agriculture to high tech: "One brother worked for Hewlett Packard, one worked for Lockheed...like my oldest son, at that age, they all went to work for Lockheed. Now my grandson is at IBM, [and] my sister's son is at IBM."[47]

But not all fruit growers readily gave up their land to developers willing to pay exorbitant sums. Several years before his death in 2005, Sakauye, mentally sharp and physically active at age eighty-nine, told a reporter, "I might profit by selling, but that isn't my enjoyment in life. I just can't give it up. Only death can take me away." At that time, Sakauye was forced to abandon his pear orchard because an office building next door blowing warm air from its huge ventilation systems changed the climate on his farm to the point that it never got cold enough for the pear trees to go dormant in the wintertime. Moreover, pear pickers were nearly impossible to obtain. Still determined to do what he loved, Sakauye continued to maintain a one-acre persimmon grove on his property.[48]

The only orchards left in the Valley today are ones that have been preserved by the county as historic landmarks, and most residents know little about the area's agricultural roots or realize the connection between the world-renowned fruit capital Santa Clara Valley and the modern-day high-technology-based "Silicon Valley." Looking at the experiences of Asian immigrants in the Valley provides a link to understanding the past and present. It is impossible to tell the history of the Santa Clara Valley without keeping the history of the Asian Americans who farmed there central to the narrative.

In the decades from 1880 to 1940, Asians made up at most 7 percent of the county population. Yet they were vital to the agricultural economy and the subjects of much debate, as well numerous pieces of legislation and court decisions designed to keep them out of farming and from immigrating in greater numbers. The Immigration Act of 1965 inaugurated a new period in the history of American immigration, profoundly affecting California. Between 1970 and 2000, the foreign-born population of San Jose grew from 7.6 percent to 36.8 percent. The Chinese and Filipino communities, tiny at the time of World War II and at midcentury, grew steadily after 1965 with the arrival of new immigrants, who were joined by other immigrants hailing from India, South Korea, Vietnam, and other countries in Southeast Asia that had not been represented previously in the population of the Santa Clara Valley. Meanwhile, the Japanese community, once the dominant Asian population in the area by far, has retained its presence, but not primarily through new immigration streams.

Currently the most populous of nine San Francisco Bay Area counties, Santa Clara County as a whole has seen a dramatic increase in its Asian and Latino populations. In 2007, Santa Clara County was just one of 10 U.S. counties where more than 50 percent of residents speak a language other than English in their households, with Spanish, Chinese, Vietnamese, and Tagalog the most common languages spoken. Census data from 2008 gave Santa Clara County the distinction of being the only "majority minority" county in the country where white, Asian, and Latino populations were evenly balanced, each comprising at least a quarter of the total population.[49] Today Asians make up 32 percent of the population of Santa Clara County (compared to 13 percent of the state and 4 percent nationally), encompassing a diverse range of ethnicities, and continue to play a major role in the economy and community.[50]

The rise of Silicon Valley as the center of microelectronics and high technology, like the rise of the Santa Clara Valley as the nation's fruit capital, depended largely on racial segmentation in the labor force and racial and gender ideology that established hierarchies and barriers to the advancement of nonwhites. In Silicon Valley today, the association of Asians with high levels of education,

Table 7.1 **Asian Population of Santa Clara County (SCC), 1950–2010**

Year	Number of Chinese (Percentage of SCC population)	Number of Japanese (Percentage of SCC population)	Number of Filipinos (Percentage of SCC population)	Number of Asian Indians (Percentage of SCC population)	Number of Koreans (Percentage of SCC population)	Number of Vietnamese (Percentage of SCC population)
1950	685 (0.2)	5,986 (2.0)	n/a	—	—	—
1960	2,394 (0.4)	10,432 (1.6)	2,333 (0.4)	—	—	—
1970	7,817 (0.7)	16,644 (1.6)	6,728 (0.6)	—	—	—
1980	22,745 (1.8)	22,262 (1.7)	28,229 (2.2)	5,187 (0.4)	6,237 (0.5)	11,156 (0.9)
1990	65,924 (4.4)	27,967 (1.9)	59,963 (4.0)	19,675 (1.3)	15,182 (1.0)	54,739 (3.7)
2000	115,781 (6.9)	27,257 (1.6)	76,060 (4.5)	66,741 (4.0)	21,647 (1.3)	99,986 (5.9)
2010	152,701 (8.6)	25,075 (1.4)	87,412 (4.9)	117,596 (6.6)	27,946 (1.6)	125,695 (7.1)

Source: U.S. Census.

technical expertise, and affluence belies not only the vast socioeconomic divides within the Asian American community, but also the long, complex history of Asian racialization that began in the "Valley of Heart's Delight" and the "Garden of the World," where agriculture drew together residents of various races, shaping identities and interactions, and redefining what it meant to be American.

ENDNOTES

Introduction

1. John Muir, *John Muir: His Life and Letters and Other Writings*, ed. Terry Gifford (Seattle: Mountaineers, 1996), 96.
2. *Picturesque San Jose and Environments: An illustrated statement of the progress, prosperity and resources of Santa Clara County, California* (San Jose: H. S. Foote and C. A. Woolfolk, 1893), n.p; *The Progressive City Beautiful: Santa Clara* (Santa Clara Chamber of Commerce, n.d.); *Read and hand to your neighbor: Catalogue of Fruit, Vegetable, Stock and Grain Farms* (San Jose, c. 1890), 15; E. Alexander Powell, "The Valley of Heart's Delight." *Sunset* 29 (August 1912), 120.
3. On the Jeffersonian agrarian ideal, see Thomas Jefferson, *Notes on the State of Virginia, Query XIX* (London: John Stockdale, 1787); Henry Nash Smith, *Virgin Land: The American West as Symbol and Myth* (New York: Vintage Books, 1950), 215; Leo Marx, *The Machine in the Garden: Technology and the Pastoral Ideal in America* (New York: Oxford University Press, 1964).
4. Santa Clara County Leases, Book O, 205, 467, Book R, 341; Santa Clara County Deeds, Book 376, 411; Santa Clara County Crop and Chattel Mortgages, Book 34, 216, Book 37, 260, Book 40, 95; Santa Clara County Official Records, Book 59, 136; 1900, 1910, 1920 Census Population Schedule, Santa Clara County; *Zaibei Nihonjin Jinmei Jiten* (San Francisco: Nichibei Shimbunsha, 1922), 242.
5. "Death Summons Pioneer Couple Within Two Days," *San Jose Mercury Herald*, January 22, 1926; 1920, 1930 Census Population Schedule, Santa Clara County; Santa Clara County Official Records, Book 764, 262, Book 1081, 52; Oral History, Tom Ezaki, January 27, 1984, and February 2, 1984. Oral History Collection, Japanese American Museum of San Jose Archives, San Jose, California. Hereafter "Oral History, name, date."
6. Neil Foley, *The White Scourge: Mexicans, Blacks, and Poor Whites in Texas Cotton Culture* (Berkeley: University of California Press, 1997), 5–12, 141.
7. Sucheng Chan, *This Bittersweet Soil: The Chinese in California Agriculture, 1860–1910* (Berkeley: University of California Press, 1986), 160–224; Eiichiro Azuma, "Japanese Immigrant Farmers and California Alien Land Laws: A Study of the Walnut Grove Japanese Community," *California History* 73 (1994), 14–29.
8. Jan Otto Marius Broek, *The Santa Clara Valley: A Study in Landscape Changes* (Utrecht, Netherlands: N.V.A. Oosthoek's Uitgevers-MIJ, 1932), 101; Yvonne Jacobson, *Passing Farms, Enduring Values: California's Santa Clara Valley* (Los Altos, CA: William Kaufmann, Inc. and the California History Center, 1984), 96. The average farm size in Santa Clara County dropped to 32 acres in 1950.

9. On the origins, perpetuation, and limits of the "factories in the field" framework of California agricultural history, see David Vaught, *Cultivating California: Growers, Specialty Crops, and Labor, 1875–1920* (Baltimore: The Johns Hopkins University Press, 1999), 1–8. See also Carey McWilliams, *Factories in the Field: The Story of Migratory Farm Labor in California* (Boston: Little, Brown and Company, 1939). Works that examine California growers' ideology and culture include Vaught, *Cultivating California*; Douglas Cazaux Sackman, *Orange Empire: California and the Fruits of Eden* (Berkeley: University of California Press, 2005); Steven Stoll, *The Fruits of Natural Advantage: Making the Industrial Countryside in California* (Berkeley: University of California Press, 1998); Ian Tyrrell, *True Gardens of the Gods: Californian-Australian Environmental Reform, 1860–1930* (Berkeley: University of California Press, 1999).

10. Studies of the history of Chinese and Japanese in California agriculture include Chan, *This Bittersweet Soil*; Valerie Matsumoto, *Farming the Home Place: A Japanese American Community in California, 1919–1982* (Ithaca, NY: Cornell University Press, 1993); Eichiro Azuma, *Between Two Empires: Race, History, and Transnationalism in Japanese America* (New York: Oxford University Press, 2005); Timothy J. Lukes and Gary Y. Okihiro, *Japanese Legacy: Farming and Community Life in California's Santa Clara Valley* (Cupertino, CA: California History Center, 1985); Masakazu Iwata, *Planted in Good Soil: The History of the Issei in United States Agriculture* (New York: Peter Lang, 1992).

11. On racialized constructions of national identity and citizenship in the twentieth century, see Mae M. Ngai, *Impossible Subjects: Illegal Aliens and the Making of Modern America* (Princeton, NJ: Princeton University Press, 2004).

12. Examples of these studies include: Foley, *The White Scourge*; Matt Garcia, *A World of Its Own: Race, Labor, and Citrus in the Making of Greater Los Angeles, 1900–1970* (Chapel Hill: The University of North Carolina Press, 2001); Moon-Ho Jung, *Coolies and Cane: Race, Labor, and Sugar in the Age of Emancipation* (Baltimore: The Johns Hopkins University Press, 2006); Devra Weber, *Dark Sweat, White Gold: California Farm Workers, Cotton, and the New Deal* (Berkeley: University of California Press, 1994).

13. Classic interpretations of anti-Asian movements include Alexander Saxton, *The Indispensable Enemy: Labor and the Anti-Chinese Movement in California* (Berkeley: University of California Press, 1971); Roger Daniels, *The Politics of Prejudice: The Anti-Japanese Movement in California and the Struggle for Japanese Exclusion* (Gloucester, MA: Peter Smith, 1966), 45–64. Though his detailed research on Japanese farmworkers in California demonstrates how much white growers depended on and benefited from the Japanese, Richard Steven Street nonetheless accepts Daniels's analysis of the alien land laws, stating that Japanese success in agriculture "angered racists and fed old fears." Richard Steven Street, *Beasts of the Field: A Narrative History of California Farmworkers, 1769–1913* (Stanford, CA: Stanford University Press, 2004), 520.

14. Gary Okihiro, "Fallow Field: The Rural Dimension of Asian American Studies," in Gail M. Nomura et al., ed., *Frontiers of Asian American Studies* (Pullman: Washington State University Press, 1989), 7.

15. Chris Friday, *Organizing Asian American Labor: The Pacific Coast Canned-Salmon Industry, 1870–1942* (Philadelphia: Temple University Press, 1994), 6.

16. Some recent works have underscored the historical interactions between minority groups in California: Shana Bernstein, *Bridges of Reform: Interracial Civil Rights Activism in Twentieth-Century Los Angeles* (New York: Oxford University Press, 2011); Scott Kurashige, *The Shifting Grounds of Race: Black and Japanese Americans in the Making of Multiethnic Los Angeles* (Princeton, NJ: Princeton University Press, 2008); Nayan Shah, *Stranger Intimacy: Contesting Race, Sexuality, and the Law in the North American West* (Berkeley: University of California Press, 2011); Allison Varzally, *Making a Non-White America: Californians Coloring Outside Ethnic Lines, 1925–1955* (Berkeley: University of California Press, 2008); Mark Wild, *Street Meeting: Multiethnic Neighborhoods in Early Twentieth-Century Los Angeles* (Berkeley: University of California Press, 2005).

17. For reflections on the landscape of Silicon Valley, see Rebecca Solnit, "The Computer: The Garden of Merging Paths," in *As Eve Said to the Serpent: On Landscape, Gender, and Art* (Athens: The University of Georgia Press, 2001), 109–122; Margaret O'Mara, "Silicon Valleys: Here, there, and everywhere," *Boom: A Journal of California* 1 (Summer 2011), 75–81.

Chapter One

1. H. S. Foote, *Pen Pictures from the "Garden of the World" or Santa Clara County, California* (Chicago: Lewis Publishing Company, 1888), 268. Andrea Malovos was born on the island of Giuppana (now Sipan, part of Croatia) in Dalmatia, Austria, a region which had been part of the republic of Venice until 1797. Andrea Malovos initially acquired Light-house Farm in 1870 by marrying Maria de Jesus Alviso, who came from a prominent Californio family, and added another one hundred acres to the property. I am indebted to Mark Malovos, great-great grandson of Andrea Malovos and Maria de Jesus Alviso, for information about his ancestors.

2. Santa Clara County Leases, Book D, 598. Santa Clara County Recorder's Office, San Jose; Santa Clara County Leases, Book J, 23–26; Patricia Loomis, "Signposts: Austrian Named Malovos Found Riches in Valley," *San Jose Evening News*, September 13, 1974; 1900 Census Population Schedule, Santa Clara County.

3. Street, *Beasts of the Field*, 312; Alexander Saxton, *The Indispensable Enemy: Labor and the Anti-Chinese Movement in California* (Berkeley: University of California Press, 1971), 209–210; Jean Pfaelzer, *Driven Out: The Forgotten War Against Chinese Americans* (New York: Random House, 2007).

4. On racialized concepts of Asian labor in the post–Civil War American South, see Jung, *Coolies and Cane*. On the politics of the anti-Chinese movement, see Saxton, *The Indispensable Enemy*; Andrew Gyory, *Closing the Gate: Race, Politics, and the Chinese Exclusion Act* (Chapel Hill: The University of North Carolina Press, 1998); Najia Aarim-Heriot, *Chinese Immigrants, African Americans, and Racial Anxiety in the United States, 1848–82* (Urbana: University of Illinois Press, 2003).

5. *Annual Report of the State Board of Horticulture of the State of California* (Sacramento: State Board of Horticulture, 1892), 241; *San Jose (San Hosay): Santa Clara County, California* (San Jose: San Jose Chamber of Commerce, 1907), 14; Broek, *The Santa Clara Valley*, 112.

6. Eugene T. Sawyer, *History of Santa Clara County, California* (Los Angeles: Historic Record Company, 1922), 135, 139–140; S. W. Shear, *Prune Supply and Price Situation* (Berkeley: Agricultural Experiment Station, 1928), 4; Broek, *The Santa Clara Valley*, 111–113.

7. Advertisements, *Sunset* 9 (June 1902); W. R. L. Jenks, "Los Gatos, Gem of the Foothills," *Sunset* 12 (December 1903), 137; "A Paradise of Prunes." *The American Farmer* 82 (June 1896), 8; Advertisement, *Sunset* 30 (March 1913), 23. Though still relatively small compared to post–World War II years, the population of Santa Clara County grew steadily in the late nineteenth and early twentieth centuries, from 35,039 in 1880, to 48,005 in 1890, 60,216 in 1900, and 83,539 in 1910. *Thirteenth Census of the United States Taken in the Year 1910. Volume II, Population* (Washington, DC: Government Printing Office, 1913), 176.

8. Stephen J. Pitti, *The Devil in Silicon Valley: Northern California, Race, and Mexican Americans* (Princeton, NJ: Princeton University Press, 2003), 11–13; Stephen M. Payne, *Santa Clara County: Harvest of Change* (Northridge, CA: Windsor Publications, 1987), 11. The Ohlone were also known as the Costanoan, derived from the Spanish word "Costeños," meaning "people of the coast."

9. Pitti, *The Devil in Silicon Valley*, 12–21; Douglas Monroy, *Thrown Among Strangers: The Making of Mexican Culture in Frontier California* (Berkeley: University of California Press, 1990), 100–117; Michael Friedly, "This Brief Eden: A History of Landscape Change in California's Santa Clara Valley" (Ph.D. dissertation, Duke University, 2000), 220–221.

10. Glenna Matthews, "Forging a Cosmopolitan Civic Culture: The Regional Identity of San Francisco and Northern California," in *Many Wests: Place, Culture, and Regional Identity*, ed. David M. Wrobel and Michael Steiner (Lawrence: University Press of Kansas, 1991), 215–223. The Murphy family held vast estates in Santa Clara County estimated to include over 70,000 acres in 1860 before they were sold in subdivisions. Jacobson, *Passing Farms, Enduring Values*, 101. See also Marjorie Pierce, *The Martin Murphy Family Saga* (Cupertino: California History Center, 2000).

11. Douglas Monroy, *Thrown Among Strangers: Making of Mexican Culture Frontier* (Berkeley: University of California Press, 1993), 233–251; Michael Friedly, "This Brief Eden: A History of Landscape Change in California's Santa Clara Valley" (Ph.D. dissertation, Duke University, 2000), 299.

12. Pitti, *The Devil in Silicon Valley*, 52–77; Milton Lanyon, *Cinnabar Hills: The Quicksilver Days of New Almaden* (Los Gatos, CA: Village Printers, 1967).

13. *Santa Clara County and Its Resources: A Souvenir of the San Jose Mercury* (San Jose: San Jose Mercury Publishing and Printing Company, 1896), 12.

14. *Santa Clara County and Its Resources*, 12; Mary Edith Griswold, "Living Water—The Romance of the New Almaden Quicksilver Mines," *Sunset* 9 (July 1902), 173.

15. *Santa Clara County and Its Resources*, 12; Harry L. Wells, "In Blossom Land: A Springtime of San Jose and Santa Clara County, California," *Sunset* 9 (May 1902), 55.

16. Leigh Irvine, *Santa Clara County, California (California Lands for Wealth, California Fruit for Health)* (San Jose: San Jose Chamber of Commerce, c. 1910), 23; *California's Richest Realm*, n.p.; Henry George, *Our Land and Land Policy: Speeches, Lectures, and Miscellaneous Writings by Henry George* (New York: Doubleday and McClure Company, 1902); Donald Worster, *A Passion for Nature: The Life of John Muir* (New York: Oxford University Press, 2008), 282–283; Jacobson, *Passing Farms, Enduring Values*, 185.

17. Tyrrell, *True Gardens of the Gods*, 8–9, 36–39; Karen R. Merrill, *Public Lands and Political Meaning: Ranchers, the Government, and the Property between Them* (Berkeley: University of California Press, 2002), 40–42.

18. Broek, *The Santa Clara Valley*, 64–65; *Historical Atlas Map of Santa Clara County* (San Francisco: Thompson and West, 1876), 17; *Annual Report of the State Board of Horticulture*, 241; Bonnie Montgomery, "The Garden City," *Content Magazine* (San Jose) 4 (Summer 2012), 18–19.

19. Robert Couchman, *The Sunsweet Story* (San Jose, CA: Sunsweet Growers, 1967), 17–19; *Picturesque San Jose*, n.p.; S. F. Leib, "Address of Welcome," in "Transactions of the Sixteenth State Fruit Growers' Convention Held at San Jose, November 15–18, 1892," 114. On a similar transition from wheat growing to fruit growing in the Sacramento Valley, see David Vaught, *After the Gold Rush: Tarnished Dreams in the Sacramento Valley* (Baltimore: The Johns Hopkins University Press, 2007), 197–219. On the origins and functions of California fruit growers' conventions, see Vaught, *Cultivating California*, 48–49; Tyrrell, *True Gardens of the Gods*, 40–41.

20. S. F. Leib, "Address of Welcome," 113. French viticulturists first settled in the Valley during the mid-1840s and planted grape cuttings from the Santa Clara mission vineyard, heralding the beginning of the region's small but thriving wine industry. See Payne, *Santa Clara County*, 76–77; Charles L. Sullivan, *Like Modern Edens: Winegrowing in Santa Clara Valley and Santa Cruz Mountains, 1798–1981* (Cupertino: California History Center, 1982).

21. William Deverell, *Whitewashed Adobe: The Rise of Los Angeles and the Remaking of Its Mexican Past* (Berkeley: University of California Press, 2004), 7–8, 59–62.

22. Wells, "In Blossom Land," 47; Irvine, *Santa Clara County*, 41.

23. Jeanette Campbell, "California Orchard Bloom," *Sunset* 9 (May 1902), 61–63.

24. On the romantic creation of southern California as a "pastoral Hispanic paradise," see Phoebe S. Kropp, *California Vieja: Culture and Memory in a Modern American Place* (Berkeley: University of California Press, 2006); Richard White, *"It's Your Misfortune and None of My Own": A New History of the American West* (Norman: University of Oklahoma Press, 1991), 425.

25. Vaught, *Cultivating California*, 48, 53. On the Southern Pacific's promotion of specialty crop agriculture, see Richard J. Orsi, *Sunset Limited: The Southern Pacific Railroad and the Development of the American West, 1850–1930* (Berkeley: University of California Press, 2005), 52–55.

26. Vaught, *Cultivating California*, 48; Charles Postel, *The Populist Vision* (New York: Oxford University Press, 2007), 109–111; John T. McGreevy, "Farmers, Nationalists, and the Origins of California Populism." *Pacific Historical Review* 58 (November 1989), 490–495.

27. *Annual Report of the State Board of Horticulture*, 245; Kevin Starr, *Inventing the Dream: California Through the Progressive Era* (New York: Oxford University Press, 1985), 137.

28. David B. Danbom, "Romantic Agrarianism in Twentieth-Century America." *Agricultural History* 65 (Fall 1991), 11–12.

29. Irvine, *Santa Clara County*, 4.

30. Carolyn Merchant, *Ecological Revolutions: Nature, Gender, and Science in New England* (Chapel Hill: The University of North Carolina Press, 1989), 100–101, 203–204; Frieda Knobloch, *The Culture of Wilderness: Agriculture as Colonization in the American West* (Chapel Hill: The University of North Carolina Press, 1996).

31. Irvine, *Santa Clara County*, 22; Gen. N. P. Chipman, "Fruit vs. Wheat" in "Transactions of the Sixteenth State Fruit Growers' Convention Held at San Jose, November 15–18, 1892," 167–168.

32. Gail Bederman, *Manliness and Civilization: A Cultural History of Gender and Race in the United States, 1880–1917* (Chicago: The University of Chicago Press, 1995), 10–15; Kristin L. Hoganson, *Fighting for American Manhood: How Gender Politics Provoked the Spanish-American and Philippine-American Wars* (New Haven, CT: Yale University Press, 1998), 11–12; Peter G. Filene, *Him/Her/Self: Gender Identities in Modern America* (Baltimore: The Johns Hopkins University Press, 1998), 79.

33. *Annual Report of the State Board of Horticulture*, 245; Filene, *Him/Her/Self*, 78–79.

34. *California's Richest Realm. Santa Clara Valley, some views of the San Martin Ranch subdivision* (c. 1901); Irvine, *Santa Clara County*, 11.

35. J. W. Nelson, "The Fruit-Grower and His Work," *Official Report of the Twenty-Sixth Fruit Growers' Convention of the State of California* (Sacramento: J. D. Young, Superintendent of State Printing, 1902), 146; *Picturesque San Jose*, n.p.

36. *Brooklodge Farm containing five hundred acres choice valley land. A beautiful country home in the garden of central California.* (San Jose: Alfred C. Eaton, 1899), n.p.; Orsi, *Sunset Limited*, 58.

37. Powell, "The Valley of Heart's Delight," 119. For a parallel argument on "homecoming" and masculinity in the West, see Louis S. Warren, "Cody's Last Stand: Masculine Anxiety, the Custer Myth, and the Frontier of Domesticity in Buffalo Bill's Wild West," *Western Historical Quarterly* 34 (Spring 2003), 49–69.

38. "Women Fruit Farmers in California," *The Chautauquan* 20 (February 1895), 597; *Santa Clara County, California* (San Jose: San Jose Board of Trade, 1887), 68; Mrs. Georgie McBride, "A Woman's Orchard," in "Transactions of the Sixteenth State Fruit Growers' Convention Held at San Jose, November 15–18, 1892," 193.

39. "Women as Fruit Growers," *California Fruit Grower* (March 14, 1896), 206. On the growing prominence of women in horticulture, see Tyrrell, *True Gardens of the Gods*, 45–46; Garcia, *A World of Its Own*, 41. On the association of women with gardening practices, see Knobloch, *The Culture of Wilderness*, 70–72.

40. McBride, "A Woman's Orchard," 193–195; Foote, *Pen Pictures from the "Garden of the World,"* 452. Another Santa Clara Valley widow who became a prune grower was featured prominently in "Women Fruit Farmers in California," 597–598.

41. *Santa Clara County, California* (1887), 76, 93.

42. Kimball, "Welcome Address," 12; Cooper quoted in Tyrrell, *True Gardens of the Gods*, 45.

43. U.S. Immigration Commission, *Reports: Immigrants in Industries*, XXIV, Vol. 1 (Washington, DC: Government Printing Office, 1911), 12. Hereafter cited, Immigration Commission,

Reports, Series, Volume, page number; "Cost of Cutting and Drying Fruit," *California Fruit Grower* 16 (May 18, 1895), 369; "Cutting and Drying California Fruits," *California Fruit Grower* 16 (May 18, 1895), 368. See, for example, the San Jose Board of Education's unanimous decision to set summer vacation during apricot, peach, and prune harvests: "Vacation Timed for Fruit Harvest," *California Fruit Grower* 16 (April 27, 1912), 14.

44. "Girls and Women in the Harvest Time," *California Fruit Grower* 21 (September 25, 1897), 2; Powell, "The Valley of Heart's Delight," 214. As with orchard fruits, hop picking also became an increasingly white, middle-class endeavor in rural California at the turn of the century, taken up by "respectable families who seek health and recreation". Vaught, *Cultivating California*, 90.

45. A. Clifford Gage, "Pueblo Santa Clara," *Sunset* 13 (July 1904), 274–275. On the use of "boys and girls" as prune pickers, see also "A Paradise of Prunes," *The American Farmer* 82 (June 1896), 8. During World War I, matron Donaldina Cameron brought residents of the San Francisco Chinese Mission Home south to the Valley to help fruit ranchers who had lost workers due to the war. In 1917, Cameron arranged for 20 girls to cut apricots in San Jose. Later, they picked prunes on the Silker Ranch near Los Gatos. Mildred Crowl Martin, *Chinatown's Angry Angel: The Story of Donaldina Cameron* (Palo Alto, CA: Pacific Books, 1977), 177–178.

46. "Women and Children in the Fruit Harvest," *California Fruit Grower* 13 (July 15, 1893), 44.

47. "Women Ranchers: What Are They Doing in California," *The Morning Call* (November 19, 1893); Foote, *Pen Pictures from the "Garden of the World*," 452.

48. "Proceedings of the Nineteenth Fruit Growers' Convention of the State of California," in *Official Report of the Nineteenth Fruit Growers' Convention of the State of California.* (Sacramento: J. D. Young, Superintendent of State Printing, 1896), 92; McBride, "A Woman's Orchard," 194.

49. Street, *Beasts of the Field*, 237–257; Ronald Takaki, *Strangers from a Different Shore: A History of Asian Americans* (Boston and New York: Little, Brown, and Company, 1998), 84–91.

50. *Statement of Summerfield Enos, Commissioner of the Bureau of Labor Statistics of the State of California to the California State Horticultural Society* (Sacramento: Superintendent of State Printing, 1886), 14. Census records for 1880 and 1890 gave 2,695 and 2,723 Chinese in the county, respectively. Though there are no exact census figures for the number of male Chinese in Santa Clara County, my calculations from the 1890 census indicate that between 83 and 95 percent of the Chinese in the county were male. The "colored" category sometimes referred to "Persons of African descent only" and other times included Asians, making exact calculations difficult. *Compendium of the Eleventh Census: 1890. Part I. Population* (Washington, DC: Government Printing Office, 1892), 477, 586–587, 769.

51. 1900 Census Population Schedule, Santa Clara County. Calculations based on a sample of 588 Chinese residents of the county.

52. Certificates of Residence, "Chinese Files," MS 1989–142, History San José; 1900 Census Population Schedule, Santa Clara County. The Geary Act of 1892, which extended the exclusion of Chinese immigrants for an additional ten years, mandated that Chinese laborers obtain certificates of residence within one year of the act's passage. This deadline was extended to May 15, 1894, which explains the flurry of certificates filed in Santa Clara County from February to April 1894. Marie Rose Wong, *Sweet Cakes, Long Journey: The Chinatowns of Portland, Oregon* (Seattle: University of Washington Press, 2004), 65; Street, *Beasts of the Field*, 377.

53. *Census Reports Volume II. Twelfth Census of the United States, Taken in the Year 1900, Population Part II* (Washington, DC: United States Census Office, 1902), l, xlix; 1900 Census Population Schedule, Santa Clara County.

54. Saxton, *The Indispensable Enemy*, 21–22, 53–66; Edna Bonacich, "Asian Labor in the Development of California and Hawaii," in *Labor Immigration under Capitalism: Asian Immigrant Workers in the United States before World War II*, ed. Lucie Cheng and Edna Bonacich (Berkeley: University of California Press, 1984), 130–178.

55. Santa Clara County Leases, Books D–M.

56. Chan, *This Bittersweet Soil*, 124. The 1860, 1870, and 1880 manuscript population census listed no white berry cultivators at all. For more on Chinese strawberry farmers in Santa Clara County, see Street, *Beasts of the Field*, 248; Kenneth Chow, "The History of the Chinese in Santa Clara County," in ed. Gloria Sun Hom, *Chinese Argonauts: An Anthology of the Chinese Contributions to the Historical Development of Santa Clara County* (Cupertino: California History Center, 1971), 7.

57. *Santa Clara County and Its Resources*, 180; Santa Clara County Leases, Book B, 72–73; Book D, 207–210; Book F, 164–166, 330–332, 519–522, 531–534; Book G, 100–102, 244–245, 385–386; Book H, 412–413; Book I, 430–432.

58. Lease Agreement, Charles Cropley and Ah Wah, Ephemera file, Ethnic groups (Chinese), History San José; Foote, *Pen Pictures from the "Garden of the World,"* 440–441.

59. Santa Clara County Leases, Book H, 359.

60. Anne B. W. Effland, Denise M. Rogers, and Valerie Grim, "Women as Agricultural Landowners: What Do We Know About Them?" *Agricultural History* 67 (Spring 1993), 236–237, 252.

61. Calculations based on the Brainard Agricultural Atlas of prime agricultural regions of the county, which did not cover urban areas or agricultural areas in the southern part of the county (present-day Morgan Hill and Gilroy). County tax assessment records for rural districts could be another source for determining this type of information, but they are unavailable for areas outside the city of San Jose in this time period. Henry A. Brainard, *Brainard Agricultural Atlas* (maps). Collection on Santa Clara County's Agricultural Past. San Jose Public Library, California Room.

62. Effland, Rogers, and Grim, "Women as Agricultural Landowners," 242. Lease figures calculated from Santa Clara County Leases, Books D–R. On the evolution of community property law in California, see Lee M. A. Simpson, *Selling the City: Gender, Class, and the California Growth Machine, 1880–1940* (Stanford, CA: Stanford University Press, 2004), 14–16.

63. Santa Clara County Leases, Book F, 164–166, 519; Book G, 100–102, 244–247, 385–386; Book N, 150–151. Before his death in 1890, Coleman Younger divided his property among his wife, Augusta, and their four children, plus his stepdaughter. Augusta Younger eventually bequeathed her share of the estate to her five children, divided equally. "Coleman Younger," Will Book G, 385–391; "Augusta Younger," Will Book O, 306–308. Records of the Santa Clara County Recorder's Office deposited at History San José.

64. "Strawberry Culture," *Palo Alto Times* (August 23, 1901); "Santa Clara County Strawberries," *California Fruit Grower* 10 (March 12, 1892), 167. On the predominance of sharecropping among Chinese farmers in Santa Clara County, see Chan, *This Bittersweet Soil*, 126–131.

65. *Santa Clara County and Its Resources*, 180; "Women Fruit Farmers in California." *The Chautauquan* 20 (February 1895), 597; Santa Clara County Crop and Chattel Mortgages, Book 16, 398.

66. H. L. Wells, "Onion Beginnings: Seeding, Packing and Shipping in California," *Sunset* 8 (January 1902), 123–125; Edward James Wickson, *The California Vegetables in Garden and Field: A Manual of Practice with and without Irrigation for Semitropical Countries* (San Francisco: Pacific Rural Press, 1917), 293–294.

67. Wells, "Onion Beginnings," 125–126; Jessie Juliet Knox, "In a Garden of Sleep: Onion Growing in the Santa Clara Valley," *Sunset* 8 (January 1902), 121.

68. For example, see the following entries: William A. Z. Edwards Diaries and Account Books, January 2, 1880, January 10, 1880, January 13, 1880. Box 2. Bancroft Library, Berkeley, California. Hereafter "Edwards Diaries," date. Tomatoes were also grown for seed on agreement with Kimberlin.

69. Santa Clara County Crop and Chattel Mortgages, Book 14, 113; Book 15, 546–547; "A Glimpse of Santa Clara History" (Santa Clara: Mission City Memorial Park, 2002) (brochure); "Death of a Leading Seed Grower," *Pacific Rural Press* 59 (May 12, 1900), 302; Foote, *Pen Pictures from the "Garden of the World,"* 561–562.

70. "Seed Growing at Santa Clara," *Pacific Rural Press* 50 (September 21, 1895), 181–182; Broek, *The Santa Clara Valley*, 114; Immigration Commission, *Reports*, XXIV, Vol. 2, 199–200.

71. Edwards Diaries, November 29–30, 1893; "W. A. Z. Edwards Life Outline as gathered from Diaries, Account Books, etc. for years 1844–1908," 10; Wright, "Thomas Foon Chew—Founder of Bayside Cannery," 27–29. On Delta asparagus, see Street, *Beasts of the Field*, 386.

72. "Testimony taken at the Inquest on the body of Ying Ong," Santa Clara County Coroner's Inquest, January 26, 1909, 6–7. History San José Research Library, San Jose, California. Lee Gun had employed Ying Ong to work the asparagus with him for four months until Ying shot himself one morning after a fire at the barn where Chinese workers boarded. Foote, *Pen Pictures from the "Garden of the World,"* 221–222.

73. Santa Clara County Leases, Book D, 208–209.

74. See, for example, Edwards Diaries, entries for August and September 1900, December 12, 1900; Ralph Rambo, *Remember When…A Boy's-Eye View of an Old Valley* (San Jose, CA: Rosicrucian Press, 1965), 22.

75. Santa Clara County Leases, Book H, 136; Sawyer, *History of Santa Clara County*, 383.

76. Santa Clara County Leases, Book I, 21; "The Chinaman in the Saddle," *California Fruit Grower* 14 (January 27, 1894), 62.

77. Edwards Diaries, February 26–March 2, 1889, December 5, 1893; John Francis Pyle Diaries and Memorandum Books, Bancroft Library, Berkeley, California. Hereafter "Pyle Diaries," date. Pyle Diaries, March 30, 1895, May 1, 1895, May 9, 1895.

78. Pyle Diaries, March 9, 1890, March 11, 1895, April 1, 1895. Pyle's diaries date from 1874 to 1921. In Edwards Diaries, entries from 1889 feature mentions of Chinese laborers almost daily.

79. W. A. Z. Edwards Life Outline, 6. Pfaelzer (*Driven Out*, 231) asserts that Edwards had been "a leader in the vigilante movement" presumably against Chinese miners during the 1850s, but I found no evidence to indicate this.

80. Edwards Diaries, October 28, 1893.

81. Santa Clara County Leases, Book H, 260–261. This lease was assigned to "Jim Mok Joey," the same individual as Jim Mock. Additional contract terms listed in contract dated December 17, 1894, Palo Alto Stock Farm Papers, Box 22, Stanford University Special Collections and University Archives. Leland Stanford Sr. died in June 1893, leaving the operation of the university and farm to his widow, Jane.

82. Him Mark Lai, *Becoming Chinese American: A History of Communities and Institutions* (Walnut Creek, CA: Alta Mira, 2004), 177, 190. Lai says Mock left Stanford's employ when the farm became a university campus, which is not likely, since Jane Stanford signed a lease with him in 1893, and the university was founded in 1891. Lai, "Flower Growers and Political Activists," 177, 190.

83. Santa Clara County Leases, Book H, 159–161, 264.

84. Santa Clara County Leases, Book E, 147–149, 374, 377.

85. Santa Clara County Leases, Book G, 502–504. Farney's first lease may not have been filed officially at the county office, as there is no record of it. Neighbor Edwards was not in the habit of filing leases with the recorder's office, though according to his diaries, he made numerous agreements with Chinese tenant farmers. In August 1908, shortly before his

death, however, Edwards did file a lease with an H. Tedesco, for the latter to farm 60 acres of Edwards's property, likely because the diarist had grown too infirm to take care of his farm. Santa Clara County Leases, Book N, 46. Edwards died on November 19, 1908.

86. Pyle Diaries, March 31, 1895.

87. Santa Clara County Leases, Book H, 260. It is unclear whether these were two separate buildings that housed different types of employees.

88. Street, *Beasts of the Field*, 322; Rambo, *Remember When*, 23; "The Present and Future of Fruit Growing in California," *California Fruit Grower* 10 (March 5, 1892), 149. On the diets of rural Chinese farm laborers, see Thad M. Van Bueren, "Late-Nineteenth-Century Chinese Farm Workers in the California Mother Lode," *Historical Archaeology* 42 (2008), 91–94.

89. For more on the history of gambling in San Jose Chinatown and white attempts to outlaw it, see Connie Young Yu, *Chinatown, San Jose, USA* (San Jose, CA: San Jose Historical Museum Association, 1991), 69–77. Chinatown residents confirmed that San Jose police, some of whom were paid off by gambling house owners, did not make many arrests for gambling. Art Eng, whose father operated a gambling business in San Jose Chinatown in the early twentieth century, recalled "The Chinatown gambling establishments were all operating and knowingly under the nose of the police....I have never heard of a raid on a gambling place although it was supposedly illegal." Yu, *Chinatown, San Jose, USA*, 74. On the issue of opium smoking as a "Chinese habit" mobilized by anti-Chinese forces, see Diana L. Ahmad, *The Opium Debate and Chinese Exclusion Laws in the Nineteenth-Century American West* (Reno: University of Nevada Press, 2007).

90. Santa Clara County Leases, Book F, 534, 519; Book D, 599; Book J, 25.

91. Yu, *Chinatown, San Jose, USA*, 36. Studies based on archaeological excavations of this site include Barbara L. Voss, "Between the Household and the World System: Social Collectivity and Community Agency in Overseas Chinese Archaeology." *Historical Archaeology* 42 (2008), 37–52, and Bryn Williams, "Chinese Masculinities and Material Culture." *Historical Archaeology* 42 (2008), 53–67.

92. "Evacuation of the Woolen Mills Chinatown (CA-SCL-807H), San Jose," Volume 1 (January 2002), prepared for California Department of Transportation by Past Forward, Inc., 9–11, 19–29.

93. Edwards Diaries, December 2, 1893; Pyle Diaries, June 23, 1902.

94. Rambo, *Remember When*, 22.

95. "Testimony taken at the Inquest on the body of Chin Yong," died May 12, 1904, 1–2, 4; *San Jose City Directory, including Santa Clara County, 1903–1904* (San Francisco: F. M. Husted, 1903), 516; "Hon. James C. Zuck" in *History of the State of California and Biographical Record of Coast Counties, California* (Chicago: The Chapman Publishing Company, 1904), 419.

96. "Testimony taken at the Inquest on the body of Chin Yong," 1–2, 7–8; "Roommate Killing," *Chung Sai Yat Po* (May 13, 1904); "Inquest Over Chinaman's Body." *San Jose Evening News* (May 13, 1904).

97. "Testimony at the Inquest of Ung Sing Bang," November 13, 1893, 2; "Testimony Taken at the Inquest on the body of Li Sack," January 9, 1901, 3. On Chinese immigrant fishermen in the Monterey Bay region and their struggle with developers over control of the coastline in the late nineteenth century, see Connie Y. Chiang, *Shaping the Shoreline: Fisheries and Tourism on the Monterey Coast* (Seattle: University of Washington Press, 2008), 13–19, 29–37.

98. "Testimony Taken at the Inquest on the Body of Yen Ohn," July 4, 1908, 2; "Testimony taken at the Inquest on the body of Ling Yen," April 10, 1913, 3–4. On the experiences of Chinese cooks in rural California, see Street, *Beasts of the Field*, 243–245.

99. Edwards Diaries, August 24, 1893.

100. Edwards Diaries, August 29, 1893, September 9, 1893, September 11, 1893. It is possible that Edwards was actually referring to Chung Kee, a San Jose Chinatown merchant who acted as a labor contractor for farmers and companies, doing business

from his cigar and candy store on Fourth and Jackson Streets. Yu, *Chinatown, San Jose, USA*, 91. Ralph Rambo identifies Charley Kow Kee as a 300-pound Chinatown pork butcher and Chung Kee as an "enterprising, self-appointed 'mayor and employment manager,'" which does not match the names in Edwards' entries. Rambo, *Remember When*, 22.

101. Edwards Diaries, December 5, 1983.
102. While tending to his in-laws' Contra Costa County farm in the 1880s and 1890s, naturalist John Muir found the management of Chinese workers one of his most vexing duties, prompting his sister Sarah Galloway to tell him she hoped the "care and oversight of those Chinamen will not upset you again". Quoted in Worster, *A Passion for Nature*, 293.
103. "The Labor Question among Vineyardists," *California Fruit Grower* 13 (August 26, 1893), 172; "White Men Inferior as Fruit Packers". *California Fruit Grower* 13 (August 26, 1893), 178; "White versus Asiatic Labor in the Fruit Harvest," *California Fruit Grower* 16 (June 15, 1895), 438; "Asiatic Help," *California Fruit Grower* 21 (September 25, 1897), 8; Vaught, *Cultivating California*, 86; Saxton, *The Indispensable Enemy*, 231–232.
104. *Statement of John Summerfield Enos*, 14.
105. Editorial, *California Fruit Grower* (August 12, 1893), 132; "The Labor Question among Vineyardists," 169.
106. Santa Clara County Coroner's Inquests, 1891–1913. History San José Research Library, San Jose, California; Sucheng Chan, "The Exclusion of Chinese Women," in *Entry Denied: Exclusion and the Chinese Community in America, 1882–1943*, ed. Sucheng Chan (Philadelphia: Temple University Press, 1991), 94–146; Lee, *At America's Gates*, 92–100. On transnational Chinese family formation and "split-household families," see Adam McKeown, "Transnational Chinese Families and Chinese Exclusion, 1875–1943," *Journal of American Ethnic History* 18 (Winter 1999): 73–110 and Madeline Hsu, *Dreaming of Gold, Dreaming of Home: Transnationalism and Migration between the United States and South China, 1882–1943* (Stanford, CA: Stanford University Press, 2000).
107. Calculations based on the 1900 Population Schedule, Santa Clara County.
108. "Testimony taken at the Inquest on the body of Chin Sui Sum," December 1902. "Costigan, John H." *San Jose City Directory, 1901–1902* (San Francisco: F. M. Husted, 1902), 586.
109. On the history of Chinese American women and the formation of families in San Francisco, see Judy Yung, *Unbound Feet: A Social History of Chinese Women in San Francisco* (Berkeley: University of California Press, 1995) and Mae Ngai, *The Lucky Ones: One Family and the Extraordinary Invention of Chinese America* (Boston and New York: Houghton Mifflin Harcourt, 2010).
110. Santa Clara County Leases, Book F, 166, 331, 522; 1900 Census Population Schedule, San Francisco County.
111. Leigh H. Irvine, ed., *A History of the New California, Its Resources and People* (New York: The Lewis Publishing Company, 1905), 529.
112. "When Chinese Labor Was Employed on the Hayes' Ranch," *San Jose Evening News*, October 27, 1904.
113. "More About the Chinks at Hayes' Ranch," *San Jose Evening News*, November 2, 1904.
114. On the history of white wage laborers' attachment to the status and privilege accrued by white racial identity, see David Roediger, *The Wages of Whiteness: Race and the Making of the American Working Class* (New York: Verso, 1991).
115. "When Chinese Labor Was Employed."
116. "Despicable Journalism," *San Jose Daily Mercury*, November 3, 1904.
117. *San Francisco Daily Clarion*, August 30, 1912; Lukes and Okihiro, *Japanese Legacy*, 46; Santa Clara County Leases, Book G, 396.

Chapter Two

1. "Katsusaburo Kawahara," in *Beginnings: Japanese Americans in San Jose, 8 Oral Histories,* Steven Misawa, ed. (San Jose, CA: San Jose Japanese American Community Senior Service, 1981), 34.
2. Calculated from the 1900 Census Population Schedule, Santa Clara County.
3. Street, *Beasts of the Field,* 409.
4. Yamato Ichihashi, *Japanese Immigration: Its Status in California* (San Francisco: The Marshall Press, 1915), 22; H. A. Millis, *The Japanese Problem in the United States* (New York: The Macmillan Company, 1915), 103; U.S. Bureau of the Census, *Sixteenth Census of the United States, 1940: Population. Volume II, Part 1, California* (Washington, DC: Government Printing Office, 1942), 518; U.S. Bureau of the Census, *United States Census of Agriculture, 1925. Part III, The Western States* (Washington, DC: Government Printing Office, 1927), 484. Statistics differentiated between the "white farm population" and "colored farm population." Since Japanese represented the only significant rural "colored" population in the county at this time (2,981 living there in 1920, compared to only 839 Chinese, who were primarily urban), calculations were made based on their population.
5. U.S. Bureau of the Census, *Report on Population of the United States at the Eleventh Census: 1890. Part I* (Washington, DC, 1892), 442; Ichihashi, *Japanese Immigration,* 22; Lukes and Okihiro, *Japanese Legacy,* 21.
6. U.S. Bureau of the Census, *Thirteenth Census of the United States Taken in the Year 1910, Volume II, Population* (Washington, DC: Government Printing Office, 1913), 157, 166, 176; Ichihashi, *Japanese Immigration,* 19.
7. Azuma, *Between Two Empires,* 27–30; Yuji Ichioka, *The Issei: The World of the First-Generation Japanese Immigrants, 1885–1924* (New York: Free Press), 40; Glenn T. Trewartha, *Japan: A Geography* (Madison: University of Wisconsin Press, 1965), 242–245; Yosaburo Yoshida, "Sources and Causes of Japanese Immigration." *Annals of the American Academy of Political and Social Science* 34 (September 1909), 160–163; Andrea Geiger, *Subverting Exclusion: Transpacific Encounters with Race, Caste, and Borders, 1885-1928* (New Haven, CT: Yale University Press, 2011), 27–35.
8. Azuma, *Between Two Empires,* 29–30; Eiichiro Azuma, "Interstitial Lives: Race, Community, and History among Japanese Immigrants Caught between Japan and the United States, 1885–1941" (Ph.D. dissertation, UCLA, 2000), 68. Yoshida's findings vary slightly with Azuma's, the former including several other prefectures and omitting Okinawa.
9. 1910 Census Population Schedule, Santa Clara County. About half of the Japanese farmers surveyed in Alviso by federal investigators in 1908 had labored on Hawaiian sugar plantations prior to residing in California. U.S. Immigration Commission, *Reports,* XXIV, Vol. 2, 447. See also Lukes and Okihiro, *Japanese Legacy,* 29, 32. On Japanese conflation of caste and class status when referring to emigrants' background in the Meiji era, see Geiger, *Subverting Exclusion,* 43–50.
10. Tabulated from the 1900 and 1910 Census Population Schedule, Santa Clara County. Chinese men counted as farmers had resided in the U.S. an average of two years longer than those called farm laborers in the census.
11. Immigration Commission, *Reports,* XXV, Vol. 2, 199–200, 203–204. On the transition from Chinese to Japanese labor in Santa Cruz County, see Kazuko Nakane, *Nothing Left in My Hands: The Issei of a Rural California Town, 1900–1942* (Berkeley: Heyday Books, 1985, 2008), 28–29.
12. 1900 and 1910 Census Population Schedule, Santa Clara County.
13. "Division Is Strictly Observed," *San Jose Mercury,* June 15, 1908. Street argues that underbidding in the 1890s allowed Japanese to replace Chinese workers, but I did not find evidence of this in the Santa Clara Valley, except for unconfirmed hearsay reported in the *Pacific Rural Press* in 1894 about "a gang of Japs in Santa Clara county working for 50 cents

per day and boarding themselves." "Meeting of the State Horticultural Society," *Pacific Rural Press* 47 (April 7, 1894), 264–265; Street, *Beasts of the Field*, 416.

14. "Case of recovering stolen money," *Chung Sai Yat Po*, July 31, 1903; "A Chinese Overseer Absconds," *San Jose Evening News*, July 31, 1903; "A Wily Mongolian Financier Made a Good Haul," *San Jose Evening News*, August 1, 1903.

15. *T. Nakashiki vs. Fook Lee*, 17761, Superior Court of the County of Santa Clara (1908). Judgment not found.

16. Street, *Beasts of the Field*, 476; "5000 Families Are Wanted Here," *San Jose Mercury*, December 6, 1906.

17. "Ephemera File: Ethnic Groups, White Labor Committee," History San José Research Library; "Coast News Items," *California Fruit Grower* 44 (August 19, 1911), 4.

18. "White Labor for the Vineyardists," *California Fruit Grower* 44 (September 30, 1911), 5; "Homer Craig Dies at Convention," *California Fruit Grower* 44 (December 23, 1911), 11.

19. Immigration Commission, *Reports*, XXV, Vol. 2, 204.

20. "Oppose the Jap Exclusion Idea," *San Francisco Chronicle*, October 9, 1906.

21. Daniels, *The Politics of Prejudice*, 25–30; Street, *Beasts of the Field*, 477–478.

22. Santa Clara County contractor notices appeared under "San Jose News" in the *Shin Sekai*. See, for example, "Recruiting workers," *Shin Sekai*, January 8, 1910; "Recruiting farm boys," *Shin Sekai*, February 17, 1910.

23. On conflicts between growers and Japanese contractors throughout the state, see Street, *Beasts of the Field*, 433–438; Vaught, *Cultivating California*, 119–120.

24. Immigration Commission, *Reports*, XXV, Vol. 2, 41–42; "Dried Fruits, Prunes and Raisins," *California Fruit Grower* 42 (December 31, 1910), 9.

25. California Commissioner of Labor, Fourteenth Biennial Report, p. 270, cited in Millis, *The Japanese Problem in the United States*, 108; Immigration Commission, *Reports*, XXV, Vol. 2, 201–202.

26. Pyle Diaries, February 9, 1907, February 15, 1907, February 22, 1907, February 28, 1907, April 29–May 11, 1907. In 1916, Mary Overfelt recorded a lease with Japanese tenant farmer H. Takaba to cultivate 19 acres of her property in San Jose. Santa Clara County Leases, Book P, 482.

27. Samuel S. Haines Papers, 1884–1922, California State Library, Sacramento. Hereafter "Haines Diaries," date. February 15, 1906, June 11, 1906, June 19–20, 1906.

28. Immigration Commission, *Reports*, XXV, Vol. 1, 67. On early Japanese labor militancy in California, see Street, *Beasts of the Field*, 413–414.

29. Immigration Commission, *Reports*, XXV, Vol. 1, 174–175.

30. "The Japanese in Hawaii," *San Francisco Chronicle*, July 2, 1909; "Hawaii Likes Chinese," *Los Angeles Times*, November 7, 1905; Masayo Umezawa Duus, *The Japanese Conspiracy: The Oahu Sugar Strike of 1920* (Berkeley: University of California Press, 1999), 18–25. See also Gary Y. Okihiro, *Cane Fires: The Anti-Japanese Movement in Hawaii, 1865–1945* (Philadelphia: Temple University Press, 1991).

31. Vaught, *Cultivating California*, 174–176, 183.

32. Edwards Diaries, June 5–9, 1905, November 16, 1905.

33. Haines Diaries, April 29, 1909, January 12, 1910, July 6, 1910.

34. Edwards Diaries, May 18, 1906.

35. Pyle Diaries, July 13, 1903, October 6, 1903, October 11, 1903, November 9, 1903, May 5, 1905; "W.A.Z. Edwards Life Outline," 1.

36. Pyle Diaries, March 27, 1908, March 30–April 9, 1908, May 24, 1907; *History of the State of California and Biographical Record*, 508–509. By the early 1920s, Pyle's cannery employed 300 people during peak season, and was run by his sons Harry and Edward. Sawyer, *History of Santa Clara County*, 301.

37. Calculations based on Santa Clara County Leases, Books J–O, Santa Clara County Recorder's Office, San Jose, California. The total acreage represented in leases dated 1900–1912 was

2,983 acres, but because five leases did not specify acreage, it is certain that the actual number of acres was well over 3,000. Rates of Japanese landownership were negligible in this period. Lukes and Okihiro estimate Japanese owned some ninety acres in the county in 1912. Lukes and Okihiro, *Japanese Legacy*, 61.

38. Santa Clara County Crop and Chattel Mortgages, Books 14–23; U.S. Bureau of the Census, *Thirteenth Decennial Census of the United States, 1910. Volume VI, Agriculture: 1909 and 1910* (Washington DC: Government Printing Office, 1913), 152. With crop mortgages, I counted the acreage containing the crops to be mortgaged specified in each agreement, cross-referencing names and properties with leases to avoid double-counting. Since many mortgages did not state the number of acres farmed even if tenant farming arrangements were implicit, it was difficult to arrive at an exact total figure. On acreage farmed by Japanese, see also U.S. Immigration Commission, *Reports*, XXIV, Vol. 2, 445, and *California and the Oriental: Japanese Chinese and Hindus. Report of the State Board of Control of California to Governor William D. Stephens* (Sacramento: California State Printing Office, 1920), 48. The U.S. Bureau of the Census made estimates regarding Japanese control of farmland, but I found that these tended to represent an undercount compared to county records. Census takers in 1910 stated that Japanese operated 2,201 acres of farmland in the county. Bureau of the Census, Department of Commerce, *Bulletin 127, Chinese and Japanese in the United States, 1910* (Washington, DC: Government Printing Office, 1914), 43, 47.

39. For a comparison of Japanese farming arrangements in Walnut Grove, where share-cropping predominated over cash leasing, see Azuma, "Japanese Immigrant Farmers and California Alien Land Laws," 14–19. On the diverse activities of ethnic and immigrant agriculturalists in the Pajaro Valley, including the Japanese, see Linda L. Ivey, "Ethnicity in the Land: Lost Stories in California Agriculture." *Agricultural History* 81 (2007), 98–124.

40. Trewartha, *Japan: A Geography*, 242–245. Trewartha notes that in the Northern Kyushu district, which coincides with Fukuoka and Yamaguchi, agriculture is somewhat less diversified, with a focus on vegetables and paddy rice. Referring to emigrant prefectures, I also include ones listed by Yosaburo Yoshida in "Sources and Causes of Japanese Immigration."

41. Trewartha, *Japan: A Geography*, 212–215.

42. Trewartha, *Japan: A Geography*, 198, 204, 207–208.

43. Ichihashi, *Japanese Immigration*, 32; Iwata, *Planted in Good Soil*, 193; Gary Y. Okihiro and David Drummond, "The Concentration Camps and Japanese Economic Losses in California Agriculture, 1900–1942," in *Japanese Americans: From Relocation to Redress*, revised edition, ed. Roger Daniels, Sandra C. Taylor, Harry H. L. Kitano (Seattle: University of Washington Press, 1991), 169. See also Robert Higgs, "Landless by Law: Japanese Immigrants in California Agriculture to 1941." *Journal of Economic History* 38 (March 1978), 205–225.

44. Azuma, "Japanese Immigrant Farmers and California Alien Land Laws," 19.

45. Santa Clara County Leases, Book K, 384–387; Ichioka, *The Issei*, 151; *San Jose City Directory, including Santa Clara County, 1901–1902* (San Francisco: F. M. Husted, 1901), 299; U.S. Immigration Commission, *Reports*, XXIV, Vol. 2, 446.

46. Santa Clara County Leases, Book N, 128, 130, 150–151.

47. 1900 Census Population Schedule, Santa Clara County; Santa Clara County Deeds, Book 356, 82, 85.

48. 1910 Census Population Schedule, Santa Clara County.

49. Santa Clara County Leases, Book O, 251; Santa Clara County Crop and Chattel Mortgages, Book 30, 245; Book 32, 298; Book 33, 118, 130.

50. Santa Clara County Leases, Book P, 67, 69, 92; 1920 Census Population Schedule, Santa Clara County.

51. 1930 Census Population Schedule, Santa Clara County; "Last of 4 Pioneer Sons Dies," *San Jose Mercury News*, December 6, 1974, 38; California Death Index, 1940–1997.

52. Foote, *Pen Pictures from the "Garden of the World,"* 268; Santa Clara County Leases, Book J, 23–26.

53. Santa Clara County Crop and Chattel Mortgages, Book 24, 338; Book 27, 329; Book 28, 420.

54. Santa Clara County Leases, Book N, 193–195, 242–243.

55. Santa Clara County Deeds, Book 392, 439. Much of the company's remaining property was sold to nearby Agnews State Hospital, a state insane asylum, to enlarge the hospital's farm to feed its growing patient population. Loomis, "Signposts: Austrian Named Malovos Found Riches in Valley," *San Jose News*, September 13, 1974; Leonard Stocking, "Report of Medical Superintendent, Agnews State Hospital, November 12, 1914," *Biennial Report of the State Commission in Lunacy* [California] 9 (1914), 67–70.

56. Santa Clara County Crop and Chattel Mortgages, Book 32, 448, 526.

57. Immigration Commission, *Reports*, XXIV, Vol. 2, 445. The ethnicity of the "business dealer" mentioned by federal investigators is unclear, as the report referenced Chinese and Japanese "dealers" in San Jose and Alviso, along with a "white dealer" in Santa Clara, all of whom provided Japanese farmers with supplies on credit.

58. Santa Clara County Leases, Book L, 198–201; Santa Clara County Crop and Chattel Mortgages, Book 22, 60–62. On Frank Zanker's father William Zanker, who settled in the county in 1857, see Foote, *Pen Pictures from the "Garden of the World,"* 544–545.

59. 1910 Census Population Schedule, Santa Clara County; Ichioka, *The Issei*, 152. On how Japanese wage earners were precluded from sending for wives from Japan, see Iwata, *Planted in Good Soil*, 114–115.

60. Santa Clara County Leases, Book M, 170–171; Book N, 11–12. See also *San Jose City Directory Including Santa Clara County, 1900–1901*, (San Jose, CA: F. M. Husted, 1900), 523, 525. Santa Clara County Great Registers, 1906, History San José. Entries for Mark Farney, Edmund Burk Farney, Paul Morphy Shearer, Frederick William Zanker, all of Alviso Precinct. On examples of Santa Clara Valley Japanese farm partnerships based on *ken*, see Lukes and Okihiro, *Japanese Legacy*, 30–31.

61. 1910 Census Population Schedule, Santa Clara County.

62. Santa Clara County Crop and Chattel Mortgages, Book 16, 441–444; 1900 Census Population Schedule, Santa Clara County; 1880 Census Population Schedule, Santa Clara County; 1870 Census Population Schedule, Santa Cruz County. Irish immigrant Charles McKiernan, husband of Barbara McKiernan, was a farmer and lumber dealer in Santa Cruz County and San Jose.

63. Santa Clara County Crop and Chattel Mortgages, Book 17, 489; Book 19, 202–204; Book 20, 175–176; Santa Clara County Leases, Book K, 456–457; Book M, 195; Book N, 469–470; 1910 Census Population Schedule, Santa Clara County; 1920 Census Population Schedule, Santa Clara County; 1930 Census Population Schedule, Santa Clara County; Santa Clara County Deeds, Book 319, 382, June 18, 1907; additional acreage purchased on February 12, 1912, Santa Clara County Deeds, Book 381, 215.

64. "Orchard Views of Santa Clara," *Pacific Rural Press* 85 (March 15, 1913), 325.

65. U.S. Immigration Commission, *Reports*, XXIV, Vol. 2, 445–446; *Bulletin 127, Chinese and Japanese in the United States, 1910*, 49; Sawyer, *History of Santa Clara County*, 139; Lukes and Okihiro, *Japanese Legacy*, 66. It does not seem likely that Japanese immigrants had much experience with berry cultivation in their native land. Prussian observer J. J. Rein noted in the late nineteenth century that "Our black mulberries, currants, gooseberries, raspberries, bilberries, and other kinds do not exist there at all, and strawberries and grapes only scantily and in poor quality." J. J. Rein, *The Industries of Japan. Together with an Account of Its Agriculture, Forestry, Arts, and Commerce* (New York: A. G. Armstrong, 1889), 82.

66. Santa Clara County Leases, Book N, 11–12; Book M, 63–66; Book N, 177; Book N, 474–476.

67. Santa Clara County Leases, Book M, 12. Santa Clara County Great Registers, 1906, History San José; Entry for Louis Zolezzi, Sunnyvale Precinct, *San Jose City Directory Including Santa Clara County, 1905–1906* (San Jose: F. M. Husted, 1905), 738; 1910 Census Population Schedule, Santa Clara County.

68. *Oda v. Laughlin Seed Co. et al*, 18570, Superior Court of the County of Santa Clara (1909); *Ishida v. John Heinlen Company*, 19664, Superior Court of the County of Santa Clara (1911).

69. "C. C. Stierlin," Will Book K, 238–241; 1910 Census Population Schedule, Santa Clara County; Foote, *Pen Pictures from the "Garden of the World,"* 669; Patricia Loomis, "Signposts: M. V. Road Named for 4 Farmers," *San Jose News*, October 8, 1971, 75. On tomato growing in the Valley, see Broek, *The Santa Clara Valley*, 114.

70. Santa Clara County Crop and Chattel Mortgages, Book 31, 439, 517, 583; Book 34, 283; Book 35, 580.

71. *California and the Oriental*, 50.

72. "Report of the California State Agricultural Society, 1908," 166–168, cited in U.S. Immigration Commission, *Reports*, XXIV, Vol. 2, 199.

73. Calculations based on the 1920 Census Population Schedule. Calculations do not include single Japanese farm laborers who were not listed as part of a household. Another 9 percent of farm families reportedly made their living by "working out" as farm laborers, and an additional 7 percent in nurseries, gardening, olives, and no listing (though another census category indicated they lived on a farm).

74. Ichioka, *The Issei*, 151.

75. Santa Clara County Leases, Book L, 404–406.

76. Santa Clara County Deeds, Book 65, 258; Book 106, 324. Santa Clara County Leases, Book N, 88–89; 1910 Census Population Schedule, Santa Clara County; J. M. Guinn, *History of the State of California and Biographical Record of Coast Counties, California* (Chicago: The Chapman Publishing Company, 1904), 469.

77. Santa Clara County Leases, Book M, 583–584.

78. Santa Clara County Deeds, Book 289, 182; Book 401, 240; *Zaibei Nihonjin Jinmei Jiten* (San Francisco: Nichibei Shimbunsha, 1922), 197. The Japanese American biographical directory said that the Horio brothers owned 50 acres of fruit orchards, but I could only verify 31.781 acres in county deed records.

79. Lukes and Okihiro go as far as to say that "Japanese farm tenancy was only a step removed from migrant labor," Lukes and Okihiro, *Japanese Legacy*, 32–33. However, evidence in lease and other property records does not support this conclusion.

80. *Ishida v. John Heinlen Company*.

81. *Oda v. Laughlin Seed Co.*

82. For similar lawsuits, see *Miyamoto v. Smith*, 20412, Superior Court of the County of Santa Clara (1912); *Esaki v. Wolpern*, 22608, Superior Court of the County of Santa Clara (1915); *Takeshita v. Greco Canning Company*, 24346, Superior Court of the County of Santa Clara (1918).

83. Santa Clara County Leases, Book O, 518; Santa Clara County Crop and Chattel Mortgages, Book 33, 276.

84. *Inouye et al. v. Younger*, 20791, Superior Court of the County of Santa Clara (1913); "Japs Seek Injunction," *San Jose Daily Mercury*, April 22, 1913.

85. *Shirachi v. Sloan*, 21284, Superior Court of the County of Santa Clara (1913).

86. *Shirachi v. Sloan*; Santa Clara County Leases, Book O, 518.

87. *Peterson v. Chakuno and Furuya*, 20348, Superior Court of the County of Santa Clara (1912); "Jap Farming Methods Are Cause of Action," *San Jose Mercury Herald*, September 12, 1912.

88. *Peterson v. Chakuno and Furuya*. A 1910 lease indicated that Peterson and her brother Vere were minors at the time they entered into an agreement with Chakuno and Furuya through their guardian, Fred Sowerby. In 1900, Lila (born in 1894) and Vere were living with their grandparents in Calaveras County. 1900 Census Population Schedule, Calaveras County. Richard L. Peterson, the widowed father of Lila and Vere, had filed a five-year agreement in 1905 with Chakuno for the same 50-acre orchard, suggesting that when the lease was renewed in 1910, Richard had passed away, leaving the property to his then-minor children. Lila, the eldest, turned eighteen in 1912, acquired her brother's interest in the property, and decided to bring suit against the Japanese lessees. Santa Clara County Leases, Book O, 199–200; Book M, 106.

89. *Peterson v. Chakuno and Furuya*. Millis found similar sentiments among white lessors in his 1915 study. One prominent Armenian farmer in Fresno told Millis that "he would rather lease his vineyards to Japanese than to farmers of his own race because they took better care of them." Millis, *The Japanese Problem in the United States*, 148.

90. *Sumida v. Takano*, 18336, Superior Court of the County of Santa Clara (1909); *Sumida v. Takano*, 18372, Superior Court of the County of Santa Clara (1909).

91. *Toda v. Takano*, 18270, Superior Court of the County of Santa Clara (1909); *Yim v. Takano*, 18276, Superior Court of the County of Santa Clara (1909). I am indebted to Bonnie Montgomery for her assistance in sorting out the intricacies of these cases.

92. *Shiraishi and Fugisaki v. Sumida et al.*, 18401, Superior Court of the County of Santa Clara (1909); *Shiraishi and Fugisaki v. Langford*, 18449, Superior Court of the County of Santa Clara (1910); *Shiraishi and Fugisaki v. Horn et al.*, 19718, Superior Court of the County of Santa Clara (1911).

93. Misawa, *Beginnings*, 40, 107; Japanese American National Museum, ed. REgenerations *Oral History Project: Rebuilding Japanese American Families, Communities, and Civil Rights in the Resettlement Era* (Los Angeles: Japanese American National Museum, 2000), 69, 141; "Division Is Strictly Observed."

94. "Division Is Strictly Observed."

95. "Japanese Boycott Has Stopped Men Gambling," *San Jose Mercury*, June 16, 1908; Azuma, *Between Two Empires*, 47–50.

96. "Chew Chun Han Passed Away," *Chung Sai Yat Po*, February 24, 1931; "Funeral Rites for Thos. Chew to be Delayed," *San Jose Mercury Herald*, February 25, 1931; "Tom Foon Chew is Called by Death," *Los Gatos Mail-News and Saratoga Star*, February 26, 1931.

97. J. C. Wright, "Thomas Foon Chew—Founder of Bayside Cannery" in Hom, ed. *Chinese Argonauts*, 22–30; Lukes and Okihiro, *Japanese Legacy*, 48–49; Santa Clara County Deeds, Book 570, 90. Although Lukes and Okihiro called Chew's corporation the "Tom Foon Ranch Company," extant business documents show it listed as the "Thomas Foon Ranch Company."

98. Street, *Beasts of the Field*, 322; Immigration Commission, *Reports*, XXV, Vol. 2, 203, 207–208.

99. Santa Clara County Crop and Chattel Mortgages, Book 33, 50; Book 31, 393.

100. Santa Clara County Crop and Chattel Mortgages, Books 31–52; Lukes and Okihiro, *Japanese Legacy*, 49, 65.

101. *Immigration Commission Reports*, XXV, Vol. 2, 447, 451.

102. "White Employees Out On Strike," *The Evening News, San Jose*, July 14, 1908; "Valley Canneries Are Busy With Early Fruit," *San Jose Mercury*, July 28, 1908; "California Capital Can Handle Big Fruit Crop," *San Jose Mercury*, July 30, 1908. On early white female labor militancy in Valley canneries during the late 1910s, see Glenna Matthews, *Silicon Valley, Women, and the California Dream: Gender, Class, and Opportunity in the Twentieth Century* (Stanford, CA: Stanford University Press, 2003), 39–44.

103. *Santa Clara County and Its Resources*, 200. The Flickinger cannery was owned by German-born Joseph Flickinger, described as "one of the best known of the pioneers and fruit growers of Santa Clara county" in his July 1897 obituary. *California Fruit Grower* 21 (July 3, 1897).

104. "5000 Families Are Wanted Here"; "Joseph H. Flickinger" in Guinn, *History of the State of California*, 496, 499.

105. "Labeling Fruit Packages," *California Fruit Grower* 31 (February 11, 1905), 2.

106. Santa Clara County Miscellaneous Records 22, 485–487; 1880, 1900, 1910 Census Population Schedule, Santa Clara County; "Wilma Tognazzini," in Bertha Marguerite Rice, *The Women of Our Valley*, vol. 2 (n.p., 1956), 28–30. A document titled "Agreement" between the J. H. Flickinger Company and Tognazzini was dated November 16, 1908 and recorded on April 5, 1909.

107. Santa Clara County Leases, Book N, 327–329. The J.H. Flickinger Company granted clear title to Tognazzini in December 1910. Santa Clara County Deeds, Book 366, 199.

Chapter Three

1. "Testimony taken at the Inquest on the body of Tomihei Hayakawa," Santa Clara County Coroner's Inquest, July 15, 1910, 6–8. History San José Research Library; 1910 Census Population Schedule, Santa Clara County; "Coldness of Bride Caused Despondency," *San Jose Daily Mercury*, July 16, 1910. The coroner's inquest identified Hayakawa's friend as "M. Muchida." Uchida's full name is taken from the Japanese language newspaper coverage of the suicide in the *Shin Sekai*, July 14–19, 1910.

2. "Was It Murder or Suicide? Tragedy Follows Wedding," *Mountain View Register-Leader*, July 13, 1910; "The Local Japanese Tragedy Is Decided To Be Suicide" in ibid., July 16, 1910.

3. With prostitutes available at nearly every Japanese settlement, venereal disease was not uncommon among Japanese men in early immigrant society, as evidenced by numerous advertisements that ran in the immigrant press for medicines claiming to cure gonorrhea and other ailments. Ichioka, *The Issei*, 89–90. According to the *Shin Sekai*, on the recommendation of Masa's cousin Toshiharu Takei, Hayakawa may have visited a doctor in Oakland on July 11, 1910, the day before his suicide. Takei noted that when Hayakawa returned to San Francisco in the afternoon, he "did not mention anything about disease" but started drinking sake and spoke of killing himself. "About Hayakawa's Suicide," *Shin Sekai*, July 18, 1910. One reporter suggested that Hayakawa suffered from syphilis. "About Hayakawa's Suicide (continued)," *Shin Sekai*, July 19, 1910.

4. "Testimony taken at the Inquest on the body of Tomihei Hayakawa," 15–20, 38–49.

5. "Suicide or Murder? Shocking Incident in Mountain View," *Shin Sekai*, July 15, 1910; "Testimony taken at the Inquest on the body of Tomihei Hayakawa," 15. Matajiro Uchida emigrated to the United States in July 1899, arriving in Seattle on a ship originating from Yokohama. U.S. National Archives and Records Administration, *Passenger and Crew Lists of Vessels Arriving in Seattle, Washington, 1890–1957* (College Park, MD: USNARA, 1957).

6. 1910 Census Population Schedule, Santa Clara County; *Thirteenth Census of the United States*, 157–158, 176–177.

7. *Thirteenth Census of the United States*, 157.

8. Compared to scholarship on the Issei, there are many more histories of second-generation Japanese Americans. See, for example, Lon Kurashige, *Japanese American Celebration and Conflict: A History of Ethnic Identity and Festival in Los Angeles, 1934–1990* (Berkeley: University of California Press, 2002); Eileen Tamura, *Americanization, Acculturation, and Ethnic Identity: The Nisei Generation in Hawaii* (Urbana: University of Illinois Press, 1994); David K. Yoo, *Growing Up Nisei: Race, Generation, and Culture among Japanese Americans of California, 1924–1949* (Urbana: University of Illinois Press, 2000).

9. Lukes and Okihiro, *Japanese Legacy*, 26–27; Charles N. Reynolds, "Oriental-White Race Relations in Santa Clara County, California" (Ph.D. dissertation, Stanford University, 1927), 146–147, 296; Peggy Pascoe, *What Comes Naturally: Miscegenation Law and the Making of Race in America* (New York: Oxford University Press, 2009), 87–91; Megumi

Dick Osumi, "Asians and California's Anti-Miscegenation Laws," in *Asian and Pacific American Experiences: Women's Perspectives*, ed. Nobuya Tsuchida (Minneapolis: Asian Pacific American Learning Resource Center and General College, University of Minnesota, 1982), 1–37.

10. Ichioka, *The Issei*, 169–172, and Azuma, *Between Two Empires*, 40. On the phenomenon of wives deserting husbands in other historical contexts in America, see Mary Beth Sievens, *Stray Wives: Marital Conflict in Early National New England* (New York: New York University Press, 2005), and Robert L. Griswold, *Family and Divorce in California, 1850–1890* (Albany: State University of New York Press, 1982), 79–81.

11. Lawrence M. Friedman and Robert V. Percival, *The Roots of Justice: Crime and Punishment in Alameda County, California, 1870–1910* (Chapel Hill: The University of North Carolina Press, 1981), 53–55.

12. Four of the 42 investigations involved Japanese female deaths (two suicides and two murders), while the rest involved the deaths of Japanese men.

13. Friedman and Percival, *The Roots of Justice*, 51–52; Lawrence M. Friedman and Paul Tabor, "A Pacific Rim: Crime and Punishment in Santa Clara County, 1922," *Law and History Review* 10 (1992), 133–137; California State Archives, "The Historical Records of County Government in California." (Sacramento: California State Archives, 2004), 39.

14. Social historians have used coroners' records to illuminate a range of topics. See, for example, Barbara A. Hanawalt, *The Ties That Bound: Peasant Families in Medieval England* (New York: Oxford University Press, 1986); Albert L. Hurtado, *Intimate Frontiers: Sex, Gender, and Culture in Old California* (Albuquerque: University of New Mexico Press, 1999), 115–128; Clare V. McKanna Jr., *Race and Homicide in Nineteenth-Century California* (Reno: University of Nevada Press, 2002); Leslie J. Reagan, *When Abortion Was a Crime: Women, Medicine, and Law in the United States, 1867–1973* (Berkeley: University of California Press, 1997), 113–131, 256.

15. "Testimony taken at the Inquest on the body of Hisagi Yamamoto," Santa Clara County Coroner's Inquest, July 25, 1908, 1–37. History San José.

16. "Fatal Fight Over Japanese Maiden," *San Jose Daily Mercury*, July 26, 1908; "Japanese Fired Fatal Shots in Self-Defense," *San Jose Daily Mercury*, July 28, 1908; "Disturbance by Pistol for Love," *Shin Sekai*, July 27, 28, 29, 30, 1908; August 2, 1908. Neither Ishizaka nor Sakata could be located in the 1910 and 1920 Santa Clara County census population schedule, suggesting that the couple moved out of San Jose after the shooting.

17. Under Albert Bessey's proprietorship, the Jubilee Incubator Company grew to such prominence that "their name on an incubator was 'much like "Sterling" on silver.'" Mary Jo Ignoffo, *Sunnyvale: From the City of Destiny to the Heart of Silicon Valley* (Cupertino: California History Center, 1994), 21.

18. "Attempted Rape Incident," *Nichibei Shimbun*, September 22, 1912. The 1910 census shows Albert Bessey living in Sunnyvale with his wife, his mother-in-law, and a Japanese servant. The Yoshidas, whose first child was not born when the census was taken, lived nearby on the same street. The census listed a "Keigo Yoshida" as Yasujiro's younger brother, but the person so designated may have actually been his nephew, Kaizo Yoshida, mentioned in the 1912 inquest. 1910 Census Population Schedule, Santa Clara County.

19. "Testimony taken at the Inquest on the body of Kamekichi Kojima," Santa Clara County Coroner's Inquest, September 21, 1912, 2–10. History San José. The coroner's inquest report transliterated Yoshida's first name as "Yusijiro." Japanese newspapers and other sources, including Yoshida's World War I draft registration card and records of the Yoshida family's internment at Heart Mountain during World War II, show that Yasujiro is more accurate and the spelling he used consistently.

20. "Testimony taken at the Inquest on the body of Kamekichi Kojima," 1–6; "Jury Finds Killing of Japanese Justifiable," *San Jose Daily Mercury*, September 22, 1912.

21. "Testimony taken at the Inquest on the body of Kamekichi Kojima," 1–6, 9–11; "Jury Finds Killing of Japanese Justifiable"; "Attempted Rape Incident"; "Post-report on the rape and gundown case," *Nichibei Shimbun*, September 27, 1912.

22. "Testimony taken at the Inquest on the body of Kitaura Fukumatsu," Santa Clara County Coroner's Inquest, December 20, 1913, 1–18. History San José; *California Polk-Husted Directory Co.'s San Jose City and Santa Clara County Directory 1911–1912* (San Jose, 1912), 553; "Jap Woman Resents an Insult with Revolver," *San Jose Mercury Herald*, December 20, 1913; "A Woman Shot Rapist to Death," *Shin Sekai*, December 21, 1913; "Outline of Gun-down Incident," *Nichibei Shimbun*, December 22, 1913.

23. "Firearms Stored in Japanese Communities," *San Jose Daily Mercury*, July 30, 1908; "Jap Gun Wielder is Caught in San Jose," *San Jose Mercury Herald*, September 12, 1912.

24. "Verdict of the Coroner's Jury" in "Testimony taken at the Inquest on the body of Kitaura Fukumatsu," no pagination. Prior to working in Edenvale, the Handas farmed in Aptos in Santa Cruz County; 1910 Population Schedule, Santa Cruz County. Rei Handa arrived in Seattle in January of 1908 at age twenty-one. U.S. National Archives, *Passenger and Crew Lists of Vessels Arriving at Seattle*.

25. "Testimony taken at the Inquest on the body of Hisagi Yamamoto," 18; "Testimony taken at the Inquest on the body of Kitaura Fukumatsu," 12; "Testimony taken at the Inquest on the body of Kamekichi Kojima," 2–5; Sharon Block, *Rape and Sexual Power in Early America* (Chapel Hill: The University of North Carolina Press, 2006), 25–27, 59.

26. A. Nicholas Groth, *Men Who Rape: The Psychology of the Offender* (New York: Plenum Press, 1979), 5. For more examples of this argument, see: Peggy Reeves Sanday, "The Socio-Cultural Context of Rape: A Cross-Cultural Study," *Journal of Social Issues* 37 (1981), 5–27; Susan Brownmiller, *Against Our Will: Men, Women and Rape* (New York: Simon and Schuster, 1975); Julia Schwendinger and Herman Schwendinger, *Rape and Inequality* (Beverly Hills, CA: Sage Publications, 1983), 27–46; Merrill D. Smith, ed., *Sex Without Consent: Rape and Sexual Coercion in America* (New York: New York University Press, 2001), 1–9; Catherine Burns, *Sexual Violence and the Law in Japan* (London: Routledge, 2005), 21–35.

27. Albert L. Hurtado, *Indian Survival on the California Frontier* (New Haven, CT: Yale University Press, 1988), 182–186. Hurtado employs arguments from Groth, *Men Who Rape*, 5, 12–13, 25–29. On rape trials involving Asian male defendants in Los Angeles, see Bonni Cermak, "In the Interest of Justice: Legal Narratives of Sex, Gender, Race and Rape in Twentieth Century Los Angeles, 1920–1960" (Ph.D. dissertation, University of Oregon, 2005), 99–110, 140–141, 181–187. Nearly all of the cases Cermak discusses involved charges of alleged statutory or interracial rape, in contrast to the attempted rapes discussed here.

28. "Testimony taken at the Inquest on the body of Kamekichi Kojima," 20; "Testimony taken at the Inquest on the body of Kitaura Fukumatsu," 19.

29. Azuma, *Between Two Empires*, 35–60, 187–207.

30. "Testimony taken at the Inquest on the body of Kamekichi Kojima," 4–6, 20; "Attempted rape incident." On Japanese immigrant fishermen in Monterey, see Chiang, *Shaping the Shoreline*, 52–54. According to Chiang, Japanese were particularly dominant in salmon fishing, operating 125 of 180 Monterey salmon boats in 1907.

31. "Attempted Rape Incident."

32. "Attempted rape and gun-down case," *Nichibei Shimbun*, September 24, 1912; "Post-report on the rape and gun-down case"; "Fact report on murder case."

33. "Testimony taken at the Inquest on the body of Kamekichi Kojima," 6. The anecdotal evidence linking financial success with a settled existence is corroborated by economist Robert Higgs's study of Japanese tenant farmers in 1909, which found a strong positive statistical correlation between a Japanese immigrant's wealth and the length of residence at his present locality. In other words, the more "settled" the immigrant, the more he was

likely to accumulate larger amounts of capital. Robert Higgs, "The Wealth of Japanese Tenant Farmers in California, 1909," *Agricultural History* 53 (1979), 492.

34. According to the 1910 manuscript census, Tsuneno and Yasujiro were twenty-eight and thirty years old, respectively; those ages, however, do not match the ages listed in the 1920 and 1930 censuses. Going by the later censuses, records of their World War II incarceration, and listings in the California death index, Tsuneno Yoshida was born in 1884, while Yasujiro Yoshida was born in 1875, which meant they were twenty-eight and thirty-seven years old, respectively, in 1912 when the assault took place. U.S. National Archives and Records Administration, *Passenger Lists of Vessels Arriving at San Francisco, 1893–1953* (Washington, DC: National Archives, 1985); War Relocation Authority, *Records About Japanese Americans Relocated During World War II* (College Park, MD: National Archives, 1988) (database).

35. Lukes and Okihiro, *Japanese Legacy*, 59–74, 106–107.

36. "Testimony taken at the Inquest on the body of Kitaura Fukumatsu," 23. The ideology of *ryosai kenbo*, or "Good Wife, Wise Mother," was sanctioned by the Meiji Civil Code of 1898 as the ideal role for female imperial subjects, who were inculcated from girlhood with "the virtues of chastity, modesty, and submissiveness." Burns, *Sexual Violence and the Law in Japan*, 27.

37. Ichioka, *The Issei*, 29–39.

38. "Testimony taken at the Inquest on the body of Kiku Tabuchi," Santa Clara County Coroner's Inquest, September 10, 1903, 1–21. History San José.

39. "Testimony taken at the Inquest on the body of Kinsaku Kuraoka," Santa Clara County Coroner's Inquest, February 17, 1905, 1–5. History San José. On American Orientalist myths and stereotypes of Japanese women as geishas at the turn of the twentieth century, see Mari Yoshihara, *Embracing the East: White Women and American Orientalism* (New York: Oxford University Press, 2003), 59–62, 68–70.

40. "Testimony taken at the Inquest on the body of Kinsaku Kuraoka," 5–7, 10. On malnutrition among Japanese farm laborers, who often subsisted on rice balls and flour dumplings in soup, see Street, *Beasts of the Field*, 425.

41. Ichioka, *The Issei*, 164–167; Evelyn Nakano Glenn, *Issei, Nisei, War Bride: Three Generations of Japanese American Women in Domestic Service* (Philadelphia: Temple University Press, 1986), 43–45, 260.

42. "Testimony taken at the Inquest on the body of Tomihei Hayakawa," 19–20, 51.

43. Ibid., 40–43.

44. "The Local Japanese Tragedy Is Decided To Be Suicide"; "Testimony taken at the Inquest on the body of Tomihei Hayakawa," 40–43; "About Hayakawa's Suicide (continued)."

45. Calculated from the 1910 Census Population Schedule, Santa Clara County; Harald Fuess, *Divorce in Japan: Family, Gender, and the State, 1600–2000* (Stanford, CA: Stanford University Press, 2004), 70–71. Misao Kondo, a teenage bride who arrived in California in 1916, recalled receiving numerous marriage proposals from men in a Japanese labor camp in Sunnyvale immediately after her husband died of influenza in the 1918 epidemic. Barbara McIntosh, "The Silence of the Issei," *San Jose Mercury News* (*West Magazine*), January 26, 1986, 19.

46. "Interlocutory Decree Granted to Japanese," *San Jose Daily Mercury*, July 6, 1912; *Ando v. Ando*, 20136, Superior Court of the County of Santa Clara (1912).

47. Harry H. L. Kitano, *Japanese Americans: The Evolution of a Subculture*, 2nd ed. (Englewood Cliffs, NJ: Prentice-Hall, 1976), 64–65, 156. Based on 1960 census statistics, Kitano calculates a divorce rate of approximately 1.6 percent for first-generation Japanese Americans.

48. Fuess, *Divorce in Japan*, 72–74, 82–98; Robert J. Smith and Ella Lury Wiswell, *The Women of Suye Mura* (Chicago: The University of Chicago Press, 1982), 151–154.

49. On the tendency of women to initiate divorce in the second half of the nineteenth century, see Robert L. Griswold, *Family and Divorce in California*, 29–30. For other examples of

divorces filed by women in a "pioneering" California community, see Vaught, *After the Gold Rush*, 110–112, 141–142.

50. *Machi Matsushita v. K. Matsushita*, 20063, Superior Court of the County of Santa Clara (1912).

51. *Hisae Kubo v. Kanematsu Kubo*, 23701, Superior Court of the County of Santa Clara (1917).

52. Glenda Riley, *Divorce: An American Tradition* (New York: Oxford University Press, 1991), 86–89. Few historians have examined divorce in nonwhite communities. For exceptions, see Omar S. Valerio-Jiménez, "New Avenues for Domestic Dispute and Divorce Lawsuits along the U.S.-Mexico Border, 1832–1893," *Journal of Women's History* 21 (Spring 2009), 10–33; Dylan C. Penningroth, "African American Divorce in Virginia and Washington, DC, 1865–1930," *Journal of Family History* 33 (January 2008), 21–35.

53. Griswold, *Family and Divorce in California*, 79–80.

54. "Wife ran away," *Shin Sekai*, July 20, 1911; "Worth of being a Japanese woman," *Shin Sekai*, October 18, 1911.

55. Ichioka states that women deserters were "ostracized and inevitably forced to move to new locales," but the scattered examples he provides do not indicate a direct correlation between social ostracism and the fact that some women moved. Ichioka, *The Issei*, 170–172.

56. *Toyo Kobayashi v. Kido Kobayashi*, 20071, Superior Court of the County of Santa Clara (1912); *Nat Ogawa v. F. Ogawa*, 21434, Superior Court of the County of Santa Clara (1914).

57. *Hirano v. Hirano*, 22012, Superior Court of the County of Santa Clara (1914).

58. *Tsuruda v. Tsuruda*, 22016, Superior Court of the County of Santa Clara (1914).

59. *Hirano v. Hirano*, 22012.

60. *Zenihiro v. Zenihiro*, 21235, Superior Court of the County of Santa Clara (1913); "Affair," *Shin Sekai*, December 8, 1913.

61. Ibid.

62. *Zenihiro v. Zenihiro*; 1910 Census Population Schedule, Santa Clara County.

63. *Zaibei Nihonjin Jinmei Jiten*, 144; Santa Clara County Marriage Records. Santa Clara County Clerk-Recorders Office, San Jose, California. Transcribed on http://files.usgwarchives.org/ca/santaclara/vitals/marriages/zab-zyc.txt.

64. "Tragedy of Life," *Shin Sekai*, April 5, 1908.

65. "Raise Your Voice without Hesitation," *Shin Sekai*, April 13, 1914; "Worth of Being a Japanese Woman".

66. "Murder Case in San José," *Shin Sekai*, February 14, 1910; "Murder Case, Victim Died Instantly," *Shin Sekai*, February 15, 1910.

67. "Testimony taken at the Inquest on the body of Kume Emoto," Santa Clara County Coroner's Inquest, February 15, 1910, 23–29. History San José; "Murder Case in San Jose." On the demand for Japanese domestic work and women's choices to enter it in the early twentieth century, see Glenn, *Issei, Nisei, War Bride*, 110–116.

68. "Testimony taken at the Inquest on the body of Kume Emoto," 25–27. The use of "consummate" by the interrogator here referred to making the marriage official to the public.

69. Ibid., 28–30. On changes in white American concepts of divorce in the late nineteenth and twentieth centuries, see Elaine Tyler May, *Great Expectations: Marriage and Divorce in Post-Victorian America* (Chicago: The University of Chicago Press, 1980), and Riley, *Divorce*, 130–131.

70. "Testimony taken at the Inquest on the body of Kume Emoto," 32–39.

71. Ibid., 41–43.

72. For example, the attack on a Japanese man in San Jose by his countrymen in 1909, according to a local reporter, "arose over a Japanese woman." "Japanese is Badly Beaten By Countrymen," *San Jose Daily Mercury*, October 14, 1909.

73. "Worthless Men," *Shin Sekai*, March 13, 1909.

74. Roger Daniels, *Asian America: Chinese and Japanese in the United States since 1850* (Seattle: University of Washington Press, 1988), 126–127.

75. Investigations of children, some of whom died by accidentally ingesting poisons used on farms or were involved in other farm-related accidents, made up about a third of the Japanese inquests from 1914 to 1930; only one child's death was investigated from 1900 to 1913. Train and automobile fatalities comprised another third, and the remaining deaths resulted from suicide and natural or other causes. It is possible that one or more of the 12 Japanese suicides investigated involved some sort of gender conflict, but there was insufficient information in the transcripts to permit any conclusions to be drawn. Santa Clara County Coroner's Inquests, History San José.

76. Ichioka, *The Issei*, 146–148; Matsumoto, *Farming the Home Place*, 25–30; "Mountain View News," *Shin Sekai*, September 30, 1912.

77. More research needs to be undertaken on the historical implications and significance of immigrant suicides. My initial findings among the Japanese of Santa Clara County indicate that single men (including men who were married but not living with their wives in America) made up the vast majority of Japanese suicides in the period from 1900 to 1930.

Chapter Four

1. *California and the Oriental: Japanese, Chinese, and Hindus. Report of the State Board of Control of California to Gov. Wm. D. Stephens* (Sacramento: California State Printing Office, 1920), 8–9. On distortions of the birthrate data in *California and the Oriental*, see Daniels, *The Politics of Prejudice*, 89.

2. "Governor Stephens and the Japanese Question," *Mountain View Register-Leader*, June 25, 1920; "Japanese Exclusion," *Mountain View Register-Leader*, July 2, 1920.

3. U.S. Bureau of the Census, *Thirteenth Census of the United States Taken in the Year 1910, Volume II, Population* (Washington, DC: Government Printing Office, 1913), 158; U.S. Bureau of the Census, *Fourteenth Census of the United States Taken in the Year 1920, Volume III, Population* (Washington, DC: Government Printing Office, 1922), 128, 132; Daniels, *Asian America*, 127, 156; *Statistics Relative to Japanese Immigration and the Japanese in California* (San Francisco: Japanese Association of America, 1920), V. The Japanese Association of America's (JAA) estimates of the Japanese population in California appear to be comparable to U.S. census numbers. The JAA counted 68,982 Japanese in California in 1918; the national census reported 71,952 in 1920. For more on the founding and activities of the Japanese Association of America, see Azuma, *Between Two Empires*, 43–46.

4. The classic account of the anti-Japanese movement in California remains Daniels, *The Politics of Prejudice*. Some interpretations tend to collapse all agitation, legislation, and ideology into one long "anti-Japanese movement." See, for example, Ronald Takaki, *Strangers from a Different Shore: A History of Asian Americans*, rev. ed. (Boston and New York: Back Bay Books, 1998), 203–209.

5. Robert Newton Lynch, "Immigration: The Anticipated Immigrant," *Sunset* 31 (December 1913), 1145.

6. *Statistics Relative to Japanese Immigration*, VII–VIII.

7. Azuma, *Between Two Empires*, 65–79 and Azuma, "Japanese Immigrant Farmers and California Alien Land Laws, 14–29.

8. "Influence of the Japanese," *Pacific Rural Press* 85 (May 24, 1913), 586–587; "The Race and Labor Problem," *Pacific Rural Press* 86 (July 26, 1913), 80. No study has been done to disaggregate support for the 1913 law by region, though Daniels suggests that much of outcry from growers came from the Central Valley. Daniels, *The Politics of Prejudice*, 45.

9. "Is Jap To Monopolize Washtub of This City?," *San Jose Daily Mercury*, April 11, 1912.

10. "Declares Japs Menace Local Laundry Industry," *San Jose Daily Mercury*, July 3, 1912; "Anti-Japanese League Has Important Meeting," *San Jose Daily Mercury*, July 18, 1912. On the

pervasive idea that Japanese were willing to "work for nothing" to drive out competition, see "Influence of the Japanese," 586.

11. "Mission Cornerstone is Laid By Japanese," *San Jose Daily Mercury*, April 21, 1913; "Legislature Will Not Back Down," *San Jose Daily Mercury*, April 22, 1913. On white Protestants' efforts to stem the anti-Japanese tide, see arguments by Sidney Gulick, a Congregational missionary who became one of the most prolific and prominent Protestant defenders of the Japanese at this time: Sidney L. Gulick, *The American Japanese Problem: A Study of the Racial Relations of the East and the West* (New York: Charles Scribner's Sons, 1914).

12. On the origins of the term "coolie" as applied to Chinese labor in the nineteenth century, see Jung, *Coolies and Cane*, 13–38; Robert G. Lee, *Orientals: Asian Americans in Popular Culture* (Philadelphia: Temple University Press, 1999), 51–82.

13. On the color line separating "whites" from the "colored races" in the early twentieth century, see Thomas A. Guglielmo, *White on Arrival: Italians, Race, Color, and Power in Chicago, 1890–1945* (New York: Oxford University Press, 2003), 6.

14. "Legislature Will Not Back Down"; "The Situation at Sacramento," *San Jose Daily Mercury*, April 30, 1913. On commentary regarding parallels between Asian labor and black slavery, see "The Race and Labor Problem," *Pacific Rural Press* 86 (July 26, 1913), 80.

15. Yamato Ichihashi, "American Views of the Japanese Question," *The Japanese American Monthly Review* 1 (July 1, 1913), 4–5; James D. Phelan to Woodrow Wilson, April 20, 1912. James D. Phelan Papers. Bancroft Library.

16. See, for example, "Coast News Items," *California Fruit Grower* 47 (February 1, 1913), 5; "Prunes," *California Fruit Grower* 47 (March 1, 1913), 10; "Early Reports of Fruit Crop Prospects," *California Fruit Grower* 47 (April 12, 1913), 1; "Prune and Other Prospects in Santa Clara," *California Fruit Grower* 47 (May 10, 1913), 3. The only piece of pending legislation mentioned in the *California Fruit Grower* in these months was a proposition for a law mandating an eight-hour work day, defeated in 1914. "Strongly Opposed to Eight Hour Restriction," *California Fruit Grower* 47 (March 1, 1913), 3; "Hearing on Eight-Hour Law at Sacramento," *California Fruit Grower* 47 (March 29, 1913), 3.

17. "The Aims of the Farmers' Union," *Pacific Rural Press* 85 (March 15, 1913), 330; "Alien Land Law Is in Favor with Farmers," *San Jose Daily Mercury*, April 27, 1913; Vaught, *Cultivating California*, 145–147.

18. "Alien Land Law Is in Favor with Farmers." On politics and negotiations between the Wilson administration and Governor Hiram Johnson over the alien land bill, see Daniels, *The Politics of Prejudice*, 52–62.

19. "Preparing to Pass an Alien Land Bill," *San Jose Daily Mercury*, April 25, 1913.

20. "Governor Signs the Land Bill," *San Jose Daily Mercury*, May 15, 1913.

21. Quote by Johnson cited in Daniels, *The Politics of Prejudice*, 64.

22. "Japanese Farming Companies," *Pacific Rural Press* 86 (August 30, 1913), 210. For a list of Japanese farm corporations in Santa Clara County in 1921, see Lukes and Okihiro, *Japanese Legacy*, 59.

23. On how this practice was contested but affirmed in favor of Japanese American defendants in *The People of California v. Jukichi Harada* (1918), see Mark Howland Rawitsch, *The House on Lemon Street: Japanese Pioneers and the American Dream* (Boulder: University Press of Colorado, 2012), 91–128.

24. *In the Matter of the Petition of Chozaburo Kumagai*, 23057, Superior Court of the County of Santa Clara (1916); *In the Matter of the Petition of Chozaburo Kumagai*, 23388, Superior Court of the County of Santa Clara (1916); Santa Clara County Deeds, Book 392, 439; Book 451, 132; Book 452, 297; Santa Clara County Leases, Book Q, 319; 1920 Census Population Schedule, Santa Clara County; *Zaibei Nihonjin Jinmei Jiten*, 323. This Japanese American directory listed the year of Chozaburo Kumagai's arrival as 1899.

25. *California and the Oriental*, 48–50.

26. Masao Suzuki, "Important or Impotent? Taking Another Look at the 1920 California Alien Land Law," *Journal of Economic History* 64 (March 2004), 128–130.

27. Daniels, *The Politics of Prejudice*, 64; Vaught, *Cultivating California*, 158–187.

28. Trewartha, *Japan: A Geography*, 198; Thomas C. Smith, *Native Sources of Japanese Industrialization, 1750–1920* (Berkeley: University of California Press, 1988), 4–5.

29. Ichioka, *The Issei*, 146–148; Matsumoto, *Farming the Home Place*, 25–30; Kesa Noda, *Yamato Colony: 1906–1960, Livingston, California* (Livingston, CA: Livingston-Merced JACL Chapter, 1981); 1920 Census Population Schedule, Santa Clara County.

30. Ichioka, *The Issei*, 164.

31. File 15322/11-2. Arrival Files, San Francisco, Records of the U.S. Immigration and Naturalization Service, RG 85, National Archives, Pacific Region, San Bruno, California. Ages calculated from INS file information and 1920 Census Population Schedule, Santa Clara County.

32. File 15287/20-22. Arrival Files, San Francisco; 1920 Census Population Schedule, Santa Clara County. On the tendency of Kumamoto natives to settle together in rural California, see David Mas Masumoto, *Country Voices: The Oral History of a Japanese American Family Farm Community* (Del Rey, CA: Inaka Countryside Publications, 1987), 8–9.

33. Tabulated from the 1910 Census Population Schedule, Santa Clara County and *Fourteenth Census of the United States Taken in the Year 1920, Volume III, Population*, 132; *United States Census of Agriculture, 1925*, Part III, 484; "Local Japanese Have Opened School for Their Children," *Mountain View Register-Leader*, July 9, 1915. I located 2,151 Japanese residents in the 1910 population schedule, 148 individuals shy of the official census figure of 2,299 Japanese in Santa Clara County.

34. 1910 Census Population Schedule, Santa Clara County; 1920 Census Population Schedule, Santa Clara County. I counted as a "family farm" any household enumerated by census takers as containing a head of household listed as a farmer by occupation and one or more dependents, usually wives and children. Individuals not listed in a household unit (e.g., single male laborers) are not included in this tabulation. Data on children based on 291 Japanese farm families with one or more children from the 1920 U.S. Census.

35. 1910 Census Population Schedule, Santa Clara County; 1920 Census Population Schedule, Santa Clara County; 1930 Census Population Schedule, Santa Clara County.

36. *California and the Oriental*, 48; John P. Irish, "The Races in the Delta," *The Japanese American Monthly Review* 1 (July 1, 1913), 8–9; *Statistics Relative to Japanese Immigration*, VIII. Tabulations of crops from 1920 Census Population Schedule, Santa Clara County based on 181 Japanese residents enumerated as farmers.

37. Santa Clara County Leases, Book P, 69, 528.

38. 1920 Census Population Schedule, Santa Clara County; *In the Matter of the Petition of Matagoro Kurasaki*, 24418, Superior Court of the County of Santa Clara (1918); Oral History, Henry Kurasaki, February 22, 1984; Lukes and Okihiro, *Japanese Legacy*, 67, 115.

39. Santa Clara County Leases, Book O, 350, 438; Book P, 126; Book Q, 80; Book Q, 157; 1910 Census Population Schedule, Santa Clara County.

40. 1920 Census Population Schedule, Santa Clara County; Lukes and Okihiro, *Japanese Legacy*, 122. Suyetaro Araki died at Heart Mountain at the age of seventy-one. Chiyo Araki was committed to Agnews State Hospital after the war and died in 1960.

41. Immigration Commission, *Reports*, XXIV, Vol. 2, 448–449.

42. Ruth Fowler, "An Attempt to Find out about the Standard of Living of the Japanese in San Jose and Santa Clara County [and obstacles to such study]," 10–11, c. 1920. Survey of Race Relations, Box 19, Folder 9. Hoover Archives, Stanford University.

43. Matsumoto, *Farming the Home Place*, 44–47; Street, *Beasts of the Field*, 521–522; Sandra O. Uyeunten, "Struggle and Survival: The History of Japanese Immigrant Families in California, 1907–1945" (Ph.D. dissertation, University of California, San Diego, 1988), 83–84.

44. *Zenihiro v. Zenihiro*; McIntosh, "The Silence of the Issei," 19.

45. Glenn, *Issei, Nisei, War Bride*, 53–54; "Harry Nishiura interview," in *Beginnings*, 80; Matsumoto, *Farming the Home Place*, 65.

46. "Testimony taken at the Inquest on the body of Kimi Yamita," Santa Clara County Coroner's Inquest, August 13, 1913; 1920 Census Population Schedule, Santa Clara County. For other cases of suicide among rural Japanese women in California, see Street, *Beasts of the Field*, 522.

47. "Details of a woman's suicide," *Nichibei Shimbun*, August 15, 1913; "Report on suicide case," *Nichibei Shimbun*, August 19, 1913; "Yanita's wife's suicide," *Shin Sekai*, August 15, 1913. Japanese newspapers confirm her surname as Yanita, not Yamita, as listed by the coroner.

48. "Testimony taken at the Inquest on the body of Masayo Ota," Santa Clara County Coroner's Inquest, April 15, 1917, 3–6. History San José. The Otas were enumerated in the 1920 census under the Heinlen household, but the census taker, who scrawled "could not speak English" on the form, neglected to include the first names of all family members. 1920 Census Population Schedule, Santa Clara County.

49. "Testimony taken at the Inquest on the body of Masayo Ota," 5–8; "Woman's violent death," *Shin Sekai*, April 17, 1917; "Funeral of Mrs. Ota," *Shin Sekai*, April 19, 1917.

50. Sherry Katz, "Socialist Women and Progressive Reform," in William Deverell and Tom Sitton, eds., *California Progressivism Revisited* (Berkeley: University of California Press, 1994), 131–132.

51. Ibid., 129–132; Linda Gordon, *Pitied But Not Entitled: Single Mothers and the History of Welfare, 1890–1935* (Cambridge: Harvard University Press, 1994), 39–41; Julie Novkov, "Historicizing the Figure of the Child in Legal Discourse," *The American Journal of Legal History* 44 (October 2000), 369–404.

52. Daniels, *The Politics of Prejudice*, 87–91.

53. *California and the Oriental*, 102; V. S. McClatchy, *Japanese Immigration and Colonization: Skeleton Brief* (Washington, DC: Government Printing Office, 1921), 20.

54. "Investigating the Japanese Menace," *Mountain View Register-Leader*, July 16, 1920; "Presence of Japanese Women in Great Numbers Assures Vast Increase in Birth-Rate," *The Sacramento Bee*, July 7, 1919; Cora M. Woodbridge, "Now's the Time to Take a Stand against the Japs," *Grizzly Bear* (October 1920), 3.

55. Broek, *The Santa Clara Valley*, 124; Jacobson, *Passing Farms, Enduring Values*, 131–133.

56. Mary Neth, *Preserving the Family Farm: Women Community, and the Foundations of Agribusiness in the Midwest, 1900–1940* (Baltimore: The Johns Hopkins University Press, 1995), 214–218; Deborah Fitzgerald, *Every Farm a Factory: The Industrial Ideal in American Agriculture* (New Haven, CT: Yale University Press, 2003).

57. *California and the Oriental*, 103. Daniels attributes the increasingly negative shift in public opinion toward Japan and the Japanese from 1913 to 1924 to factors other than the backlash against the rise of Japanese farm families, citing "a racist ideology, a growing uneasiness about Japanese military prowess and aggression, and the consistent anti-Japanese propaganda of the California exclusionists." Daniels, *The Politics of Prejudice*, 65.

58. Azuma, *Between Two Empires*, 56–57; Kiichi Kanzaki, *California and the Japanese* (San Francisco: Japanese Association of America, 1921), 4.

59. T. Iyenaga and Kenoske Sato, *Japan and the California Problem* (New York: G. P. Putnam's Sons, 1921), 134–135.

60. Colonel John P. Irish, "The Range of California Orientation," *The Monthly Bulletin*, California State Department of Agriculture, Vol. 8, November–December, 1919, Proceedings of the Fifty-Second Convention of the Fruit Growers and Farmers Held under the auspices of the California State Department of Agriculture, Sacramento, 719, 721.

61. McClatchy, *Japanese Immigration and Colonization*, 11–13; "Concerning the Japanese Question," *San Jose Mercury Herald*, January 14, 1920.

62. "Phelan in New Move Against Japs," *San Jose Evening News*, January 21, 1920; "Presence of Japanese Women in Great Numbers Assures Vast Increase in Birth-Rate"; "Production of Orientals Tremendous," *San Jose Evening News*, January 29, 1920.

63. McClatchy, *Japanese Immigration and Colonization*, 11–13, 37–39; "Japanese Birthrate Makes Dominance Sure," *San Jose Mercury Herald*, August 29, 1919. Daniels calls McClatchy and Hiram Johnson (who served as California's governor and as U.S. senator) "the general staff of the exclusionist forces." Daniels, *The Politics of Prejudice*, 91.

64. *California and the Oriental*, 37–38; McClatchy, *Japanese Immigration and Colonization*, 39. On similar concerns over Japanese birthrates expressed by Los Angeles County health officials, see Natalia Molina, *Fit To Be Citizens?: Public Health and Race in Los Angeles, 1879–1939* (Berkeley: University of California Press, 2006), 56–57, 106–110.

65. My sample of 1,958 Japanese in Santa Clara County from the 1920 Census Population Schedule shows 573 individuals age 10 and under born in California and 451 women age eighteen and over, giving a ratio of approximately 1.27. I use this to give an estimated Japanese "birthrate" in Santa Clara County, but it is possible that some of these children were not born in the county but moved from elsewhere in California between 1910 and 1920.

66. "Welcome Address," *The Monthly Bulletin*, California State Department of Agriculture Vol. 8, November–December, 1919, Proceedings of the Fifty-Second Convention of the Fruit Growers and Farmers Held under the auspices of the California State Department of Agriculture, Sacramento, 619.

67. "Fifty-Second State Fruit Growers and Farmers Convention," *California Fruit News* 60 (November 22, 1919), 3–4.

68. K. K. Kawakami, *The Real Japanese Question* (New York: The Macmillan Company), 40; Kanzaki, *California and the Japanese*, 10–12. Kawakami held a master's degree from the University of Iowa and had been the general secretary for the Japanese Association of America. On collaborations between the Japanese state and Issei leadership to produce pro-Japanese English-language materials, see Azuma, *Between Two Empires*, 52.

69. Brian J. Gaines and Wendy K. Tam Cho, "On California's 1920 Alien Land Law: The Psychology and Economics of Racial Discrimination," *State Politics and Policy Quarterly* 4 (Fall 2004), 276–279; Lukes and Okihiro, *Japanese Legacy*, 58; Daniels, *The Politics of Prejudice*, 21, 29–30; "American Legion Protests," *Mountain View Register-Leader*, August 6, 1920.

70. "A White Man's Country," *Mountain View Register-Leader*, September 3, 1920; "Production of Orientals Tremendous"; "Would Debar Japs But Admit Chinese Laborers," *Daily Palo Alto Times*, January 29, 1920. On how Japanese farmers in Mountain View pledged more than a thousand dollars toward World War I savings stamps, see "Loyal Japanese," *Mountain View Register-Leader*, July 5, 1918.

71. On white fruit growers' varied opinions on the Japanese issue, see: "Governor of California Calls Attention of Federal Government to Oriental Immigration," *California Fruit News* 61 (July 24, 1920), 3–4; "Farmers Want Laws Passed to Remedy These Evils," *Pacific Rural Press* 100 (December 11, 1920), 758. On the Santa Clara Valley's successful 1919 and 1920 growing seasons, see, for example, "Santa Clara Valley a Big Canning Center," *California Fruit News* 60 (July 5, 1919), 3; "Federal Crop Report for California," *California Fruit News* 60 (August 16, 1919), 7; "Dried Fruit Production Last year Shows Larger Tonnage Than Was Estimated," *California Fruit News* 62 (August 21, 1920), 5.

72. Azuma, "Japanese Immigrant Farmers and California Alien Land Laws," 28–29; Azuma, *Between Two Empires*, 68–69; Shah, *Stranger Intimacy*, 123–124. These views sharply contrast with Roger Daniels's conclusion that the 1920 measure was an "empty gesture, an ineffective irritant" that did not significantly affect land tenure in California. Daniels, *The Politics of Prejudice*, 88.

73. Ichioka, *The Issei*, 155; Robert Higgs, "Landless by Law: Japanese Immigrants in California Agriculture to 1941," *Journal of Economic History* 38 (March 1978), 220–221; Suzuki, "Important or Impotent?" 136–137; "Katsusaburo Kawahara," in *Beginnings*, 36.

74. "Santa Clara Valley a Big Canning Center," 3. On the growth of other canneries in Santa Clara County, see, for example: "Big Cannery Project for San Jose," *California Fruit News* 57 (May 4, 1918), 13; "Coast News in Brief," *California Fruit News* 59 (February 1, 1919), 3.

75. Sawyer, *History of Santa Clara County*, 135; Matthews, *Silicon Valley, Women, and the California Dream*, 34.

76. Santa Clara County Miscellaneous Records, Book 36, 520; Santa Clara County Crop and Chattel Mortgages, Book 43, 102, 364, 430, Book 46, 287.

77. Santa Clara County Crop and Chattel Mortgages, Book 45, 402, 416, 440.

78. Santa Clara County Crop and Chattel Mortgages, Book 51, 461; Santa Clara County Official Records, Book 100, 5.

79. Santa Clara County Official Records, Book 153, 569; *R. G. Fontana et al. v. Y. Oku*, 31901, Superior Court of the County of Santa Clara (1925).

80. Major Document 333, "Cooperative Movement among Japanese Farmers in California," 30–32. Survey of Race Relations (hereafter SRR), Box 31, Hoover Institution Archives, Stanford University; Gunki Kai, "Economic Status of the Japanese in California," (M.A. thesis, Stanford University, 1920), 61; Lukes and Okihiro, *Japanese Legacy*, 70.

81. California Pear Growers Association Minutes, Volume 1, January 20, 1919; Volume 2, January 17, 1922; Volume 2, January 20, 1925; Volume 3, May 22, 1922. Bancroft Library.

82. Major Document 333, "Cooperative Movement among Japanese Farmers in California," 37–38; "Strawberry Growers Organized with 75 percent," *Pacific Rural Press* 93 (March 31, 1917), 415; "America Must Lower Alien Bars, Insists Stanford Man," *San Francisco Chronicle*, July 5, 1927.

83. "Growers Form New Co-Operative Society," *Daily Palo Alto Times*, May 18, 1922.

84. Ichioka, *The Issei*, 153–156; Azuma, "Japanese Immigrant Farmers and California Alien Land Laws," 21–22.

85. Santa Clara County Leases, Book P, 52.

86. Ichioka, *The Issei*, 228–229. For more on this grassroots mobilization and the creation of a racialized Issei identity in the aftermath, see Azuma, *Between Two Empires*, 69–74.

87. Louis Marshall, "Appellee's Points," *Webb v. O'Brien*. 267 U.S. Supreme Court, October Term 1922; 1920 Census Population Schedule, Santa Clara County.

88. *Inouye et al. v. Youngers*, 20791, Superior Court of the County of Santa Clara (1913); Santa Clara County Deeds, Book 521, 370.

89. Marshall, "Appellee's Points"; Azuma, "Japanese Immigrant Farmers and California Alien Land Laws," 26.

90. "Brakes on Peaceful Penetration: Pacific Coast Alien Land Laws," *Harvard Law Review* 37 (1923–1924), 373–374.

91. Marshall, "Appellee's Points"; 1920 Census Population Schedule, Santa Clara County; *Zaibei Nihonjin Jinmei Jiten*, 218.

92. *Webb v. O'Brien*. 263 U.S. 313, 44 Supreme Court 112, November 19, 1923.

93. "Mr. Hayes Discusses the Japanese Menace," *San Jose Mercury Herald*, January 8, 1920.

94. Marshall, "Appellee's Points."

95. "Brief for Appellants," 47–48. *Webb v. O'Brien*. 267 U.S. Supreme Court, October Term 1922.

96. "The Anti-Alien Decision," *San Jose Mercury Herald*, November 21, 1923; "Decision Made by Supreme Court on Local Case Makes Land Law Wholly Effective," *San Jose Mercury Herald*, November 20, 1923.

Chapter Five

1. On the construction of "Asian" as a "peculiarly American racial category" by the Immigration Act of 1924, see Ngai, *Impossible Subjects*, 37–50.

2. Azuma, *Between Two Empires*, 111–113.

3. The origins of the Santa Clara Valley's popular nickname can be found in the poem "Valley of Heart's Delight" in Clara Louise Lawrence, *Poems Along the Way* (San Jose: Tucker Printing Company, 1927).

4. Ichioka, *The Issei*, 23. Ichioka notes that no precise figures can be obtained on the acreage Issei farmers cultivated through alternative methods in each community.

5. Azuma, *Between Two Empires*, 73; Major Document 327, "Public opinion of the Oriental in San Jose," 3–4. SRR, Box 31; Ruth Miriam Fowler, "Some Aspects of Public Opinion Concerning the Japanese in Santa Clara County" (M.A. thesis, Stanford University, 1924), 28.

6. Santa Clara County Leases, Book O, 205, 467, Book R, 341; *Zaibei Nihonjin Jinmei Jiten*, 242; 1910, 1920, 1930 Census Population Schedule, Santa Clara County; Santa Clara County Official Records, Book 488, 163; Oral History, Tom Ezaki, January 27, 1984, and February 2, 1984.

7. Santa Clara County Official Records, Book 282, 283; Santa Clara County Official Records, Book 498, 171–173; 1930 Census Population Schedule, Santa Clara County.

8. Santa Clara County Official Records, Book 764, 262, Book 1081, 52; Oral History, Tom Ezaki, January 27, 1984, and February 2, 1984. Ezaki said the family owned approximately 25 acres by World War II, though records show the brothers had purchased 28 acres from the Nelsons.

9. Santa Clara County Official Records, Book 416, 304–306; 1910 Census Population Schedule, Santa Clara County; 1920 Census Population Schedule, Santa Clara County; 1930 Census Population Schedule, Santa Clara County.

10. "Hatsu (Matsumoto) Kanemoto interview," in *REgenerations*, 132.

11. On the use of the "middleman arrangement" in Walnut Grove, California, see Azuma, "Japanese Immigrant Farmers and California Alien Land Laws," 28.

12. Audrie Girdner and Anne Loftis, *The Great Betrayal: The Evacuation of the Japanese-Americans during World War II* (London: The Macmillan Company, 1969), 64–65; "I. K. 'Ishi' Ishimatsu, 1899–2000," *San Jose Mercury News*, June 27, 2000; Ichioka, *The Issei*, 237.

13. Ichioka, *The Issei*, 238–239; Azuma, "Japanese Immigrant Farmers and California Alien Land Laws," 28.

14. *Zaibei Nihonjin Jinmei Jiten*, 218; Santa Clara County Official Records, Book 44, 122; Santa Clara County Official Records, Book 825, 302; Curt Fukuda, Correspondence, June 3, 2009.

15. Lukes and Okihiro, *Japanese Legacy*, 60, 115–116; 1920 Census Population Schedule, Santa Clara County; Oral History, Katsusaburo Kawahara, January 25, 1984; Oral History, Hisao Omori, November 2, 1983.

16. Oral History, Katsusaburo Kawahara, January 25, 1984, and February 8, 1984; Ichioka, *The Issei*, 239.

17. Azuma, *Between Two Empires*, 92–96.

18. J. Merle Davis, "We Said: 'Let's Find the Facts' and This is What They Answered—First and Last—on the Coast," *Survey Graphic* IX (May 1926), 202.

19. J. Merle Davis to Ray Lyman Wilbur, August 23, 1924. Ray Lyman Wilbur Personal Papers, Box 57, "Oriental Survey Exclusion Relations" Folder. Special Collections, Stanford University.

20. Gordon H. Chang, *Morning Glory, Evening Shadow: Yamato Ichihashi and His Internment Writings, 1942–1945* (Stanford, CA: Stanford University Press, 1997), 22, 59; Yamato Ichihashi, *Japanese in the United States: A Critical Study of the Problems of the Japanese Immigrants and Their Children* (Stanford, CA: Stanford University Press, 1932).

21. Letter to Mr. William L. Chandler, San Jose, October 9, 1924. SRR, Box 13, Folder 11. Davis is presumed to be the author of this unsigned letter, which appears with similar correspondence. Major publications by intellectuals who worked on the Survey include: Emory S. Bogardus, *Immigration and Race Attitudes* (New York: D. C. Heath and Company, 1928), Roderick McKenzie, *Oriental Exclusion: The Effect of American Immigration Laws,*

Regulations, and Judicial Decisions Upon the Chinese and Japanese on the American Pacific Coast (Chicago: The University of Chicago Press, 1928), Eliot Grinnell Mears, *Resident Orientals on the American Pacific Coast: Their Legal and Economic Status* (Chicago: The University of Chicago Press, 1928), William C. Smith, *Americans in Progress: A Study of Our Citizens of Oriental Ancestry* (Ann Arbor, MI: Edwards Bros., 1937). See also the May 1926 issue of *Survey Graphic* and the 1925–1926 issue of the *Journal of Applied Sociology*, which published Survey findings. Though he intended to, Park never wrote a book based on the Survey. On the Survey's demise, see Henry Yu, *Thinking Orientals: Migration, Contact, and Exoticism in Modern America* (New York: Oxford University Press, 2001), 73–74.

22. "Public Opinion of the Oriental in San Jose," Question 13. SRR, Box 17, Folder 8.

23. Major Document 327, "Public opinion of the Oriental in San Jose," 3–4; "Tentative Findings of the Survey of Race Relations: A Canadian-American Study of the Oriental on the Pacific Coast" (paper presented at the Findings Conference at Stanford University, Stanford, California, 1925), 15.

24. Fowler, "Some Aspects of Public Opinion," 178, 153; Eliot Grinnell Mears, "The Land, the Crops and the Oriental: A Study of Race Relations in Terms of the Map," *Survey Graphic* IX (May 1926), 149.

25. "Public Opinion of the Oriental in San Jose," Question 8; Major Document 327, "Public opinion of the Oriental in San Jose," 4. Chinese and Japanese in the Monterey fishing industry at this time faced similar accusations of being "destructive fishers" who depleted various seafood species with their aggressive practices. Chiang, *Shaping the Shoreline*, 15–19, 53–55.

26. "Public Opinion of the Oriental in San Jose," Questions 4 and 5. My tabulations from the surveys differ slightly from Fowler's, who correlated different questions and concluded that of the 41 employers, "only a little over half in both groups" found the Japanese to be good workmen. Fowler also based her results on an unpublished monograph written by Ida Case entitled "Public Opinion of the Oriental in San Jose," as was Major Document 327 and the questionnaire itself, both already cited. This monograph has not been located in Stanford University Archives. Fowler, "Some Aspects of Public Opinion," 211, 214.

27. Major Document 132, "Interview on Asiatic labor with Neumann, manager of Lyndon Hotel, Los Gatos, California," April 5, 1924, SRR, Box 26.

28. Major Document 327, "Public opinion of the Oriental in San Jose," 2; "Public Opinion of the Oriental in San Jose," Question 14. Census takers counted 839 Chinese in Santa Clara County in 1920, and 761 in 1930.

29. "Public Opinion of the Oriental in San Jose," Question 5, SRR; Fowler, "Some Aspects of Public Opinion," 155, 177.

30. Ibid., 155, 177–178. For more on the history of contract ideology and its importance to American identity, see Amy Dru Stanley, *From Bondage to Contract: Wage Labor, Marriage, and the Market in the Age of Slave Emancipation* (Cambridge: Cambridge University Press, 1998). On labor contract practices in rice growing in Japan during the interwar years, see John F. Embree, *Suye Mura: A Japanese Village* (Chicago: The University of Chicago Press, 1939), 132–138.

31. Fowler, "Some Aspects of Public Opinion," 226–227.

32. Ibid., 171.

33. Ibid., 48; *San Jose Mercury Herald*, March 15, 1912. In 1912 Misa Seki married G. S. Okamoto, a Japanese merchant who owned a large store on South Second Street in San Jose.

34. "Public Opinion of the Oriental in San Jose," Question 3.

35. Fowler, "Some Aspects of Public Opinion," 131, 134–135, 153–156. On medical discourse in Los Angeles County that painted the living conditions of rural Japanese as unsanitary, see Molina, *Fit To Be Citizens?*, 58–59.

36. Fowler, "Some Aspects of Public Opinion," 137, 156; Charles N. Reynolds, "Oriental-White Race Relations in Santa Clara County, California" (Ph.D. dissertation, Stanford University, 1927), 382.

37. On the solidification of hierarchies based on race and nationality in the 1924 Immigration Act, see Ngai, *Impossible Subjects*, 21–55.

38. "A Far Reaching Law," *Daily Palo Alto Times*, May 27, 1924; "Public Opinion of the Oriental in San Jose," Question 3. On turn-of-the-century views of "new immigrants" from southern and eastern Europe, see Matthew Frye Jacobson, *Barbarian Virtues: The United States Encounters Foreign Peoples at Home and Abroad, 1876–1917* (New York: Hill and Wang, 2000).

39. Laura E. Gomez, *Manifest Destinies: The Making of the Mexican American Race* (New York: New York University Press, 2008). On how public health officials in Los Angeles developed a slightly different hierarchy of racialization in the 1910s, see Molina, *Fit To Be Citizens?*, 46–74.

40. Pitti, *The Devil in Silicon Valley*, 86, 89–91.

41. "Production of Orientals Tremendous," *San Jose Evening News*, January 29, 1920.

42. Major Document 327, "Public opinion of the Oriental in San Jose," 3.

43. Ngai, *Impossible Subjects*, 50–55, 64–71; Kelly Lytle Hernández, *Migra! A History of the U.S. Border Patrol* (Berkeley: University of California Press, 2010), 88–93.

44. Major Document 328, "Statement regarding schools in the vicinity of San Jose in the midst of a large foreign population," by William C. Allen, May 9, 1925, 4. SRR, Box 31.

45. Major Document 327, "Public opinion of the Oriental in San Jose," 3; Pitti, *The Devil in Silicon Valley*, 87–88.

46. "Tentative Findings of the Survey of Race Relations," 12; "Dr. Park's Proposal to the California Development Association," June 13, 1924. SRR, Box 16, Folder 27.

47. J. Merle Davis, "The Orientals," in *Immigrant Backgrounds*, ed. Henry Pratt Fairchild (New York: John Wiley and Sons, Inc., 1927), 185; "Dr. Park's Proposal to the California Development Association," June 13, 1924. SRR, Box 16, Folder 27.

48. On how white sharecroppers in Texas in the 1920s alluded to their experience with blacks when they spoke of Mexicans as a "second color menace," see Foley, *The White Scourge*, 62–63.

49. Major Document 327, "Public opinion of the Oriental in San Jose," 3.

50. "Tentative Findings of the Survey of Race Relations," 12.

51. "Dr. Park's Proposal to the California Development Association"; "Production of Orientals Tremendous"; Molina, *Fit To Be Citizens?*, 61–115.

52. Nayan Shah, *Contagious Divides: Epidemics and Race in San Francisco's Chinatown* (Berkeley: University of California Press, 2001), 17–44; "Tentative Findings of the Survey of Race Relations," 12; Major Document 328, "Statement regarding schools in the vicinity of San Jose," 4; Molina, *Fit To Be Citizens?*, 128–129.

53. On the longstanding paradoxical perception of Asians as a racial "problem" and a racial "solution" in America, see Yu, *Thinking Orientals*, 7.

54. "Hatsu (Matsumoto) Kanemoto interview," in *REgenerations*, 139; Fowler, "Some Aspects of Public Opinion," 34. On teachers regarded Japanese American students in a positive light, see Thomas James, *Exile Within: The Schooling of Japanese Americans, 1942–1945* (Cambridge, MA: Harvard University Press, 1987), 13–14.

55. Major Document 327, "Public opinion of the Oriental in San Jose," 3–5; Fowler, "Some Aspects of Public Opinion," 156.

56. "Public Opinion of the Oriental in San Jose," Question 6.

57. Major Document 328, "Statement regarding schools in the vicinity of San Jose," 1. Allen noted on this report for the Survey of Race Relations that his observations were "Not for publication unless names of towns and schools are omitted," underlined and in capital letters. Allen later published an article using his report from Santa Clara County almost verbatim, and including observations from other school visits in the California desert and Arizona. William C. Allen, "Americanization in Some of Our Public Schools," *School and Society* 22 (October 1925), 422–425.

58. It is unclear how the categories of "Spanish and Mexican" and "Mexican" were differentiated here. It is possible that the former indicated children of Californio descent, while the latter referred to those who had emigrated more recently from Mexico.

59. Major Document 328, "Statement regarding schools in the vicinity of San Jose," 1–2.

60. Alvin Ray Graves, *The Portuguese Californians: Immigrants in Agriculture* (San Jose: Portuguese Heritage Publications of California, Inc., 2004), 34–36, 62. Santa Clara County recorded a population of 8,192 Portuguese in 1930, with 2,891 foreign-born and a sizable native-born second generation of 5,301.

61. Major Document 328, "Statement regarding schools in the vicinity of San Jose," 3–4.

62. Guglielmo, *White on Arrival*, 80–83.

63. Hans Christian Palmer, "Italian Immigration and the Development of California Agriculture" (Ph.D. dissertation, University of California, Berkeley, 1965), 122.

64. Ruth Thayer Wilson, "Delinquency Areas in San Jose" (M.A. thesis, Stanford University, 1934), 19–20.

65. Davis, "The Orientals," 185. Davis resided in Santa Clara County during 1923–24, primarily in Saratoga at the home of his minister friend Roscoe D. Douglass. Davis also worked closely with Stanford graduate students on the Survey of Race Relations.

66. Guglielmo, *White on Arrival*, 85; Major Document 328, "Statement regarding schools in the vicinity of San Jose," 3–4.

67. "San Jose Public Schools: Annual Report of the Board of Education and Superintendent." (San Jose: Board of Education, c. 1921), 142.

68. Wilson, "Delinquency Areas in San Jose." 26.

69. Major Document 327, "Public opinion of the Oriental in San Jose," 5.

70. Fowler, "Some Aspects of Public Opinion," 35; Reynolds, "Oriental-White Race Relations in Santa Clara County," 267.

71. Davis, "The Orientals," 185–187.

72. William C. Smith, "The Second Generation Oriental-American," *Journal of Applied Sociology* X (1925–1926), 160–161; Edward K. Strong, Jr., *The Second-Generation Japanese Problem* (Stanford, CA: Stanford University Press, 1934); Yu, *Thinking Orientals*, 108–109.

73. "Tentative Findings of the Survey of Race Relations," 20.

74. Reynolds, "Oriental-White Race Relations in Santa Clara County," 380.

75. Fowler, "Some Aspects of Public Opinion," 164–165, 137. The 1932 Stanford alumni directory reported that Fowler was living in San Jose and teaching at Santa Clara Union. *Stanford University Alumni Directory*, 275; William C. Smith, "Changing Personality Traits of Second Generation Orientals in America," *The American Journal of Sociology* 33 (1928), 926. On the varied friendship and school experiences of nonwhite children growing up in multiethnic neighborhoods of prewar Los Angeles, see Mark Wild, *Street Meeting: Multiethnic Neighborhoods in Early Twentieth-Century Los Angeles* (Berkeley: University of California Press, 2005), 94–120.

76. Major Document 327, "Public opinion of the Oriental in San Jose," 5. Jefferson became a segregated school when the trustees of the Agnew and Brawley refused to enroll Japanese pupils. In the 1920s, only two or three of the thirty students at Jefferson were reported to be "American."

77. Fowler, "Some Aspects of Public Opinion," 37.

78. Reynolds, "Oriental-White Race Relations in Santa Clara County," 267; Fowler, "Some Aspects of Public Opinion," 126–127.

79. Fowler, "Some Aspects of Public Opinion," 38–29, 126–127.

80. On popular culture images of "'Oriental' men preying on helpless 'white' women," see Henry Yu, "Mixing Bodies and Culture: The Meaning of America's Fascination with Sex between 'Orientals' and 'Whites'" in *Sex, Love, Race: Crossing Boundaries in North American History*, ed. Martha Hodes (New York: New York University Press, 1999), 449–450.

81. Fowler, "Some Aspects of Public Opinion," 207; Reynolds, "Oriental-White Race Relations in Santa Clara County," 269.

82. Fowler, "Some Aspects of Public Opinion," 235–201. On the experiences of Asian mixed-race children in prewar California, see Allison Varzally, *Making a Non-White America: Californians Coloring Outside Ethnic Lines, 1925–1955* (Berkeley: University of California Press, 2008), 110–117.

83. Yu, "Mixing Bodies and Culture," 450–454. Yu notes that sociologists did carefully use the "burning" interest in intermarriage to "provoke interest and generate funding for the survey." Davis made hundreds of copies of a document on "interracial marriage" by Park to solicit donations, noting that in Seattle, "practically everyone is crazy to get a copy."

84. "America Must Lower Alien Bars, Insists Stanford Man," *San Francisco Chronicle*, July 5, 1927. On social scientists' predictions that "kindlier feelings" towards Asians would continue to increase with the passage of toughened alien land laws and the 1924 Immigration Act, see Yu, *Thinking Orientals*, 73–74.

Chapter Six

1. "Night Riders Force Flight of Workers; Farm Dynamited in Race War," *San Francisco Chronicle*, October 5, 1933; "Dynamite Wrecks House," *San Jose Evening News*, October 4, 1933; "Dynamite Found by Filipino Pea Picker in Oven," *San Jose Mercury Herald*, October 4, 1933.

2. See, for example, "Japanese To Give Christmas Program," *Daily Palo Alto Times*, December 23, 1933; "Novel Japanese Entertainment Offered Tonight," *San Jose Mercury Herald*, April 12, 1934; "Tokio Club Upset by Locals," *San Jose News*, May 28, 1935; "Japanese Christian Church Asks Help of Americans in Financing New Building," *Daily Palo Alto Times*, December 19, 1938.

3. Couchman, *The Sunsweet Story*, 89–90; Matthews, *Silicon Valley, Women, and the California Dream*, 49–50.

4. James N. Gregory, *American Exodus: The Dust Bowl Migration and Okie Culture in California* (New York: Oxford University Press, 1989), 23; Kevin Starr, *Endangered Dreams: The Great Depression in California* (New York: Oxford University Press, 1996), 67.

5. Gregory, *American Exodus*, 11.

6. Ngai, *Impossible Subjects*. 101–103; Bruno Lasker, *Filipino Immigration to Continental United States and to Hawaii* (Chicago: The University of Chicago Press, 1931), 347–348.

7. Linda España-Maram, *Creating Masculinity in Los Angeles's Little Manila: Working-Class Filipinos and Popular Culture, 1920s–1950s* (New York: Columbia University Press, 2006), 17–19. Of the Filipino residents of Santa Clara County in the 1930 census sample with "mother tongue" listed, Ilocano was by far the most common response (73), followed by Visayan, spoken in the Cebuano provinces (43). Census takers also recorded Spanish, Tagalog, and "Filipino dialect" as responses for "mother tongue" by Filipinos.

8. James Earl Wood interview notes, 23. Box 2, Folder 2:7, James Earl Wood Collection, Bancroft Library. Hereafter "Wood interview notes, page(s)."

9. State of California, Department of Industrial Relations, *Facts About Filipino Immigration Into California, Special Bulletin No. 3* (San Francisco: California State Printing Office, 1930), 11–12; U.S. Bureau of the Census, *Fifteenth Census of the United States: 1930, Volume III, Part 1* (Washington, DC: Government Printing Office, 1932), 233, 253. The 1930 census no longer included the categories "Indian," "Chinese," and "Japanese" in its enumeration of "color" by county. Instead, it used only the categories "native white," "foreign-born white," "Negro," and "other races," and thus could not be relied on to obtain population figures for Filipinos in Santa Clara County.

10. County population estimates from chart in Wood's papers, Box 1, Folder 17. James Earl Wood Collection, Bancroft Library. According to Wood's research, Los Angeles and San

Francisco Counties had the highest Filipino populations in 1930, at 4,591 and 4,576, respectively.

11. Calculations based on 1930 Census Population Schedule, Santa Clara County from a sample of 780 Filipino residents, 849 Japanese residents, and 110 Chinese residents.

12. "31,000 Island Natives Here," *San Francisco Examiner*, April 10, 1930.

13. Wood interview notes, 10–11.

14. Wood interview notes, 7–9; 1930 Census Population Schedule, Santa Clara County. Of Japanese men over eighteen years of age, 5.7 percent worked as servants in private households and 4.7 percent in the service industry.

15. Emory S. Bogardus, "American Attitudes Towards Filipinos," *Sociology and Social Research* 14, (September–October 1929), 3.

16. Fred Cordova, *Filipinos: Forgotten Asian Americans, A Pictorial Essay, 1763-circa 1963* (Dubuque, IA: Kendall/Hunt Publishing Company, 1983), 123–130; España-Maram, *Creating Masculinity in Los Angeles's Little Manila*, 23–24.

17. Oral history, Mariano Catolico, typed and handwritten transcript. Courtesy of Patricia Catolico.

18. Wood interview notes, 7–9; Bogardus, "American Attitudes Towards Filipinos," 3.

19. 1930 Census Population Schedule, Santa Clara County. I included in this figure only individuals whose occupation was listed as "farm laborer" or as a laborer in a particular agricultural industry. In addition, another approximately 10 percent of Filipinos were enumerated as "laborers" with no industry specified in the census. If a portion of these individuals were also farm laborers, the percentage of Filipinos who were agricultural workers in the county was probably substantially higher than 56.

20. Wood interview notes, 3–4, 6, 13.

21. *The People of the State of California v. C. Cabaltero* et al., 26, 113½, Superior Court of the County of Santa Clara (1937). Reporter's Transcript, 92.

22. Wood interview notes, 10–11; John Pusateri, S-261 Class III B—Ethnography, "Mexicans in San Jose," April 19, 1936 in Mrs. Fremont Older, "When Santa Clara County Was Young" (binder), Cupertino Library, Cupertino, California; Gilbert González, *Labor and Community: Mexican Citrus Workers in a Southern California Colony*. Urbana: University of Illinois Press, 1994), 36–37.

23. Oral History, Katsusaburo Kawahara, February 8, 1984.

24. Oral History, Harry Araki, March 13, 1984.

25. Wood interview notes, 4, 21.

26. Wood interview notes, 4; William F. James and George H. McMurry, *History of San Jose, California: Narrative and Biographical* (San Jose: A. H. Cawston, 1933), 193–194; "Share It with Barrett: Max Watson's Pet Tree," *San Jose Mercury News*, February 16, 1958.

27. 1930 Census Population Schedule, Santa Clara County; "Thomas Flores," Hawaii County Draft Board 2, July 31, 1917, *World War I Selective Service System Draft Registration Cards, 1917–1918* (National Archives and Records Administration Microfilm Publication M1509, roll HI3), card 1722. Records of the Selective Service System, Record Group 163; *SS President Lincoln Passenger Manifest, April 21, 1926, Passenger Lists of Vessels Arriving at San Francisco, 1893–1953* (National Archives Microfilm Publication M1410, roll 296), 114. Records of the Immigration and Naturalization Service, Record Group 85; Ngai, *Impossible Subjects*, 101–103; Wood interview notes, 19.

28. Wood interview notes, 5, 21; Manuel Buaken, *I Have Lived with the American People* (Caldwell, ID: Caxton Printers, 1948), 63.

29. Rufino Deogracias, "Filipino Agricultural Workers Must Fight Against the Contract System," *The Agricultural Worker* 1 (December 20, 1933), 6. In June 1932, a dispute over wages ended in murder near Salinas when Gregorio Powel shot his Filipino labor contractor S. Lorenzo. "Filipino Slain By Employee," *San Francisco Examiner*, June 11, 1932. Two Filipino contractors were slain by employees at the ranch of Allen Hoover, son of

former president Herbert Hoover, in May 1936. "Hoover Farm Killing," *San Francisco Examiner*, May 27, 1936.

30. "Who is Filipino Labor Chamber," *The Agricultural Worker* (February 20, 1934); Carey McWilliams, "Exit the Filipino," *The Nation* 141 (September 4, 1935), 265.

31. Wood interview notes, 24; España-Maram, *Creating Masculinity in Los Angeles's Little Manila*, 45–47.

32. Azuma, *Between Two Empires*, 189–195. See also Arleen De Vera, "The Tapia-Saiki Incident: Interethnic Conflict and Filipino Responses to the Anti-Filipino Exclusion Movement" in *Over the Edge: Remapping the American West*, ed. Valerie J. Matsumoto and Blake Allmendinger (Berkeley: University of California Press, 1999), 201–214.

33. Wood interview notes, 14–15, 24; Cinco quote from untitled newspaper clipping, c. February 12, 1930, Box 2, Folder 4, James Earl Wood Collection, Bancroft Library.

34. Ngai, *Impossible Subjects*, 110–116; España-Maram, *Creating Masculinity in Los Angeles's Little Manila*, 111–118; Rick Baldoz, *The Third Asiatic Invasion: Empire and Migration in Filipino America, 1898–1946* (New York: New York University Press, 2011), 128–135; Rhacel Salazar Parrenas, "'White Trash' Meets the 'Little Brown Monkeys': The Taxi Dance Hall as a Site of Interracial and Gender Alliances between White Working Class Women and Filipino Immigrant Men in the 1920s and 30s," *Amerasia Journal* 24, no. 2 (1998), 115–133.

35. Ngai, *Impossible Subjects*, 113–114; Baldoz, *The Third Asiatic Invasion*, 138–143; Howard A. DeWitt, "The Watsonville Anti-Filipino Riot of 1930: A Case Study of the Great Depression and Ethnic Conflict in California," *Southern California Quarterly* 61 (September 1979), 291–302.

36. "Pajaro Filipinos Flogged, Beaten in New Rioting," *San Jose Mercury Herald*, January 23, 1930; "Veterans Patrol Pajaro Valley to Quell Riots," *San Jose Mercury Herald*, January 24, 1930; "Police Guarding Colony in Gilroy," *San Jose Mercury Herald*, January 24, 1930.

37. "White Man Is Stabbed During Filipino Race Rioting Here," *San Jose Mercury Herald*, January 24, 1930; "Periled Firemen Rescue Two Overcome in $250,000 SJ Hotel, Hardware Store Blaze," *San Jose Mercury Herald*, January 26, 1930; "Holmes Plan to Replace Gutted Building at Once," *San Jose Mercury Herald*, January 27, 1930.

38. "The Filipino Quarrel," *San Jose Evening News*, January 24, 1930; "Local Filipinos at Meeting Pledge to Avoid Discord," *San Jose Mercury Herald*, January 25, 1930; "Editorial Analysis," *San Jose Mercury Herald*, January 25, 1930.

39. "Editorial Analysis"; "Officials Held to Blame by Filipinos For Pajaro Riots," *San Jose Mercury Herald*, January 25, 1930; "Gilroy Bans 50 Whites, Filipinos," *San Jose Mercury Herald*, January 27, 1930.

40. Wood interview notes, 1.

41. Wood interview notes, 7.

42. "Local Filipinos at Meeting Pledge to Avoid Discord"; Wood interview notes, 24; 1930 Census Population Schedule, Santa Clara County.

43. "Police Continue to Guard Against Possible Renewal of Race Rioting," *San Jose Mercury Herald*, January 28, 1930.

44. Howard A. DeWitt, *Violence in the Fields: California Filipino Farm Labor Unionization During the Great Depression* (Saratoga, CA: Century Twenty One Publishing Company, 1980). 44–45.

45. Wood interview notes, 1–2; Shah, *Stranger Intimacy*, 31–35, 74–79.

46. Wood interview notes, 7–8.

47. "The Frances Trimillos Interview," *Lost Generation: Filipino Journal* 1 (1991), 48.

48. Wood interview notes, 8–9. On other instances of consensual relationships between Filipino men and white women turned into sensational public discourse, see Baldoz, *The Third Asiatic Invasion*, 124–128.

49. Pascoe, *What Comes Naturally*, 92–93, 158–159.

50. DeWitt, "The Watsonville Anti-Filipino Riot of 1930," 293–298; Ngai, *Impossible Subjects*, 106–109; Baldoz, *The Third Asiatic Invasion*, 148–152.

51. "Shot Fired at Filipinos in Yerba Race Feud," *San Francisco Examiner*, July 20, 1930; "Filipino Farm Laborers Flee as Outbreaks Occur," *Oakland Tribune*, July 21, 1930; "Filipinos Quit Trouble Area," *San Francisco Examiner*, July 24, 1930.

52. Lasker, *Filipino Immigration*, 48.

53. "Valley Filipino Labor Dropped Under Threats," *San Jose Mercury Herald*, August 14, 1930. Watson's note and another note addressed to the Sunnyvale Chief of Police found in Wood's files, Box 2, Folder 2:18. James Earl Wood Collection, Bancroft Library.

54. Santa Clara County Coroner's Official Register, August 13, 1930.

55. "Filipino Dies in Fire; Probe Bares Threats to Employers," *San Jose Mercury Herald*, August 13, 1930; "Missing Filipino Held Fire Victim," *San Jose Mercury Herald*, August 14, 1930; "Filipinos Are Discharged As Threat Result," *San Jose Evening News*, August 14, 1930.

56. "Valley Filipino Labor Dropped Under Threats," *San Jose Mercury Herald*, August 14, 1930; Wood interview notes, 9, 18, 21.

57. Ngai, *Impossible Subjects*, 107–109; Dorothy B. Fujita-Rony, *American Workers, Colonial Power: Philippine Seattle and the Transpacific West: 1919–1941* (Berkeley: University of California Press, 2003), 172; DeWitt, *Violence in the Fields*, 78.

58. Weber, *Dark Sweat, White Gold*, 13, 124–126; Gregory, *American Exodus*, 160–163. See also Walter J. Stein, *California and the Dust Bowl Migration* (Westport, CT: Greenwood Press, 1973).

59. Similarly, Neil Foley observes that the Southern Tenant Farmers' Union did not make inroads in central Texas, where most share tenants were white and viewed themselves as superior to the largely black and Mexican population of sharecroppers and wage laborers. Foley, *The White Scourge*, 185–194.

60. Matthews, *Silicon Valley, Women, and the California Dream*, 54–55; Pitti, *The Devil in Silicon Valley*, 111–113.

61. On the CAWIU cotton strike, see Weber, *Dark Sweat, White Gold*, 79–111, and Cletus E. Daniel, *Bitter Harvest: A History of California Farmworkers, 1870–1941* (Ithaca, NY: Cornell University Press, 1981), 167–221.

62. "Eight Jailed In Drive on Pea Field Terrorists," *San Jose Mercury Herald*, April 18, 1933; Daniel, *Bitter Harvest*, 143–145; Matthews, *Silicon Valley, Women, and the California Dream*, 59.

63. Matthews, *Silicon Valley, Women, and the California Dream*, 59; "27 Agitators in Cherry District Jailed, Militia Threat Made to Check Cherry Strike," *San Jose Mercury Herald*, June 18, 1933; Irving J. Woodin, "Summary of the 1932 California Deciduous Movement," *The Blue Anchor* 9 (December 1932), 3.

64. Daniel, *Bitter Harvest*, 150–151; Minutes of the Cannery and Agricultural Worker's Industrial Union, San Jose, August 5, 1933. Federal Writers' Project. Box 34, Folder P-97. Bancroft Library.

65. Minutes of the Cannery and Agricultural Worker's Industrial Union, San Jose, August 5, 1933. Decker may have been referring to the Filipino Labor Supply Association, essentially an employers' organization that did not represent the interests of ethnic labor. DeWitt, *Violence in the Fields*, 84–85.

66. Patrick H. Mooney and Theo J. Majka, *Farmers' and Farm Workers' Movements: Social Protest in American Agriculture* (New York: Twayne Publishers, 1995), 130; Starr, *Endangered Dreams*, 82.

67. "Pictorial Review," *The Agricultural Worker* 1 (February 20, 1934); Minutes of the Cannery and Agricultural Worker's Industrial Union, San Jose, August 5, 1933.

68. "Injunctions Bar Pear Strikers' Picketing Here," *San Jose Mercury Herald*, August 17, 1933.

69. "Pear Growers Raising Wages, Refuse to Deal with Strikers," *San Jose Mercury Herald*, August 18, 1933. On growers' perspectives on the 1933 pear season, see Dr. S. W. Shear, "The California Bartlett Pear Situation," *The Blue Anchor* 10 (February 1933), 15.

70. Matthews, *Silicon Valley, Women, and the California Dream*, 59–60; Daniel, *Bitter Harvest*, 155–156; Anne Loftis, *Witnesses to the Struggle: Imaging the 1930s California Labor Movement* (Reno: University of Nevada Press, 1998), 17.

71. Deogracias, "Filipino Agricultural Workers Must Fight Against the Contract System," 6; "Mexican Pickers Arriving Here To Harvest Pea Crop," *San Jose Mercury Herald*, April 8, 1934.

72. Matthews, *Silicon Valley, Women, and the California Dream*, 61–62; Brian McGinty, "Shadows in St. James Park," *California Historical Society Quarterly* 57 (1978–1979), 290–307.

73. "Bosses Prepare to Lynch Union Leaders! Anti-Lynch Meet in Jan," *The Agricultural Worker* 1 (December 20, 1933).

74. "Filipino Jap Riot Feared," *San Francisco Examiner*, January 24, 1934; "Spinach Strike District Quiet," *San Francisco Examiner*, January 25, 1935; "First Asparagus Strike Starts," *San Francisco Examiner*, March 15, 1934; "Unionization of Filipinos in California Agriculture," Monographs Prepared for a Documentary History of Migratory Farm Labor in California (Oakland, CA: Federal Writers' Project, 1938), 12. Bancroft Library.

75. DeWitt, *Violence in the Fields*, 78–85; "Summary of Events Which Took Place in Salinas Strike Area," *Union Gazette*, October 26, 1934; Fujita-Rony, *American Workers, Colonial Power*, 108; Howard DeWitt, "The Filipino Labor Union: The Salinas Lettuce Strike of 1934," *Amerasia Journal* 5 (1978), 1–22.

76. "Spinach Pickers Get 5 c. Raise," *Farm Labor News*, April 16, 1937.

77. Minutes of the Cannery and Agricultural Worker's Industrial Union, San Jose, August 5, 1933; Azuma, *Between Two Empires*, 196.

78. "Chinese Meat Markets Menace Must be Met. Chinese Markets Multiplying at San Jose Makes It a Local Issue," *Union Gazette*, November 2, 1934; "How Non-Union Chinese Butcher Shops Ruin American Standards," *Union Gazette*, November 23, 1934.

79. "Oriental Menace Returning to California Unless We Wake Up," *Union Gazette*, December 14, 1934; "Chinese Markets Feel Effects of San Jose Battle," *Union Gazette*, January 25, 1935.

80. "One Chinese Market Closed At San Jose," *Union Gazette*, May 31, 1935; "Union Meat Market Opened at Location Vacated by Chinese," *Union Gazette*, June 28, 1935.

81. Charles C. Derby Diaries and Typescripts, 1911–1941. Bancroft Library. Entries for July 16, 1934, July 18, 1934. Hereafter abbreviated "Derby Diaries," date.

82. John Terry, "The Terror in San Jose," *The Nation* (August 8, 1934), 161; Pitti, *The Devil in Silicon Valley*, 113.

83. Kathryn Olmsted, "Quelling Dissent: The Sacramento Conspiracy Trial and the Birth of the New Right," *Boom: A Journal of California* 1 (Summer 2011), 59–74.

84. "Vigilantes Raid Filipino Camp, Woman Perishes," *San Jose Mercury Herald*, September 22, 1934.

85. "Summary of Events Which Took Place in Salinas Strike Area," *Union Gazette*, October 26, 1934; Pitti, *The Devil in Silicon Valley*, 113.

86. Ngai, *Impossible Subjects*, 119–120; Baldoz, *The Third Asiatic Invasion*, 188–193.

87. McWilliams, "Exit the Filipino," 265.

88. Pitti, *The Devil in Silicon Valley*, 115–120; Vicki Ruiz, *Cannery Women, Cannery Lives: Mexican Women, Unionization, and the California Food Processing Industry, 1930–1950* (Albuquerque: University of New Mexico Press, 1987), 74–77; Weber, *Dark Sweat, White Gold*, 164–199.

89. "Petition Seeks To Close Alviso Dance Resorts," *San Jose Mercury Herald*, June 30, 1935; "Girls Help Keep Boys At Work, Judge Says," *San Jose Mercury Herald*, July 9, 1935. On taxi dancing as a profitable occupation for women during the Depression, see España-Maram, *Creating Masculinity in Los Angeles's Little Manila*, 121–122.

90. *The People v. P. Bagasol*, 22 Cal. App. 2d 327 (1937).

91. "Filipino Holdup, Murder Goes To Jurors Today," *San Jose Mercury Herald* (April 2, 1937); "Filipino Robber Gang Guilty, Five Given Life Term," *San Jose Mercury Herald* (April 3, 1937). The defendants appealed the case to no avail. The Court of Appeal of California cited section 189 of the Penal Code, which held that all murders committed in the perpetration of another crime, including robbery, qualify as murder of the first degree, regardless of whether a given death was accidental or premeditated. *The People v. C. Cabaltero* et al., Crim. No. 1974, Court of Appeal of California, First Appellate District, Division One (1939).

92. *People v. C. Cabaltero* et al. Reporter's Transcript, 9–10, 12; 1930 Census Population Schedule, Santa Clara County. Jitsuo, Kimiyo, and Naomi Nishida appear twice in the 1930 census, likely because census takers caught them on different days at two separate locations, since they operated multiple farms. There was some confusion in the court transcripts about how the Avelinos were related, but it appeared that Fred and Marcella were cousins, and another man involved, Robert Avelino, was Marcella's brother.

93. *People v. C. Cabaltero* et al. Reporter's Transcript, 12, 145. On the "Back-to-the-Farm" movement launched by Issei in 1935 to persuade Nisei to remain in farming, see Azuma, *Between Two Empires*, 114–118.

94. *People v. C. Cabaltero* et al. Reporter's Transcript, 90–102.

95. War Relocation Authority, *Records About Japanese Americans Relocated During World War II* (College Park, MD: National Archives, 1988) (database); 1940 Census Population Schedule, Santa Clara County.

96. Derby Diaries, April 2, 1937, April 5, 1937, May 5, 1937. On the formation of the Associated Farmers of California, see Daniel, *Bitter Harvest*, 251–254.

97. See, for example, "Burglar, Auto Thief Sent to Prison," *San Jose Evening News*, August 28, 1936; "Editorial: Increase in Alcoholic Cases," *San Jose Mercury Herald*, August 31, 1936.

98. "Woman Injured By Fruit Crew," *San Jose Mercury Herald*, August 29, 1936; "Woman Hurt by Farm Raid Mob," *San Francisco Examiner*, August 28, 1936; Sawyer, *History of Santa Clara County*, 338, 596.

99. "Valley Prune Market Quiet," *San Jose Mercury Herald*, August 28, 1936; "Harvest Loans on Prune Crop Now Available," *San Jose Mercury Herald*, August 30, 1936.

100. Linda Gordon, *Dorothea Lange: A Life Beyond Limits* (New York: W. W. Norton, 2009), 225.

101. John Steinbeck, "The Harvest Gypsies: Beaten, Bewildered and Half-Starved, They Wander the Trails of the Fruit Season; What Can Be Done to Aid Them?" *San Francisco News* (October 5, 1936). The entire series was published between October 5 and 12, 1936, and also reprinted as a pamphlet by the Simon J. Lubin Society. John Steinbeck, *Their Blood Is Strong* (San Francisco: Simon J. Lubin Society of California, Inc., 1938).

102. Though Steinbeck picked the Salinas and Central Valleys as the settings for most of his fiction, his connection to the Santa Clara Valley was strong. Both his mother, Olive Hamilton, and his first wife, Carol Henning, were born in San Jose; he attended Stanford University sporadically from 1919 to 1925 and lived in Los Gatos from 1936 to 1940, a period that ranked "as the most professionally satisfying of his entire life" and saw the publication of best-sellers such as *Of Mice and Men*, *The Long Valley*, and *The Grapes of Wrath*. John Steinbeck, *Working Days: The Journals of* The Grapes of Wrath, *1938–1941*, ed. Robert DeMott (New York: Viking, 1989), xi.

103. "Here's a Challenge," *San Francisco News*, October 6, 1936.

104. Foley, *The White Scourge*, 201; Gordon, *Dorothea Lange*, 226.

105. "Labor Council Adopts a Program for Relief of Dust Bowl Refugees," *Union Gazette*, August 6, 1937.

106. "No Housing For Farm Workers; Must Shift for Themselves When Not Needed in Harvest," *Union Gazette*, August 20, 1937.

107. "Labor in Field and Orchard! A call to organize!," pamphlet (San Jose, CA: Central Labor Council, 1937). Federal Writers' Project. Box 33, Folder P-15 B. Bancroft Library; "Farm Labor Issues Told at Session," *San Francisco Examiner*, January 13, 1937.

108. Memo for Mr. John C. Henderson, Chief, Migratory Labor Section from F. N. Mortenson, n.d. (c. 1939). Folder, San Jose Migratory Camp. RG 96. National Archives, San Bruno; Gordon, *Dorothea Lange*, 227.

109. Gordon, *Dorothea Lange*, 229; Letter to Harvey M. Coverley from F. N. Mortenson, December 3, 1941. Folder, San Jose Migratory Labor Camp RR-CF 39 201-01, RG 96. National Archives, San Bruno, California.

110. Petition, residents in vicinity of Moreland School, n.d. Folder, San Jose Migratory Labor Camp. RG 96. National Archives, San Bruno, California; 1920 Census Population Schedule, Santa Clara County; Santa Clara County Leases, Book P, 69, 528; Lukes and Okihiro, *Japanese Legacy*, 67, 115; Henry Kurasaki, Oral History, February 22, 1984.

111. Ralph M. Pearce, *From Asahi to Zebras: Japanese American Baseball in San Jose, California* (San Jose: Japanese American Museum of San Jose, 2005), 11–12, 32; "Tokio Club Upset by Locals"; 1930 Census Population Schedule, Santa Clara County; *Zaibei Nihonjin Jinmei Jiten*, 197. On the early history of baseball in rural California, see David Vaught, "'Our Players are Mostly Farmers': Baseball in Rural California, 1850–1890," in *Baseball in America and America in Baseball,* ed. Donald G. Kyle and Robert B. Fairbanks (College Station: Texas A&M University Press, 2008), 8–31.

Epilogue

1. Yu, *Chinatown San Jose, USA*, 110; "Theodore Chan, Obituary," *San Jose Mercury News*, April 10, 2003; "Toi Lonnie Young, Obituary," *San Jose Mercury News*, March 2, 2004; "Toi L. Young was a 'Rosie' in W. W. II," *San Jose Mercury News*, March 2, 2004; "James C. Y. Leung, Obituary," *San Jose Mercury News*, October 5, 1989.

2. Oral history, Mariano Catolico.

3. "Closed Encounters," *Cupertino Courier*, February 23, 2005.

4. "S.J. group weathers pains of W.W. II, marks 70th year," *San Jose Mercury News*, February 2, 1993.

5. Lukes and Okihiro, *Japanese Legacy*, 117; "Hatsu (Matsumoto) Kanemoto interview," in *REgenerations*, 147–149.

6. "S.J. group weathers pains of W.W. II, marks 70th year"; "Eiichi Edward Sakauye interview," in *REgenerations*, 403. Sakauye passed away in November 2005, at the age of 93. "Rich Legacy of Ex-Internee—Eiichi Edward Sakauye, 1912–2005," *San Jose Mercury News*, December 1, 2005.

7. "Evacuation Not An Easy 'Pill,'" *San Jose Mercury Herald*, March 26, 1942.

8. "Katsusaburo Kawahara," in *Beginnings*, 42; Letter, Hisajiro Inouye to Mrs. Weston, November 5, 1943. Ethel Bull Stamp Collection, History San José Research Library.

9. Oral History, Katsusaburo Kawahara, February 8, 1984; Frank J. Taylor, "Home Again," *Collier's* (February 15, 1947), 35.

10. "First Evacuees Leave Today," *San Jose Mercury Herald*, May 26, 1942.

11. Lukes and Okihiro, *Japanese Legacy*, 119; "Katsusaburo Kawahara," in *Beginnings*, 42.

12. Chang, *Morning Glory, Evening Shadow*, 101, 104. The Ichihashis were transferred from Santa Anita to Tule Lake, where Yamato Ichihashi was arrested and detained at Sharp Park (in present-day Pacifica, California). Investigated as a "suspect enemy alien" who might be a threat to domestic security, he was released after six weeks and returned to Tule Lake.

13. "Who We Are: Voices of Diversity," *San Jose Mercury News* (*West Magazine*), January 15, 1995, 20.

14. "Hironaka interview," in *REgenerations*, 92.

15. "Katsusaburo Kawahara," in *Beginnings*, 44. For more on the establishment of Heart Mountain, see Douglas W. Nelson, *Heart Mountain: The History of an American Concentration Camp* (Madison: The State Historical Society of Wisconsin, 1976).

16. Established on March 18, 1942, the WRA was a civilian agency in charge of running the permanent relocation centers. The army stationed armed guards on camp perimeters.

17. "Masuo Akizuki interview," in *Beginnings*, 18; "Harry Nishiura interview," in *Beginnings*, 78; "Sakauye interview," in *REgenerations*, 355.

18. "Sakauye interview," in *REgenerations*, 357–361; "Rich Legacy of Ex-Internee."

19. Record of *Heart Mountain Relocation Center vs. Yasutaro B. Oku*, March 28, 1945. Shigeichi Kawano Papers, Box 14, Folder 13. Department of Special Collections, Charles E. Young Research Library, UCLA.

20. "Harry Nishiura interview," in *Beginnings*, 78.

21. "The Loyal Opposition," *San Jose Mercury News* (*West Magazine*), January 31, 1993; Eric L. Muller, *Free to Die for Their Country: The Story of the Japanese American Draft Resisters in World War II* (Chicago: The University of Chicago Press, 2003).

22. Lukes and Okihiro, *Japanese Legacy*, 121–123; "Japanese Farmer Sakauye," videotaped interview, 1980. California History Center, De Anza College, Cupertino, California.

23. "Hironaka interview," in *REgenerations*, 103.

24. "County's Japanese-Americans Had Their Day of Infamy, Too," *San Jose Mercury News*, January 29, 1967. Mineta served as a congressional representative from the Santa Clara Valley from 1975 to 1995, prior to becoming secretary of commerce under President Bill Clinton and then secretary of transportation from 2001 to 2006.

25. Taylor, "Home Again," 36.

26. Lukes and Okihiro, *Japanese Legacy*, 124. On the "easy transition from antagonistic to congenial images" of the Japanese after the war, see John W. Dower, *War Without Mercy: Race and Power in the Pacific War* (New York: Pantheon Books, 1986), 301–311, and Naoko Shibusawa, *America's Geisha Ally: Reimagining the Japanese Enemy* (Cambridge, MA: Harvard University Press, 2006).

27. War Relocation Authority, *People in Motion* (Washington, DC: Government Printing Office, 1947), 61.

28. Lukes and Okihiro, *Japanese Legacy*, 125.

29. "Kanemoto interview," in *REgenerations*, 156; "Bunrei Utsunomiya interview," in *Beginnings*, 98.

30. WRA, *People in Motion*, 66; Oral History, Henry Kurasaki, February 22, 1984, and February 23, 1984.

31. Mel Inouye and Curt Fukuda, Correspondence, August 27, 2011.

32. WRA, *People in Motion*, 66; "War internees had a lawyer on their side," *San Jose Mercury News*, August 4, 1987.

33. "West Coast Incidents Involving Persons of Japanese Ancestry." Pacific Coast Committee on American Principles and Fair Play Records. Carton 1, Folder 56. Bancroft Library.

34. "Sakauye interview," in *REgenerations*, 390–391.

35. "Midori Kimura interview," in *Beginnings*, 72; "Remembering the Lost Years," *San Jose Mercury News* (*West Magazine*), February 22, 1987, 24.

36. "San Joseans among plaintiffs," *San Jose Mercury News*, November 9, 1986; "Relieving the wrongs of wartime," *San Jose Mercury News*, October 13, 1990. Kimura died in San Jose in 1996. "Midori Kimura, 98, Survivor of W. W. II Internment Camp," *San Jose Mercury News*, May 31, 1996. On the redress and reparations movement, see Alice Yang Murray, *Historical Memories of the Japanese American Internment and the Struggle for Redress* (Stanford, CA: Stanford University Press, 2008); Robert Sadamu Shimabukuro, *Born in Seattle: The Campaign for Japanese American Redress* (Seattle: University of Washington Press, 2001); Yasuko I. Takezawa, *Breaking the Silence: Redress and Japanese American Ethnicity* (Ithaca, NY: Cornell University Press, 1995).

37. WRA, *People in Motion*, 49, 53, 66.

38. "Isamu Kawamura interview," in *REgenerations*, 48. On the legal battles leading up to the repeal, see Mark Brilliant, *The Color of America Has Changed: How Racial Diversity Shaped Civil Rights Reform in California: 1941–1978* (New York: Oxford University Press, 2010), 28–57; Rawitsch, *The House on Lemon Street*, 134–136.

39. Matthews, *Silicon Valley, Women, and the California Dream*, 81.

40. Ibid., 117. See also Rebecca S. Lowen, *Creating the Cold War University: The Transformation of Stanford* (Berkeley: University of California Press, 1997); Margaret Pugh O'Mara, *Cities of Knowledge: Cold War Science and the Search for the Next Silicon Valley* (Princeton, NJ: Princeton University Press, 2004).

41. Paul F. Griffin and Ronald L. Chatham, "Urban Impact on Agriculture in Santa Clara County, California," *Annals of the Association of American Geographers* 48 (September 1958), 203.

42. Jacobson, *Passing Farms, Enduring Values*, 231–236; "From Fertile Fields, a High-Tech Harvest," *San Jose Mercury News*, June 20, 2001.

43. Oral history, Mariano Catolico; Interview, Patricia Catolico, September 4, 2012, Mountain View, California.

44. Jacobson, *Passing Farms, Enduring Values*, 230.

45. Ibid., 231.

46. "Japanese Farmer Sakauye," videotaped interview, 1980; "From Fertile Fields, a High-Tech Harvest"; U.S. Census Bureau, "Small Area Income and Poverty Estimates": http://www.census.gov/did/www/saipe/index.html.

47. "Kanemoto interview," in *REgenerations*, 152, 165.

48. "From Fertile Fields, a High-Tech Harvest."

49. Matthews, *Silicon Valley, Women, and the California Dream*, 147; "Majority of Santa Clara County families speak foreign language at home," *San Jose Mercury News*, September 22, 2008; "Data shows nearly even racial mix in Silicon Valley," *San Jose Mercury News*, August 7, 2008.

50. Santa Clara County's Asian population grew by 18,000 from 2006 to 2007, representing the largest gain by a U.S. county for the second consecutive year. "Data shows nearly even racial mix in Silicon Valley."

BIBLIOGRAPHY

Manuscript and Archival Collections

California Joint Immigration Committee Collection, 1924–1936. Bancroft Library, University of California, Berkeley.

California Pear Growers' Association. Minutes, 1916–1925. Bancroft Library, University of California, Berkeley.

Charles C. Derby Diaries. Bancroft Library, University of California, Berkeley.

Certificates of Residence. "Chinese Files," MS 1989–142. History San José.

Coroners' Inquests, Santa Clara County. History San José.

William A. Z. Edwards Diaries and Account Books. Bancroft Library, University of California, Berkeley.

Federal Writers' Project on Migratory Labor, District no. 8, 1936–1939. Bancroft Library, University of California, Berkeley.

Samuel S. Haines Papers. California State Library. Sacramento.

Ralph W. Hollenberg Papers, Materials Relating to the Farm Security Administration, Region IX, 1924–1949. Bancroft Library, University of California, Berkeley.

Yamato Ichihashi Papers. Special Collections and University Archives, Stanford University.

Jessie Juliet Knox Scrapbooks. History San José.

Ng Shing Gung Temple Reconstruction Records. History San José.

Oral History Collection. Japanese American Museum of San Jose Archives, San Jose, California.

Palo Alto Stock Farm Papers. Special Collections and University Archives, Stanford University.

John Francis Pyle Diaries and Memorandum Books. Bancroft Library, University of California, Berkeley.

W. R. Ralston Papers. Bancroft Library, University of California, Berkeley.

Records of the U.S. Immigration and Naturalization Service. Japanese Arrival Files. Record Group 85. National Archives, Pacific Region, San Bruno, California.

Records of the Farmers Home Administration. Record Group 96. National Archives, Pacific Region, San Bruno, California.

Fred Ross Papers. Special Collections and University Archives, Stanford University.

Santa Clara County Crop and Chattel Mortgages, Deeds, Leases, Miscellaneous Records, and Official Records. Santa Clara County Recorder's Office, San Jose.

Santa Clara County Superior Court Records. History San José and Santa Clara County Superior Court, San Jose, California.

Survey of Race Relations. Hoover Archives, Stanford University.

Ray Lyman Wilbur Papers. Special Collections and University Archives, Stanford University.

James Earl Wood Collection. Bancroft Library, University of California, Berkeley.

Newspapers and Periodicals

The Agricultural Worker
The Blue Anchor
California Fruit Grower
California Fruit News
Daily Palo Alto Times (1905–1943)
Los Gatos Mail-News and Saratoga Star
Palo Alto Times (1893–1905)
San Francisco Chronicle
San Francisco Examiner
San Jose Daily Mercury (1885–1899)
San Jose Evening News
San Jose Mercury (1899–1913, 1950–1983)
San Jose Mercury Herald(1913–1950)
San Jose Mercury News (1983–present)
San Jose Morning Times
Sunset
Survey Graphic
Union Gazette

Published Government Documents

Bureau of the Census. "Bulletin 127, Chinese and Japanese in the United States, 1910." Washington, DC: Government Printing Office, 1914.

———. *United States Census of Agriculture, 1925.* Part III, *The Western States.* Washington, DC: Government Printing Office, 1927.

———. *United States Census of Agriculture, 1935.* Washington, DC: Government Printing Office, 1936.

———. *United States Census of Agriculture, 1945.* Washington, DC: Government Printing Office, 1946.

California State Board of Control. *California and the Oriental: Japanese, Chinese, and Hindus.* Sacramento: California State Printing Office, 1922.

California State Department of Industrial Relations. *Facts about Filipino Immigration into California.* San Francisco: Department of Industrial Relations, 1930.

"Statement of John Summerfield Enos, Commissioner of the Bureau of Labor Statistics of the State of California to the California State Horticultural Society." Sacramento: Superintendent of State Printing, 1886.

U.S. Immigration Commission. *Immigrants in Industries. Part 25: Japanese and Other Immigrant Races in the Pacific Coast and Rocky Mountain States.* Washington, DC: Government Printing Office, 1911.

War Relocation Authority. *The Wartime Handling of Evacuee Property.* Washington, DC: Government Printing Office, 1946.

———. *People in Motion.* Washington, DC: Government Printing Office, 1947.

Selected Primary Sources

Advantages of the City of San Jose, California as a Manufacturing Center. Society for the Promotion of Manufactures, c. 1884.

Anthony, Donald. "Labor Conditions in the Canning Industry in the Santa Clara Valley of the State of California." Ph.D. dissertation, Stanford University, 1928.

Beach, Walter G. *Oriental Crime in California: A Study of Offenses Committed by Orientals in That State, 1900–1927*. New York: AMS Press, 1932.

Benham, George B. *The Asiatic Problem and American Opinions*. San Francisco: Asiatic Exclusion League, 1908.

Blossom Trolley Trip, Santa Clara County. n.d., 1910–1920.

Bogardus, Emory S. *Immigration and Race Attitudes*. New York: D. C. Heath and Company, 1928.

Broek, Jan Otto Marius. *The Santa Clara Valley: A Study in Landscape Changes*. Utrecht, Netherlands: N.V.A. Oosthoek's Uitgevers-MIJ, 1932.

Brooklodge Farm containing five hundred acres choice valley land. San Jose: Alfred C. Eaton, 1899.

Bunje, Emil T. H. *The Story of Japanese Farming in California. Produced on a U.S. Works Progress Administration Project*. Berkeley: University of California, 1937.

Byrn, John William. "A Junior High School in Action: A Survey of Roosevelt Junior High School of San Jose, California." M.A. thesis, Stanford University, 1932.

California's Richest Realm. Santa Clara Valley, some views of the San Martin Ranch subdivision. c. 1901.

Carroll, Mary Bowden. *Ten Years in Paradise: Leaves from a Society Reporter's Notebook*. San Jose: Popp & Hogan, 1903.

Consulate-General of Japan, ed. *Documental History of Law Cases Affecting Japanese in the United States*. Vol. II: *Japanese Land Cases*. San Francisco: The Consulate-General of Japan, 1925.

Davis, J. Merle. "The Orientals." In *Immigrant Backgrounds*, edited by Henry Pratt Fairchild. New York: John Wiley and Sons, Inc., 1927.

Elliot, Albert H., and Guy C. Calden, compilers, ed. *The Law Affecting Japanese Residing in the State of California*. San Francisco: Albert H. Elliot and Guy C. Calden, 1929.

Federal Writers' Project of the Works Progress Administration for the State of California. *The WPA Guide to California*. New York: Pantheon Books, 1939.

Foote, H. S. *Pen Pictures from the "Garden of the World" or Santa Clara County, California*. Chicago: Lewis Publishing Company, 1888.

Fowler, Ruth Miriam. "Some Aspects of Public Opinion Concerning the Japanese in Santa Clara County." M.A. thesis, Stanford University, 1934.

George, Henry. *Our Land and Land Policy: Speeches, Lectures, and Miscellaneous Writings by Henry George*. New York: Doubleday and McClure Company, 1902.

Guinn, J. M. *History of the State of California and Biographical Record of Coast Counties, California*. Chicago: The Chapman Publishing Company, 1904.

Gulick, Sidney L. *The American Japanese Problem: A Study of the Racial Relations of the East and the West*. New York: Charles Scribner's Sons, 1914.

Hall, Frederic. *The History of San Jose*. San Francisco: A. L. Bancroft and Co., 1871.

Harrison, E. S. *Central California, Santa Clara Valley. Its resources, advantages and prospects. Homes for a million*. San Jose: McNeil Bros., c. 1888.

Historical Atlas Map of Santa Clara County. San Francisco: Thompson and West, 1876.

History of the State of California and Biographical Record of Coast Counties, California. Chicago: The Chapman Publishing Company, 1904.

Ichihashi, Yamato. *Japanese Immigration: Its Status in California*. San Francisco: The Marshall Press, 1915.

———. *Japanese in the United States: A Critical Study of the Problems of the Japanese Immigrants and Their Children*. Stanford, CA: Stanford University Press, 1932.

Irvine, Leigh, ed. *A History of the New California, Its Resources and People*. New York: The Lewis Publishing Company, 1905.

Irvine, Leigh. *Santa Clara County, California (California Lands for Wealth, California Fruit for Health)*. San Jose: San Jose Chamber of Commerce, c. 1910.

Iyenaga, T., and Kenoske Sato. *Japan and the California Problem*. New York: G. P. Putnam's Sons, 1921.

James, William F., and George H. McMurry. *History of San Jose, California: Narrative and Biographical* (San Jose: A. H. Cawston, 1933).

Japanese Agricultural Association. *Japanese Farmers in California*. San Francisco: Japanese Agricultural Association, 1918.

Johnson, Herbert B. *Discrimination Against the Japanese in California: A Review of the Real Situation*. Berkeley: The Courier Publishing Company, 1907.

Kanzaki, Kiichi. *California and the Japanese*. San Francisco: Japanese Association of America, 1921.

Kawakami, K. K. *The Real Japanese Question*. New York: The Macmillan Company, 1921.

Kimberlin, Dorotha Electa Ball. "Children of the Unemployed in the Junior High School, San Jose, California." M.A. thesis, Stanford University, 1934.

Lange, Dorothea, and Paul Schuster Taylor. *An American Exodus: A Record of Human Erosion*. New York: Reynal and Hitchcock, 1939.

Lasker, Bruno. *Filipino Immigration to Continental United States and to Hawaii*. Chicago: The University of Chicago Press, 1931.

McKenzie, Roderick. *Oriental Exclusion: The Effect of American Immigration Laws, Regulations, and Judicial Decisions upon the Chinese and Japanese on the American Pacific Coast*. Chicago: The University of Chicago Press, 1928.

McWilliams, Carey. *Factories in the Field: The Story of Migratory Farm Labor in California*. Boston: Little, Brown and Company, 1939.

Mears, Eliot Grinnell. *Resident Orientals on the American Pacific Coast: Their Legal and Economic Status*. Chicago: The University of Chicago Press, 1928.

Meriwether, Lee. *The Tramp at Home*. New York: Harper & Brothers, 1889.

Millis, H. A. *The Japanese Problem in the United States: An Investigation for the Commission on Relations with Japan Appointed by the Federal Council of Churches of Christ in America*. New York: The Macmillan Company, 1915.

Misaki, Hisakichi. "The Effect of Language Handicap on Intelligence Tests of Japanese Children." M.A. thesis, Stanford University, 1927.

Naka, Kaizo. "Social and Economic Conditions Among Japanese Farmers in California." M.S. thesis, University of California, Berkeley, 1913.

Picturesque San Jose and Environments: an illustrated statement of the progress, prosperity and resources of Santa Clara County, California. San Jose: H. S. Foote and C. A. Woolfolk, 1893.

The Progressive City Beautiful: Santa Clara. Santa Clara: Santa Clara Chamber of Commerce, n.d.

Rein, J. J. *The Industries of Japan. Together with an Account of Its Agriculture, Forestry, Arts, and Commerce*. New York: A. G. Armstrong, 1889.

Reynolds, Charles N. "Oriental-White Race Relations in Santa Clara County, California." Ph.D. dissertation, Stanford University, 1927.

San Jose Chamber of Commerce. *Santa Clara County, California*. San Jose: San Jose Chamber of Commerce and Santa Clara County Board of Supervisors, c. 1936.

"San Jose Public Schools: Annual Report of the Board of Education and Superintendent." San Jose, 1908–1909.

"San Jose Public Schools: Annual Report of the Board of Education and Superintendent." San Jose, 1911–1912.

"San Jose Public Schools: Annual Report of the Board of Education and Superintendent." San Jose: Board of Education, c. 1921.

San José (San Hosay): Santa Clara County, California. San Jose: San Jose Chamber of Commerce, 1907.

Santa Clara County and Its Resources: A Souvenir of the San Jose Mercury. San Jose: San Jose Mercury Publishing Co., 1896.

Santa Clara County, California. San Jose: Board of Trade of San Jose, 1887.

Santa Clara, the city of homes. Santa Clara: Commercial League, n.d.

Sawyer, Eugene T. *History of Santa Clara County with Biographical Sketches*. Los Angeles: Historic Record Company, 1922.

Smith, William C. *Americans in Progress: A Study of Our Citizens of Oriental Ancestry*. Ann Arbor, MI: Edwards Bros., 1937.

Statistics Relative to Japanese Immigration and the Japanese in California. San Francisco: Japanese Association of America, 1920.

Steinbeck, John. *In Dubious Battle*. New York: Covici, Friede, Inc., 1936.

——. *The Long Valley*. New York: Viking Press, 1938.

——. *Their Blood Is Strong*. San Francisco: Simon J. Lubin Society of California, Inc., 1938.

——. *The Grapes of Wrath*. New York: Viking Press, 1939.

——. *The Harvest Gypsies: On the Road to the Grapes of Wrath*. Berkeley: Heyday Books, 1988.

——. *Working Days: The Journals of The Grapes of Wrath, 1938–1941*. Edited by Robert DeMott. New York: Viking, 1989.

——. *America and Americans and Selected Nonfiction*. Edited by Susan Shillinglaw and Jackson J. Benson. New York: Viking Press, 2002.

Stevens-Walter, Carrie. *In California's Garden: Santa Clara Valley*. San Jose: Board of Supervisors of Santa Clara County, 1897.

Strong, Edward K., Jr. *The Second-Generation Japanese Problem*. Stanford, CA: Stanford University Press, 1934.

"Survey of Race Relations: A Study of Orientals on the Pacific Coast, jointly undertaken by the Institute of Social and Religious Research and Five Pacific Coast Regional Committees." Southern California Regional Committee, c. 1925.

"Tentative Findings of the Survey of Race Relations: A Canadian-American Study of the Oriental on the Pacific Coast." Paper presented at the Findings Conference at Stanford University, Stanford, California, 1925.

Wickson, Edward J. *The California Fruits and How To Grow Them*. San Francisco: Dewey & Co., 1891.

Wilson, Ruth Thayer. "Delinquency Areas in San Jose." M.A. thesis, Stanford University, 1934.

Young, Kimball. *Mental Differences in Certain Immigrant Groups; Psychological Tests of South Europeans in Typical California Schools with Bearing on the Educational Policy and on the Problems of Racial Contacts in this Country*. Eugene: University of Oregon, 1922.

Selected Secondary Sources

Aarim-Heriot, Najia. *Chinese Immigrants, African Americans, and Racial Anxiety in the United States, 1848-82*. Urbana: University of Illinois Press, 2003.

Ahmad, Diana L. *The Opium Debate and Chinese Exclusion Laws in the Nineteenth-Century American West*. Reno: University of Nevada Press, 2007.

Almaguer, Tomas. *Racial Fault Lines: The Historical Origins of White Supremacy in California*. Berkeley: University of California Press, 1994.

Arbuckle, Clyde. *Clyde Arbuckle's History of San Jose*. San Jose: Smith and McKay, 1986.

Azuma, Eiichiro. "Japanese Immigrant Farmers and California Alien Land Laws: A Study of the Walnut Grove Japanese Community." *California History* 73 (1994): 14–29.

——. "Racial Struggle, Immigrant Nationalism, and Ethnic Identity: Japanese and Filipinos in the California Delta." *Pacific Historical Review* 67 (May 1998): 163–199.

——. "Interstitial Lives: Race, Community, and History among Japanese Immigrants Caught between Japan and the United States, 1885–1941." Ph.D. dissertation, UCLA, 2000.

——. *Between Two Empires: Race, History, and Transnationalism in Japanese America*. New York: Oxford University Press, 2005.

Baldoz, Rick. "Valorizing racial boundaries: Hegemony and conflict in the racialization of Filipino migrant labour in the United States." *Ethnic and Racial Studies* 27 (November 2004): 969–986.

——. *The Third Asiatic Invasion: Empire and Migration in Filipino America, 1898–1946*. (New York: New York University Press, 2011).

Barron, Hal S. *Mixed Harvest: The Second Great Transformation in the Rural North, 1870–1930*. Chapel Hill: The University of North Carolina Press, 1997.

Bederman, Gail. *Manliness and Civilization: A Cultural History of Gender and Race in the United States, 1880–1917*. Chicago: The University of Chicago Press, 1995.

Bernstein, Shana. *Bridges of Reform: Interracial Civil Rights Activism in Twentieth-Century Los Angeles.* New York: Oxford University Press, 2011.

Block, Sharon. *Rape and Sexual Power in Early America.* Chapel Hill: The University of North Carolina Press, 2006.

Brilliant, Mark. *The Color of America Has Changed: How Racial Diversity Shaped Civil Rights Reform in California, 1941–1978.* New York: Oxford University Press, 2010.

Buaken, Manuel. *I Have Lived with the American People.* Caldwell, ID: Caxton Printers, 1948.

Burns, Catherine. *Sexual Violence and the Law in Japan.* London: RoutledgeCurzon, 2005.

Calles, Rudy. *Champion Prune Pickers: Migrant Worker's Dilemma.* Los Alamitos, CA: Hwong Publishing Company, 1979.

Camarillo, Albert M. *Chicanos in a Changing Society: From Mexican Pueblos to American Barrios in Santa Barbara and Southern California, 1848–1930.* Cambridge, MA: Harvard University Press, 1979.

Carstensen, Frederick V., Morton Rothstein, and Joseph A. Swanson, eds. *Outstanding in His Field: Perspectives on American Agriculture in Honor of Wayne D. Rasmussen.* Ames: Iowa State University Press, 1993.

Chan, Sucheng. *This Bittersweet Soil: The Chinese in California Agriculture, 1860–1910.* Berkeley: University of California Press, 1986.

———. *Asian Americans: An Interpretive History.* Boston: Twayne, 1991.

———. *Entry Denied: Exclusion and the Chinese Community in America, 1882–1943.* Philadelphia: Temple University Press, 1991.

———, ed. *Chinese American Transnationalism: The Flow of People, Resources, and Ideas between China and America during the Exclusion Era.* Philadelphia: Temple University Press, 2006.

———., and Madeline Y. Hsu, eds. *Chinese Americans and the Politics of Race and Culture.* Philadelphia: Temple University Press, 2008.

Chang, Gordon H. *Morning Glory, Evening Shadow: Yamato Ichihashi and His Internment Writings, 1942–1945.* Stanford, CA: Stanford University Press, 1997.

Chapman, Paul Davis. *Schools as Sorters: Lewis M. Terman, Applied Psychology, and the Intelligence Testing Movement, 1890–1930.* New York: New York University Press, 1988.

Chen, Yong. *Chinese San Francisco, 1850–1943: A Trans-Pacific Community.* Stanford, CA: Stanford University Press, 2000.

Chiang, Connie Y. *Shaping the Shoreline: Fisheries and Tourism on the Monterey Coast.* Seattle: University of Washington Press, 2008.

Chuman, Frank F. *The Bamboo People: The Law and Japanese-Americans.* Del Mar, CA: Publisher's Inc., 1976.

Cinel, Dino. *From Italy to San Francisco: The Immigrant Experience.* Stanford, CA: Stanford University Press, 1982.

Cordova, Fred. *Filipinos: Forgotten Asian Americans, A Pictorial Essay, 1763-circa 1963.* Dubuque, IA: Kendall/Hunt Publishing Company, 1983.

Couchman, Robert. *The Sunsweet Story.* San Jose, CA: Sunsweet Growers, 1967.

Danbom, David B. *The Resisted Revolution: Urban America and the Industrialization of Agriculture, 1900–1930.* Ames: The Iowa State University Press, 1979.

———. "Romantic Agrarianism in Twentieth-Century America." *Agricultural History* 65 (Fall 1991): 1–12.

———. *Born in the Country: A History of Rural America.* Baltimore: The Johns Hopkins University Press, 1995.

Daniel, Cletus E. *Bitter Harvest: A History of California Farmworkers, 1870–1941.* Ithaca, NY: Cornell University Press, 1981.

Daniels, Roger. *The Politics of Prejudice: The Anti-Japanese Movement in California and the Struggle for Japanese Exclusion.* Gloucester, MA: Peter Smith, 1966.

———. *Asian America: Chinese and Japanese in the United States since 1850.* Seattle: University of Washington Press, 1988.

De Vera, Arleen. "The Tapia-Saiki Incident: Interethnic Conflict and Filipino Responses to the Anti-Filipino Exclusion Movement." In *Over the Edge: Remapping the American West*, edited by Valerie J. Matsumoto and Blake Allmendinger. Berkeley: University of California Press, 1999.

Deutsch, Sarah. *No Separate Refuge: Culture, Class, and Gender on an Anglo-Hispanic Frontier in the American Southwest, 1880–1940*. New York: Oxford University Press, 1987.

Deverell, William. *Whitewashed Adobe: The Rise of Los Angeles and the Remaking of Its Mexican Past*. Berkeley: University of California Press, 2004.

DeWitt, Howard A. *Anti-Filipino Movements in California: A History, Bibliography and Study Guide*. San Francisco: R and E Research Associates, 1976.

———. "The Filipino Labor Union: The Salinas Lettuce Strike of 1934." *Amerasia Journal* 5 (1978): 1–22.

———. *Violence in the Fields: California Filipino Farm Labor Unionization During the Great Depression*. Saratoga, CA: Century Twenty One Publishing Company, 1980.

Dower, John W. *War without Mercy: Race and Power in the Pacific War*. New York: Pantheon Books, 1986.

Duus, Masayo Umezawa. *The Japanese Conspiracy: The Oahu Sugar Strike of 1920*. Berkeley: University of California Press, 1999.

Embree, John F. *Suye Mura: A Japanese Village*. Chicago: The University of Chicago Press, 1939.

España-Maram, Linda. *Creating Masculinity in Los Angeles's Little Manila: Working-Class Filipinos and Popular Culture, 1920s–1950s*. New York: Columbia University Press, 2006.

Faragher, John Mack. *Sugar Creek: Life on the Illinois Prairie*. New Haven, CT: Yale University Press, 1986.

Fiege, Mark. *Irrigated Eden: The Making of an Agricultural Landscape in the American West*. Seattle: University of Washington Press, 2000.

Filene, Peter G. *Him/Her/Self: Gender Identities in Modern America*. 3rd ed. Baltimore: The Johns Hopkins University Press, 1998.

Findlay, John M. *Magic Lands: Western Cityscapes and American Culture After 1940*. Berkeley: University of California Press, 1992.

Fitzgerald, Deborah. *Every Farm a Factory: The Industrial Ideal in American Agriculture*. New Haven, CT: Yale University Press, 2003.

Foley, Neil. *The White Scourge: Mexicans, Blacks, and Poor Whites in Texas Cotton Culture*. Berkeley: University of California Press, 1997.

Freedman, Estelle B., and John D'Emilio. *Intimate Matters: A History of Sexuality in America*. New York: Harper and Row, 1988.

Friedly, Michael. "This Brief Eden: A History of Landscape Change in California's Santa Clara Valley." Ph.D. dissertation, Duke University, 2000.

Friedman, Lawrence M., and Robert V. Percival. *The Roots of Justice: Crime and Punishment in Alameda County, California, 1870–1910*. Chapel Hill: The University of North Carolina Press, 1981.

Fuess, Harald. *Divorce in Japan: Family, Gender, and the State, 1600–2000*. Chicago: The University of Chicago Press, 2004.

Fujita-Rony, Dorothy B. *American Workers, Colonial Power: Philippine Seattle and the Transpacific West, 1919–1941*. Berkeley: University of California Press, 2003.

Gaines, Brian J., and Wendy K. Tam Cho, "On California's 1920 Alien Land Law: The Psychology and Economics of Racial Discrimination." *State Politics and Policy Quarterly* 4 (Fall 2004): 276–279.

Garcia, Matt. *A World of Its Own: Race, Labor, and Citrus in the Making of Greater Los Angeles, 1900–1970*. Chapel Hill: The University of North Carolina Press, 2001.

Geiger, Andrea. *Subverting Exclusion: Transpacific Encounters with Race, Caste, and Borders, 1885–1928*. New Haven, CT: Yale University Press, 2011.

Gillenkirk, Jeff. *Bitter Melon: Stories from the Last Rural Chinese Town in America*. Seattle: University of Washington Press, 1987.

Giovinco, Joseph. "'Success in the Sun'? California's Italians during the Progressive Era." In *Struggle and Success: An Anthology of the Italian Immigrant Experience in California*, edited by Paola A. Sensi-Isolani and Phylis Cancilla Martinelli. New York: Center for Migration Studies, 1993.

Girdner, Audrie, and Anne Loftis. *The Great Betrayal: The Evacuation of the Japanese-Americans During World War II*. London: The Macmillan Company, 1969.

Gjerde, Jon. *The Minds of the West: Ethnocultural Evolution in the Rural Middle West, 1830–1917*. Chapel Hill: The University of North Carolina Press, 1997.

———. "New Growth on Old Vines—The State of the Field: The Social History of Immigration to and Ethnicity in the United States." *Journal of American Ethnic History* 18 (Summer 1999): 40–65.

Glenn, Evelyn Nakano. *Issei, Nisei, War Bride: Three Generations of Japanese American Women in Domestic Service*. Philadelphia: Temple University Press, 1986.

———. *Unequal Freedom: How Race and Gender Shaped American Citizenship and Labor*. Cambridge, MA: Harvard University Press, 2002.

Gomez, Laura E. *Manifest Destinies: The Making of the Mexican American Race*. New York: New York University Press, 2008.

González, Gilbert. *Labor and Community: Mexican Citrus Workers in a Southern California Colony*. Urbana: The University of Illinois Press, 1994.

Gordon, Linda. *Pitied But Not Entitled: Single Mothers and the History of Welfare, 1890–1935*. Cambridge, MA: Harvard University Press, 1994.

———. *The Great Arizona Orphan Abduction*. Cambridge, MA: Harvard University Press, 1999.

———. *Dorothea Lange: A Life Beyond Limits*. New York: W. W. Norton, 2009.

Grant, Michael Johnston. *Down and Out on the Family Farm: Rural Rehabilitation in the Great Plains, 1929–1945*. Lincoln: University of Nebraska Press, 2002.

Graves, Alvin Ray. *The Portuguese Californians: Immigrants in Agriculture*. San Jose: Portuguese Heritage Publications of California, Inc., 2004.

Greenberg, Jaclyn. "Industry in the Garden: A Social History of the Canning Industry and Cannery Workers in the Santa Clara Valley, California, 1870–1920." Ph.D. dissertation, UCLA, 1985.

Gregory, James N. *American Exodus: The Dust Bowl Migration and Okie Culture in California*. New York: Oxford University Press, 1989.

Griswold, Robert L. *Family and Divorce in California, 1850–1890: Victorian Illusion and Everyday Realities*. Albany: State University of New York Press, 1982.

Guerin-Gonzales, Camille. *Mexican Workers and American Dreams: Immigration, Repatriation, and California Farm Labor, 1900–1939*. New Brunswick, NJ: Rutgers University Press, 1994.

Guglielmo, Thomas A. *White on Arrival: Italians, Race, Color, and Power in Chicago, 1890–1945*. New York: Oxford University Press, 2003.

Gyory, Andrew. *Closing the Gates: Race, Politics, and the Chinese Exclusion Act*. Chapel Hill: The University of North Carolina Press, 1998.

Haas, Lisbeth. *Conquests and Historical Identities in California, 1769–1936*. Berkeley: University of California Press, 1995.

Higgs, Robert. "Landless by Law: Japanese Immigrants in California Agriculture to 1941." *Journal of Economic History* 38 (March 1978): 205–225.

Higham, John. *Strangers in the Land: Patterns of American Nativism, 1860–1925*. New Brunswick, NJ: Rutgers University Press, 1955.

Hirobe, Izumi. *Japanese Pride, American Prejudice: Modifying the Exclusion Clause of the 1924 Immigration Act*. Stanford, CA: Stanford University Press, 2001.

Hofstadter, Richard. *The Age of Reform: From Bryan to FDR*. New York: Vintage Books, 1955.

Hoganson, Kristin L. *Fighting for American Manhood: How Gender Politics Provoked the Spanish-American and Philippine-American Wars*. New Haven, CT: Yale University Press, 1998.

Hom, Gloria S., ed. *Chinese Argonauts: An Anthology of the Chinese Contributions to the Historical Development of Santa Clara County*. Los Altos: California History Center, Foothill Community College District, 1971.

Hsu, Madeline Y. *Dreaming of Gold, Dreaming of Home: Transnationalism and Migration between the United States and South China, 1882–1943*. Stanford, CA: Stanford University Press, 2000.

Hurtado, Albert L. *Indian Survival on the California Frontier*. New Haven, CT: Yale University Press, 1988.

———. *Intimate Frontiers: Sex, Gender, and Culture in Old California*. Albuquerque: University of New Mexico Press, 1999.

Ichioka, Yuji. "Japanese Associations and the Japanese Government: A Special Relationship, 1909–1926." *Pacific Historical Review* 46 (1977): 409–438.

———. *The Issei: The World of the First Generation Japanese Immigrants, 1885–1924*. New York: Free Press, 1988.

Ignoffo, Mary Jo. *Sunnyvale: From the City of Destiny to the Heart of Silicon Valley*. Cupertino: California History Center, 1994.

Irons, Peter. *Justice At War*. New York: Oxford University Press, 1983.

Ito, Kazuo. *Issei: A History of Japanese Immigrants in North America*. Translated by Shinichiro Nakamura and Jean S. Gerard. Seattle: Japanese Community Service, 1973.

Iwata, Masakazu. *Planted in Good Soil: The Issei in United States Agriculture*. 2 vols. New York: Peter Lang, 1992.

Jackson, Kenneth. *Crabgrass Frontier: The Suburbanization of the United States*. New York: Oxford University Press, 1985.

Jacobson, Matthew Frye. *Whiteness of a Different Color: European Immigrants and the Alchemy of Race*. Cambridge, MA: Harvard University Press, 1998.

———. *Barbarian Virtues: The United States Encounters Foreign Peoples at Home and Abroad, 1876–1917*. New York: Hill and Wang, 2000.

Jacobson, Yvonne. *Passing Farms, Enduring Values: California's Santa Clara Valley*. Los Altos, CA: William Kaufmann, Inc. In Cooperation with the California History Center, De Anza College, Cupertino, 1984.

James, Thomas. *Exile Within: The Schooling of Japanese Americans, 1942–1945*. Cambridge, MA: Harvard University Press, 1987.

Japanese American National Museum, ed. *REgenerations Oral History Project: Rebuilding Japanese American Families, Communities, and Civil Rights in the Resettlement Era*. Los Angeles: Japanese American National Museum, 2000.

Jensen, Joan. *Loosening the Bonds: Mid-Atlantic Farm Women, 1750–1850*. New Haven, CT: Yale University Press, 1986.

Jung, Moon-Ho. *Coolies and Cane: Race, Labor, and Sugar in the Age of Emancipation*. Baltimore: The Johns Hopkins University Press, 2006.

Kitano, Harry H. L. *Japanese Americans: The Evolution of a Subculture*. 2nd ed. Englewood Cliffs, NJ: Prentice-Hall, 1976.

Knobloch, Frieda. *The Culture of Wilderness: Agriculture as Colonization in the American West*. Chapel Hill: The University of North Carolina Press, 1996.

Kurashige, Lon. *Japanese American Celebration and Conflict: A History of Ethnic Identity and Festival in Los Angeles, 1934–1990*. Berkeley: University of California Press, 2002.

Kurashige, Scott. *The Shifting Grounds of Race: Black and Japanese Americans in the Making of Multiethnic Los Angeles*. Princeton, NJ: Princeton University Press, 2008.

Kurtz, Lester R. *Evaluating Chicago Sociology: A Guide to the Literature, with an Annotated Bibliography*. Chicago: The University of Chicago Press, 1984.

Lai, Him Mark. *Becoming Chinese American: A History of Communities and Institutions*. Walnut Creek, CA: Alta Mira, 2004.

Lal, Barbara Ballis. *The Romance of Culture in an Urban Civilization: Robert E. Park and Ethnic Relations in Cities*. London: Routledge, 1990.

Lanyon, Milton. *Cinnabar Hills: The Quicksilver Days of New Almaden*. Los Gatos, CA: Village Printers, 1967.

Lee, Erika. *At America's Gates: Chinese Immigration during the Exclusion Era, 1882–1943*. Chapel Hill: The University of North Carolina Press, 2003.

Lee, Robert G. *Orientals: Asian Americans in Popular Culture*. Philadelphia: Temple University Press, 1999.

Leonard, Karen Isaksen. *Making Ethnic Choices: California's Punjabi Mexican Americans*. Philadelphia: Temple University Press, 1992.

Leong, Karen J. *The China Mystique: Pearl S. Buck, Anna May Wong, Mayling Soong, and the Transformation of American Orientalism*. Berkeley: University of California Press, 2005.

Leung, Peter C. Y. *One Day, One Dollar: Locke, California, and the Chinese Farming Experience in the Sacramento Delta*. El Cerrito, CA: Chinese/Chinese American History Project, 1984.

Loftis, Anne. *Witness to the Struggle: Imaging the 1930s California Labor Movement*. Reno: University of Nevada Press, 1998.

———, and Audrie Girdner. *The Great Betrayal: The Evacuation of the Japanese-Americans During World War II*. London: The Macmillan Company, 1969.

Lowen, Rebecca S. *Creating the Cold War University: The Transformation of Stanford*. Berkeley: University of California Press, 1997.

Lukes, Timothy J., and Gary Y. Okihiro. *Japanese Legacy: Farming and Community Life in California's Santa Clara Valley*. Cupertino: California History Center, 1985.

Lye, Colleen. *America's Asia: Racial Form and American Literature, 1893–1945*. Princeton, NJ: Princeton University Press, 2005.

Lynn-Sherow, Bonnie. *Red Earth: Race and Agriculture in Oklahoma Territory*. Lawrence: University Press of Kansas, 2004.

Marchetti, Gina. *Romance and the "Yellow Peril": Race, Sex, and Discursive Strategies in Hollywood Fiction*. Berkeley: University of California Press, 1993.

Marsh, Margaret. *Suburban Lives*. New Brunswick, NJ: Rutgers University Press, 1988.

———. "Suburban Men and Masculine Domesticity, 1870–1915." *American Quarterly* 40 (Summer 1988): 165–186.

Marx, Leo. *The Machine in the Garden: Technology and the Pastoral Ideal in America*. New York: Oxford University Press, 1964.

Masumoto, David Mas. *Country Voices: The Oral History of a Japanese American Family Farm Community*. Del Rey, CA: Inaka Countryside Publications, 1987.

Matsumoto, Valerie J. *Farming the Home Place: A Japanese American Community in California, 1919–1982*. Ithaca, NY: Cornell University Press, 1993.

Matthew, Fred H. *Quest for an American Sociology: Robert E. Park and the Chicago School*. Montreal: McGill University Press, 1977.

Matthews, Glenna. "A California Middletown: The Social History of San Jose in the Depression." Ph.D. dissertation, Stanford University, 1976.

———. "Forging a Cosmopolitan Civic Culture: The Regional Identity of San Francisco and Northern California." In *Many Wests: Place, Culture, and Regional Identity*, edited by David M. Wrobel and Michael C. Steiner, 211–234. Lawrence: University Press of Kansas, 1997.

———. "'The Los Angeles of the North': San Jose's Transition from Fruit Capital to High-Tech Metropolis." *Journal of Urban History* 25 (1999): 459–476.

———. *Silicon Valley, Women, and the California Dream: Gender, Class, and Opportunity in the Twentieth Century*. Stanford, CA: Stanford University Press, 2003.

May, Elaine Tyler. *Great Expectations: Marriage and Divorce in Post-Victorian America*. Chicago: The University of Chicago Press, 1980.

McClain, Charles J. *In Search of Equality: The Chinese Struggle Against Discrimination in Nineteenth-Century America*. Berkeley: University of California Press, 1994.

McKanna, Clare V. Jr. *Race and Homicide in Nineteenth-Century California*. Reno: University of Nevada Press, 2002.

McKeown, Adam. "Transnational Chinese Families and Chinese Exclusion, 1875–1943." *Journal of American Ethnic History* 18 (Winter 1999): 73–110.

———. *Chinese Migrant Networks and Cultural Change: Peru, Chicago, Hawaii, 1900–1936*. Chicago: The University of Chicago Press, 2001.

Meloy, Michael J. "The Long Road to Manzanar: Politics, Land, and Race in the Japanese Exclusion Movement, 1900–1942." Ph.D. dissertation, University of California, Davis, 2004.

Merchant, Carolyn. *Ecological Revolutions: Nature, Gender, and Science in New England.* Chapel Hill: The University of North Carolina Press, 1989.

Merrill, Karen R. *Public Lands and Political Meaning: Ranchers, the Government, and the Property between Them.* Berkeley: University of California Press, 2002.

Miller, Stuart Creighton. *The Unwelcome Immigrant: The American Image of the Chinese, 1785–1882.* Berkeley: University of California Press, 1969.

Mintz, Steven, and Susan Kellogg. *Domestic Revolutions: A Social History of American Family Life.* New York: Free Press, 1988.

Misawa, Steven, ed. *Beginnings: Japanese Americans in San Jose, 8 Oral Histories.* San Jose, CA: San Jose Japanese American Community Senior Service, 1981.

Mitchell, Don. *The Lie of the Land: Migrant Workers and the California Landscape.* Minneapolis: University of Minnesota Press, 1996.

Molina, Natalia. *Fit to Be Citizens?: Public Health and Race in Los Angeles, 1879–1939.* Berkeley: University of California Press, 2006.

Monrayo, Angeles, and Rizaline R. Raymundo, ed. *Tomorrow's Memories: A Diary, 1924–1928.* Honolulu: University of Hawai'i Press, 2003.

Monroy, Douglas. *Thrown Among Strangers: Making of Mexican Culture Frontier.* Berkeley: University of California Press, 1993.

Mooney, Patrick H., and Theo J. Majka. *Farmers' and Farm Workers' Movements: Social Protest in American Agriculture.* New York: Twayne Publishers, 1995.

Muller, Eric L. *Free to Die for Their Country: The Story of the Japanese American Draft Resisters in World War II.* Chicago: The University of Chicago Press, 2003.

Murray, Alice Yang. *Historical Memories of the Japanese American Internment and the Struggle for Redress.* Stanford, CA: Stanford University Press, 2008.

Nakane, Kazuko. *Nothing Left in My Hands: The Issei of a Rural California Town, 1900–1942.* Berkeley, CA: Heyday Books, 1985.

Neth, Mary. *Preserving the Family Farm: Women Community, and the Foundations of Agribusiness in the Midwest, 1900–1940.* Baltimore: The Johns Hopkins University Press, 1995.

Ngai, Mae M. *Impossible Subjects: Illegal Aliens and the Making of Modern America.* Princeton, NJ: Princeton University Press, 2004.

———. *The Lucky Ones: One Family and the Extraordinary Invention of Chinese America.* Boston and New York: Houghton Mifflin Harcourt, 2010.

Noda, Kesa. *Yamato Colony: 1906–1960, Livingston, California.* Livingston: Livingston-Merced Japanese American Citizens League Chapter, 1981.

Nomura, Gail M. "Significant Lives: Asian and Asian Americans in the History of the U.S. West." *Western Historical Quarterly* 25 (Spring 1994): 69–88.

O'Mara, Margaret Pugh. *Cities of Knowledge: Cold War Science and the Search for the Next Silicon Valley.* Princeton, NJ: Princeton University Press, 2004.

Okihiro, Gary Y. *Cane Fires: The Anti-Japanese Movement in Hawaii, 1865–1945.* Philadelphia: Temple University Press, 1991.

———. *Margins and Mainstreams: Asians in American History and Culture.* Seattle: University of Washington Press, 1994.

———, and David Drummond. "The Concentration Camps and Japanese Economic Losses in California Agriculture, 1900–1942." In *Japanese Americans: From Relocation to Redress,* revised ed., edited by Roger Daniels, Sandra C. Taylor, and Harry H. L. Kitano. Seattle: University of Washington Press, 1991.

Orsi, Richard J. "Selling the Golden State: A Study of Boosterism in Nineteenth-Century California." Ph.D. dissertation, University of Wisconsin, 1973.

———. *Sunset Limited: The Southern Pacific Railroad and the Development of the American West, 1850–1930.* Berkeley: University of California Press, 2005.

Osterud, Nancy Grey. *Bonds of Community: The Lives of Farm Women in Nineteenth-Century New York.* Ithaca, NY: Cornell University Press, 1991.

Osumi, Megumi Dick. "Asians and California's Anti-Miscegenation Laws." In *Asian and Pacific American Experiences: Women's Perspectives,* edited by Nobuya Tsuchida. Minneapolis: Asian/

Pacific American Learning Resource Center and General College, University of Minnesota, 1982.

Palmer, Hans Christian. "Italian Immigration and the Development of California Agriculture." Ph.D. dissertation, University of California, Berkeley, 1965.

Pascoe, Peggy. *Relations of Rescue: The Search for Female Moral Authority in the American West, 1874–1939*. New York: Oxford University Press, 1990.

———. "Miscegenation Law, Court Cases, and Ideologies of 'Race' in Twentieth-Century America." *Journal of American History* 83 (June 1996): 44–69.

———. "Race, Gender, and the Privileges of Property: On the Significance of Miscegenation Law in the U.S. West." In *Over the Edge: Remapping the American West*, edited by Valerie J. Matsumoto and Blake Allmendinger. Berkeley: University of California Press, 1999.

———. *What Comes Naturally: Miscegenation Law and the Making of Race in America*. New York: Oxford University Press, 2009.

Payne, Stephen M. *Santa Clara County: Harvest of Change*. Northridge, CA: Windsor Publications, 1987.

Pearce, Ralph M. *From Asahi to Zebras: Japanese American Baseball in San Jose, California*. San Jose: Japanese American Museum of San Jose, 2005.

Penrose, Eldon R. *California Nativism: Organized Opposition to the Japanese, 1890–1913*. San Francisco: R and E Research Associates, 1973.

Pfaelzer, Jean. *Driven Out: The Forgotten War Against Chinese Americans*. New York: Random House, 2007.

Pierce, Marjorie. *The Martin Murphy Family Saga*. Cupertino: California History Center, 2000.

Pitti, Stephen J. *The Devil in Silicon Valley: Northern California, Race, and Mexican Americans*. Princeton, NJ: Princeton University Press, 2003.

Postel, Charles. *The Populist Vision*. New York: Oxford University Press, 2007.

Rambo, Ralph. *Remember When . . . A Boy's-Eye View of an Old Valley*. San Jose, CA: Rosicrucian Press, 1965.

Rauchway, Eric. *The Refuge of Affections: Family and American Reform Politics, 1900–1920*. New York: Columbia University Press, 2001.

Rawitsch, Mark. *The House on Lemon Street: Japanese Pioneers and the American Dream*. Boulder: University Press of Colorado, 2012.

Reagan, Leslie J. *When Abortion Was a Crime: Women, Medicine, and Law in the United States, 1867–1973*. Berkeley: University of California Press, 1997.

Rice, Bertha Marguerite. *The Women of Our Valley*, vol. 2. n.p., 1956.

Rice, Richard B., William A. Bullough, Richard J. Orsi, and Mary Ann Irwin. *The Elusive Eden: A New History of California*. 4th ed. New York: McGraw Hill, 2011.

Riley, Glenda. *Divorce: An American Tradition*. New York: Oxford University Press, 1991.

Roediger, David R. *The Wages of Whiteness: Race and the Making of the American Working Class*. New York: Verso, 1991.

———. *Working Toward Whiteness: How America's Immigrants Became White. The Strange Journey from Ellis Island to the Suburbs*. New York: Basic Books, 2005.

Rotundo, E. Anthony. *American Manhood: Transformations in Masculinity from the Revolution to the Modern Era*. New York: Basic Books, 1993.

Ruiz, Vicki. *Cannery Women, Cannery Lives: Mexican Women, Unionization, and the California Food Processing Industry, 1930–1950*. Albuquerque: University of New Mexico Press, 1987.

Sackman, Douglas Cazaux. *Orange Empire: California and the Fruits of Eden*. Berkeley: University of California Press, 2005.

Saxenian, AnnaLee. *Regional Advantage: Culture and Competition in Silicon Valley and Route 128*. Cambridge, MA: Harvard University Press, 1994.

Saxton, Alexander. *The Indispensable Enemy: Labor and the Anti-Chinese Movement in California*. Berkeley: University of California Press, 1971.

———. "In Dubious Battle: Looking Backward." *Pacific Historical Review* 73 (May 2004): 249–262.

Scott, Joan. "Gender: A Useful Category of Historical Analysis." *American Historical Review* 91 (December 1986): 1053–1075.

Shah, Nayan. *Contagious Divides: Epidemics and Race in San Francisco's Chinatown*. Berkeley: University of California Press, 2001.

———. *Stranger Intimacy: Contesting Race, Sexuality, and the Law in the North American West*. Berkeley: University of California Press, 2011.

Shibusawa, Naoko. *America's Geisha Ally: Reimagining the Japanese Enemy*. Cambridge, MA: Harvard University Press, 2006.

Shimabukuro, Robert Sadamu. *Born in Seattle: The Campaign for Japanese American Redress*. Seattle: University of Washington Press, 2001.

Simpson, Lee M. A. *Selling the City: Gender, Class, and the California Growth Machine, 1880–1940*. Stanford, CA: Stanford University Press, 2004.

Smith, Henry Nash. *Virgin Land: The American West as Symbol and Myth*. Cambridge, MA: Harvard University Press, 1950.

Smith, Merrill D., ed. *Sex Without Consent: Rape and Sexual Coercion in America*. New York: New York University Press, 2001.

Smith, Robert J., and Ella Lury Wiswell. *The Women of Suye Mura*. Chicago: The University of Chicago Press, 1982.

Smith, Thomas C. *Native Sources of Japanese Industrialization, 1750–1920*. Berkeley: University of California Press, 1988.

Solnit, Rebecca. *As Eve Said to the Serpent: On Landscape, Gender, and Art*. Athens: The University of Georgia Press, 2001.

Stanley, Amy Dru. *From Bondage to Contract: Wage Labor, Marriage, and the Market in the Age of Slave Emancipation*. Cambridge: Cambridge University Press, 1998.

Starr, Kevin. *Inventing the Dream: California Through the Progressive Era*. New York: Oxford University Press, 1985.

———. *Endangered Dreams: The Great Depression in California*. New York: Oxford University Press, 1996.

Stein, Walter J. *California and the Dust Bowl Migration*. Westport, CT.: Greenwood Press, Inc., 1973.

Stilgoe, John. *Common Landscape of America, 1580–1845*. New Haven, CT: Yale University Press, 1982.

———. *Borderland: Origins of the American Suburb, 1820–1939*. New Haven, CT: Yale University Press, 1988.

Stoll, Steven. *The Fruits of Natural Advantage: Making the Industrial Countryside in California*. Berkeley: University of California Press, 1998.

Street, Richard Steven. *Beasts of the Field: A Narrative History of California Farmworkers, 1769–1913*. Stanford, CA: Stanford University Press, 2004.

Sullivan, Charles L. *Like Modern Edens: Winegrowing in Santa Clara Valley and Santa Cruz Mountains, 1798–1981*. Cupertino: California History Center, 1982.

Sunset Magazine, A Century of Western Living, 1898–1998: Historical Portraits and a Chronological Bibliography of Selected Topics. Stanford, CA: Stanford University Libraries, 1998.

Takaki, Ronald. *Iron Cages: Race and Culture in Nineteenth-Century America*. New York: Alfred A. Knopf, 1979.

———. *Strangers from a Different Shore: A History of Asian Americans*. revised ed. Boston and New York: Back Bay Books, 1998.

Takezara, Yasuko I. *Breaking the Silence: Redress and Japanese American Ethnicity*. Ithaca, NY: Cornell University Press, 1995.

Tamura, Eileen. *Americanization, Acculturation, and Ethnic Identity: The Nisei Generation in Hawaii*. Urbana: University of Illinois Press, 1994.

Trachtenberg, Alan. *The Incorporation of America: Culture and Society in the Gilded Age*. New York: Hill and Wang, 1982.

Trewartha, Glenn T. *Japan: A Geography*. Madison: University of Wisconsin Press, 1965.

Tyrrell, Ian. *True Gardens of the Gods: Californian-Australian Environmental Reform, 1860–1930.* Berkeley: University of California Press, 1999.

Uyeunten, Sandra O. "Struggle and Survival: The History of Japanese Immigrant Families in California, 1907–1945." Ph.D. dissertation, University of California, San Diego, 1988.

Valencius, Conevery Bolton. *The Health of the Country: How American Settlers Understood Themselves and Their Land.* New York: Basic Books, 2002.

Van Nuys, Frank W. "A Progressive Confronts the Race Question: Chester Rowell, the California Alien Land Act of 1913, and the Contradictions of Early Twentieth-Century Racial Thought." *California History* 73 (1994): 2–13.

Varzally, Allison. *Making a Non-White America: Californians Coloring Outside Ethnic Lines, 1925–1955.* Berkeley: University of California Press, 2008.

Vaught, David. "Factories in the Field Revisited." *Pacific Historical Review* 66 (May 1997): 149–184.

———. *Cultivating California: Growers, Specialty Crops, and Labor, 1875–1920.* Baltimore: The Johns Hopkins University Press, 1999.

———. "State of the Art—Rural History, or Why Is There No Rural History of California?" *Agricultural History* 74 (Fall 2000): 759–774.

———. *After the Gold Rush: Tarnished Dreams in the Sacramento Valley.* Baltimore: The Johns Hopkins University Press, 2007.

———. "'Our Players are Mostly Farmers': Baseball in Rural California, 1850–1890." In *Baseball in America and America in Baseball,* edited by Donald G. Kyle and Robert B. Fairbanks. College Station: Texas A&M University Press, 2008.

Warren, Louis S. "Cody's Last Stand: Masculine Anxiety, the Custer Myth, and the Frontier of Domesticity in Buffalo Bill's Wild West." *Western Historical Quarterly* 34 (Spring 2003): 49–69.

———. *Buffalo Bill's America: William Cody and the Wild West Show.* New York: Alfred A. Knopf, 2005.

Weber, Devra. *Dark Sweat, White Gold: California Farm Workers, Cotton, and the New Deal.* Berkeley: University of California Press, 1994.

White, Richard. *"It's Your Misfortune and None of My Own": A New History of the American West.* Norman: University of Oklahoma Press, 1991.

Wild, Mark. *Street Meeting: Multiethnic Neighborhoods in Early Twentieth-Century Los Angeles.* Berkeley: University of California Press, 2005.

Wong, Marie Rose. *Sweet Cakes, Long Journey: The Chinatowns of Portland, Oregon.* Seattle: University of Washington Press, 2004.

Worster, Donald. *A Passion for Nature: The Life of John Muir.* New York: Oxford University Press, 2008.

Wu, Frank H. *Yellow: Race in America Beyond Black and White.* New York: Basic Books, 2002.

Yoo, David K. *Growing Up Nisei: Race, Generation, and Culture among Japanese Americans of California, 1924–1949.* Urbana: The University of Illinois Press, 2000.

Yoshihara, Mari. *Embracing the East: White Women and American Orientalism.* New York: New York University Press, 2003.

Yu, Connie Young. *Chinatown, San Jose, USA.* San Jose, CA: San Jose Historical Museum Association, 1991.

Yu, Henry. "Mixing Bodies and Cultures: The Meaning of America's Fascination with Sex between 'Orientals' and 'Whites'." In *Sex, Love, Race: Crossing Boundaries in North American History,* edited by Martha Hodes. New York: New York University Press, 1999.

———. *Thinking Orientals: Migration, Contact, and Exoticism in Modern America.* New York: Oxford University Press, 2001.

Yun, Judy. *Unbound Feet: A Social History of Chinese Women in San Francisco.* Berkeley: University of California Press, 1995.

Zavella, Patricia. *Women's Work and Chicano Families: Cannery Workers of the Santa Clara Valley.* Ithaca, NY: Cornell University Press, 1987.

INDEX